COMEDY SAMURAI

COMEDY SAMURAI

FORTY YEARS OF BLOOD, GUTS, AND LAUGHTER

LARRY CHARLES

GRAND
CENTRAL
NEW YORK BOSTON

Grand Central Publishing
Hachette Book Group
1290 Avenue of the Americas, New York, NY 10104
grandcentralpublishing.com
@grandcentralpub

First Edition: June 2025

Grand Central Publishing is a division of Hachette Book Group, Inc. The Grand Central Publishing name and logo is a registered trademark of Hachette Book Group, Inc.

The publisher is not responsible for websites (or their content) that are not owned by the publisher.

The Hachette Speakers Bureau provides a wide range of authors for speaking events. To find out more, go to hachettespeakersbureau.com or email HachetteSpeakers@hbgusa.com.

Grand Central Publishing books may be purchased in bulk for business, educational, or promotional use. For information, please contact your local bookseller or the Hachette Book Group Special Markets Department at special.markets@hbgusa.com.

Print book interior design by Marie Mundaca

Library of Congress Cataloging-in-Publication Data

Names: Charles, Larry, 1956- author.
Title: Comedy samurai : forty years of blood, guts, and laughter / Larry Charles.
Description: First edition. | New York : GCP, 2025.
Identifiers: LCCN 2024059416 | ISBN 9781538771549 (hardcover) | ISBN 9781538771563 (ebook)
Subjects: LCSH: Charles, Larry, 1956- | Television comedy writers—United States—Biography. | Screenwriters—United States—Biography. | Television producers and directors—United States—Biography. | Motion picture producers and directors—United States—Biography.
Classification: LCC PN1992.4.C48 A3 2025 | DDC 791.4502/32092 [B]—dc23/eng/20250212
LC record available at https://lccn.loc.gov/2024059416

ISBNs: 9781538771549 (hardcover), 9781538771563 (ebook)

Printed in Canada

MRQ-T

1 2025

To my wife/rock, Keely.
It is not hyperbole to say I wouldn't be here without her.

CONTENTS

PROLOGUE

IS THIS THE END?

March 27, 2024

It seemed like just another typical Friday night at the Charles house. Dinner from DoorDash in front of the TV watching a movie or show with my wife, Keely, and our son, McLain, twenty, while our two big black Malinois, Rama and Kali, whimpered and barked and humped each other to guarantee distraction. Since the pandemic, Keely and I had pretty much stopped going out. We were not social animals to begin with so we sort of loved the excuse to stay home. And that continued once the pandemic ended. Did it end?

I had been diagnosed as an adult-onset type 1 diabetic back when I was about forty, and though it is a life-changing diagnosis, one I had struggled with especially in those first few years, now at sixty-seven I had finally figured out how to deal with it, as imperfect as that process must inevitably be. Calculating carbohydrates, and units of insulin. Many thousands of pinpricks to monitor blood sugar and the needles. It takes its toll. Sometimes more mentally and emotionally than physically. At first. Weirdly, in many ways, I was healthier as a result of my diagnosis. It forced me to be serious about exercise and diet and, as best I could, my mental state. But based on my regular visits to my endocrinologist, I was in great health. All the possible ramifications and consequences of diabetes hadn't hit me. My heart and brain and circulation and eyesight were all great and had hardly changed in twenty-seven years.

I didn't like to share my diagnosis with my professional colleagues and kept it hidden from most. Of course, every time I direct a movie, I must have a physical for insurance purposes and have never been denied. So those doctors, and I guess, the producers who had access to those reports knew. And I would usually tell my assistant director, the AD, the right-hand person to a director on set, so that if by chance, anything would happen to me, they'd have that vital piece of information.

I don't believe I ever told Sacha through our three movies together. Or Paul and Helen on *Mad About You*. Or the *Entourage* guys. Or Billy Crystal. Or Nic Cage. I don't remember ever mentioning it to Bill Maher once until recently. What for? I didn't want them to judge me or have a lack of faith or confidence in my ability.

I did mention it to Larry David, who was a close friend and mentor, on more than one occasion, but every time I brought it up, he would say, shocked and surprised as if it were the first time I'd mentioned it, "You're diabetic?!"—until I simply stopped saying it.

Of course, he and Bill were always quick to share their health problems with me, and I was always discreet with that information, not sharing it with anyone. Old Jews talk about their health. But I didn't.

As I reached my sixties, it seemed like I might be the lucky one who escapes or sidesteps the consequences of this condition. I felt great. And so I began to get lazy.

My A1C crept up. My blood pressure crept up. My weight crept up. I was on many annoying medications. But like the insulin injections, I had gotten used to them and thought that, as long as I stay on that routine, I should be okay.

I had stopped smoking cigarettes for good a decade before, after many years of stopping and starting. But I was still smoking pot. Sometimes a lot. Like that night.

And Keely and I and McLain were having a great time on that Friday night. My recent obsession had become obscure Eastern European vodka. I was so proud, I had taken to collecting the unique bottles. And they were adding up. I enjoyed pretending that I was a Russian peasant knocking back straight shots while I ate food from the old country (smoked fish, pickles, etc.). Not every day. Not even necessarily every week. But that week I had done it twice in a row. The vodka that night was Stumbras, an organic vodka from Lithuania.

And I felt fine when later I climbed the stairs to our bedroom and flopped into bed. Then it hit me. Not pain. But a pressure I had never experienced before. It wasn't just my chest. It was my entire upper torso. And my head! I knew I was in trouble. Keely knew something was wrong as well. She asked if she needed to call 911. I hated the idea of calling 911. I said no at first, thinking it was going to pass. Thinking I could will it to go away. But it didn't. My Apple Watch told us that I was in A-fib. My heart rate was in radical fluctuation from high to low. I finally acquiesced. "Call 911."

We live at the top of a canyon, and there is no shortcut to get here so it took a few minutes for the ambulance to arrive. I worried about things like the neighbors knowing something was wrong. We had been so private. Now I would be carried out on a stretcher for all to see. I was embarrassed.

But there was no greater sense of relief than when the EMTs came rushing up to my bedroom. They were like a football team or an army platoon. I knew they'd take care of me. And I didn't care who knew what.

They carried me down the stairs. One of the paramedics saw the posters on my walls. A *Masked and Anonymous* poster from Japan. An original *Religulous* poster. And a large poster of Jean-Luc Godard's *Weekend* given to me as a gift from my eldest daughter, Sophie. As they lowered me down the staircase, he asked if I was a Godard fan. I said yes! And *Weekend* might be my all-time favorite movie. He concurred. We traded laudatory references to some of Godard's other celebrated work, such as *Contempt* and *Alphaville*, and I thought, *A paramedic who's into Godard. How cool!*

With Keely sitting up front with the driver, suffering vicariously with me, I retched into a plastic bag as the ambulance careened down our canyon road, past damaged or destroyed or nonexistent guardrails over which cars that had not successfully negotiated the windy hairpin turns went off the side.

One of the paramedics was named Steelhammer. That was the name on his name plate. It sounded like an action hero from the '70s or at least a parody of an action hero from the '70s. In between retching, I asked him if that was real and he said, as he must've a thousand times before, "Yup, that's my name," while he monitored my plummeting blood pressure.

We finally made it to the Pacific Coast Highway.

The juxtaposition of being in a racing ambulance on PCH was not lost on me either. I had never sat backward on this road so I saw it from a brand-new perspective. It was beautiful. Would it be the last time I would see it? I had lost control of my narrative.

How did I get here? I had wandered through the comedy desert. I had come to the promised land, but like a comedy Moses, I could not enter. I had come to the banks of the River of Comedy that separated the Almosts from the Alreadys, but like the restless outsider I was and would always be, I knew I would never wade in, never cross it. I had encountered the inadvertent oracles who generously shared their wisdom and prophecy with me and changed and shaped me and also warned me, warnings I had often ignored, without them even knowing it. I did what I could do and didn't what I couldn't. I had destroyed the golden calves, the false idols, but could not change my fate.

I took a violent approach to comedy. A seriousness. An intensity. I treated comedy like life and death. Honor and dishonor. Pride and shame. Triumph or humiliating failure. This wasn't a pretense. I didn't know how to be pretentious. I came from the streets of Brooklyn and everything was on the line. Laughter had to hurt. Laughter had to kill. It had to mean something. It had to mean that much. It had to be as important and impactful as crying. As dying. Comedy had to be as serious as drama. I came from the working classes. I didn't come from the ruling classes. The elite. The privileged. The aristocracy. I was given nothing, handed nothing. If I wanted it I would have to take it. And when others needed help, I would be there. Without hesitation. A Comedy Samurai. I was a soldier and I had a job to do. And when that job was done, I moved on. Every project was a village in need of saving. And I was there to do nothing less than to save it. To rescue it from death. By killing. With laughter. It was the comedy version of the Bushido Code.

It seemed like only yesterday that I was a clueless kid from Brooklyn who'd come out to LA to find fame and fortune and had succeeded but not in any way I could've imagined. It was the beginning of this life, and now, alas, this could be the end.

CHAPTER 1

"THE BAD NEWS IS, YOU'RE HIRED." (FRIDAYS)

*C*hristmas time, 1978. I had just turned twenty-two. I had abruptly left Hollywood, for no reason, on the brink of a break-through, as what, something in show business, a writer, I don't even know, to be a bellhop at the Brickman Hotel in South Fallsburg, New York. And now, a year later, just turning twenty-three, after visiting my mother in Florida, and weeping over my abject failure, I returned to Hollywood, the scene of my existential crime.

To do what? And how? I truly had no idea. I had left town the year before so abruptly, I didn't feel comfortable calling people who had helped me already and that I never got back in touch with. People like Jay Leno, who had bought my first joke, handwritten on a piece of legal paper, as I stood in front of The Comedy Store. Or Stan Burns, the veteran comedy writer who had taken me under his wing even though he had no idea who I was. That left me with virtu-ally nobody. I hadn't heard anything from or about Darrow Igus, the comedian and one of the stars of *Car Wash*, whom I met on Venice Beach as I walked home from my night shift as a parking attendant at the Marina City Club and wound up writing material for. In all the time I was gone, he hadn't become a big comedian, I hadn't seen him on *The Tonight Show* or any other venue, or in any movies or TV shows. But I checked the masthead at *Chic* magazine, the Larry Flynt publication I occasionally wrote freelance pieces for, and Darrow's wife, Toi, was still an editor. My thought was, I'd call her and try to pitch some freelance humor assignments for the magazine. Hopefully she'd be responsive.

When I called, she seemed surprisingly happy to hear from me. She said sure, I could write something freelance for the magazine, but as it happened, Darrow was sitting with her in the office right then. I thought he might be pissed and I wouldn't blame him.

He got on the phone and immediately asked what the hell happened to me. Before I could finish my lengthy explanation, he told me he had been cast on a new Los Angeles–based late-night comedy show modeled after *Saturday Night Live* and they were looking for writers and he had told them about me but he had no idea where I was or how to get in touch with me. But the timing was great. If I could get my shit together, the producers would look at it and there might be a staff-writing job still available.

My life totally changed in that moment. I told him I would get my material together and call the office. I never pitched the freelance ideas to Toi.

Instead I gathered the material I had, some handwritten, some badly typed and/or copied, and submitted it. In just a few days, amazingly, miraculously, Darrow told me that the producers would like to see me. I called the office. They were actually expecting my call. They arranged a time for me to come in and meet.

I know it sounds crazy, but in a rush of ambition before the meeting, I even hurriedly wrote a couple of new pieces to bring to the interview in an effort to put my best foot forward. I put on a nice shirt, grabbed my unruly sheath of material including the new pieces, and hitchhiked from Hollywood to the ABC Television Center in Los Feliz for the interview.

I remember the guy who picked me up asked what I did for a living and I told him, "I'll know in an hour."

Sitting in the office waiting for me were the three producers: Bill

Lee, John Moffitt, and Jack Burns. When I was a kid back in Trump Village, Brooklyn, and show business was a vague dream, I would memorize the credits to all the TV shows and movies I watched and knew both Moffitt and Lee as a successful producer-director team from numerous variety specials.

Beyond that, and not that he remembered it, but as a kid, I'd met John Moffitt when my father would take me to the *Ed Sullivan* rehearsals to see his buddy Tony Jordan, the production manager.

Jack Burns was a comedy icon. He had been George Carlin's original partner in a short-lived team that had been discovered by Lenny Bruce. He went on to replace Don Knotts as Andy's deputy on *The Andy Griffith Show*. After that, he and Avery Schreiber were a very successful comedy team, appearing everywhere and even having their own show. Their routine about the cab driver picking up the out-of-town conventioneer was a classic. He also produced and wrote for *Hee Haw* and *The Muppet Show*, both long running and wildly successful. I was a fan.

I sat down. I was hyped up. But not really nervous. I felt this was a long shot, but the fact that I had made it this far was a good portent, a sign of good things to come. That was all I was expecting. I was resigned to not getting the job. Just being up for something like this seemed like an important step.

There was some small talk. They spoke positively about my material. I told them that I had brought a new piece just for the meeting. They were impressed. Jack took the pages from me. Jack, as I would find out later, was considered one of the great cold readers. He would read the new sketch out loud playing all the parts and see how it sounded.

He began and almost immediately I wasn't happy with his reading. This was a crossroads moment. Before he got to the end of the first page, I stopped him. I don't know where I got the temerity, but I told him that he was reading it wrong. I reached out and took the pages back from him and volunteered to read it out loud myself. They didn't stop me. This could be a gamble, a roll of the dice I might regret my entire life.

Instead the sketch killed. They loved it. They seemed very happy. But it was show business, and I was still wary. The meeting was almost over, and I took another big leap. I actually said to them, pretty much verbatim, "Thank you for seeing me, I understand how these things work, and it's okay if I don't get the job. All I ask is that you let me know. Don't leave me hanging. Just tell me one way or another. Don't drag it out. I can take it."

Could I? Could I take it? Or would this rejection break me, destroy me? I didn't know. What made me say that? No idea. But with that last statement, I thanked them and left. I hitchhiked home. When I walked into the apartment, the phone was ringing. It was Jack Burns: "I have good news and I have bad news. The good news is that we're getting back to you quickly..." My heart sank. "The bad news is, you're hired."

•••

The first writers' meeting was an exciting, chaotic affair. I have found after years of doing this that writers enter these first meetings with the personas they want to project—cool, reserved, aggressive, etc.—but after a few weeks of grinding under pressurized deadlines, the masks are discarded and you are who you are. And that's a relief. Because to interact as a staff and produce the best-quality work, it's important that people be authentic. Even and maybe especially writers.

I was dressed in black pants, a white shirt, and a black leather jacket. I was wearing sunglasses. To hide the fear.

It was a uniform of sorts. Something I would seek and experiment with all my life. In a world in which I often felt overwhelmed, it would at least simplify something: what to wear.

Like a rabbi. A car valet. A bus boy. A punk. Like me.

I was a raw primitive compared to most. My last job had been as a bellhop. In fact, my hair and beard would not be this short and neat again until I directed *Borat*. I was now making ten times more money. Now that I was writer, I had to figure out how to be a writer.

I had been writing my entire life, lived in my imagination, but it was nothing like this. This was a very new world.

In this world, you had to conjure those ideas quickly and somehow coalesce them into a sketch form. Sketches had certain rules of character, of dialogue, of physical and visual and verbal humor, and a certain length and structure. And most important, big laughs and a big finish. And you needed to have them ready to read and be judged by a certain time, and because the show was live, there was very little margin for error. And if you survived that gauntlet every week and like an athlete had a good percentage of sketches that made it to air, then you were a success. And if you didn't, you were gone.

I had an innate sense of these rules from my years glued to variety shows. Almost immediately and I don't know why, I set out to succeed by those rules and break them at the same time.

In dreams begin responsibilities, indeed.

As I surveyed the people in the room, I immediately gravitated to certain writers at that first meeting, never imagining that some of them would change my life.

Elaine Pope, a Canadian who had worked with Lily Tomlin, was immediately like a big sister. Many years later, we'd win an Emmy together on *Seinfeld*.

Steve Adams, from Massachusetts, who it turned out was the nephew of one of my favorite authors, Kurt Vonnegut, was a sort of high school star quarterback who had become a hippie, and immediately became like a big brother to me. We became office mates. And he was like a teacher, literally teaching me to write, to take ideas and concepts and turn them into fleshed-out sketches, as we went along.

Bruce Kirschbaum and I immediately found common ground in our esoteric high-brow/low-brow cultural references in movies, TV, and music. We would wind up writing a lot of sketches and snorting a lot of cocaine together.

Bryan Gordon was another adult who seemed to have a healthy attitude about being there. He would be the first writer I knew to become a director. That would be inspirational to me later. I immediately liked and, more important, respected him. He was the least competitive person in the room and didn't need to be. Three of the actors were also hired as writers.

Bruce Mahler, who was a sweet and gentle and almost naive person but with a very specific and singular voice, specializing in conceptual routines. He was also a piano virtuoso and thought musically. I would often notice his scripts were dotted with musical notation so he'd know when to go up or down on a line.

Then there was the force of nature, Michael Richards. A tall, gangly coiled snake of a man. An adult. Yet there was something very childlike about him. Like he didn't understand anything. My immediate first reaction before I knew anything was that this guy was a genius. He was incapable of small talk; in fact, conversation itself was awkward. But when he embodied a character, he disappeared within it and spoke through it in the most original and intense ways. He didn't portray characters, he channeled them, became them. It was the only way he could express himself. It was almost like he was humorless when he wasn't in character. But he always seemed ready to erupt, explode, not in anger, but in cosmic comic energy. And I think his characters were a way to release that pent-up tension and anxiety.

And then I heard the voice of Brooklyn on the other side of the room. Loud, brash, opinionated, but good-natured and not didactic or dogmatic. Suddenly I was transported back to the streets of Brighton. Hearing that voice and feeling that feeling gave me an unconscious confidence. I belonged here too. I had found my comedy muse. My inadvertent mentor. As it turned out, for life, really. He was a balding, bespectacled grown-up in a Chicago Blackhawks jacket. That was Larry David.

Although there was nearly a decade of difference in our ages, we were even from the same neighborhood. And that transcended age. I immediately stayed close to him in the hopes that I would absorb some of his streetwise wisdom and vision. And he was generous enough to share it.

Although we couldn't have looked more different, he and I were from Brooklyn and therefore ready for a fight. With anybody. About almost anything. That's how you bond in Brooklyn. And when it came to his material, Larry's point of view was as ingrained in him as Michael's characters and no less unique. He trusted his judgment or at least trusted it more than anyone else's. And the result was something singular, which was apparent even then. An attitude that seemed to seamlessly synthesize street smarts, literary and cinematic intelligence, and a well-honed natural almost "Brooklynesque" comedy sensibility and attitude.

There were others, all nice people. Joe Shulkin, the head writer, a withdrawn, intellectual, acid-eating Deadhead. Sam Hefter, a wonderful warm, nurturing person who already had a family and who harbored the horrible secret that he had stolen someone else's material to get the job. Fred Raker, a punster, whose impressions rivaled the cast's but who had trouble getting sketches on the show. When Reagan was running and John Roarke the brilliant impressionist was assigned to play him, Fred was given the job of playing Jimmy Carter when they'd have to be in the same sketch. And Fred watched that 1980 election with a more desperate eye than the rest of us, knowing inherently that if Carter lost, he would lose his job.

There was Tom Kramer, the only writer younger than me. He was the resident filmmaker, which Bruce and I resented, having our own film ideas.

After a few episodes, a writing team joined the staff. Rod Ash and Marc Curtis. They approached me on the first day and said, "So you're the one." When I asked what they meant, they explained that they had been hired but were notified that their hiring was rescinded because they had found someone else instead. Me. But here they were now and we became good friends too.

This was my first television-writing job. Bruce and Steve had worked on Donny and Marie Osmond's variety show and had lived in Provo, Utah. And that made them among the most experienced on the staff. Yet without cachet, we were uncompromising firebrands.

The first issue was the name of the show. It was still unanswered when we were hired and even first assembled. So it was put to us to come up with a title befitting this show. One thing we were all hyper-aware of was the inevitable accusation that we would be perceived as a *Saturday Night Live* rip-off and that was abhorrent to every single writer. So we went off and came up with titles for the show that would set it apart from anything that had ever been on the air. There were long, absurd, Pythonesque titles; and short, one-word titles; and sometimes not even words. We were excited by the freedom and abandon when we submitted them and imagining how cool it would be for a show to have any of these titles. It would throw down the gauntlet about the kind of show we intended.

When the producers came back and said the name of the show would be *Fridays*, we were not just taken aback, but in disbelief and anger. There was already a logo, stationery, binders, jackets. It was a wake-up call. Our opinions would be tolerated and even indulged but not listened to. This was another corporate hierarchy. Calling it *Fridays* couldn't have made a louder statement that we were nothing but an *SNL* rip-off. We were embarrassed by the name.

Weirdly, for myself and some others, it made our commitment to even more radical work even deeper. If it was going to be called *Fridays*, then each week we had to do all we could to offend and even destroy the status quo. It might've seemed naive then, but I still believe it and live by that philosophy today.

•••

I loved the freedom of writing sketches. I soon discovered there were literally no rules—if it worked. No time limits, no structural restrictions, whatever genre, whatever was on my mind, grabbed my attention, struck my fancy, if I could figure out a way to manifest it as a sketch, it was potentially valid.

Later I would be forced into the rules and structure of sitcoms, where you had to service characters and story and some sort of grounded emotional reality, but I got lucky enough to work with Larry and Jerry, who encouraged me to stretch, bend, and break those rules and see what happened.

Another great thing about sketch writing, and I imagine this was true in most sketch shows, was that in essence you were your producer and director as well as writer. On *Fridays*, you were expected to supervise every aspect of your sketch from costumes and sets to camera angles to performances. Our sketch was our temporary fiefdom, and we were the kings.

But I had trouble cracking the code on the first two episodes. I couldn't get a sketch in the show. It was quite frustrating, and not being represented in the show makes one feel insecure and left out. And even in employment jeopardy. That's the competitive nature of the show. By the same token, I thought what was being produced was rather lame and tame. I was committed to a more extreme vision.

The third episode's musical guests were the Clash. They may have been my favorite band, and they were at the height of their powers. I really wanted to be part of that episode.

I wrote a sketch called "Diner of the Living Dead." I was a big George Romero fan. I loved the original *Night of the Living Dead*. But I especially liked the 1978 follow-up, *Dawn of the Dead*. It contained an element of satire, drawing parallels between our mindless consumerist culture and the undead. I was very struck by that metaphor in a sketch format, and "Diner of the Living Dead" seemed like a perfect follow-up. It had all the elements.

We had a cast and crew read-through every week. Despite the entire cast and all the writers being there, Jack always read each sketch aloud himself, playing every part. It was kind of strange and there was grumbling about it, but it was an accepted ritual. It happened that my sketch did great at the read-through. Everyone could see and was excited by it. This would be my first sketch. And it would be on the same episode as the Clash.

Also on that show was a Steve Adams piece. Steve's pieces were quiet and seemingly normal with one strange twist. In this case, it was a talk show called *Women Who Spit*. It was just a mundane talk show with women discussing mundane issues but spitting like guys at various points.

The Clash performed their already instant classics: "London Calling," "Clampdown," "Train in Vain," and "The Guns of Brixton." Coincidentally, Joe Strummer also quite spontaneously spit during one of the songs.

Of the first three shows, this one stood out. For me, the audience, the public.

Later at Yamashiro, the vast Japanese restaurant in the Hollywood Hills where we sometimes held the weekly wrap parties, I got to smoke large spliffs with the band and declare our commitment to radicalism and celebrate our triumph. It wasn't just Yamashiro's location overlooking the city, but I felt on top of the world. This was my life. Not carrying bags or driving cabs or washing dishes. And this was what this show could be. Anarchic, radical, extreme. Not corporate. Not safe.

This became a running theme in my work. In my choices. I fancied myself, in my head at least, as the outsider artist on the inside. This was an inescapable path to futility filled with thwarted desire and suffering that can never truly be reconciled. And many artists, inside, outside, have grappled with the question, only to find there is no answer. Could I have it all? And what the fuck was "all" anyway? An illusion and seduction that are hard to resist.

Indeed.

The next day almost all the ABC affiliates in the South dropped the show. I was proud. Fuck the South. But the producers and especially ABC were extremely unhappy and anxious and frightened. Yet at the same time, the show got tremendous attention for the controversy. And that episode remains one of the best we ever did.

The writers had been relegated to a cinderblock sub-basement in a building on the lot at ABC Television Center. This lot seemed more geared to live or live-on-tape shows. The local news was done there. ABC's West Coast soap operas were done there. Some sitcoms, like *Benson*, ABC's spin-off of the hit show *Soap*, were done there. *Benson* starred Robert Guillaume as the aide-de-camp to the governor character, both of whom had appeared on *Soap*.

The writers would spend a lot of time out of our windowless

prisonlike offices, fucking around in the long hallways, racing, throwing a ball, playing football with a piece of balled-up garbage, throwing coins down the hall for money.

At the end of the hall, a couple of the lesser characters of *Benson* had their dressing rooms. They were as far from their action as we were from ours. But more isolated. After all, the *Fridays* writers were hanging out, sharing ideas, and eventually drugs. Very communal and fraternal. These supporting actors would sit in their "cells" all day waiting.

One short-lived character on *Benson* was a comedian–joke writer for the governor. The part lasted only a few episodes. Sometimes the actor would sit forlornly in his dressing room. If I was down there at the far end of the hallway, I would engage him in conversation. He was unhappy being there and soon would be gone. I never thought in that moment that we would run into each other again. That was Jerry Seinfeld.

At that time he was a beleaguered comedian forced to recite sub-standard sitcom jokes for a steady paycheck. He was one of many who dotted the TV landscape in the '70s and '80s. They aspired to their own shows based on their stand-ups and some got that chance and quickly failed. Then what? What do you do when your "life" fails? Jerry was about to be cast adrift from a minor role on a mediocre sitcom. Far removed from a show based on his life and his stand-up. It might seem hard to believe, but he was nervous about his future.

●●●

In order to produce and remain prolific on *Fridays* and survive, essentially living in that sub-basement, in order to have a live show every week, cocaine was introduced into the mix. We needed to pull all-nighters and turn around the day after the show and start all over again for weeks and weeks at a time. Although most of us were young and strong, your brain, your creativity wears down under that kind of duress, and coke helped keep it perked up. And it gave you the confidence you didn't really possess. And it was absurdly fun. At first.

The producers couldn't have us driving all over town to various dealers to cop so a system was worked out where we had grams of coke literally delivered to our desks like pizza on a regular basis. This became a survival tool, and indeed for those who did not partake, their work suffered and they couldn't keep up the pace and most of them fell by the wayside.

But for those of us becoming steadily and increasingly addicted, it became a bonding agent. We all carried little metal spoons with us and would spoon each other before the show. Soon it was before, during, and after and sometimes in between sketches of the show. And soon after that, it was simply all the time, even on the rare days off, until the bonding ended and was replaced by each of us going into our offices, alone, paranoid, locking the door, and snorting a few lines ourselves.

The producers were as bad as we were. Jack Burns's personality in particular underwent a transformation. He was upbeat, funny, supportive, but soon he could only be found brooding in his darkened office wearing a large Stetson cowboy hat and massive sunglasses. He was like a comedic Kurtz. You dreaded being beckoned in because he would literally start to mumble gibberish and gobbledygook, and you didn't know if it was the drugs or he was having a stroke. It was scary.

Some of the cast managed to stay relatively straight, including Larry and Michael. Some indulged but managed to handle it without going over the edge. But not everyone. I'm not sure all of them realized they were performing coke-fueled sketches. Much of our material became drug drenched.

But before it all went south, it was an exhilarating environment and corresponded to the increasing success of the show. Suddenly West Coast celebrities were coming to the show just to hang out and party.

Once Larry Flynt, confined permanently to a wheelchair following the attempted assassination on his life, with his wife, Althea, came to the show. They brought Jimmy Carter's sister, Ruth Carter Stapleton, with them as well as a large entourage of bikers and hangers-on. Flynt has recently converted inexplicably to born-again Christianity, and the president's sister, also inexplicably, was his spiritual adviser.

The word filtered down to the sub-basement that Flynt and his entourage wanted a joint. I quickly and excitedly volunteered and rolled one up to bring to them in the green room. I was moving at breakneck speed through the whole process, running up the flights of stairs to the green room, joint in hand. I raced to the open door, through which I could see Flynt in his wheelchair along with Althea and the president's sister, but as I leapt through the portal, I found myself on the ground, taken down by two Secret Service agents who had positioned themselves on either side of the entrance. They held me down until I exclaimed, "I have a joint for the president's sister!" I displayed the hastily rolled spliff and they helped me up and I delivered it, taking in the surreal scene. Everyone seemed quite fucked up and out of it already, before I returned to the sub-basement.

●●●

Jack wanted *Fridays* to be an outlaw show. And indeed, the more coke got trafficked, the more we were breaking the law.

But nothing fed Jack's desire to produce an outlaw show, even if it was funded by one of the largest corporations in the world, more than a letter I received one day. It was from a federal prisoner in Missouri. His name was Larry Scott Andersen, and he had chosen my name out of the dozen or so writers because I, too, was a Larry.

The letter, well written and well typed, which I still have, said that he, too, was a writer. That he had been framed for his crime. That his goal was to embark upon a writing career when he got out of the pen. And he was hoping I might be able to help.

Jack was exhilarated by this correspondence. He vociferously encouraged me to continue the correspondence. Soon I was receiving collect calls from the prison, too. This went on for at least a couple of months. I'd have to stop whatever I was doing and take a call from the prison.

But then they stopped. In a way I was relieved. But also curious.

One weekday morning, earlier than I would've normally gotten up, I received a phone call telling me to quickly turn on the TV to *The Today Show*. There was Larry Scott Andersen being interviewed by one of the hosts. He talked confidentially about his fledgling writing career and the help and encouragement he was receiving from such notables as Neil Simon and Cheech and Chong. He was parlaying that support into an early release from prison and hoped to start his writing career in earnest once that occurred.

I confess, I was a bit offended. After all, he hadn't mentioned me. I was a bit skeptical. Would these prominent people really help him? And though Jack was disappointed, mainly I was relieved. Having moved on to greener pastures, he stopped contacting me. And I thought that was the end of the chapter. But it wasn't.

A couple of months later, someone showed me a newspaper article. Larry Scott Andersen had been rearrested while on parole and would be imprisoned for a long time.

•••

The jewel in the crown of the late-night shows was the opening sketch. It reached the widest viewership and thus had the most impact. And because of that, budgets for the opening sketches were quite a bit more generous than the weird esoteric sketch that played at ten to one in the morning.

But the formula for the opening sketch still seemed elusive. At one of the writers' meetings, Larry David, who felt the show was often not putting its best foot forward and instead did a lot of cheap and exploitive material while quality stuff wasn't getting on or being relegated to the end of the show, went off on a harangue about the bullshit of the opening sketch.

I remember him saying that the opening sketch was just about a play on words of a popular movie. And he gave some examples that Joe Shulkin had written and were produced. And he was right. Like *Star Wars Memories*, which combined a *Star Wars* parody with the Woody Allen movie *Stardust Memories*. Often these sketches' biggest laughs came on the titles or the appearance of a celebrity portrayed by our skilled impressionists, including Larry. Otherwise the sketches were less than inspired.

In his ire, off the top of his head, Larry gave an example of a title without a sketch. With Reagan having defeated Carter in 1980, Larry blurted out, "*The Ronnie Horror Picture Show.*" A takeoff on *The Rocky Horror Picture Show.* He said it off the cuff in passing and with some disdain, and everyone sort of smiled and moved on. Except for Bruce Kirschbaum and me. We were able to immediately see a full-fledged sketch, plus play with the music, something we each harbored fantasies about, and we immediately volunteered to write it.

"*The Ronnie Horror Picture Show*" turned out to be the crowning achievement of *Fridays*. A twenty-plus-minute musical sketch, performed live. It received a tremendous amount of attention. So much so that the producer of the actual *Rocky Horror Picture Show*, Lou Adler, threatened to sue for not getting the proper permissions. Instead of fighting it, the corporate lawyers immediately buckled and the sketch would never be seen again. But it also contributed to a surge in the ratings, which had the media giving us a second look beyond the trite *Saturday Night Live* rip-off charges. This, coupled with what were the weakest seasons of *Saturday Night Live*, allowed us to dominate for a moment the late-night comedy conversation.

This attention would be parlayed just a few weeks later by the now infamous Andy Kaufman episode.

•••

Andy was admired by virtually everyone on the show. He was not just the most radical conceptual artist of his time but he was also the lovable Latka on the hit series *Taxi*. So there was excitement about having him on the show. For Jack, it was another opportunity to break all the rules. His coke-fueled desire to tear everything down dovetailed nicely with Andy's desire to push through all known boundaries in comedy. Andy was a philosopher of comedy. He asked, What is funny?

I believe he told us himself at the first writers' meeting with him that his desire was to interrupt a sketch. Bruce K and I were both like beatniks attending a poetry reading at a coffeehouse, snapping our fingers and "gronking." There were those who had mixed feelings, some even negative, but Jack took over and made the deciding vote. We were going to disrupt a sketch on live network TV. He was super excited. Andy's ideas were so avant-garde, yet his affect didn't change much. But his ideas were savagely savant-like and idiosyncratic, just bouncing off the top of his head, but perhaps bouncing around inside his mind for his entire life.

The decision was made to use a sketch by Steve Adams, which was a simple dinner sketch in a restaurant with a simple twist. Each member of the dinner party unbeknownst to the others would excuse themselves to smoke pot in the bathroom. The transgressive action took place off camera. Our audience quite indiscriminately loved drug humor, and in many sketches, their laughter was replaced by whistles, noises, and howls.

But this would be a domestic relationship sketch. Two couples at a restaurant, a relatable situation that included drug references, during which Andy, at some point in the sketch, would choose a moment to stop following the script. And then see what happens. How will the actors react? How will the audience react? How will the audience at home react?

Andy did other sketches that night. All equally radical, but more containable and staying within the confines of one reality, regardless of that reality. For instance, another memorable piece involved Andy as himself and a guest, the masked magician played by Bob Zmuda. The masked magician was going to reveal trade secrets. This made Andy uncomfortable. He didn't like violating the "Magician's Code." So when the magician swallowed his sword, Andy jabbed it and it went in too far down the magician's throat and the magician spit up blood. It was the perfect exploration and deconstruction of an audience's expectation of what was acceptable to be funny. When is something still a laugh? Even when you gasp or scream and cry? Or perhaps those are even deeper laughs that conjure up myriad emotions and reactions.

These were the laughs, the comedy, that I would try to pursue all my life. The deeper codes of comedy. Thoughts and reflections that reached their apex first through Larry David and then Bob Dylan and finally Sacha. These three would be teachers.

As the sketch approached, all those who knew what was coming and were fortified by coke, none more than Jack, held our breaths in anticipation.

But there were many who didn't have a clue what was to come, including the other actors in the sketch with the exception of Michael Richards, though even he didn't know exactly how all this would play itself out. Also the crew. One thing I've learned from doing this for many decades now is that crews will follow you to the ends of the earth. There are always exceptions but as a group they are the most loyal people I've ever dealt with. And of course the audience, the live audience there to see a show and have an experience and the home audience, somewhat detached but still involved.

So even though it was Andy Kaufman, the sketch, two couples at a restaurant, sneaking off one at a time to smoke a joint, lulled everyone into a sense of complacency. Their expectations weren't very high. The other actors had done this so many times before by now. The crew knew there were no elaborate camera moves or special effects or stunts. And the audience, familiar with couples in restaurants and always enamored of a drug reference, imagined something quite safe.

First, Maryedith Burrell left to smoke and came back high. She didn't play an obvious stoner, instead highlighting the shifting and heightened perceptions of someone who was high, noticing things that the others were baffled by.

Andy was next. He exited and then returned to his seat. He seemingly tried to soldier on with the sketch, but within seconds it was abundantly clear that he was not going to do that. He broke the fourth wall of the sketch by glancing at the audience with his patented bemusement. Michael, like the caged comedy beast he always was, simply waited to see where Andy would go. Maryedith seemed to get that something was off right away and began to laugh, though

I never quite believed the laugh was sincere. It had a nervous quality to it and I wouldn't blame her—though she was a skilled improv comedian, she was entering uncharted territory. Melanie Chartoff seemed truly confused, trying at first to get Andy back into it and then stunned when she realized that was not going to happen.

But the truth was it was a middling sketch, getting more whistles for the drug references than laughs. And so it took a minute for the audience to even realize something was off. The whistles and "whoops" died down as confusion set in. Finally Andy explained calmly that he couldn't do the sketch, that he couldn't play stoned. It kind of ground everything to an awkward halt, which I believe was Andy's goal. I believe he would've been happy creating an unprecedented but quietly awkward moment and then perhaps walking off.

But Michael hopped out of his chair and darted off camera and returned with the cue cards, which he dumped in front of Andy. Andy picked up the cudgel and gently spilled water from his glass onto Michael, who avoided most of it as he jumped out of the way. Melanie seemed annoyed and threw some butter at Andy, which he played as if he was now pissed and threatened to shove the butter back in her face and you can see her flinch. She doesn't want that to happen.

The brilliant Mark Blankfield, playing the waiter, never broke stride and continued filling water glasses and tending to the extras playing the other patrons.

But Andy, true to his comedy aesthetic, was not at that point looking for fireworks. Just the upending of comic expectations. Is this funny? That's what he was curious about. But for the actors and audience, they wanted laughs and, if not laughs, action.

It was too late for laughs. Andy had successfully soured the audience, and winning them back was not in the cards, nor on his agenda. But this weird anticlimax, this small-scale conflict of a moment, was not sufficient for live TV, and Jack Burns perceived that. You can first see him in the corner of the screen trying to intervene and really trying to spur someone to action. But Melanie was backing away in fear, Maryedith kept laughing, and Michael, an avant-garde artist in his own right, was okay just letting it be what it was and not contriving it any further.

So Jack entered the scene. He was yelling for Bobby, our director Bob Bowker, to go to a commercial, but Bob knew not to cut away too quickly. Jack then upped the ante by instigating an altercation with Andy. Within seconds the loyal crew, thinking the sketch, indeed the show, was being ruined by this interloper, rushed the stage and swarmed Andy, ready to hurt him if necessary. As the struggle ensued, the curtain was pulled, Bobby cut to a long shot, and indeed we went to a commercial.

At that point Jack had to let the crew know it was all planned so they didn't lynch Andy. But people were pissed anyway.

Honestly, I can't really remember whether the show continued or whether that was the last sketch. But clearly, the moment not really intended to be a national sensation became just that. We have seen Carol Burnett and Harvey Korman and Tim Conway and Vicki Lawrence break character on *The Carol Burnett Show*. They would try to restrain themselves but suddenly burst into laughter. And indeed the audience loved these moments of supposed spontaneity. Late-night comedy writers were less enamored of perceiving it as a way to get laughs when the material was weak.

But this was different. The goal was not to up the laugh quotient but to break it apart, deconstruct it, question and analyze it. It was not funny. But in some ways it was better than funny. And it used the medium, the liveness, which is usually a facade where everything is really planned to the second to its fullest extent. Live finally meant reality and reality can't be predicted.

At the after-party that night, a few of the writers gravitated to Andy. I thought he was a visionary and genius, which were not two words usually applied to comedians. I remember casually saying to him, How do you top this, what do you do next, you'll have to stage your own death. It was a tossed-off comment though many great comedic concepts grew out of such comments. He wasn't the kind of person who needed outsiders pitching him ideas. He had his own ideas of what he would do next.

As he appeared in *Fridays* twice more and then began his illustrious wrestling career I didn't think about that conversation again until May 16, 1984. The day Andy died.

•••

One Monday night, December 8, 1980, while Boston-born Bruce and I were writing together in our office, feeling the weekly pressure of an unrealistic deadline that could only be met with the assistance of artificial substances, Bruce excused himself to go upstairs to our main offices, where there was a TV, to check in on the Patriots, who were on *Monday Night Football*. I wasn't happy because of all the work we had ahead of us, but he wasn't gone too long. However, when he returned, he was weeping. Glibly, I asked him if the Patriots were losing. He told me that John Lennon had been killed. I didn't cry. But I was shocked and stunned and saddened. It seemed like a permanent end to something. Something mythical and magical but obviously not real. John himself had said just a few years before, the dream is over. And now it really was. And with it, all our illusions.

I don't remember exactly when Jack was fired. It seemed in retrospect, like the death of Lennon, inevitable. Jack had lost control. Of the show and himself. And though I would always think of him as more than a mentor, a father figure really, and me to him, something of a son figure, that was now over too.

Bill Lee's drug use masked a virulent cancer. He called the writing staff in to his hospital room at Cedars-Sinai, but rather than rail at the random inequities of life, he chastised us for not coming up with more memorable repeatable sketch characters. He died soon after. A producer till the end.

Suddenly loss snuck its way into the show and hung over it like a dark cloud. The combination of the new news show *Nightline*'s strange success exploiting the Iran hostage crisis, and the fact that, unlike *Fridays*, it was owned by the network, made it easy to hand them the coveted 11:30 time slot and push us back to midnight. And our failure to hold on to their lead, led inevitably to our demise.

There was a lame toothless attempt to do a prime-time special to see if the show could catch on at a more family-friendly hour, but both Bruce and I refused to do it. However, Bruce demanded that we get paid anyway, per some weird clause in the basic WGA contract. And we were. That would be the last money I would earn for a long time. A long time.

CHAPTER 2

COMEDY MOSES, OR WANDERING IN THE COMEDY DESERT

*T*he year was 1982. I was unemployed. And I would essentially wander in the comedy desert for the next seven years.

The comedy desert is vast and desolate. Nothingness without any guarantee of "somethingness." Jobs, gigs, even possibilities, merely mirages on the horizon. And the worst part is, you don't know you're in the desert until it's too late. You must go through to the oasis if there is one. There is no going back. And along the way, the comedy desert is littered with corpses of actors and comedians and writers and producers who thought they were doing well. Thought the mirage was real. Thought they could make it to the other side.

As is often the case when a show fails, everyone dispersed, tried to get as far away from the stench of failure as possible. Larry David moved back to New York and had an infamously miserable year writing on *Saturday Night Live*. That misery would be put to good use years later on *Seinfeld*.

I quit coke, pot, and cigarettes. All at about the same time. All cold turkey. I was hyperfocused.

I'd never even thought about a career until after *Fridays* was over, but I soon realized that if I didn't think about it, nobody else would either.

I was a runner in those days and would walk over to Fairfax High and run around their track. I was obsessed with Bruce Springsteen and listened incessantly to "The River" on a cassette in my Walkman while I ran. Some songs set a perfect pace for me. One day "Crush on You" was serving that purpose. I would sing along quietly to myself, *"Ooh, ooh, I got a crush on you…"* It was dusk as I rounded the track mouthing the words to the song and saw another lone figure ahead of me. It was unmistakable. It was the Boss himself getting in his laps. I thought, *C'mon, I'm listening to his music and it was like I conjured him up. Here he is!* I quickened my pace to pull up alongside him.

Bruce and I exchanged no words. I merely took off my headphones as I ran next to him so that he could hear what I was listening to, we exchanged a knowing glance and a chuckle at the sweet synchronicity, and then I blew past him.

Thinking perhaps delusionally that *Fridays* would be some sort of stepping stone, I wasn't entirely wrong. Except that the steps led down.

I hadn't had an agent until the very end of *Fridays* and only because it seemed like the thing to do. My first agent was a cool Asian-American fellow named Paul Yamamoto and his associate, very preppy and white, Pat Faulstitch. They seemed like they were incredibly enthusiastic and excited at the prospect of representing me. It seemed like there would be no limits I could reach with such supportive representation. But when I gave them my first post-*Fridays* screenplay, I didn't hear anything for a long while. I've come to learn that not hearing anything is like hearing something. Only something not good. Something like, *What the fuck am I supposed to do with this?* But at the time, I didn't know that.

Then one day they asked if they could come to my house. I didn't really want to socialize, just get some action on the screenplay or any cool work for that matter. But nevertheless, they showed up after hours. Even at that point I still thought, *They have some exciting news for me, and they want to tell me in person.*

I'll never forget, I sat in this slightly past its peak big easy chair procured at a garage sale. It was grand in design but very used and frayed. And Paul and Pat kneeled on either side of me and told me in the most somber tones there was nothing they could do with the screenplay. Nothing? There was nobody to show it to? No notes? No thoughts? Just nothing.

Almost immediately after this fiasco, Paul came to me and said he was no longer interested in being an agent. He needed to find himself. And he abruptly left the business. This began what I call my *Spinal Tap* drummer series of agents.

Over the next several years, I had an agent get busted for coke just as I signed with him, an agent tragically die of AIDS just as I signed with him, and an agent who was the victim of a bizarre home invasion robbery that traumatized him for many years just as I signed with him. A string of bad luck for them for sure. But also for me.

I came out of *Fridays* extremely uncompromising and, as it turned out, extremely unrealistic. I viewed working anything in prime time as selling out. I viewed working on sitcoms as selling out. And essentially that didn't change until *Seinfeld*.

A series of jobs came along, some through these agents, some by word of mouth. Some seemed promising but weren't.

A writer acquaintance of mine who wanted to segue into directing had secured a directing job on an anthology series called *Monsters*. He asked me quite generously to write the episode, which I did. But I was very unhappy with the results. I felt, quite arrogantly, I could do better, but worse, I realized not only how far I was from a good writing job, but how distant the dream of directing was.

After that, I was hired to write *Elvira's Halloween Special*. I believe it was for some nascent cable outfit at the time. But it didn't matter. I was quickly fired for being too edgy. For Elvira.

Bruce Kirschbaum, my former *Fridays* colleague, had hooked up with two of Orson Welles's last associates, Paul Hunt and Gary Graver. They had helped Orson through some of his last projects. In fact, Gary had shot what was then the still unfinished fragments of Welles's final film, *The Other Side of the Wind*.

But as cool as it was to work for and with Welles, it didn't pay the bills for Gary or Paul. And so they had dabbled in soft-core porn, rip-offs of more popular genre movies, and when I met them, straight-to-video B-horror movies. This was a world I was very interested in. Making movies, even bad ones, seemed like fun. And I knew from Bogdanovich to Coppola, this was also a way to segue into directing.

I know this sounds crazy but it's true. First, I truly had no idea how to "become" a director. But perhaps more important, I was far too embarrassed to ever say out loud, "I want to direct." It sounded absurd and idiotic when I imagined it coming out of my mouth, and so I kept it a secret locked up in my imagination until I could figure out how I could be one, a director, without saying it.

Somewhere around this time, five years from when I had regularly harassed him as a parking valet and stole roaches out of his ashtray while he patiently waited for his car in Century City, I found myself writing for David Steinberg. Writing material. He was doing stand-up again after a career peak in the late '60s, when he had hit albums, made notorious appearances on *The Smothers Brothers Comedy Hour*, and even had his own short-lived summer show (that was a thing then) and had segued into directing and being producing partners with, of all people, Burt Reynolds. He needed new stuff. All of this with the understanding that, if possible, we'd turn this into something greater, like a movie or TV show or special.

I loved writing for David. He had become very political and, in fact, had made it onto Nixon's enemy list, a badge of honor for a comedian, and was now doing semi-regular *Tonight Show* appearances. He was one of Johnny's favorite guests, combining erudition with comedy and current events. David was funny and smart.

So he and I would discuss various topics that seemed to be trending in the news and then just riff until we hit upon a concept that could be developed. It was done under the deadline of an upcoming *Tonight Show* appearance, which lent urgency to the proceedings.

I would often accompany David to the show and had the great luck and pleasure of meeting Johnny himself on a few occasions. He would come into David's dressing room for a few minutes before the show to shoot the shit and even try out some jokes on us. I always felt there was a great disparity between his on-camera physicality and his in-person physicality. On TV he seemed like a slight person. You might have a sense of his formal almost military stiffness of his body language. In person, that stiffness was present too, but he was a big strapping guy. He looked like a high-ranking officer in the military. But it was Johnny.

David brought me along on a number of gigs, and though it was a far cry from what I had envisioned for myself, I was grateful to be busy, make a little money, and have some fun and creatively challenging opportunities.

David was going to direct a Cinemax show starring the legendary yet still cult comedian Richard Belzer, and he recommended me for a writing gig. I went to meet Belzer. Like David, who lived in a lavish mini estate in the hills of Sherman Oaks, drove a classic car, and had full-time help so he and his wife could navigate their life, Belzer also enjoyed the finer things. I couldn't really relate to this. I had been broke most of my life, and for the short time I earned good money on *Fridays*, I still lived in the same apartment and drove the same car. Later I would come closer to this lifestyle, fall into the same traps, and realize the sad irony of it.

Belzer, The Belz, put the "culture" in the term "cult comedian." An influencer before the word was popularized. People, comedians would come to see him in clubs just to watch him work. His spontaneity and wit were without precedent, and he could spend an hour or more just talking to the audience, asking them questions, making jokes at their expense, in an endless stream of literary-referenced-yet-laugh-out-loud comedy. But his success had been limited because he wasn't able to translate that very specific gift to the mediums of television or movies or even larger live venues, where material needed to be written and rehearsed and memorized and repeated take after take, night after night.

He was like a great jazz musician doing comedy. He may have been the coolest cat I'd ever met.

This show might be an opportunity to fuse what Belzer was with a more disciplined approach required of the medium. I was excited.

Comedians like Robin Williams worshipped him, but Belzer, though known and successful to a point, had certainly not reached those heights. Belzer's issue was he liked to live as if he did.

So I didn't meet him in an agent's office or conference room. I met him at the Beverly Hills Hotel, where he was staying in a suite.

In the room were some of the other people who would be involved in the show and had already been deeply involved in Belz's life. Tom Leopold, who during these years was probably the funniest person I knew. He was a writer and sometime performer and never really quite figured out how to conjure that magic in front of the camera but he could have an entire table convulsed with laughter at lunch. He called himself a "shticktician." He and Belzer together were an explosion of spontaneous hilarity. And he would be co-starring in the show. Cool.

Also there was Belzer's older brother, Len, a sweet, smart, supportive man who lived seemingly amiably in Belzer's shadow, yet it was his own shadow he couldn't escape. Years later, like their father before them, Len would take his own life.

In addition, there was Seth Greenland, a writer whose dad owned an eponymous and prestigious ad agency in New York. After dabbling in television and movies, Seth would eventually settle in the world of prose.

And hovering in the background, Rick Newman, the nurturing and pioneering owner of Catch a Rising Star and Belzer's manager, who had lost an eye when it was poked by the sharp tip of a chair in the club. I'm fascinated and transfixed by the stories behind missing limbs and organs. Eyes are a particular obsession.

I felt very detached from this crowd at first, even as Richard was incredibly warm to me. There was too much laughing but not enough funny ideas. I kept my mouth shut. Though I knew I wouldn't be able to do that forever. Belz held court as a parade of friends and associates came in to pitch ideas. Some were cool. Some were amusing. Some were funny or had potential. Some were unfunny and had no potential. But they were all greeted with this overly enthusiastic guffawing.

I remember Christopher Guest coming in. He had the coolest pedigree of virtually anyone in comedy. I can't remember if this was just before or just after *Spinal Tap*. But as I remember, *Spinal Tap* didn't make an immediate splash. Instead in the best traditions of cult movies, *Spinal Tap* is probably more popular now than when it came out. But Guest was already a legend among comedy people for his seminal contributions to the *National Lampoon Radio Hour* and the off-Broadway *Lampoon* show, *Lemmings*.

And this was at least ten years before he started making his own movies.

As I remember, his pitch was for a private detective parody. It was thrilling to watch him perform the entire piece in this small room.

I remember that, despite the overly raucous laughter, we never heard about the piece again once he'd left. Had they not wanted to pay him? Had he decided to keep it for himself? I never knew.

After avoiding it for most of the session and being uncharacteristically quiet, Belzer finally asked me what I thought. About everything. I took a deep breath and told the truth. I found most of what was discussed and pitched to be fairly weak. I gave a critique of the various pieces, and the room grew quiet. Then Belzer said he agreed with me and everyone chimed in, admitting they felt the same way. Great. Now we could get to work.

I think I gained Belzer's respect after that, and he and I worked together off and on for many years.

The show we did, cleverly titled *The Richard Belzer Show*, consisted of six episodes for Cinemax and was fun to make. David directed. It was a mix of improv, sketches, and music. We had one-of-a-kind comedy meteors as guest stars such as Robin Williams and Gilbert Gottfried.

I remember the show coming out, and then I remember it being over. Very unceremonious. And something I would have to get used to but honestly never have.

•••

Shows are picked up with great fanfare. But dropped off like unwanted dogs on abandoned streets. With as little attention as possible. I've never been coddled over a cancellation. In fact, I've never had anybody ever say to me, "The show is canceled." It was more like, "Huh, we don't seem to be doing it anymore." The offices were closed. Everyone was gone. Eventually you got the message without any specific person having to be the bad guy.

But my relationship with Belzer and Steinberg continued. Steinberg was hired to emcee and Belzer to appear on Playboy's *Tommy Chong Roast*, to be filmed in Las Vegas. This was during that period between *The Dean Martin Celebrity Roasts* and Comedy Central's very successful revival. And both David and Belzer hired me to write their material.

Although I didn't think there was anyone on the dais who knew Tommy Chong personally, that didn't really seem to matter, as long as you could say something insulting and funny about him. It brought together a dazzling array of wildly disparate performers. Old-time comic Slappy White. One of the last professional stand-up comedy teams, Mack and Jamie. Sitcom star and comedian Marsha Warfield. I'm not even sure I said a word to any of them. But also on the bill was Jerry Seinfeld. I seem to remember us greeting each other initially at McCarran Airport. Our common ground was that sub-basement. But escaping it was the best thing that ever happened to him. He was grateful to be fired from *Benson*. It allowed his stand-up career to flourish. And here he was.

It was a surreal experience. I was holed up in a penthouse in the Desert Inn, one of the hotels from the glory days of the rat pack that had been owned by Howard Hughes and was about to be torn down. There, as I stared through a panoramic window that looked out on all of Las Vegas, I wrote the dirty, filthy, but hopefully hilarious material for David and Richard. If this were 1964, I would say, "This is the life." But it wasn't. It was the mid-eighties, and I was hyperaware of something slipping away that I never had a grasp on. I wanted more. I expected more. But it was becoming painfully apparent that there was no correlation between my desires, my hunger, and reality.

Also on the bill was one of my comedy idols, Dick Shawn. Dick was an unusual and conceptual and intense comedian, especially for his time. He used his body and wasn't afraid to not be funny, sometimes for a long time, until his payoff. He was a mainstay on TV in the '60s and '70s. I loved watching his stand-up. He was weird and wild, even though his hair was professionally coiffed and he wore a tuxedo. And he showed up, though usually underutilized, in movies like *It's a Mad, Mad, Mad, Mad World*. His most famous movie role is as LSD in Mel Brooks's original 1967 *The Producers*, where he sang the classic song "Love Power."

He was the last guest on the dais to speak that night. It had been a night of depraved and obscene language. All limits had been reached and breached. Shawn approached the podium and stood silently for a moment. Then projectile-vomited across the dais and into the audience. It was pea soup but his point was made. He was a comedian and how was he supposed to top what had preceded him without taking it to the next level? And that's why I loved Dick Shawn. Because that's how he thought. What's the next level?

A year later, he would literally collapse and die onstage, but because of his comic philosophy, people thought it was part of his act, until it was too late.

After that, David was hired to direct and I was hired to write a Belzer comedy special from the Bottom Line in New York City. This was a fun time. I wanted the special to be "written." Sharp material based on Belzer's life. More like Richard Pryor than his off-the-cuff ad-libbing with the audience. And Belzer had the life for it. Drug problems. Drinking problems. Woman problems. He worked as a gopher for Miles Davis. His father committed suicide. He was with Belushi the night he died. Not bits but a coordinated life story. A concert with a certain coherence and narrative story line. With drama as well as comedy.

The problem was, Pryor worked on his material for a couple of years, honing it and shaping it and ordering and structuring it. We'd have only a few weeks. No tryouts. Just do it.

And I was able to write the material, but it was voluminous and it was impossible for Belzer to get familiar enough with it within the time limits imposed on it. So the concert had some of that material. But also bits and routines, some new, some tried-and-true, all funny, but disparate. No theme running through them.

After that, David had an opportunity to make his own stand-up special and asked me to write that too. It would be directed by one of David's other constant associates in those days, Hank Polonsky. He was a great guy, and this might've been his first opportunity to direct, having been primarily an editor up until then. Hank's dad was Abraham Polonsky, one of the most prominent of the blacklisted writers. He had written the classic John Garfield movie *Body and Soul* and wrote and directed the follow-up, *Force of Evil*, before he was blacklisted. He wrote the great racially tinged crime drama *Odds Against Tomorrow* under an assumed name.

I remember thinking of the irony of my worship of Elia Kazan, and now meeting someone who was a direct victim of Kazan's infamous naming names. Abraham Polonsky had to move his family, including a young Hank, to England in order to make a living, and it took him many years before he could come back and reestablish his career. There had certainly been a price to pay. Yet Hank bore no malice or bitterness toward anybody. His father survived to thrive again, and Hank saw his life and his story as ultimately an unusual but good one.

But the special came and went, and like the temp worker I really was, I was once again out of work with zero possibilities.

•••

Being unemployed in LA leaves you with a lot of time on your hands. Days to fill in with thinking and wasting time. Sometimes the thinking was a waste of time, and sometimes the waste of time led to very fruitful thoughts.

I loved driving in LA. It was a meditative time for me. And it was how I learned about this labyrinth of a city pre-GPS. I would drive as far as I could in one direction or another and then try to wend my way back home.

I realized that people had LA all wrong. The first mistake was comparing it to New York. New York with its skyline and classic iconic architecture was renaissance art. You could look at it and know immediately why it was beautiful. LA was modern art. Jagged and jarring, risking ugliness and formlessness, but if you looked at it long enough and deeply enough, the beauty emerged. And soon the world caught up to that.

As someone who grew up glued to the TV watching cheap B-movies and TV shows that didn't have budgets for sets, and thus were forced to shoot on location, like *Indestructible Man* with Lon Chaney Jr. as a death row prisoner put to death but brought back to life seeking vengeance on the streets of Bunker Hill, which I watched transfixed dozens of times, I knew LA long before I arrived.

There were many landmarks that were iconic to me. None more than the *Daily Planet* building from the George Reeves TV *Superman*, which is actually Los Angeles City Hall. And *Dragnet* prided itself on its diverse Los Angeles locations. There were the early comedies of Laurel and Hardy like *The Music Box* or Charlie Chaplin's two-reelers, all shot on the streets in the days before getting permission became a big pain in the ass. They would just take a camera and go.

And then there was the golden age of 1970s cinema, which produced such seminal films as Altman's *The Long Goodbye* and Mazursky's *Alex In Wonderland*, which traversed the city in a stoned way that it hadn't been portrayed before. I found it all very inspiring. You can be sure I soaked that shit up all my life and really felt at home in LA, even embracing its innate alienation and disorientation.

I had read Raymond Chandler, too, back in Brooklyn and Florida, but now with time on my hands, I got into Fante and Bukowski. This was where they lived and what they wrote about long before it was cool.

•••

Sometime in the mid to late eighties, David Steinberg had mentioned that if I wrote a spec script, we could potentially get a movie made. That was all the motivation I needed. I sat down with a tape recorder and came up with a simple premise. A young comedian is about to do a road tour just as his mother, a rowdy dirty comedian from the old club days gets thrown out of her nursing home. *Great Exits.* I thought about Garry Shandling as the young comic and someone like Bette Midler or Barbra Streisand as the mother. He is forced to take her on the road with him. I improvised the entire thing into the tape recorder in three days. I'm not saying it was a masterpiece or didn't need work, but the first sixty or seventy pages were pretty good.

The movie never got made but it became my calling card. First, somehow, it seemed like Elizabeth Taylor was looking for some kind of vehicle and was interested. David was friends with a confidante of hers. We met with him, not Liz, a few times but like so much in Hollywood, it sort of stopped. It certainly would have been an interesting experience.

It also somehow got to Garry Shandling when he was doing *It's Garry Shandling's Show,* an early radical sitcom experiment that predated *The Larry Sanders Show.* Alan Zweibel, who was one of the original *SNL* writers, was working on the show, and he was at the meeting. I can't remember much about the meeting except they were both very nice and respectful but nothing came of it. I got to know Garry much better years later when he had evolved into a sort of comedy shaman when I was working with Sacha. He would show up at screenings and offer his inimitable, though-sometimes-hard-to-decipher deep analysis and wisdom. I really respected and liked him and wished we had worked together somewhere. And I got to know Alan better when he appeared many years later on *Curb Your Enthusiasm.* He had written much seminal comedy, yet was a completely unpretentious approachable and supportive guy.

●●●

Jerry Seinfeld hosted Super Bowl parties in the early '90s. They were fun. Not lavish affairs but cool get-togethers to eat, drink, and watch the game. Garry was at one. I said, "It's nice to meet you." He said, "We've met before." I said, "No we haven't. I'd remember." He insisted and finally we were distracted by other things. And for years after that, I thought he had me confused with someone else, until I remembered coming to see him at his show for that meeting in the mid-eighties. He was right. I think I must've blocked the specifics because all I can remember of the meeting was that it took place. And he must've thought I was an asshole for not remembering. And I was.

I was scraping by, doing little punch-up jobs on a few movies. I worked on Eddie Murphy's *The Distinguished Gentleman,* not one of his most distinguished efforts. This was when Eddie Murphy was trying to be mature. You get a lot of bad advice in Hollywood. I worked on *Problem Child,* but honestly I'm not sure if it was *One* or *Two.* My memory of these gigs was the struggle to get paid and never really getting paid what I was promised.

I got a call from an executive at one of the big movie studios. He asked me to come in and listen to a pitch of theirs for me to potentially write. This sounded promising. An artistic challenge. Some money. I went to the meeting. There they told me a comic fable about a mischievous older aunt who constantly got her niece and nephew in trouble.

I liked it and went home to work on it. That day, when I returned home, I picked up the *New York Times* and saw a review of a French comedy, *Tatie Danielle.* It was about a mischievous older aunt who constantly got her niece and nephew in trouble.

I was so naive, I kid you not, that when I read that, I thought, *Wow what a crazy coincidence.* I immediately called the executive, who actually got on the phone. I said, "You're not going to believe this but there's a French comedy with exactly the same plot as what you pitched me." He abruptly hung up. Like that. I ended my sentence, and there was a literal click. And I never heard anything from anybody again. And the movie didn't get made.

It was almost 1989, and it looked like the decade would end with me out of work and not only directionless but also not even close to being a director. Or anything, for that matter.

And then Arsenio called.

CHAPTER 3

"YEAH, IT'S FUNNY..."
(THE ARSENIO HALL SHOW)

*I*n the midst of my Sisyphean flailing, Bryan Gordon, one of the mentor writers, along with Larry David and Steve Adams from *Fridays*, called me. I don't know how he heard about it, but he had somehow recommended me for a staff-writing job on the fairly new *Arsenio Hall Show*. At one point I would've been thrilled to be a monologue writer for a late-night show, but now I wanted much more. By the same token, I was in desperate straights, and being lucky enough to have a job where you wrote jokes for a living was not something I could ignore. Growing up, those were men, and yes, admittedly they were predominately men, and white men at that, that I admired, from *Laugh-In* or *The Tonight Show*. These were comedy-writing dream jobs. But as my dream grew, my job prospects shrank in direct proportion, and now writing jokes for a late-night show represented something else. Some sort of end of the line. Far from the world of writing sitcoms or movies and a planet away from directing. I was still trying to figure out what I'd done wrong when the answer was nothing. Life just works that way sometimes. Some people are lucky, and some people, large pools of people—in fact, entire regions of the earth—are fucked.

The *Arsenio* offices were in a very decrepit old building on the Paramount lot that had a lot of history and a lot of death, but these buildings are not designed to memorialize anything in particular but to be redone again and again in the image of the new tenants who come and go every generation. So the building was ancient but also represented change. Still, like all offices at that time on the Paramount lot, they were dank. That's what movie lots are first and foremost. A self-contained industrial hub with not just glamorous offices and stages, but wood shops and metal shops and a gas station, a power station, package delivery, food choices, and parking. Of course, there were corridors of power where the executives and stars comfortably resided, hidden from the masses. But unless you were one of the elite, you would never experience these luxury enclaves. You barely walked by them or even knew they existed. There were two different worlds behind the same wall.

Walking into the *Arsenio* offices would serve as one of the many unexpected revelations of this experience. It was a virtually all African-American office staff. There were exceptions, including the executive producer and director. But populated by a preponderance of African-Americans, something I had never experienced.

Unfortunately show business is really no different or better than any other American subculture. We are still naturally segregated. When I have worked with Larry or Sacha, it's something we always try to remedy by seeking out an integrated crew, but with the exception of a token, we always fail. Most of those crews and most crews I have worked with happen because of friendships, comfort, familiarity, and history. The only way to change an ingrained culture is to take more extreme measures. From the Voting Rights Act to quota systems, we do what we can as a society to force these issues to that level to make change. Otherwise it won't happen. And it's the same for equal employment in Hollywood. It will have to be forced. Or we can hope that evolution goes in the right direction. Maybe most of these jobs will be eliminated in the future, the workers replaced by robots.

Years later, one of the many reasons I did a pilot with Kanye was to consciously try to alter that culture. The Kanye pilot, over a decade later, would be the first time I could originate a show culture and make that a priority. And starting from there, using the same process, we wound up with an overwhelmingly black crew. Shifting the paradigm was challenging but could be done.

One of the great things about working in different countries is the diverse crews. I have worked with crews from Uruguay and Argentina and Morocco and Spain and Thailand and the Czech Republic and Nigeria and more. And they are usually made up of people from multiple countries the way we are from multiple states.

But here in *Arsenio's* office suite, it was a different picture. Most people working there were black, and I had the experience of a multilevel complex diverse black majority. A situation most white Americans simply don't find themselves in.

Just because people were black didn't mean they identified as the same. Their differences were striking. And I thought it would be educational for white people to see how complex black society is. It was for me. People from different parts of the country, different levels of education, different ages and genders.

I saw the conflicts between the different strata of African-Americans, depending on education, region of origin, and yes, even skin shade. But as diverse as they were, they would be judged and reduced and generalized about as a group, as they had through history, simply because they shared a skin color.

I navigated my way across the long room, which ended at Arsenio's private office. I needed this job but still wasn't sure I wanted it. I entered. He sat behind a shiny desk. We are the same age. In comedy, that provides shortcuts to reference points that you share and can be cited. And so we talked about comedy, wending our way back to Richard Pryor. I explained my pitch. I thought Arsenio was in a unique position with a national late-night forum, so why not take advantage of it and do a nightly pointed Pryor-type monologue? Far-ranging, from current events to personal crisis. Share what's in your mind and it will be unique and unprecedented.

Granted, I was a white guy sharing my perspective on the racial gulf and other issues through Arsenio, and that in itself could be construed as institutional racism. Not that much different than the predominately white writing staffs of *Good Times* or *Sanford and Son*.

But Arsenio had learned his craft at the comedy clubs, like The Comedy Store, where comedians of all ethnicities and backgrounds and genders were forced to intermingle in a cool fashion. Clubs like The Comedy Store became bastions of integrated progressive America without even trying.

Still, he was also a comedian who justifiably also wanted laughs.

The show had not been on long, but just by virtue of being the first African-American-hosted late-night talk show, it was getting buzz. But over the year I spent on the show, it would become a global phenomenon, with all the accompanying baggage.

I wrote more story-oriented, less jokey material, and to his credit, Arsenio jumped in with both feet. But it clearly was less favored by the audience, and he began to relegate his monologues to easy and cheap jokes about pop culture reference points, like Roseanne's weight.

Roseanne was still a mainstream cultural icon at that point and thus an easy target. Together with Tom Arnold, they formed an early version of the trash tabloid couple. It used to be couples like Richard Burton and Elizabeth Taylor, erudite elitists with expensive jewelry and world travel. It seems to have returned to that again. But for a while the working class, like Roseanne and Tom, were the objects of scrutiny.

Arsenio's relentless mocking of Roseanne's weight led to a rather juvenile desperate attention-seeking feud by the then manically aggressive Tom Arnold, who threatened to come over to our lot and beat up Arsenio.

Arsenio, like Johnny Carson, looked a lot slighter on TV than he was in real life. In reality, he was physically formidable and in good shape. But eventually all the conflict wore off and faded away. In fact, ironically Tom and Roseanne wound up being guests on the show. It was all show business.

Arsenio was tapping into some sort of zeitgeist while having guests and musicians on regularly who'd never been on TV at all. He was in a very unique position, and therefore, it was hard for anyone to stand in his shoes and know what he was going through. And the media, while fascinated and transfixed, also denigrated and belittled Arsenio. I was struck by the unfounded criticism leveled at him—he was too fawning, an ass kisser, a bad interviewer, all bullshit—and I could only attribute it to the institutional racism of the media. Yet his popularity grew.

One thing, however, was undeniable. The bigger he got, the fewer of my jokes he was using.

Slowly but steadily, my joke-to-air ratio began to dwindle, and I became very disappointed and confused. This also coincided with the meteoric rise of the show into some sort of cultural touch point. About that aspect, I was fascinated. It was a phenomenon that I would observe and witness. It gave me a taste and a perspective on what that experience would be like in the future although I had no idea that's what my future would be.

Arsenio was a fan of mine and let me know it in many different ways. Like when a joke did get a shocked reaction, he would sometimes drag me out in front of the cameras from offstage, long hair and beard, shades, leather jacket, and tell the audience that I was Satan and that Satan was on the writing staff and all evil bad jokes were my fault.

But rather than push forward at the time when the audience seemed willing and open to listen to anything Arsenio would say, he was choosing to assiduously avoid any controversy.

I would soon find out perhaps the most profound underlying reason for Arsenio to avoid controversy. Arsenio himself, a black talk show host, was controversy.

The writers rotated the responsibility of dropping off the material to Arsenio every day. Arsenio would take the reams of jokes and pitches and shape them into his monologue. You rarely got to see Arsenio. You would primarily drop the jokes on the desk of one of his many assistants, Velma.

At that particular time, Mike Tyson was at his most ferocious. He was "alpha-maled" out. He exuded menace. This was prior to his utter collapse, so there was no chink in the armor yet.

He had taken a liking to Velma during the numerous times he had been on the show. And he would often come in the afternoon with his two vastly larger bodyguards and loiter by her desk. The desk where I would have to drop off the jokes.

I remember walking up to the desk one day when Tyson and his cohorts were hovering, seeing that no matter what I did, I'd be interrupting. As I was about to lay the sheath of papers on Velma's desk, Tyson, who was much shorter than me, glowered at me menacingly and it seemed, not that he was taller than me, but that I was enveloped within him. I'd already been consumed and didn't know it. The bodyguards watched carefully in case this moment somehow slipped into violent confrontation, not unusual for Mike in those days. Very unusual for me. But Tyson simply glared at me. It seemed like if I uttered even a joke, they had tacit permission to beat the living fuck out of me.

I dropped the material on Velma's desk and backed out of the room like there was an unleashed tiger ready to attack.

But it was on my next excursion to the desk that my eyes wound up opening to reality.

As I was dropping off the monologue jokes, someone at the desk was going through fan mail. I was curious and asked if I could see something. She showed me large stacks of mail that were piled everywhere as if to say, "Help yourself." I assumed it was the usual fawning fan mail until I grabbed a random stack to read.

These emails were written by the most virulent out-of-control psychotic sadistic racist homophobic hateful violent maniacs I had never seen or even imagined. They were so vivid in their violent threats that visions of blood-soaked massacres flooded your mind. Knives, guns, and other sharp objects and weapons randomly shoved up his ass or in his mouth. This was not hate mail, but hate crime mail. It was like violent rape porn with murder at the conclusion. It was like a snuff movie on paper. And in these violent racist fantasies, Arsenio was always the victim.

I was stunned by the level and depth of hate. I held on to a couple of pieces just because it's hard to imagine, and people don't even believe how deep and wide racial hatred runs in this country. It's as much of the foundation of our country as anything. And in those days, the majority of it was handwritten, and sometimes in crayon, so you could literally feel the person who had written it. It made the stench of hate harder to wash off.

And it came by the stack. Every time Arsenio got too topical or political, he got more hate mail. And in a sense, everything he did, no matter how innocuous or inoffensive, was topical and political. When he'd shake the hand of or hug a white female guest, the switchboard lit up, the hate mail surged. Hate mail and hate phone calls. They were the social media of the day.

A black male host greeting a white female guest was a politically radical act in late-1980s America.

But it made me realize the pressure he was under. To be a black star meant getting threatened every day. It was, and still is, hard to believe the casual institutional racism that exists so blatantly in the society. And if you don't think there's institutional racism, ask a black man. Every black guy on this show, even Arsenio, was routinely stopped by the police. One day, I walked into an elevator with one of the black writers who was dressed in expensive and dressy clothes while I wore sweatpants and a T-shirt, and you could feel the people on the elevator get uptight about him. It was like a psychological experiment. Which was one of the great by-products of working on that show.

Like so much in my life, it wound up being a much deeper experience than I'd anticipated or even sought. But I was smart enough or curious enough or something to realize the uniqueness of this environment, with me incongruously dropped in the middle of it like some sort of modern Mark Twain story, and I observed it carefully.

For safety and security reasons, Arsenio soon abandoned any semblance of controversy in the monologue unless it had to do with how graphic he would get about describing Roseanne's corpulence. We even had to have metal screeners for the audience. And it yielded many weapons per night.

Six months into a one-year contract, I virtually completely ceased getting jokes on the air. I couldn't solve the formula of writing the kind of jokes he needed. Though I was profoundly disappointed, I somehow also didn't take it personally. I was weirdly flattered that my jokes were too harsh, and I knew on some level this wasn't where I belonged. Though I had no idea where I did belong.

And I never held it against Arsenio. He was always a cool guy, and actually we had a great rapport. He would sometimes come to my windowless office in the triple-wide to tell me how funny one joke or another was but that he would never do it on the air. And I got it. I gave him the best I had, and it wasn't suiting his needs. But what would I do next?

My one-year contract was almost up, and I knew I was in trouble. There would be no good reason to keep me on once my contract was up. I was going to be "not renewed." A euphemism for "You're fired." Moreover, I didn't want to stay either but had absolutely no prospects whatsoever. Again. I was tired of it but had no clue how to break through. I felt like I was beginning to lose the game, the race. I wasn't going to get to where I wanted to go, where I belonged, and I wasn't even sure where that was.

Paramount Studios was a historic but overcrowded facility. Great historical buildings and locations were haphazardly juxtaposed with hastily dropped triple-wide trailers like the one the Arsenio writers worked in.

One day, despondent and self-pitying about my fate—I had no money, and no discernible future—I stood outside the writers' triple-wide trailer and desperately looked for a sign. What should I do? I had gotten married to my first wife, Barbara, in 1986 and now had a child and no way to provide. And this is the show business bargain that you make. You might wind up at this point. I already had. And would again. There are no guarantees. There is no security. You make it, whatever the fuck that is, and as I learned, it's just another illusion, or you don't, you fail, also an illusion foisted upon us, and you get out of the way. And Los Angeles is a city littered with those broken dreams and the broken people who dream them.

One person who lived his dream to the hilt was Jack Nicholson. A bit actor whose career was at a nadir when he played the small role in *Easy Rider* that catapulted him to fame. He rode the wave. He played the game and won. And seemingly did it his way as well. And further, paid dues, major dues, but kept going. He went from Roger Corman movies, no small accomplishment, to the most prestigious films with the most prestigious directors.

I knew that Jack Nicholson was on the lot editing his sequel to *Chinatown, The Two Jakes*. After much pressure for many years, Nicholson decided to revisit the world of the classic Polanski-directed masterpiece. This time, it would be Jack himself who would direct the sequel. And the buzz was he was on the Paramount lot doing postproduction. I wandered the lot quite a bit, and finally I had seen his parking space and sometimes even his Mercedes convertible parked in it and knew he was around. He always struck me as somebody who had figured it out. I admired him tremendously.

This day as I stood outside the triple-wide trailer, feeling as lost as I could remember, contemplating a bleak future, no answers, not even questions, I saw a car approaching very slowly. It felt like I was watching it on a telephoto lens in slow motion. It was moving so slow. But it was the Mercedes I recognized from the parking space. And sure enough, behind the wheel in a Lakers cap and shades was Jack. He slowly cruised by me. Jack Nicholson. He had everything. He had beaten the system. Did it his way. And was reaping the rewards. We exchanged glances, both of us in shades, held each other's gaze for an eternal moment, and then for no reason, we both suddenly burst out laughing, and without stopping, without missing a beat, as if it had been scripted, as he slowly glided past me, he nodded knowingly and said, "Yeah, it's funny . . . ," and drove off.

And I got it immediately. An epiphany provided by an inadvertent oracle. This was Jack. And this was the word of Jack. Someone who had wandered this path barefoot and now cruised it in a classic Mercedes. "Of course it's absurd. It's ridiculous. Its meaninglessness is what's meaningful. It's everything, it's nothing. Embrace it."

And I knew that was the answer. I saw the light. I saw the path. I saw the way. Lit by the headlights of Jack's Mercedes. I knew that's what I would do. Follow the light. Embrace the journey, not the destination. Embrace the absurdity.

I was fired the next day.

CHAPTER 4

"NOT THAT THERE'S ANYTHING WRONG WITH THAT..." (SEINFELD)

I managed to never need to fully absorb the devastation of being fired off one of the hottest shows on television. Specifically, it was thanks to a couple of lucky breaks, which occurred on the heels of that traumatic event of my losing my livelihood.

The first was being stood up by Keenen Ivory Wayans. The other was a phone call from Larry David.

Somehow, and I have no idea at this point how, I wangled an interview for *In Living Color*. It was a breakthrough sketch show and was to my mind the perfect show to work on. I could return to the freedom of sketches. The cast was amazing and much more diverse than *Fridays*. I really wanted this job and thought being fired from *Arsenio* was leading me to this place. Everything was working out just by me taking Jack Nicholson's inadvertently oracular telepathic advice and remembering *It's a game, it's absurd*, and fully embracing that concept.

Unfortunately my Zen transcendence doesn't last long. I arrive at the *In Living Color* offices for a meeting with Keenen Ivory Wayans himself. But when I arrive, I am not expected. There is no record of a meeting. Further, Keenen isn't even there.

If I had been smart and cool at that moment, I would've taken a deep breath and rescheduled and left, comforting myself that a snafu like that could happen to anybody. But I wasn't like that.

I lost my shit. I didn't freak out on the receptionist, but I told her not to bother rescheduling or even getting to the bottom of it. Fuck it. Then I stalked out of the offices swearing never to return.

As soon as I left, I had a sense that I had acted far too impulsively and just possibly blew a chance at what would be, for me, a dream job.

I returned home, rather embarrassed. What was I supposed to do now?

Soon after returning home, the phone rang. It was Larry David. He asked what I was up to, and I responded with an emphatic, "Nothing."

He reminded me of the pilot he had done with Jerry Seinfeld a year or two before that had remained in limbo for a year. And that when it was finally picked up, it was for a measly four episodes. He had tried to hire me at that point, but NBC and Castle Rock said no because I had no sitcom experience. Who could argue with Castle Rock, headed by Rob Reiner? They were a wildly successful production company at the time, having made the Stephen King adaptations *Stand by Me* and *Misery*, both directed by Rob. They could do no wrong. And they didn't want me. Amazingly, although Larry was the co-creator of the show, he had show runners hovering over him who were making the final decisions. This made him very uncomfortable.

I remember when he had come to town with those first *Seinfeld* scripts. I sat in the lobby of his hotel, the now defunct Bel Age in West Hollywood, and read "Male Unbonding," "The Stake Out," "The Busboy," "The Chinese Restaurant," one after the other. And guffawing heartily out loud, much to the amusement of the hotel guests.

But now miraculously the show had gotten picked up again. This time for thirteen episodes. Amazingly, that thirteen-episode pickup had taken almost three years. And one of the prerequisites is that Larry himself was now the show runner. Larry was in charge. And his first act as a show runner was to hire me as a writer. I remember his sales pitch vividly: "We'll do thirteen episodes, we'll make a little money, and then it will be canceled and then we'll be free and we can go on with our lives."

I said yes.

The next day, the phone rang. It was a very cool and contrite Keenen Ivory Wayans, who apologized profusely for any confusion. He really wanted me to work on the show and would I please come in and try again. I was very moved by this call. And troubled. I hadn't really been in the privileged position of turning down work that I wanted. But I had to be straight with him and told him I'd said "yes" to this sitcom. He understood and was disappointed. So was I. Had I made a mistake? Had he? Only time would tell.

Larry had already taken me under his wing at *Fridays*. Now that mentorship would manifest. He literally plucked me from among his many creative associates to help him make *Seinfeld*. This would be the first of two times Larry changed the direction of my life.

It's important to say here that I've prided myself on never asking anybody for anything. I don't like selling myself. And I don't like asking or owing favors. Larry asked me to work on *Seinfeld*. And that would occur again when he suggested out of the blue that I direct *Curb Your Enthusiasm*. Same with Sacha. I was approached. In all cases, I never asked, never begged, never groveled for virtually anything. I'd rather fail on my feet than succeed on my knees.

It's a testament to their instincts to have chosen me. And a testament to mine that I agreed.

•••

Things got off to a rough start. They always have with me. The key is surviving the obstacle course of your mind.

Larry and Jerry were the only other people around. There was another writer, a great and talented guy named Matt Goldman, who was simply too nice a guy to write this show. Jerry, Larry, and I had easy access to our inner pricks. But Matt was a good and decent person and, thus, couldn't delve into that darkness. He was soon gone.

I struggled at first. What was a *Seinfeld*? I would read and reread Larry's scripts, but they really defied description in many ways. What they all possessed was a truth and honesty about human nature and life in the lower regions of both our mind and our economics. Although it was for a network sitcom, when I read those scripts, I thought of Bukowski and Pekar and even Zola and Gorky. These were not rich people, and these were not good people. But they weren't bad people.

The show was about that morality, the question of ethics, questions of faith and belief, existence, ambiguity. As I've often said, far from a show about nothing, *Seinfeld* was a show about everything. It's one of the reasons it still resonates. It's seeking some deeper truth but you'd never know it.

I loved this challenge and was determined to find my way through the boundaries and structures of an acceptable *Seinfeld* script. But at the same time not merely replicating Jerry and Larry's work but somehow putting my imprint on it. But how? I mean, we did work on the same show. So I supposed it should resemble that, but I was committed to experimenting within this form. Exploring darker themes that wouldn't normally be fodder for sitcom humor. And Jerry and Larry didn't push me or pressure me. They let me find my way. And once they saw that nascent epiphany in my writing, they fully encouraged it.

But cracking the *Seinfeld* code would prove to be daunting. First, neither Jerry, Larry, or myself had ever worked substantially on a sitcom. We had no idea what we were doing. Add to that our fatalistic attitude and we wound up making a show that we liked. That made us laugh. That we would watch. That show turned out to be *Seinfeld*.

Often it's best to know the rules before you break them. But this wasn't like that. It was counterintuitive. Not knowing the rules was liberation. Despite people on all strata telling us how to be and how rigid the rules were, we saw how malleable the form actually was.

That was of particular interest to me. Expanding the form. What is a sitcom? How far can it veer and still be called that? And does it need to be called that? Words become antiquated. We don't talk about burlesque or vaudeville except in the very past tense. Soon the word "sitcom," like "variety show," will be a relic of a bygone era.

And yes, of course, Jerry, Larry, and I, to one degree or another, had all spent far too much time in front of TVs watching most of the same things over and over again until they were ingrained in us and in a way that was internalizing those rules. But we were also three people who saw the absurdity of those rules and who had the creative courage to ask why it must be that way. Of course, as we discovered, it didn't have to be that way. It just had to be great.

This was a characteristic I would love in Sacha as well. When everybody tells you the way it is, the way it's supposed to be, the way it has to be, having the courage to ask why and finding out there is no good reason, it's just the way it's always been, and then creating a new path in a new direction.

Sitcoms for the most part up until then were essentially extended vaudeville sketches. Proscenium stages, audiences, and writing and performances geared to appeal to that audience.

Sitcom veterans James L. Brooks and Norman Lear came along and started expanding that narrow definition, one with more naturalistic behavior like *Mary Tyler Moore* and one with more controversial content, like *All in the Family*.

But even those sitcoms adhered to certain rules. The typical structure of sitcoms up until *Seinfeld* was to do no more than six scenes, sometimes less. And these scenes would take place in limited areas. Home base, the home or workplace set, and a swing set, a set that could be reconfigured every week to be another store or apartment.

Most action took place off camera with characters rushing into the home base set to announce what had just happened.

We loved those urgent "burst into the room" monologues, and as comedians and comedy writers, we would naturally gravitate to that memorable monologue form and fashion our own more modern self-aware, self-conscious variations. Like Kramer "bursting" into the apartment to recount the harrowing adventure of saving Toby's toe after its amputation by the bus in "The Fire." Or "bursting" into the apartment and slapping his wager on the kitchen counter and announcing proudly, "I'm out!" in "The Contest."

But that *Abbott and Costello* energy was often a two-man job and so many great *Seinfeld* moments borrow from that tradition as well. Two-man postmodern vaudeville routines often with a dollop of Beckett. Especially in my episodes, which tended to a certain bleakness and darkness, an adjunct reality of the *Seinfeld* world. They were on some level trapped. Trapped inside the apartment. Trapped inside the coffee shop. Trapped inside their own sitcom. And the unseen outside world was chaos. It was existential. Not a show about nothing. A show about nothingness.

Watching Jerry and Jason in those moments was like seeing the great comedy teams in their prime. And then throw a third person into the mix to up the comic conflicts and stakes, and in this case that third person wasn't Sidney Fields from *Abbott and Costello* but Kramer.

Kramer, in Larry and Jerry's eyes in his original incarnation, was more like a traditional neighbor, entering from next door with some comic relief. But I was aware of the ferocity within Michael Richards and his one-of-a-kind comic energy and wanted to unleash him. And I was given the opportunity in such episodes as "The Statue," in which he impersonates a cop to retrieve the statue. Or "The Baby Shower," in which he is responsible for the death of Jerry, his little "cable boy." Or his pinball-like energy as he tries to grab a seat in "The Subway."

At the same time, I could project and channel more of my interests and neuroses and obsessions into Kramer than the other characters. I mean, Jerry and Larry were Jerry and George, and though I could contribute to that, Kramer gave me more carte blanche to explore. And in the process, I expanded the boundaries of Kramer. His outside world, his unseen friends, his more conspiratorial mindset. Those were things I was able to imbue the character with, along with the unpredictable intensity of Michael's performance, which others were able to expand upon and make Kramer both singular and an equal to the other characters. And in doing so, this made the show better and richer as well.

This in some ways led to a trilogy I wrote for the show. Sort of my own little *Seinfeld* movie that featured Kramer more on his own. It gave both Michael and me a chance to expand the *Seinfeld* universe. *Seinfeld*, but on an epic scale of comic madness. It was Abbott and Costello meet *The Day of the Locust*. The first episode was "The Keys," the finale of Season 3, and it was followed by the two-part Season 4 premiere, "The Trip," where Kramer is mistaken for a serial killer, and Clint Howard plays the actual killer, Tobias Lehigh Nagy. All shot on location in LA, like the film noir B-movies of my youth.

These episodes had many meta moments. Elaine was writing a *Murphy Brown* script, the sitcom starring Candice Bergen on another network, CBS. Later, Kramer wound up with a part on the show. That was the first time that I know of where a character from one show appeared on another show on an entirely different network.

But the episodes came together due to unforeseen circumstances. NBC would be broadcasting the '92 Summer Olympics and wanted Larry to produce two extra episodes that would air during the Olympics. This was part of the cross-promotional frenzy of network TV at that time. Something that Larry abhorred. Even though all the other sitcoms had agreed, he refused. So, with Larry's approval, I volunteered to do it.

Although I didn't direct it, I was as specific as I could be on paper, and because we were so far outside the norms of a typical sitcom episode, even for *Seinfeld*, my input was needed, required, and gladly supplied. I was able to draw on my many influences beyond the three-wall sets of a sitcom.

Jerry, Larry, and I didn't know how to write traditional sitcoms. Not really. We'd all drifted past sitcoms in one way or another. Jerry on *Benson*. Larry with a failed Gilbert Gottfried pilot, and me with many original and experimental TV scripts that were never produced. And we barely watched contemporary sitcoms.

But Larry and Jerry had confidence in their vision, in their innate knowledge of what was funny, and quickly found an organic solution to the structural issues. They ignored it. That meant sometimes a show might take place entirely in the apartment, like "The Tape," or entirely in the eponymous "Chinese Restaurant."

I enjoyed and was encouraged to draw on elements from genres with no connection to *Seinfeld* or even comedy, and try to make them funny. That has always been a comedy challenge I have tried to face. The alchemy of comedy. Make the unfunny funny. Turn comedy shit into comedy gold.

In my first produced, but not first broadcast, episode, "The Baby Shower," Jerry's reluctant acceptance of Kramer's offer of free illegal cable leads to him being shot down by the FBI in slow motion like a Sam Peckinpah movie. I killed Jerry in my first episode!

I referenced one of my favorite surreal epics of the '70s, Lindsay Anderson's insane picaresque, *O Lucky Man!*, starring Malcolm McDowell, when I used the pigman story in "The Bris" episode.

Or I used film noir techniques to tell a sitcom story, like "The Opera," featuring Joe Davola, the psychotic clown stalking Elaine in echoes of the opera they are attending, *Pagliacci*.

Of course, another big influence on Jerry, Larry, and myself, but really, especially me, was the dry, clipped, truculent, laconic, and supremely and hilariously corny cop show *Dragnet*. And when I read about a decades-long delinquent library book and the potential fine, I saw dialectic elements that I could turn into an original synthesis. And I began imagining the humorless no-nonsense Joe Friday like library cop Lieutenant Bookman.

The scene where Bookman confronts Jerry for the first time remains some of my best writing. But as funny and distinctive as I believed that scene was, I could never imagine the heights it would reach once Philip Baker Hall embodied the role. Once the words were coming out of his mouth, the synthesis was complete. We had created comedy magic.

From "The Pony Remark" on, death hovered over *Seinfeld*. Ironically, death as a subject in sitcoms was actually introduced by

Brooks's "Chuckles the Clown" episode of *Mary Tyler Moore* and Edith's death on Lear's *All in the Family*. But they were treated as special episodes that wound up breaking new ground. Most sitcoms were still afraid to deal with it even in the aftermath of those two groundbreaking shows. But it wasn't till *Seinfeld* that it was treated like everything else, a part of our daily reality. Again *Seinfeld* was a show that found comedy in places where it normally wouldn't be looked for. And I loved that. And as much as Jerry and Larry pushed me, I pushed them to embrace these themes. Laughing at things you shouldn't will elicit the deepest response. Masturbation, Nazis, rude handicapped people, stalking, suicide, murder, and general sometimes unforgivable bad behavior.

•••

The structural confines of a *Seinfeld*, like the structure of a song, gave me the foundation and the freedom to explore ideas without limitations. To be audacious in both conception and execution. Yet even within that liberating environment, I confronted some unexpected censorship. We weren't the kind of show that was salacious or heavily double-entendred like so many sitcoms. Character and patience and honesty in building to a massive wave of laughter sacrificed for cheap, quick, easy, contrived, and ultimately disposable jokes. Think about it. There were no network notes for Larry's "The Contest," perhaps the most perfect piece of sitcom writing there is. The censorship we felt, well, I felt really, was about ideas.

And strangely, they all involved Elaine stories.

In "The Subway," Elaine's original story was that she hops on the wrong train and finds herself on the express to 125th Street in Harlem. Suddenly, it dawns on her that she is the only white person on the train, and she internally freaks out as she tries to remain cool on the outside. This was a glimpse at the ingrained conditioned racism we all suffer from but hate to admit.

Interesting side note, my father had told me this crazy story about being on the subway in the 1960s. It was a full car, and like many people do, he conked out in his seat for a bit. When he awoke, everyone in the subway car was crowded into one corner, cowering, and opposite my father sat a completely naked man. That story, which I had carried around since I was a kid, became the Jerry story in "The Subway." The thrill of being able to do something like that can't be measured in money or fame. It's a different, perhaps deeper, sense of satisfaction. I'd hoped it would make my father happy, but it seemed like he may never have seen the episode, which was disappointingly his approach to most of my work.

In "The Airport," Elaine's original story, and this was based on a true incident, she is relegated to coach while Jerry lives it up in first class. Mid-flight, the passenger next to Elaine dies. The airplane has no place to put him so they drape a blanket over him and leave him there, next to Elaine! This was true and seemed so horrendously hilarious. But others disagreed.

In both cases, these stories were deemed too dark and harsh and unsettling, and I was forced to rewrite them to make them more palatable, which also rendered them more sanitized though, admittedly, still quite funny.

So instead of Elaine having a bout of racial paranoia in "The Subway," there is a long train delay in the tunnel and she becomes anxious and claustrophobic. And in "The Airport," the passenger next to her is not dead, just merely obnoxious.

But perhaps the most notorious censorship on the show surrounded an episode I wrote called "The Bet." At the time, there was much media attention devoted to the subject of women purchasing guns. I immediately thought this could be a provocative and funny topic for an Elaine story. Elaine buys a gun. You can see it, can't you? Elaine getting paranoid on the streets of New York. Kramer has a friend...etc.

Jerry and Larry agreed enough, seeing the potential despite some obvious pitfalls, for me to write a draft. With that script in hand, we set about casting the outside supporting characters and constructing the sets. But at the read-through, there was obvious palpable discomfort. On many people's part. I got it. In fairness, the script simply didn't transcend the problems it faced. It wasn't funny enough to surmount those obstacles, so it was scrapped.

By the same token, an episode like the Emmy-winning "The Contest," which sidestepped any network notes, was my Emmy-nominated script "The Outing." "The Outing" took two seasons to finally get filmed. There was simply too much nervousness surrounding the subject, as it drew from popular rumors of the time that Jerry was gay. But it wasn't Jerry who had a problem with it. This was still the early nineties, and the network chafed at gay-themed stories altogether.

But for me, it seemed like the logical next question for Abbott and Costello. You live in the same room, sleep in the same bed. *Are you fucking?*

The network was not convinced until "Not that there's anything wrong with that." Once that phrase found its way into the script once or twice, Jerry and Larry realized it was the key, and instead of just a qualifier for Jerry and George's gay denials, it became a running joke and, by today's standards, a meme that could be applied to virtually anything. Once introduced, it struck a key that opened the door to the comedy of that episode.

Although Jerry's managers were primarily concerned with Jerry winding up "smelling like a rose" at the end of each episode, an epigraph along with a caricature of "lovable Jerry" I immortalized on the whiteboard in Larry and Jerry's office, I felt they underestimated Jerry's power and the audience's trust in him. My argument was that Jerry was sort of our comedic Rod Serling. We trusted him to lead us down a dark labyrinth of comedy and come out the other side. And Jerry not only embraced that notion. He relished it.

But it took me a number of tries to get to that point. I had much failure. Entire scripts thrown out, rejected. But I think Jerry and Larry knew more than I did that I was on to something.

At one point, Larry walked into my office, where I was despondent, stuck, sitting and struggling with a script. I looked up and said, "You know, I never thought of myself as a comedy writer." And Larry said, "I wish you had told me that before."

The elements finally came together in my first produced but not broadcast script, "The Statue."

A friend of mine, John Mascaro, a teacher, had innocently told me a story of having a moving-out party from his place in Philadelphia. At the party, one of the students had admired this relatively worthless statuette that sat on the fireplace mantel. My friend thought nothing of it until he was packing up a few days later and noticed the statue was gone. At the time, he shrugged it off but then found himself at a party at this very same student's house, and lo and behold, there was the statue brazenly displayed. When he confronted him, the student insisted it was a different statue.

This was a situation I could easily see Jerry and George sliding into. It had some classic comical conflict possibilities.

One of the common issues in writing a script is the so-called third act. I'm not a big believer in rigid structure, but network sitcoms demanded it to some degree, based on, if nothing else, an extremely specific allotted running time that could not be exceeded. But intersecting things in a way that isn't seen, only to be revealed in a climax, is a challenge every script faces. And some never get past it.

But the predictability and the satisfaction of anticipation are two reasons sitcoms are popular. A successful sitcom is like church. People gather every Sunday to essentially hear variations of the same story.

I chafed under this inherent limitation of the form initially, particularly in a network context, where there were already too many rules.

Jerry and Larry and I all struggled with structure in the early days. It was like a laboratory. The experimenting with the structure eventually led to a successful formula that could be replicated.

Remember, even though it is so familiar now, *Seinfeld* didn't exist yet. There was no *Seinfeld*. It was being invented.

Today, people quote it, swear by it, live by it, draw upon it for inspiration and daily sustenance, act as if it's always been here. As ubiquitous and great as *I Love Lucy* was, I don't think it permeated the consciousness and changed it the way *Seinfeld* has.

Because we hadn't watched many contemporary sitcoms, our

references were resolutely set in our childhoods. *Abbott and Costello,*
The Three Stooges, Superman, Dragnet. And it was the surreal dynamics of those shows that made us laugh then and even today. We
hadn't watched *Cheers* or *Taxi.* And thus they had no influence on
Seinfeld.

So what were these elements that emerged in the early stages of
the show that eventually in the right amounts produced the *Seinfeld*
formula?

Larry and Jerry were originally content with doing a less-story-
oriented, less-plot-driven show. The way I read those original scripts
by Larry, I thought of Jim Jarmusch much more than Jim Brooks.
People hanging out and having wide-ranging, self-conscious
super-funny original relatable conversations in real-life situations.

Each week we would have a meeting after the read-through in
the office that Larry and Jerry shared. At these meetings, Larry and
Jerry would sit opposite each other at their desks at the opposite
end from the door. Behind Jerry in chairs were usually his managers
and also executive producers, George Shapiro and Howard West,
although their main job was looking out for Jerry's interests. Behind
Larry, I sat on a cabinet. Never a chair. Around the rest of the room
were the executives from Castle Rock: Jeff Stott; Glenn Padnick,
who's distinct cackle can be heard on almost all *Seinfeld* episodes;
Alan Horn, who went on to be president of Warner; Andrew Scheinman, who at that time was a creative muse to all the Castle Rock
filmmakers who were making critical and commercial hits. But his
creative instincts for the show did not mesh with Larry's at all. Rob
Reiner was a partner but rarely attended the meetings.

Also at the meetings were the president of NBC, Warren Littlefield, portrayed by Bob Balaban during Season 3, and Rick Ludwig,
the earnest executive who had some intuitive sense about the show
and would not let it die. And his associate Jeremiah Bosgang. Also
both gently lampooned in that season.

Those meetings would sometimes get contentious. There were
usually three sides. Castle Rock and NBC pushing us to give the
show a more traditional sitcom structure. That seemed clichéd to

me. Larry would intensely resist, and I would get vociferously vocal about it. Was I completely out of place? What gave me the temerity to assume equality in this room? It didn't even occur to me though perhaps it should've. I'm sure I didn't make any fans in that room. But I just never worried about those sort of things. At least not until long after. Like now.

I didn't know why—maybe it was because we believed the show was going to get canceled anyway—but both Larry and I engaged in heated arguments with the executives about this point. It was a theme of these early meetings. And to some degree, the "No Hugging, No Learning" motto emerged as an aphoristic explanation of what made *Seinfeld* different than all shows that came before it. There were no false morality lessons or fake happy endings. You felt that life would go on, but perhaps each episode took a certain toll too. And I believed in that vision and was unfailingly loyal to Larry. I always stood up on his behalf. And he earned it. But did I help? I thought I was helping but perhaps I did not. Regardless, my passion for this path was pure. I could see what he and Jerry saw. And I would see it again. The future.

Jerry himself was not very garrulous at these early meetings. He was absorbing and observing. He was probably feeling some ambiguity about all these choices, and as I've said, none of us really knew what we were doing. He always remained equanimous, which is in one word how I would describe Jerry. We certainly didn't know what was right and wrong and would only find out once the show was on the air.

Larry finally said that if we were going to be forced to have stories, the stories themselves needed to be funny. This was an interesting challenge. To place a framework of farce over the naturalism of the dialogue and see what that synthesis would yield. And it yielded something relatively unique and innovative and to some degree accidental and lucky. It yielded *Seinfeld*.

How was this layer added? I think of a few crossroads moments that began to define that style.

First was "The Chinese Restaurant." I remember Rick Ludwig in one of these meetings pleading with Larry to consider some actual story element. I really felt it was brilliant and groundbreaking as it was. What was more existential and relatable than waiting for a table and feeling you were getting ignored? But Rick was a good guy and hard to ignore, and I could see Larry started to relent. Rick suggested to at least consider some kind of clock on the story to add pressure to the action. We talked about catching a movie, but you can always catch another showing, so I suggested the movie was the cult classic *Plan 9 from Outer Space* and was only playing for one night at a revival theater. That seemed to satisfy everyone's needs. Personally I felt the episode was pure in its original form and wasn't vastly improved by the addition of a clock.

For me, the second evolutionary leap came in an unexpected form. Larry and I spent a lot of time in those early days discussing story structure. How do two pieces fit in an unpredictable way so the journey of the story was as much fun and as funny as what went on within each scene?

We fell into a habit of midday walks around the Studio City neighborhood that housed the Radford Lot, where we shot *Seinfeld*. But as time went on, we got more ambitious. The walks extended farther and farther. Sometimes we'd get stuck in an inconvenient spot when needing to relieve ourselves. Sometimes we simply walked too far and had to have someone come retrieve us with a vehicle. Then we got into hiking the hills in Fryman Canyon Park. We didn't bring water. There were no cell phones. We wore our work clothes and we would walk until drenched with perspiration discussing and experimenting with various plot twists for that week's script.

There was something about the strenuousness of the walks, the oxygenating of our brains, that allowed us to ponder and contemplate far wilder and more unexpected scenarios for the story.

The stories began to overlap and intersect in surprising ways. And we embraced it.

Early on, you will see episodes where the intersecting stories are still showing their seams and acting as if almost traditional sitcom A and B stories, shoved uneasily together. But soon, the surprise and eventually the anticipation of the connection became part of the fun.

The third element that contributed to the unique storytelling of *Seinfeld* began with Julia Louis-Dreyfus. Concerned and frankly upset that she was being underutilized in the show, she came to Jerry and Larry weeping, while I was sitting with them in their office. Her distress was justified. She was right. We had not yet tapped in to the magical formula for Elaine or for unleashing Julia. And we were aware of it. Not proud. Maybe embarrassed slightly. But certainly aware. And being guilt-ridden men, we assured her that she would be more integrated into the show even though we clearly had no idea how to do it. Between sketches, stand-up, and even our own spec scripts, we had never had a need to write for three-dimensional women, and it was a failure of ours and the male hierarchy in general.

Without having a plan or a solution, we began in very rudimentary fashion. Larry actually drew a chart on the whiteboard and listed all four characters. From then on, a script wasn't a script until all four characters had a story. Preferably one that overlapped or intersected with the others. It forced us to be comically resourceful even out of our wheelhouse of comedy, which felt right and was exhilarating. We were innovating, but for ourselves. Suddenly these layers began to reveal themselves, and the scripts rose to another level.

Though things improved, there was still a feeling that Julia's prodigious comic gifts were still not being fully exploited. This awareness along with the chart led to an epiphany. Why not give Elaine one of George's stories? There was never a shortage of George stories. His character had the most comic facets and possibilities, and Larry could draw from his vast warehouse of personal experiences.

So one week, a story originally earmarked for George and based on a true incident was given to Elaine. Larry had had a girlfriend fly in to visit him for a weekend some years before, but by the time the weekend was over, Larry was looking forward to her leaving. Instead she decided to stay longer, which in the story leads George to try to concoct ways to get rid of her. Classic George story.

But giving it to Elaine was easily one of the most important and seminal moments in the show. It gave Elaine an inner life. It was not a happy one. It was as dark as the guys. She was capable of the same social crimes as they were. Though she was attractive and personable, she was a mess. Suddenly Elaine was born. Both in the writing and in Julia's performance. Julia was liberated and uninhibited and inhabited the possibilities of that character and made them her own in the same way as Michael and Jason did with Kramer and George. She became an iconic character. A breakthrough character.

So rather than being saddled by these creaky old sitcom conventions, we subverted them, distorted them, and often ignored them. Our fatalistic attitude about the fate of the show allowed us to make a show that we thought funny. The funnier we thought it was, the quicker its demise. But it turned out to be the opposite.

The show broke all the rules because we didn't know the rules. But we delivered the goods. Whatever else it was, it was always funny first and foremost. And that was the goal. And that provided the audience with enough familiarity to accept a radically new paradigm for the sitcom form. One that I would argue led to *Curb* and beyond.

Yet in the middle of this, we were easily distracted. Sometimes Larry and I would walk from our offices over to Ventura and Laurel Canyon, where stood a substantial newsstand. Larry and I were luddites of a sort, writing long hand and assiduously avoiding computers. The plethora of newsstands and magazines were my internet. With so many eclectic titles and weird subcultures and subjects the focus of magazines, it was my version of scrolling and clicking. And being inspired.

But Larry and I had gotten into the habit of discussing Sunday's football on Monday morning and feeling like we had some great insights. Like, almost in a *Seinfeld*-ian way, putting together the disparate pieces, making the connections. Remember, Larry felt he would've been a great general manager for the Yankees, which we depicted on the show.

Larry had a friend who knew a bookie, and before you know it, we were betting on football.

Amazingly our instincts were right and we were quite good at it. But for me, it quickly became obsessive. I would be dropping off or picking up my kids at a birthday party on a Sunday and would pull over to the side of the road to listen to the radio and see if a last second field goal was going to fuck me on the spread.

Larry and I began walking up to the newsstand, not to buy *Time* or *Newsweek* or look for material, but in order to buy the football betting tout sheets. We started to take it seriously. Too seriously. And we were winning and felt we had figured it out.

We'd sit in Larry's office poring over the tout sheets while scripts in need of rewriting began to pile up on Larry's desk. Finally Jerry came in one day and said, "What happened to the show?" It was like being snapped out of it. We had become consumed with football betting. It's a lot easier than writing and producing the show. So we dropped betting completely and began focusing again.

Our naivety was an unexpected key to unlocking the *Seinfeld* formula. It required a certain innocence, a lack of cynicism about the possibilities of the medium. Not to create a successful sitcom, but the funniest show of all time. Many things that I've worked on have had that mission statement, and arguably, some have fulfilled it.

But it came with a price and a learning curve as well. Although the show was perennially losing in the ratings to *Jake and the Fatman* on Wednesday nights, we knew something we were doing was resonating with someone. Soon after the show premiered, the "*Seinfeld* spec" quickly became the script to write. Suddenly we were inundated with spec *Seinfeld* scripts, literally dozens, from highly polished successful Hollywood writers to people in the farthest reaches of the country.

I was assigned the task of reading them, reading them all, and responding. And through that first season, in addition to my normal duties, I read every *Seinfeld* spec that came in, from wherever it might have come from. This was an opportunity for me to treat other writers the way I would want to be treated. I had been lucky and had been treated well much of my career, but you never forget rejections or assholism or arrogance or apathy. I first tried to respond with a full critique of the script and suggestions for how to improve it. It was 1990, and I didn't use a computer. So I felt the best route was simply to call the author myself and discuss it.

People were amazed when they picked up the phone. I realized how meaningful that gesture alone was. And then they were stunned when I would spend an hour on the phone going over their script with them. People were incredibly grateful, as I would've been, to be treated with a little dignity and respect.

But no good deed goes unpunished as we learned on *Seinfeld*, and my altruism came at a price.

First, let me say that most, if not virtually all, with one or two exceptions, of the *Seinfeld* spec scripts that came in were so far from right, it was sometimes challenging to find encouraging words and be honest.

A couple of seasons later, Larry had come up with the idea of Jerry and George selling the show about nothing as a sort of season-long arc. I was reminded that a couple of years before, I had read a relatively unsalvageable script that had as its plot line that George and Jerry make a pilot. Beyond that momentary overlap, nothing about the two episodes overlapped, and moreover, the script was poorly written and disappeared into obscurity with most of the rest. So as with the vast majority of these spec scripts that didn't merit further discussion, I said nothing about this one.

But uncharacteristically, two years later NBC publicity announced that we would be doing a season based on the actual story of Larry and Jerry selling *Seinfeld*. And we got sued.

Plagiarism is an "unwritten" sin in comedy writing so we were affronted by the suggestion that we would swipe something from this mediocre script. It would have been easier to buy the script. We relished the thought of testifying and presenting our side of the story. But it wasn't meant to be. Apparently in these situations, petty nuisance suits, the corporate policy is to settle. We were more outraged by that.

I was entrusted with searching out writers from more conventional sources, and I knew it would be difficult. Any script would now have to be submitted through an agent with a release form per standard procedure. I just knew not everyone could write a *Seinfeld* script. I still read many of them. Almost none of them were good. The exceptions were hired.

I also felt it was important to reach out beyond the television-writing world. One day I was driving and listening to NPR and heard David Sedaris do an essay. It was about writing for *Giantess* magazine, a specialized periodical for men whose fetish was dressing up and acting like babies. He also talked about cleaning houses for a living and cleaning a celebrity's house and setting it on fire. All very unique and original with a deeply sardonic point of view. Long before David Sedaris became a best-selling literary celebrity.

Both stories made me laugh, and I could see George or Kramer involved with stuff like this. I told Jerry and Larry, and they encouraged me to pursue it. But when I called David, he was apathetic. He hadn't heard of the show. Couldn't care less. And had no interest in writing for TV. And ultimately that worked out very well for him.

•••

I sat in on every casting session of the show for the first few seasons and strongly pushed for actors with the most gravitas and intensity (including Wayne Knight as Newman) rather than the usual sitcom glibness. Larry and Jerry trusted me, and we were almost always in agreement on our choices, most of which were inspired and ultimately memorable. Lawrence Tierney, who played Elaine's curmudgeonly father in "The Jacket," was someone I had seen in many B-movies and film noirs, including *Dillinger*. He was a rough-hewn character in real life and was based loosely on the writer Richard Yates, whose daughter, Monica, had been a girlfriend of Larry's. (And gender reversal inspiration for the Elaine story in "The Busboy.") Tierney was about to experience a career renaissance a year later when he starred in *Reservoir Dogs* as Joe Cabot. He scared everyone on the set (yet had memorized the entire script); his tough guy image was not a performance. It was him. When Jerry and George are intimidated by him, it was real. He was as anti-sitcom as you could get. And that's what made it work. Though he was never asked back.

Philip Baker Hall was another example of an intense dramatic actor, who didn't even really seem to possess a sense of humor, and had never done or even been thought of for sitcoms until he came in to audition and ultimately own Lieutenant Bookman in "The Library." He played it super straight, yet his acting instincts intrinsically understood the comic timing of the scenes, and he created an indelible character that people still talk about today. We all loved him, and years later, Larry and I jumped at the chance to use him in *Curb* as the doctor who does battle over doctor's office decorum in the premiere episode of Season 4, "Mel's Offer."

But things don't always work out. When I wrote "The Bris," I had a very specific idea for the part of the mohel. It was independent film stalwart Allen Garfield. He had appeared in some of my favorite movies of the seventies, including Robert Downey Sr.'s *Putney Swope* (okay, 1969), Coppola's *The Conversation*, and Robert Altman's *Nashville*. I heard his voice when I wrote the dialogue and made an impassioned plea with Larry and Jerry to just offer him the role without an audition. With some hesitation, they agreed. I was very excited.

Things quickly fell apart on the first day of rehearsal. Larry received an alarmed call from the set. He grabbed me and we ran onto the stage to witness Allen leading the cast in a series of improvs. The actors all shot us "help" glances when we arrived. Director Tom Cherones stood to the side simply befuddled. When they took a break, Jerry came to Larry and me and told us it was a disaster and in no uncertain terms said that he needed to go. We discussed how to do it, but Larry and Jerry were unanimous in their solution. I pushed for him, I had to fire him. As Jerry returned to the set to call a "break" in rehearsals, I looked down at Larry's chair and my own. On each seat was an envelope. When I opened it, it was a Happy Rosh Hashanah (Jewish New Year) card from Allen with an incredibly heartfelt, sincere, and long handwritten note written into it, expressing his undying gratitude for the blessing of being cast in the show. Fuck.

Before I knew it, everybody was gone but Allen and me. We

walked outside as I gingerly broached the subject. I told him that we loved him, and he was special and one of a kind, but he wasn't right for the role. He burst into tears, sobbing uncontrollably as I stood there ashamed and embarrassed. It was horrible. I slowly talked him down off the ledge, telling him that it was only a minor setback and we would find something even better for him to play in the near future. He embraced me tightly and slowly, reluctantly accepted the news with that buffer. He staggered away, his body still heaving from the wailing. Needless to say, if you know the history of *Seinfeld*, you know he never appeared on the show.

●●●

We would eat at a 24-hour deli called Jerry's right down the street from the studio after each taping. This became a ritual right from the beginning of the show. This was before Jerry became an icon so we were able to sit in a booth relatively undisturbed. But the meals were surreal anyway. Often Andy Kaufman would be there working a shift as a busboy as a conceptual comedic conceit. He wore the hat and apron and carried the bus box, filling it with dirty dishes, bringing waters and sodas and coffee. There was no attitude. No attempt to be funny. Just doing his job like all the other busboys. He would never break character, even though George Shapiro, who was his manager as well as Jerry's, was always at the table. If he smiled, it was the smile of an anonymous busboy to a table of strangers who were dining. It was one of the most brilliant things I'd ever seen.

I don't know how this part of the ritual began—I imagine it was a spontaneous gesture—but always weekly, after our meal at Jerry's, we would get in our cars and Jerry and I, who both lived on the other side of the hills, would race up Laurel Canyon from Ventura to Mulholland. Now when I say race, let me clarify. Jerry would give me a substantial head start, allowing me to wend my way up Laurel Canyon to Mulholland without him even really trying to catch up. Then just as I was approaching Mulholland and thought I would cross over before he did, I would see his headlights behind me in the distance getting closer and closer, zigging and zagging around the curves until I could hear the roar of his engine. We would both go over the crest at Mulholland at high speeds, often leaving the ground. But when we came down, Jerry was always in front of me. Now I was driving my only car, a Saab 900, and he was driving one of his many Porsches. Eventually I traded up to a Saab 9000, but it made no difference. Sometimes as our cars went airborne at the crest, I wondered how I'd explain or rationalize a horrible accident.

Larry and Jerry had a large office with a private bathroom. There was a smaller middle office, not usually in use, and an equally small corner office, which was mine. There was a bullpen, where our two writers' assistants sat. It also had couches for whatever, auditions, appointments, hanging out.

We were always on our guard for material. We had to be. The show was voracious. When we first moved into these offices, I spent a lot of time with Larry and Jerry just talking out the broad strokes of the original set of stories. And I might use their private bathroom while we were doing it. Otherwise, I would be relegated like everyone else to the hallway bathroom.

I continued using their bathroom even when I was in my own office. I thought nothing of coming into their room, after knocking—I was nothing if not polite—and then allow myself into their bathroom. And I wasn't just taking a quick piss as my reading material would attest to. I remember Larry and Jerry looking at each other quizzically but not saying anything and I didn't think anything of it.

Neither wanted to say out loud to me to stop using their bathroom for my long, leisurely shits. So instead they wrote a script about George abusing his boss's bathroom and getting fired. I got the message.

One day I came to work. It was a normal day. I had to explain yet again to the guard at the gate who I was and why was I there. I'd park in a spot far, far from the offices. I entered our office, past the writers' assistants, entered my darkened room, and as customary, closed my door. As I put my stuff down on my desk, there was a voice behind me from the shadows.

"Do you remember me?"

Uh-oh, I've just been thrust back into the film noir version of my life.

Indeed I knew who it was without even turning around. It was Larry Scott Andersen, the convict I had corresponded with a decade earlier on *Fridays*. He had returned to prison, and yet here he was, sitting on the couch, just waiting for me.

My next thought was, how did he just waltz in here? I get stopped almost every day by the gate security. Everyone's always asking me what I'm doing there or if they can help me in that threatening way that really means get the fuck out of here.

But this guy is here. Sitting in the shadows. Looking normal and anonymous enough and practiced enough to sidle past security undetected by exactly the same people that hassle me.

I try to be casual. I say his name. He is impressed that I remember. He fills in the time between our last conversation and this moment.

He was poised to be released from prison. He was never guilty of the crime he had been convicted of anyway. He had all those contacts he had made from prison, like Cheech and Chong and Neil Simon and me, all set up so when he was free, he could pursue his comedy-writing career. But his plans were derailed by another arrest almost immediately upon his release, and he wound up in prison for an even longer stint.

I had spent enough time around convicts and criminals to be instinctively wary of his version of events. Undoubtedly some of it was true. But the important parts, his guilt or innocence, that's where he wavered in my eyes. I could feel he was not there for a friendly visit. I could feel he was there because he wanted something. And everything had to be heard through that filter.

As proof of his dedication while he was away, he told me, he had continued honing his craft. As proof, he offered me two neatly bound sitcom scripts. One was for *Roseanne* and the other was for Burt Reynolds's *Evening Shade*. Coincidentally, we shared this building with both of those shows.

I took them and told him I would read them. I hinted that I

had to get to work. He told me he had no car. I did not offer him a ride. He rose to leave and asked me for money. I had a crumpled five-dollar bill and gave it to him. He exited.

I walked into the waiting area after he left and asked anyone who was there if they noticed what had just happened. No one had. I wondered for a moment but just for a moment if I had imagined the whole thing. Then reality returned.

One of the staff came to the door and announced that they had seen Larry Scott Andersen fishing in the recycling bins outside our offices where many scripts were discarded and had pulled out two and tucked them under his arm before he entered. *Roseanne* and *Evening Shade*. Nothing if not opportunistic.

Just at that moment, another member of the staff entered the office and announced that Larry Scott Andersen hadn't headed for the exit but in the opposite direction. Toward the stages. And disappeared.

Oh shit, I thought. *There's a stalker on the lot. And I put him here.* What if he killed Jerry? I had to do something. I couldn't keep it to myself. I sat down with the line producers and Jerry and Larry and told them the whole saga up until Larry Scott Andersen disappearing in the lot.

A search was conducted, but it turned up nothing. It was decided that we'd hire a bodyguard for Jerry. Something he had never done before. There had been no need before. I can't remember the guy's name, but it was Frank or Sal, and he was cool and an ex-cop. I, too, stayed close to Jerry when we ventured from the offices across the parking lot to the stage, perusing the panorama of parked cars for a glimpse of the culprit. But there was no sign of him.

Finally, it was show night. Jerry was his customarily cool self. He had to be able to focus on what he was doing. I'm not sure who knew what was transpiring and who didn't. I remember walking out of the offices to the stage for the show. It was just beyond dusk but not fully dark. We made a phalanx around Jerry as we marched to the stage.

There was security outside the stage. And everyone was searched before entering. Security ringed the perimeter of the interior as well. As we entered, one of Frank/Sal's colleagues approached. They had apprehended Larry Scott Andersen just before they let the audience in. He had been sleeping on the stages all week. But he wasn't arrested or detained. He was just escorted off the premises.

So he could be literally waiting for me on the street when I left after the show. Great.

Although I scanned my surroundings with greater acuity and checked my rearview mirror for a couple of days, he was gone. I never knew what became of him, and my attempts to find out online have borne no fruit.

Sadly, ironically, security hassled me at the gate the very next day.

•••

The day of the premiere of *Seinfeld*, January 16, 1991, a Wednesday at 9:30 p.m., everyone had gathered in Larry and Jerry's office to watch together. As we waited for the show to come on, we were surprised to hear the announcement that the show would be preempted. And it wasn't just any preemption. Desert Storm had been launched. We had been preempted by war. The premiere of *Seinfeld* was preempted by the Gulf War. This was as inauspicious a beginning as a show could have.

Things didn't get much better. We were consistently losing to almost all the competition, perhaps most embarrassingly, William Conrad's swan song, *Jake and the Fatman*. A routine and absurd and derivative cop show seemingly from a different era in which the hook was that the cop, though a tough veteran of the streets, was fat. Losing to that show particularly galled me.

But there was something in the show's failure that gave the executives hope. *Seinfeld* did very well with a demographic that wasn't really being serviced. It was an audience NBC wanted. So the notion arose of moving the show from its loser time slot on Wednesday nights to Thursday night behind the still powerhouse *Cheers*.

When Warren Littlefield, the president of the network, presented this idea to Larry, his legendary response was, "If they don't want to watch us on Wednesday, fuck 'em!"

But there was a unanimous consensus that we should do it, and Larry was soon convinced it was the right thing for the show. And indeed the first week behind *Cheers* and the show was a smash hit.

Success brought with it unwanted stresses and conflicts.

Even though Larry had not wanted to use the actual name "Kramer," and in fact, Michael's character is called Kessler in the pilot, Jerry insisted and Larry relented. Larry, knowing Kramer—the "real" Kramer, Kenny Kramer, comedian, "entrepreneur," and Larry's neighbor back in Manhattan Plaza—would try to exploit the exposure and indeed he did. But Larry's initial reticence about that evaporated quickly, and soon as he drew stories from his life, he utilized real people's names, people from his past and even his present, to name his characters, sometimes in roles that resembled the real person but often just to name an incongruous character.

While working on "The Fix-Up," I thought of a plot about faulty condoms. And I thought of Kramer's bootleg black-market world—a world that resembled more mine and then Kramer's than Jerry's or Larry's but one that they immediately and instinctively embraced—as being a key to Kramer. The murky netherworld of his other life.

Inspired by Larry's open use of real names for which people were flattered, I thought that the guy who gets Kramer the irregular condoms is his unseen pal, Bob Sacamano.

Robert Saccomanno, always Robert in real life, never Bob, was a childhood friend with a great name. I thought he would be pleased to be name-dropped on the show as was the virtually unanimous verdict of everyone else it happened to. It soon became a badge of honor for most. But surprisingly my friend, known on the show as Bob Sacomano, was unhappy. And it led to the dissolution of our friendship.

It was intended as a one-off, but for some reason, the unseen Bob Sacamano became a popular character on the show.

It's so ironic that anywhere in the world that *Seinfeld* plays, the people know the name of Bob Sacamano.

I was one of the strangest-looking comedy writers at that time. I had a long beard and hair and wore sunglasses more often than I should've yet people got used to it too. For a long time I wore only pajamas. Peter Farrelly in his semi-autobiographical novel, *The Comedy Writer*, described me as a cross between Jerry Garcia and Charles Manson, and I would have to say that was accurate.

I wound up appearing on the shows in a little walk-on or a walk-by cameo. I was the man who ignores Elaine's pleas to help save her fish in the parking garage. I, along with Larry David, was a Greenpeace member on a raft who watched Russell Dalrymple fall off and disappear into the ocean. And with Larry David, I filled out the background when Kramer was arrested as a suspected serial killer in my self-penned "The Trip."

Perhaps my most prominent cameo happened, like the others, quite inadvertently. I had written an episode called "The Airport." In it, Elaine is waiting desperately to use the bathroom. After an inordinately long amount of time, the door swings open and I burst out, surrounded by a tsunami of foul odor. For a long time, "Shitty Man" was my most famous onscreen credit. But that was good for me. It was "on brand." I was a professional freak. I was proud.

Once the show was a hit, my life pretty much changed. It certainly changed me and in some cases changed those around me. My father, suddenly for the first time, took some interest in my career. He never really wanted to know how I was doing. He wanted to know how my career was doing. My mother was genuinely thrilled. And I think that her excitement about my success made her anxious. But I was happy my working on *Seinfeld* gave her status at the condo she and my stepfather, Marvin, had moved to in Boynton Beach after my brother and I moved out. I think my parents, like many parents, lived some of their unrealized dreams through me.

However grandiose my own self-image might've been, there were always reminders to keep you modest. Like my Aunt Jean was in a nursing home in Coney Island at the end of her life. Aspects of her memory had begun to slip. And one day my father brought me to see her. When we entered, she was in a wheelchair in discussion with a group of women in wheelchairs. She immediately brightened when she saw me and proudly announced: "Look! It's my nephew, Larry David!"

So my father and my stepmother, Rosalie, finally decided to pay a visit to Southern California. They would see the grandkids, yes. But also go to Palm Springs and Vegas and San Francisco. Most important, my father needed a picture with Jerry Seinfeld.

This became my father's obsession for the week he was here. At first I shot it down unceremoniously. "Dad, that's not how I operate. I don't ask for favors. I don't want to owe anybody anything." But he didn't understand or care about my ethical dilemma or code for living. He wanted a picture with Jerry and he was relentless. Every day I would go to work and he'd ask, "Can I get a picture with Jerry?" and every day I said "No." Monday through Thursday. Friday I weakened under the weight of his final assault. I brought my father and his camera, which he didn't know how to operate, to work with me.

We went to work and everything was cordial and I finally saw Jerry and I sort of sidled up to him and said, "You know, my father is here and he really wants a picture and I would normally never..." But Jerry, ever graceful, agreed before I could finish. The three of us went outside, and Karen the writer's assistant who joined us was entrusted to snap the actual photo. I couldn't take the responsibility.

Before the first picture, Jerry said to me, "Larry why don't you get in here? We'll take it with the three of us." So I did. Then my father said, "Let me just get one with Jerry." And Jerry graciously acceded to his wish.

A year later I was in my father's house, and there, proudly and prominently displayed on a shelf, was the framed enlarged photo from that day of my father and Jerry. Not me.

•••

There were three economic tiers of *Seinfeld*. The bourgeois class represented by Jerry's great apartment without a need for steady employment. Had his parents helped him out at some point? Even though there was an attempt to portray Jerry as a "struggling" comedian, he always came off as far more successful. He never seemed desperate for money. Then George, who was from a lower middle class, more Larry David–like background, and Elaine, with no mention of a mother but a father who was a renowned if not best-selling author, constantly scrambling to make ends meet. But in conventional ways. Office jobs, publishing. Then Kramer, the underground man. Somehow thriving in the black-market economy. Hustling, scrambling, scheming, more desperate but also willing to take more risks. But in the end, also a mystery how he made ends meet.

My episodes tended to be drawn from the lower depths. From outside the mainstream. Whether it be illegal cable ("The Baby Shower"), or homeless people loitering on the library steps ("The Library"), or selling used records ("The Old Man"), or stalkers ("The Opera"), or the Hollywood underbelly ("The Trip" parts 1 and 2), or the mysterious unseen Bob Sacamano ("The Fix-Up"), it was a netherworld of bohemians, artists, eccentrics, schemers, and weirdos who gloriously, proudly didn't fit in.

The episode that perhaps most and best epitomized this was "The Subway," where all the stories took place underground on the train among desperate people and more desperate people. Kramer overhears a horse-racing tip and tries to place a bet. But he is observed and followed and when he wins, someone tries to rob him. Finally a blind beggar comes to his rescue and it's revealed he is really an undercover cop. This was my world but not the world of Jerry and Larry. Though they loved and enjoyed it like voyeurs and encouraged me to keep exploring.

But a shift in the direction of the show started to occur around Season 4. I started to feel creatively separated when more of the shows had to do with a different class of people. Larry and Jerry's real world as opposed to mine. This was due in large part to expanding the writing staff, which inevitably included a more affluent class of writers. Better homes, better schools, intact families, etc. It was a far more yuppified version of *Seinfeld*. Suddenly, rather than drawing from the wide swath of the struggling masses, we had corporate magnates like Calvin Klein, J. Peterman, and George Steinbrenner as supporting players. And indeed Jerry, who grew up in a private house on Long Island, and even Larry were from higher economic strata than I was. I was truly a kid from the streets.

Perhaps the best example of this shift was "The Hamptons." It was funny, clever, full of fresh ideas and word play ("shrinkage") but it depicted a world of people who lived aboveground. Who had nice apartments with views, not the basement. Who had second houses. Unheard of. People were eating lobster instead of trying to figure out how to get their next meal. In the episode "The Smelly Car," they valet their car only to have it be returned to them stinking of the valet's body odor. This was a very "bougie" LA problem. I had actually been a sweaty car valet and it was a bit classist and condescending and very different than my point of view and the Bukowski/Harvey Pekar dynamic that attracted me to the show. During this time both George and Elaine actually got good jobs. It was all legitimate and funny. But much less urgent and desperate and I just related to it less.

I could've stayed with *Seinfeld* as long as I wanted. But as I've stated elsewhere, I didn't get into this business for security. Yes, I had won Emmys and had some financial security and status. But those were also inadequate to address my increasing creative malaise and my wanderlust. Many would question that move. But I didn't and never would. I knew instinctively my time at *Seinfeld* was drawing to a close despite its phenomenal success. My only move was moving on.

•••

After about eighty episodes, I felt like I had hit numerous walls. It was made clear to me that, despite my seminal contribution to the show, contributing much of what it became known for, I would never really be rewarded in kind. I'd never be made executive producer and all that came with that title, particularly creative responsibility. Larry had already had a meltdown about having George Shapiro and his partner, Howard West, and Castle Rock executive Andrew Scheinman given executive producer credit when they were never even present for any of the hard work nor contributed in any way to the arduous creative process. I wouldn't be rewarded financially, which was a measure of appreciation. I always felt the Castle Rock executives resented me and my presence. They saw me as a fly in the ointment that preached revolution when they wanted safety, subversion instead of adherence to their status quo.

After Larry, Jerry, and the cast became frustrated with the extremely gentile Tom Cherones's lack of comedic instincts and sensibilities, both visually and verbally, the decision was made to try some new directors. David Steinberg was one, and an old friend of Larry's, Joshua White, was another. I thought perhaps this would be an opportunity for me to volunteer. But David and Josh wound up being one-offs. Even Jason Alexander directed an episode, but afterward, the awkward silence spoke volumes. He never asked and was never asked again. Larry and the cast didn't like the disruption, and felt like they could at least do what they wanted without input from Tom, and Tom was fine with that, so he remained and my momentary pipe dream was extinguished. I wouldn't get to direct these amazing one-of-a-kind actors until much later on *Curb*.

They would all get rich. They would all be owners. Jerry and Larry, of course, and deservedly so. But erstwhile executive producers, and Jerry's managers, George Shapiro and Howard West and the Castle Rock partners. Later I heard even Steve Bannon became wealthy from *Seinfeld*. But I would always be relegated to the labor class. A worker. A temp worker. A good one. A valued one. But no more, never more than that.

I suppose there was no better illustration of that than the events surrounding the writing Emmy I won with Elaine Pope for "The Fix-Up," which rather than a cause for celebration, was a catalyst for recriminations and resentments.

Tom Leopold, the consummate "shticktician," had joined the *Seinfeld* writing staff. At that time, Season 3, that staff consisted of me, Peter Mehlman, Elaine Pope, and Tom.

But if Tom had a failing at that time, it was vanity and pride and a somewhat fragile ego. That is not to say that we don't all suffer from these traits on occasion. But in my estimation, Tom let it get the best of him. Yet you could argue as well that he wasn't at fault at all in the incident I'm about to describe to you. Perhaps no one was.

Tom had told us a story about a café across the street from his apartment in the West Village. It was one of the places that were just a dead space. Nothing ever succeeded there. It was a black hole for small businesses. The idea of Jerry giving advice to the Pakistani café owner who needed it and soon went out of business, holding Jerry responsible, seemed organic and outrageous.

Tom wrote a draft.

Often *Seinfeld* scripts were heavily rewritten by Larry. And in truth, he was a brilliant writer who made almost everything better and certainly more *Seinfeld*-ian.

Larry and Jerry did not mess much with my scripts. They enjoyed my writing and wanted that voice to be part of the tapestry of the show, and thus had few notes or thoughts. My episodes had a flavor, a taste that tickled both of them, and though on the same matrix, after all they were *Seinfeld* episodes, very different than what they did. But they clearly appreciated it. And when Larry needed to revise or rewrite or add or subtract, it always benefitted the script and I was appreciative.

But Larry found Tom's first draft wanting and set about to rewrite it. Pretty extensively. Though for me, I was never fully comfortable with anyone rewriting my work, even in the case of Larry when he sometimes vastly improved it. But Tom was a veteran of the sitcom wars and understood how the system worked. A system that Larry and Jerry did not know anything about and, further, did not care about. They didn't get to where they are by standing on ceremony.

So when Larry finished his rewrite of the Tom script, Tom assumed, based on the past status quo on sitcom writing staffs, that the author of the first draft received sole credit even if it was acknowledged that the executive producer, in this case Larry David, might have truly been its co-author. But Tom had walked into a con-fluence of unfortunate events.

Larry was already feeling the crushing pressure of doing the show. And he had growing resentment toward not only Howard and George but even Jerry. He came into my office on many occasions in those days to complain about Howard and George receiving executive producer credit, though he felt strongly that they did not ethically deserve it.

More than that, at that time, Larry had a rising animus for Jerry, who up until that point had been taking co-writing credit though Larry felt his contribution did not warrant it. Larry felt that he had done all the work and Jerry came in afterward and did what was essentially a polish, a punch-up. But Larry had conveniently forgotten how often he and I discussed his and other writers' story ideas and my contributions were taken for granted.

I never asked for anything, and I never got it.

Further, I sat in Larry and Jerry's office many times when the three of us broke stories together, Larry jotting down the bullet points on the whiteboard.

Despite Jerry's accurate assessment of what dynamic was necessary to continue both the success and the harmony of the show and no longer taking writing credit, Larry was feeling that things were woefully unbalanced, yet his power to do something about it was limited. He flailed, confided in me, but as is Larry's mien, rather than simply approaching the problem honestly and head-on, he chose to make Tom's script, "The Cafe," his Waterloo. He insisted on a co-writer credit.

This, of course, flew in the face of conventional practices. One of the legitimate reasons the system was set up that way was to protect writers from predatory executive producers, but that was obviously not the case with Larry. Some unscrupulous executive producers would use writing credits to make extra money or get medical insurance or residuals, which all came out of the original writer's cut. But in this case, and many others, Larry did a page one rewrite.

No, Larry truly felt it was fair. And he was certainly right on a certain level. Why shouldn't everyone who contributed get credit? And underneath that, for Larry: "I'm tired of not getting credit for my work." Again one could argue he was the co-creator of the show, but no one could foresee at that moment how valuable that would prove to be. Especially Larry, who took the longest to come around to accepting the phenomenon that *Seinfeld* was becoming.

Tom would have been wise to acquiesce to Larry's request. They were old friends. Older than my friendships with either of them. And Tom knew the rules were sort of bullshit too. But he dug in stubbornly and would not relent. We were at a stalemate.

Jerry would occasionally like to play Solomon and have these biblical tribunals, where true justice could be meted out. Our caterer, whose lies about fat content in the lunches she prepared were exposed and "served" as one of the inspirations for "The Non-Fat Yogurt" episode, was tried at such a tribunal made up of the writing staff, and found guilty and dismissed.

Now Jerry decided that this would be the method to determine the right course of action. He would gather the writers, and they would have to give their opinion out loud in front of both Larry and Tom. You don't think about being queasy or cringing as a comedy writer, but here we were, sitting in Larry and Jerry's office about to give out personal verdicts on who was right, which essentially was a loyalty pledge to Larry or the end of our tenure on *Seinfeld*.

Peter, Elaine, and myself all sided with Larry. We felt he was legitimately right but also we weren't fools.

Tom felt like a pariah, which was understandable. But though it was uncomfortable, it seemed like another shibboleth worth shattering. Fair credit for fair work. And Tom in this moment had a choice. And it's a choice I myself have had to exhibit on many challenging occasions. Resilience. To take failure and disappointments as opportunities to rise even further. But many talented people I knew did not possess that trait.

Failure is a crucial component of success. There is no success without failure. I've worked with some of the greats, and their failures are legion. Publicly humiliating failures. But they were not deterred. But rejection is crippling for some of equal talent and vision and destroys their ability to move on.

I myself have experienced crushing failure, and *Seinfeld* was no exception. But I was determined not to take it personally and looked at it as a challenge to succeed. And I did. At least at *Seinfeld*.

Tom chose to withdraw and play out his string on the show.

And Larry, left with a sour taste in his mouth from the whole ordeal, withdrew his demand for co-writing credit.

But this conflict and the confusion and delays it caused created the need for another script to stay on schedule. A script that would have to be written quickly, in a day or two, literally.

Elaine Pope and I volunteered.

Elaine, the namesake of the *Seinfeld* character, was part of the large mosaic that may have served as some inspiration for Elaine. Keep in mind, the character was somewhat of a blank until the epiphany of giving her George's story, which ignited the flame that became Julia Louis-Dreyfus.

But Elaine Pope was also very different from Elaine Benes. A Canadian lesbian living openly in the semi-accepting, though still hypocritical, atmosphere of Hollywood. She, in a sense, had become Larry's muse and confidante on *Fridays*. That was a dynamic Larry had with a lot of women and which he relied upon. They often wrote together. And even the three of us would collaborate on occasion.

Elaine and I were very close from the beginning. As I said, from *Fridays* on, she played an older sister/mentor role for me for which I've probably never adequately thanked her.

We had discussed a story that we were in the middle of experiencing. Her friend, Cindy, who was experimenting with being straight and my friend, yes, Robert Saccomanno, were both single lonely people. Elaine and I thought it would be brilliant to bring them together. They had a lot in common and might just hit it off, and we'd be genius matchmakers. But if you've seen the episode, you know the whole plan unravels and Elaine and I began blaming each other's friend for the failure, which led to our own fight. All this worked perfectly for our characters; Elaine and Jerry were the matchmakers for George and Maggie Wheeler as Cynthia. And Kramer weirdly enough was the perceptive voice of reason.

We finished the script in less than two days. It was funny and very shootable but also definitely a first draft. We knew that and even encouraged Larry to take a pass at it. In fact, we both said to Larry repeatedly, we'd be happy to share the credit with you. We have no problem with that. It would be fun for us all to collaborate again. But again and again, Larry demurred. He didn't want to talk about this subject. He didn't want to think about it anymore. He didn't want any part of it.

When it came time to submit episodes for the Emmys, everyone was encouraged to submit their favorite episode. I would never have chosen "The Fix-Up," which, though wildly memorably funny was a more traditional version of *Seinfeld*, excited me less than some of the other episodes I had done that season. I was particularly proud of "The Subway," since the simple yet open-ended device of the subway seemed like an ambitious concept for a sitcom episode. One I had never seen before. Far more unique and experimental and radical and dark than "The Fix-Up." And I had written "The Subway" myself. I submitted "The Subway."

Naturally, "The Subway" wasn't nominated. But "The Fix-Up," which Elaine had submitted, was. In addition, Larry's episodes, "The Tape" (with Bob Shaw and Don McEnery) and "The Parking Garage," had both been nominated.

Larry took no pride in the show dominating the writing category with three of the five nominations. Nor did he find any solace in his own two nominations or any of the others that year. Instead he was bitter and angry about "The Fix-Up." It was an extremely unpleasant environment for quite a long time after the nominations. Then, to make matters worse, as the awards approached, word was leaked from the blue ribbon panel that "The Fix-Up" had won. A moment I could only imagine, a moment in my Trump Village mind, of potential unbridled and unabashed joy became in reality a moment of misery as Larry made his unhappiness very known. I don't know what sort of conversations Elaine had with Larry, but I felt compelled to speak with him. I said, first, I did not submit this episode. I submitted "The Subway." And I wouldn't have submitted this episode. Second, despite all that, we did offer repeatedly to share the credit with you, and you refused. It seemed to give him perspective, and after that, his rancor toward me quickly evaporated.

But I think Elaine, like Tom, a veteran of these battles, stood her ground and defended her position and wouldn't back down. It certainly drove a wedge between her and Larry. And like Tom, rather than bounce back with an indisputably great episode, she retreated.

Because of the stress and pain of the experience, neither Elaine nor I bothered to write an acceptance speech even though we knew we were winning. Now, here we are in the back of the limo in tux and gown on our way to the show, trying to concoct some sort of impromptu speech. Only it's timing out at four minutes rather than the forty seconds allotted. I am in a flop sweat.

We knew that Jerry was giving the award in this category, so we seized upon the idea of having Jerry read our speech and we would write it so he would wind up taking credit for the episode. And then we wouldn't have to speak.

The bit got a laugh and we managed to get offstage with a funny moment and relatively unscathed. After you win, you are escorted to the pressroom, where you are led onto a raised platform where dozens if not hundreds of photographers are snapping your picture. Elaine and I laughed at this spectacle. I asked the photographers where they ever dreamed all these photos would be used. They just kept flashing.

The next day, one of those thousands of pictures I derided wound up as the cover photo of *The Hollywood Reporter.* Why? Well, as it turned out, their photographer lost his other roll of film. The one with the photos of the big stars. And we were what he had left.

Both Elaine and Tom left at the end of the season.

I often compared the *Seinfeld* experience to the Beatles, where I was George Harrison but I worked under John and Paul. I had a lot of great songs. But they were John and Paul. Super talented. But also the leaders of the band. In control. So the most I could ever hope for would only be one or maybe two songs on an album, maybe even classic songs, but if I really wanted more, if I wanted to make my own album, I would have to branch out.

Many rode it out till the end, complacent with the status and money and safety it brought them. They had a steady gig on perhaps the greatest sitcom of all time. And had no interest in jumping ship. But Jerry and Larry knew me, even felt my hunger and dissatisfaction, and knew therefore that casting my lot in the outside world, not staying safely cocooned on a hit show, would one day be my fate.

And that day came.

Many questioned my decision. But I never did. Even if I never had that level of success again, what was it? It certainly wasn't mine. I had failed before. I would fail again. But I knew I would survive, and I knew that tapping into my muse and staying true to it was the only road to survival and redemption. I trusted myself. I trusted my instincts. Even though I had no idea where they would lead me. This was the nascent code of the Comedy Samurai.

CHAPTER 5

ZEN SHO RUNNER, OR SCENES FROM A SITCOM MARRIAGE (MAD ABOUT YOU)

I had done *Seinfeld* and I would always have that credit, but now it was time to explore new worlds and take on new challenges and face new risks. And possibly reap new rewards. For me that was exhilarating.

When I identified the holes I was trying to fill with my next gig, I knew it involved three things: something that challenged me as a writer and pushed me beyond my boundaries, show runner status, and more money.

I immediately stumbled out of the gate with a series of failed pilots including one, *Middleman*, that starred Wayne Knight. It was an almost live action cartoon. Surreal and weird. I quickly found out that, though I had left *Seinfeld*, it wasn't as easy for others to perceive me as anything other than an ex-*Seinfeld* writer. I was expected to clone *Seinfeld*, which was anathema to me. Why leave, just to copy what you were escaping from? I had to forge my own path. But I was expected to replicate *Seinfeld* in whatever I did next, and that would never be an option for me.

I was approaching forty and had no clear path to directing, which I was beginning to accept. That dream was fading, I thought. Show runner status gave me much if not more of the things you would traditionally have in a directorial role if you were making your own movie. And I thought perhaps this was meant to be my version of directing. In television at that time and often still true today, the writer-producer, the show runner, is the top of the hierarchy.

The show runner writes, co-writes, or rewrites every script of a television season. They supervise every casting session. Every editing session. Every rehearsal. The director in television, unless it's his own work, is often serving the needs of the show runner. It's the ultimate power on a set, not to be abused, but utilized and implemented to keep the vision realized close to the vision imagined.

But every show has an irreplaceable part. Somebody who simply can't be replaced. It's usually, but not always, the star or stars of a show. The irreplaceable part holds the ultimate power. Everyone else is replaceable. As important as I was here and in many other places, I wouldn't be the irreplaceable part for some time.

My agent, Gavin Polone, had become a manager. I had convinced Larry David, who was unhappy with his representation while at *Seinfeld*, to sign with Gavin, who I always thought had a stubborn integrity. Naturally, when Larry became wealthy from *Seinfeld*, so did Gavin. Meanwhile, I was looking for work. Perhaps out of guilt, Gavin came to me with an offer.

I hadn't been a big fan of *Mad About You*. I found their young marrieds in love, glib, happy go lucky, light as a feather witty romanticism and banter well made but unrelatable. My own marriage was nothing like that. By then I had three daughters, and my relationship with my wife veered closer to *Who's Afraid of Virginia Woolf?* than a sitcom. And precisely because of that, I thought it would be a challenge. Could I bring a darker hue, and higher emotional stakes? Bergman's *Scenes from a Marriage* as a sitcom? If Paul Reiser and Helen Hunt were willing to do it. And they were. And if I could do it. I had never written emotionally honest and real multifaceted characters. After all, our motto at *Seinfeld* was "No Hugging, No Learning."

Mad About You had been almost too much "hugging and learn-ing." Further, despite overseeing the show's evolution to a more sophisticated and mature version of itself, the executives also made their mandate clear: Return the show to its past ratings glory and blaze into a fruitful syndication future. It was to succeed or be canceled.

The show was faltering in the ratings in its fourth year. That was often a make-or-break time for a show. It might not be worth spend-ing any more money on it if it's not going to be a syndication hit. Better to pull the plug now. But *Mad About You* had been a hit in the ratings, and maybe it needed a jolt to get back to its previous status. The show had not reached the magical 100 episodes, which would ensure it a lucrative syndication deal, and I was specifically tasked with getting the show there.

I pitched Paul and Helen a two-season arc that would involve a breakdown of their marriage, infidelity, hopelessness, and then rec-onciliation culminating in a pregnancy. And be funny? Yeah, that would be the hard part. But unlike *Seinfeld*, Paul and Helen weren't as invested in that as they were exploring these ideas honestly within this usually restrictive format.

I was essentially pitching them a sitcom version of my life. The truth about long-term relationships, overwhelmed, disappointed, settling, compromising, dreams deferred, pleasures rare, ingrained habits but with laughs.

After turning down many job offers, I said "yes" to *Mad About You*. I was a show runner.

I entered the stage at Culver Studios with quite a bit of trepida-tion. Could I do this? Could I lead an army?

One hundred people stopped what they were doing and turned to face me. The look on their faces was: "Help us. Just tell us what to do."

Paul and Helen broke rank and welcomed and hugged me. I noticed Paul had a somewhat amused expression as he embraced me.

Back then I had gotten into the habit of wearing pajamas every day. Full-on pajamas. Not fancy Hugh Hefner pajamas. Just sturdy reliable Everyman pajamas. Sometimes matching sets, in light blue hues, like a mental patient who had escaped from a hospital. Sometimes, plaid flannel, which made me look like a Bay City Roller. I often wore a bowler like Alex in *A Clockwork Orange*. I also had hair and a beard each halfway down my torso. And a lot of beads. Did they think I was the show runner, or was I here to sage the stage?

Later, Paul explained that the last time I had seen him was at the Emmys a few years before when I weighed at least fifty pounds more and I was wearing a tuxedo. So when I walked in, he suddenly panicked that he had hired the wrong person.

I walked through the stage, answering a nonstop barrage of questions. That's what being a show runner is. Answering questions. Solving problems. Making creative decisions. And you hope that you're right enough of the time to make the show a hit.

Sony and NBC had been so desperate to salvage the show that I was brought in after the fifth episode. There had been births and deaths on the show before I got there that sent people reeling. A "pall," no pun intended, hung over the stage. The original show runner and co-creator, Danny Jacobson, had drifted away and left the ship rudderless and leaderless. Into the vacuum many had tried to step, all unsuccessfully. To add to the complications of my first week, the guest star was Yoko Ono. With a husband who had been tragically murdered and her signature being anguished screaming, she was not exactly a comedy dynamo. Yes, one would defer to Yoko Ono's opinion in many areas of life. But not sitcom dialogue.

Asking Paul and Helen to do a two-season-long arc where America's favorite couple would separate only to reconcile, and after numerous failed attempts get pregnant, made everyone but them quite nervous. This had been what they were looking for. The dark bitter coffee beneath the froth of their characters. At a certain point we'd be sloughing off laughs to dig deeper into the emotional honesty.

I thought about writing a book called *Zen Sho Runner*. But my assistant reminded me that I'm "not that Zen." And she was right. I was a spiritual materialist. A fraud. A charlatan. Living an ideal

I could never live up to. I read and reread the Bodhisattva Vow. I could even talk the talk. But the Bodhisattva Vow is about putting the enlightenment of others before your own. I was still too selfish and ambitious and acquisitive to truly live by that vow.

But I would learn things and grow and expand and be challenged during my tenure at *Mad About You* that I could have never anticipated.

First, I had to learn to deal with writers as the boss, as a leader. On *Seinfeld*, there was no writers' room, which was a staple of sitcoms of the '80s, '90s, and beyond, and eventually movies as well. Gangs of writers all pitching ideas desperately, because their jobs depended on it, that rarely meshed. For me, it diluted the singular voice of the show, any show, and reduced it to a corporate echo of what the show should be. This became standard operating procedure everywhere but notably not at *Seinfeld*.

The writers' room was an early low-tech version of AI.

Indeed at *Mad About You*, I was now in charge of over a dozen quite disparate writers, including such future superstar creators as Brenda Hampton, who created *7th Heaven* and literally dashed off the pilot for that show while she was doing *Mad About You*, and Jenji Kohan, who left the show at the same time I did and quickly went on to create both *Weeds* and *Orange Is the New Black*. These women were on the forefront of the next generation of TV, but they were joined by and often clashed with the old guard writers, who saw the world from a more traditional white male point of view, which was beginning to reek of insipient moldiness, even then. My job was to synthesize those many voices into one cohesive form. I was expected to "run the room." That is, orchestrate and choreograph the egos and competitiveness and insecurity of the writers and execute the needed changes to the script and know when to order dinner.

As I had observed at my first writers' meeting on *Fridays*, and was still true, everybody entered a writers' room projecting the persona they want others to perceive. It's a mask. This is the cool one, this one is always on, this one is quiet, etc., but eventually, huddled around a circular table in a small room for endless hours engulfed in the stale and fetid air of too many humans together for too long, the masks start to slip and you become who you are. Which is much better for the writing.

Making sitcoms became a very alchemical experience for me. On many levels. Often taking nothing, or just as often taking shit, and turning it into gold was my job. Taking contrasting or under-developed creative comedic conceits and turning them into a seam-less synthesis. But it was true of the people management too. Creating chemistry and harmony from drastically dissimilar personalities in conflict and competition. And I did relish that challenge.

It was a revelatory experience to write dialogue that didn't always have to be funny.

As many thoughts as I had about character and performance and directorial choices on *Seinfeld*, there was a hierarchy to follow. That meant there were literally rules that kept my interaction with the actors somewhat limited. I had to convey much of my thoughts to Larry as we would watch rehearsals and even shooting. And he would combine them with his own thoughts and convey them to the cast and the director.

So I learned how to talk to actors. How to communicate. How to listen. And help guide and craft performances from actors who were looking for one small key to unlock the truth of their performance. Actors who were willing to go out on a limb, not just comedically, but dramatically as well, and be concerned with the emotional hon-esty, the psychological reality, or the absurdity of their character's choices.

Although the directors would do their cut of a show per the union requirement, it was generally a quick assembly and up to the show runner to really edit it into an episode that was of a piece with the series.

•••

My own personal life had veered far from *Seinfeld* territory many years before. So I found I had a wellspring of dysfunctional dynamics to draw from. But *Mad About You*, like most comedies, was required to have a happy albeit hopefully well-earned happy ending. I didn't see my own life going that way.

We essentially had four directors during my two seasons at *Mad About You*, all of whom I worked with closely and respected. Gordon Hunt, Helen's father, whose eclectic résumé served him well as did his unflappable demeanor. Michael Lembeck, the son of Harvey Lembeck, most famous for his portrayal of Eric Von Zipper in the beach party movies of the '60s. Tommy Schlamme, who would go on to produce and direct *The West Wing*, among many others. And finally, perhaps my original inadvertent oracle and muse and mentor, David Steinberg, who in a strange twist of fate was now working for me.

Being on the set with these guys, watching them work, watching the distinctive energy and strengths they would bring to the set each in their own unique way, watching them interact with the actors and the crew—although I said at some point when I took this job that I'd given up on directing completely, but now ironically I was in a graduate director's program as the show runner of this show.

Gordon, who had such a varied résumé, was a consummate actor's director. Gordon was a listener. The actors always felt heard. And he was always willing to explore ideas and thoughts. My epiphany from him was, if you want actors to take chances and make leaps, you must make them feel secure, and each reaches that point a different way. It is a very intuitive almost mystical process on that level. And his relationship with Helen embodied that. The seasons that I was there, I insisted on pushing Helen and Paul as characters and also as actors. And Helen in particular was suffering some of the torment in her struggle to separate herself from the character. Sometimes a great challenge for an intense actor immersed in their part.

There was a necessary and constant examination of who Helen and Paul were, who Jamie and Paul were. How did they get there? What went wrong and right? Judging and weighing the emotional honesty of every situation. The personal and the professional morphing together to make a show.

Michael Lembeck brought a vitality and energy to the set that I haven't witnessed since, even when I try to emulate him. He was a natural performer, and had been a regular on the original *One Day at a Time*, but had also absorbed the lessons of being on the set with his dad and as a young actor so he knew the ins and outs of directing. He was a camp counselor and it was infectious. And actors rewarded him as well for his support. Michael rarely sat, was always moving, always upbeat positive and optimistic. Although I can be downbeat negative and pessimistic, I still found it inspiring and aspirational.

Tommy Schlamme brought something mind-blowing to the *Mad About You* set that he would apply in many shows of his that followed. He shot the sitcom in an almost revolutionary way. Rather than staying within the confines of the proscenium and shooting the episode like a play, he would get inside the set, sometimes taking the camera himself, and with handheld and even the mounted cameras, shot a much more dynamic version of the show, adding an urgency to the shooting that continues to have a huge impact on me.

●●●

The first season I was there (of two), we would wrap, and while the staff and actors reviewed and critiqued and sometimes celebrated the show, Helen would be whisked to another soundstage to be hoisted on a harness twenty or thirty feet in the air in front of a massive green screen for *Twister*. She won the Emmy that year.

The next season, she actually had to be written out of a few shows because she was shooting James L. Brooks's *As Good as It Gets* with Jack Nicholson. She was dealing with enormous pressure. Juggling these very different parts and the demands it put on her physically and emotionally. She won the Emmy and the Oscar that year.

We hadn't really had prominent guest stars on *Seinfeld* during my time there. It just wasn't the focus of the stories. That would change later on after I left. But *Mad About You* had a history of guest stars and cameos. Although Yoko Ono was the guest star the week I arrived, and Jerry Lewis and Carl Reiner among others had been guests before I showed up, and Michael Richards had even showed up in an episode as Kramer, the major guest star during my tenure was like a dream come true. Mel Brooks. I would come to actually know Mel Brooks. An idol. To work with him. To talk to him. He was working on *The Producers* musical at the time, which would play a crucial role in my second professional encounter with him where I got to direct him for an entire season on *Curb* when Larry was to star in *The Producers* on Broadway.

When Paul Reiser, and writers Vic Levin, Billy Grundfest, and myself, sat down to work on the script with Mel, it was hard to put aside that we were writing with the man who created the *2000 Year Old Man* and *Blazing Saddles* and *Young Frankenstein*, and well, you know, Mel Brooks! Truly a legend. A major reason I was even sitting there. Perhaps the OG inadvertent oracle. Seeing him and his work made me dream. And Mel is exactly what he seems to be. Sweet and generous and wickedly funny. He was sunny and cheery and sincere. But he was also Mel Brooks. He was way past jokes. Way past setups and punchlines. He was simply funny in ways you could never predict. His improv skills were stunning, and I loved watching him riff the way people loved watching Coltrane. And for his work on *Mad About You*, Mel won his first performing Emmy.

But the show took its toll. It was a demanding show to write. I often spent eighteen-hour days, sometimes seven days a week, to get the scripts done for read-through so the crew could prep the show. It was a crushing deadline that in the world of the network sitcom never goes away. I had a beautiful bungalow on the Culver Lot, but it was essentially adjacent to the stage in which we shot, and that was the extent of my movements. Bungalow to stage and back, interrupted by casting and editing sessions. I became a rare presence at home, and as Jamie and Paul's marriage strained, so did ours. I became a shadow figure in my own house. I was told that one of my daughters remarked, "I think I saw Daddy this morning."

And although for the sake of the sitcom, Jamie and Paul reconcile and reunite and get pregnant, Barbara and I never really reconciled though it took ten more years before we separated. But she did get pregnant with our fourth child after Sophie, Pearl, and Zelda.

We had literally just found out a week or two before that she was pregnant, and that further, this time, for the first time, we were having a boy. But it was so early and so many things can happen that we told no one.

Hank Azaria, Helen's husband at the time and an accomplished actor in his own right, had been playing a recurring part on the show as a friendly innocent dog walker. Hank's sister Stephanie was a world-renowned astrologer. She lived in New Jersey but was in town. Everyone on the show, and indeed many other prominent celebrities, had readings done by her. I was a skeptic. I tried to avoid getting caught up in it. But Helen and Hank and Paul but also almost everyone else insisted that I let Stephanie do a reading. Reluctantly, I agreed and provided Stephanie with the cursory information she needed to do my charts. It seemed like an inconvenience and a sort of waste of time, considering how much work the show required, but it also seemed that I would be making the wrong statement to Helen and Paul by saying no.

When I went to see her a few days later, I was skeptical but trying to be open-minded. We sat down, and she pulled out a surprisingly thick file with star charts and constellations and equations and other diagrams and charts and began the reading. It was the size of the *Oxford Dictionary*. She thumbed through a couple of pages, and then abruptly, she put the papers down. Then she said, "I don't usually do this, but I have the strangest feeling that you and your wife are pregnant and you're having a boy."

I was flabbergasted. Speechless. She was right, of course. It was a dramatic moment that reminded me that we don't know everything. Reality is a much more elusive force than we can even comprehend. Had she taken a guess, had it been the astrological charts, or did she possess a certain well-honed intuitive clairvoyance? Or all of the above? One thing for sure, I couldn't deny the truth of this moment.

Francesco was born that June. Like Pearl and Zelda, both born in May, he was a hiatus baby. Get pregnant before the season starts. Give birth when the season ended. Only Sophie, our eldest, was born in October and that was because I was out of work.

•••

I had successfully gotten the show to 100 episodes and had enhanced its value by returning it to the top of the ratings and multiple Emmy nominations, and subsequently it was sold into syndication in a very lucrative deal that made everyone rich except me again for some reason. Once again, my agent had negotiated a deal in which I was an employee. Albeit, a highly paid employee. A mercenary. A Comedy Samurai brought in to do a job. But not to benefit from the riches I generated. I was still a temp worker. Oh well. I had decided long ago that money was a weak motivation for anything and often led to ruin and regret. Of course, I've also learned that not having it can be a total drag too.

I realized I had reached another crossroads. As with *Seinfeld*, I could've stayed with *Mad About You* as long as it lasted or I wanted. But I was hungry and restless again. And my work at *Mad About You* was really done. I had led the show back to number one. A triumph that I am still proud of. The cast and crew showed their appreciation by honoring me with a pajama day. But like any good Comedy Samurai, you don't hang around and receive accolades. You move on to the next challenge.

It was time to direct.

CHAPTER 6

THE BEL AIR HILLBILLIES

I had a large family now, three girls and a little boy, and though our house in Hollywood was great, the neighborhood surrounding it was not. I would take the girls out for a walk and we'd inevitably be sidestepping creeps. Not just homeless people. That I could handle. But people who were out of control. With bad intentions. Scary people. Every night we'd have multiple helicopters whirring loudly overhead shining floodlights in the backyards of the neighborhood including ours, seeking some escaped something. I knew if we were being attacked, our screams for help wouldn't be heard because of the copter noise.

Every garbage night we'd have people coming to the door in the middle of the night, banging and ranting. At first I'd try to engage them but they quickly spiraled into irrational hallucinations and I simply hoped they'd go away.

Finally we had a Halloween party for the kids, and before we knew it, a female crack addict with her shirt wide open exposing herself wandered into the house, forcing Barbara and me and some friends to forcibly remove her from the premises. She wound up kicking in one of the large stained glass panes that had been part of the house since it was built in 1911, shattering it all over the floor.

We were forced to call the cops, who eventually apprehended her, but to what end? This was the neighborhood.

Yes, Reagan had released needy patients onto the streets everywhere, including Hollywood, with no adequate infrastructure, and that was a fucking tragedy. But we were forced to deal with it every night. As much as Barbara and I sympathized, we were concerned for the safety of the kids.

We had to move.

We looked for a year until our real estate agent, Denny, brought us to a house that wasn't yet on the market. It was in Bel Air.

When we pulled up to the house, which was on a street called Ottone off Stone Canyon Road, and he told us the surprising un–Bel Air price, I said yes without even walking in. It was a cool house built in the '30s in the moderne style and had been lived in and died in by only one person. It had an acre of land, no nearby neighbors, and was in the fashionable section known as Lower Bel Air, within walking distance of the Hotel Bel-Air. Every house around us was worth ten times more. Amazingly I could afford it.

More amazingly, by the time we moved out, I was broke.

Of course, the house needed remodeling and we lived in the house during this. It was a stressful time. And like all of these projects, despite what might have been well-meaning participants, it went vastly overbudget.

But Barbara and I were committed to maintaining the status quo. To keep up appearances. Not for the outside world so much. But for our own sanity. So our solution to everything during this time was to avoid reality and simply throw money at any problem, including our marriage, which was already in a hopeless place for me, but I didn't have the courage to face it. That meant pouring money into the house, schools, lessons, vacations. The superficial trappings of an affluent but empty life.

And despite my protests to the contrary, despite my seeing my father as the anti–role model, despite my swearing to myself never to fall into those traps, I became my father, addicted to infidelity, compensating for my dying dreams and dragging anyone I was involved with down with me. I was desperately lonely and empty but also embarrassed and ashamed. I had accomplished one thing for sure. I had become a cliché.

Barbara was also compensating in her own weird way. We were in over our heads in every way imaginable. And groping for something. But not each other.

Barbara and I went to see a marriage counselor, as my parents did, but rather than laughing at and deriding the whole process as my father had famously done so derisively before they finally divorced, I lost my temper and the therapist refused to see me again. Instead she recommended a psychiatrist. He was a Jungian, an Italian Jew and one of the most brilliant people I ever met. He might've saved my life. His name was Zanini.

He became a lifeline as I drifted in and out of relationships and projects.

•••

Living in Bel Air was surreal. Barbara and I really didn't belong there. We were like the Bel Air Hillbillies. It is unquestionably a beautiful spot with a reservoir at the top of Stone Canyon, where wildlife grazed and old-growth trees dotted the streets along with some stunning architecture both old and new. But its blatant wealth and privilege and exclusivity was something neither of us could ever get comfortable with. We were the people who had slept on mattresses we had found discarded in dumpsters when we first got together. I only knew this lifestyle from watching it on TV. It didn't feel luxurious. It felt burdensome.

One of the signs to the rest of the community that we didn't belong were our dogs. Barbara had never been a dog lover. At best, she had apathy to dogs. But my daughter Zelda had requested for her birthday a trip to the pound. Something happened to Barbara that day. They came home with a dog. But soon many more followed. When it was six and people thought we were simply Bel Air eccentrics when we took them out walking, that was one thing. But soon Barbara became deeply involved in the rescue movement. Deeply and then obsessively. Again, a noble pursuit, and God knows, like unwanted and abused children, there are far too many abandoned dogs, but when we had twenty-five dogs, we could no longer walk them, and though they were of many different derivations and mixed breeds and overall they got along well and behaved like a pack, it was still total bedlam in the house. There were fights, almost impossible to break up, and we all got bit at one point or another. And God help you if you came to our door. The cacophonous barking alone reduced delivery people to tears. My kids didn't like it. Even Zelda. She wanted one small dog. My kids still don't have dogs today, and I would imagine it had something to do with that environment.

Another event that did nothing to endear us to the neighbors occurred one random night. I was home. I decided to watch TV downstairs so as not to disturb anybody. Everyone was asleep upstairs except Sophie, who slept in a bedroom downstairs but in another wing of the house as far from where I was as possible. Behind me about twenty feet as I watched TV was a two-story glass wall with doors in it that had been added when we did the remodeling. They say, people who live in glass houses but in truth no neighbor could see us and it was pitch black outside. I did something I had never done before this and have never done after. I started watching a *Seinfeld* rerun. I always thought it was the height of hubris and nostalgia to watch my old work so I avoided it assiduously. But this night there wasn't much else on and it was an episode I wrote so I thought, *What the hell*, and began to watch.

And it was funny, and I said to myself, *You know, this is pretty funny*. This is good. And just as I started to relax and enjoy it, there was a banging on the glass doors attached to the two-story glass wall. I turned to see a group of shadowy men. Men in the shadows. Impossible to identify. What were a group of men doing at my door this late at night? I came closer and still could not discern who they were and certainly had no idea what was going on or what they wanted. But as I approached the door, one man screamed with frightening intensity, "Open your door! Your children are in danger!"

I just couldn't imagine I heard that right and said, "What?"

And he repeated with the same urgency, "Open the door! Your children are in danger!"

My mind and heart were racing. Was there a serial killer, a child rapist loose in the neighborhood? Had he snuck into my house?

Once again, with life and death seemingly in the balance, the man shouted, "Hurry! Your children are in danger!"

I could now see the glint of a badge and behind him twenty or thirty other men and women with badges. It seemed to be the police.

What do you do? Ignore them and go back to the show? I opened the door and before I finished asking, "What is going on?" they pushed past me and rushed into the house and fanned out in every direction.

Is there a child rapist in the house? Is there a killer stalking us?

But rather than answering my questions or even volunteering any information, they grabbed me and brusquely sat me on a kitchen chair with a phalanx of cops standing over me.

"Who else is in the house?"

"What?"

"WHO ELSE IS IN THE HOUSE?"

I quickly told them: the four kids and Barbara. They were all asleep. "Where is your wife?" "She's upstairs..." But before I could finish that sentence, I was interrupted. One said to the other, "Get her," and they began to rush upstairs to our bedroom while I remained closely guarded in the kitchen.

I said emphatically enough to slow them down, "Wait! She's fast asleep, and if you burst into the room, she'll have a heart attack. Let me at least go to the foot of the stairs and wake her."

They led me to the foot of our staircase and I shouted tentatively, "Barbara, wake up, the police are here."

Barbara eventually emerged groggily from the bedroom onto the catwalk and was quickly grabbed by other policemen and taken to an opposite end of the house. I didn't see her again for the next two hours.

I still didn't know what was going on.

Meanwhile the police had entered all my children's rooms and begun to question them without either of us present. I had no idea what was being asked or answered. I was still completely and utterly baffled.

After a while a cop finally asked me a question: "What do you know about the photographs?"

"The photographs? I don't know anything about 'the photographs.' I don't know what you're talking about."

"You don't know anything about the photographs?"

"No, Officer, I don't know anything about 'the photographs.'"

The questioning ended. The cop was clearly dissatisfied with my answer.

Finally after two hours, the police brought Barbara into the kitchen and sat her down.

Barbara was pissed. I was shocked. My goal was, no matter what they think is going on, I know they're wrong and I must convince them it's a mistake and get them out of here.

They asked us both again about the photographs, and we both said we had no idea what they were talking about.

Finally a female detective entered the kitchen. She was clutching a large stack of recently developed photos.

"You don't know anything about these photographs?" she asked incredulously.

She flipped through a few. We both recognized them. I was almost relieved. My eldest daughter, Sophie, who was probably no more than thirteen, had taken a photography class at the ArtCenter College of Design in Pasadena. One of her assignments was to explore the effect of the media on female body image. So she had taken a series of photos of her two much younger sisters, Pearl, who was seven, and Zelda, who was four. And because she didn't want to embarrass them, she wrapped them in tape. For modesty's sake.

I guess without knowing any context, it might look like they were posing in bondage or against their will. But once you knew the context, it was obvious Sophie's intention was innocent. Guilty of only the naivety of an older sister trying to protect her younger sisters' demureness.

But she then gave the roll of film to our housekeeper, who took it to the local drugstore for developing. Yes, this was how long ago this was. Photos were taken with a camera that wasn't a phone and then brought to a place to be developed and then you would get actual physical photos back.

But when the person at the drugstore saw the photos, they called the police.

This was at a time when there was a targeting of celebrities for being involved with any untoward or pornographic materials of any kind. In fact, Pee Wee Herman had recently been publicly busted for some minor infraction like masturbating inside a porno theater during a movie, which captivated the media's attention. As you could imagine, both of these "crimes" wouldn't happen with today's technology.

Anyway, once I saw the pictures, I felt confident I could explain it as I've explained it here. Plus I was concerned that I would be busted and the headlines the next day would be something like, SEINFELD WRITER BUSTED IN CHILD PORNO RING, thus ending my career. So I was motivated to assure them it was simply a big misunderstanding.

Barbara, on the other hand, was simply outraged and angry and went into a vituperative harangue about invading our privacy and violating our rights. It involved much obscenity and invectives.

I tried to calm her down, but she wouldn't hear of it and told the police to "Get the fuck out of our house."

By this time they had thoroughly searched the house, gone through our computers and files and drawers. Looked everywhere. They even asked my four-year-old daughter, Zelda, if anyone had touched her private parts. Her response? "What are my private parts?"

As I learned later, by letting them in, I gave the police free rein to search. However by the same token, I also had the right to stop the search at any time. Which I didn't. But maybe Barbara telling them to get the fuck out did.

Inadvertently letting them in helped us because despite their extensive hours-long search, of course they could find no other evidence of child pornography.

The police were angry too. This was a big raid and it turned up this small stack of photos taken by a teenage girl of her sisters for an assignment at art school.

After many hours, they left. But they said as they were leaving that they were not dropping the case. They would give it to the district attorney's office, and it would be up to them.

We were forced to hire a criminal attorney for Barbara and myself in case charges were brought and to monitor the case and I guess what's called a habeas corpus attorney in case the children were forcibly taken away by child protective services. Both of these investigations could be long and costly regardless of the outcomes, and they were.

It took six months, but the investigation was finally dropped. I never watched a *Seinfeld* rerun again.

CHAPTER 7

"YOU SHOULD DIRECT ONE OF THESE THINGS..."
(CURB, PART 1)

I was becoming a very successful show runner in the competitive world of television and needed to start being okay with that. Despite the success and power that accompany the crown of show runner, I knew it wasn't me. But the bigger question loomed. What was me?

Perhaps I was meant to wander. A Comedy Samurai. Going from show to show, project to project, saving them with my mind and my pen, and then moving on. I had started to romanticize or at least delude myself with this Comedy Samurai label.

Around this time, the turn of the century, Larry David had decided with great ambivalence to return to stand-up. Jeff Garlin, who I had cast on *Mad About You* back in the late nineties, knew Larry and was working on a project down the hall from him at Castle Rock, where Larry had an office after *Seinfeld*. Hearing of Larry's plans, Jeff suggested to Larry that he film the process. This seemingly simple idea evolved into something fairly revolutionary. Going back to the time of *Nanook of the North*, the silent documentary by Robert Flaherty, through the work of French ethnographer Jean Rouch in the '50s and '60s nonfiction, the documentary form had often mixed in, sometimes openly, sometimes furtively, elements of fiction. By the same token, Rob Reiner and then Chris Guest were among the first to apply the documentary form to a comical, totally improvised, primarily fictional story, in 1984's *This Is Spinal Tap* and then *Waiting for Guffman* in 1996. But the combination of fiction and nonfiction elements in a television comedy seemed, in my memory, unprecedented. I loved the idea. In fact, it excited me. And I thought, through a series of random circumstances as with *Seinfeld* in the sitcom, Larry David may have deconstructed and then reinvented the form. Ironically, in England at around the same time, a similar epiphany had occurred, which led to Sacha's *Da Ali G Show*.

I didn't think much about it beyond that except to be eager to see it when it was done. Surprisingly, Larry asked me, not to direct it, for I wasn't even a director yet and as stated before had pretty much abandoned that dream, but to play myself in a small talking head cameo, describing Larry.

The pilot was a wild hit and was quickly picked up by HBO for a series, even though Larry himself still wasn't completely certain what or how that would work.

As I've explained, I've had people come into my life. Purposeful and accidental mentors and inadvertent oracles who have suddenly and abruptly pointed me in the right direction. Larry David, perhaps more than any of those many mentors and oracles, kept appearing at crucial points in my life and changing my course.

And this was one of the moments. As he told me about the show getting picked up and having to figure out how it would work, he casually tossed off, "You should direct one of these things." I was taken aback, trying to make sure I processed that comment correctly, but it still took only a second for me to respond, "Yes. Definitely. Okay."

And that was it. I was hired to direct an episode of the first season of *Curb Your Enthusiasm*.

I was ready in many ways to direct. I had been directing in one form or another all my life. I felt confidence in every area except technically. But I approached it seriously. Overpreparing. Like a test I was determined to pass with flying colors.

Since I'd never directed before, I didn't know all I didn't know. And *Curb* was a good laboratory to figure it out. There would be no script. Only, at that time, about a six-page outline.

The job of the director on *Curb* was to cover the action and keep ramping up the situation, the conflict until it achieved maximum comedy overload.

Larry only cared about the abstract essentials of the acting and the lines and the concept and the story. As long as those worked, he didn't care what it looked like.

(And ironically, that mundane, cover-the-action mentality created its own aesthetic, which was carried over and then maximized further in *Borat*.)

My job as director was really to imagine. Imagine the scene. What do I need to see? What's the tone? What else is going on?

Letting my mind drift through the scene enabled me to see it clearly. And from that clear vision I was able to concoct shot lists, drawings, and storyboards when necessary, while being open to and realizing that it all might go out the window and, like the action in front of the camera, I might be improvising.

I thrived in this environment. But it wasn't without its technical snafus.

I was born Lawrence Charles Wengrod but part of my show business dream was to change my name, like Lenny Bruce, Woody Allen, and Mel Brooks, my holy trinity of comedy. I had been reticent, hesitant, maybe even lazy in changing it legally. But I had made the decision that fateful night at The Comedy Store back in '76, to declare myself Larry Charles when I sold my first joke to Jay Leno and he asked my name. It quickly caught on and after that I was often referred to as simply LC. However, the first few days on the *Curb* set, they seemed far too eager to refer to me as LC.

Eventually my AD, Dale Stern, who was rewarded by his loyalty and expertise with an invitation to work with me later on *Borat* and *Brüno* and has gone on to great success as a director in his own right, but here was the AD on my very first directorial job, told me the real reason for the crew calling me LC.

I had a few beefs with one of the producers of the first season show about "Line Crossing." It's sort of a technical term in this context, not a behavioral one. And a cardinal sin in mainstream filmmaking. It has to do with who looks where as you shoot a scene with multiple people talking, and for me though I knew what it was, the first time, it was confusing.

I remember the producer saying, "You're crossing the line." And I responded, "So what? Godard does it all the time." And he did. But Godard did it on purpose and I was doing it accidentally.

Long after the conflicts over that issue on that episode, long after that producer was gone and I had becomes not just a director but the executive producer of the show, Dale finally told me. When they called me LC, it derisively meant "Line Cross."

I pledged to myself that I would never have that issue again. But I did. And I do. Hmm, maybe I should've at least finished that first semester at film school.

Despite my technical limitations, my vision of the shots, the scenes, that first directorial effort, "The Wire," was very strong. I could draw out what I wanted, or make ambitious shot lists, but often I didn't want to know what was going to happen, forcing the cameramen to find it, thus creating an extra layer of urgency, which amplified the comedy.

I loved the vitality and physicality of directing. The interactions, the changing, shifting environment forced me to become hyperaware and observant and draw from everything around me and catch that lightning in front of the camera.

Everything in *Curb* was about the moment. The script, the thought, nothing mattered but what was captured in front of the camera.

By its very nature, great live music is different and unique and personal every time you experience it, no matter who the artist or what the genre. But in film and television, even the most supposedly spontaneous moments have traditionally been scripted, rehearsed, and contrived. There were many reasons for this, including economics. But now a filmmaking style was emerging that was modern. Not just cool shots. But what I called the "ugly aesthetic." It was raw, hand-held, intense, intimate, unwavering, honest, beyond sets or wardrobe or marks or camera movement. It transcended all of the traditional elements of film and TV and spoke more directly to the audience, who was hungry for the next level of interaction with their entertainment.

It was not pretty but had its own beauty. And it was fresh. No false separation between the show and the viewer. No beauty shots, no special lighting. Work with what was presented to you. Functional austere filmmaking in service of this most original content. Content that did not exist before "action" was called and the cameras rolled.

It was about surprise and discovery. Not fulfilling expectations but upending them and surpassing them.

It was a lean machine too. As few crew as we were allowed so that actors could slip right into the scene without much preparation. Not indulgent. We only did shots that could happen with a handheld camera. Everything had to be covered that way. That forced choices as so many restrictions on creativity do, that lead to innovative solutions. No waste. When we had it, we knew and we moved on. We didn't shoot endless takes that drained the scene of its spirit and exuberance.

Curb was a fun set. The pressure was only to make it good.

There were no notes. And despite Larry's arbitrary obsession with keeping the show length at thirty minutes despite first cuts that often hovered around an hour, HBO was okay with us turning in an episode of virtually any length. And as time went on, Larry was able to occasionally be persuaded to let the show run a little long.

Once I got past the technical limitations, Larry increasingly gave me the most complex large-scale episodes where practicing this dogma style verity filmmaking became more of a challenge, which I relished.

Each episode that involved special effects or large-scale stunts or action expanded my directorial language. I didn't know it at the time but while staying in the *Curb* moment, I was also inadvertently prepping for future projects.

No one was ever in a bad mood on *Curb*. The line between off camera and on camera was blurred so the shows not only seemed documentary-like, but they were. Here were these actors you love, pretending to be versions of themselves in some made-up situations. That's the documentary called *Curb Your Enthusiasm*.

It was, and is, more real than most reality TV.

And when you had people like Susie Essman and Jeff Garlin and Richard Lewis and eventually Bob Einstein and JB Smoove, and for a shorter time, Ben Stiller and David Schwimmer, not to mention an entire season with Mel Brooks and Paul Mazursky, witty banter was readily available, and the only challenge was to get them to hold a thought, save the anecdote, and get back to the scene. Or even sometimes, use it in the scene.

Casting in a comedy is an essential but relatively unsung element. As on *Seinfeld* with the legendary casting director, Marc Hirschfeld, we had an amazing casting director for *Curb*, Allison Jones. For the first few seasons, the mandate was to maintain verisimilitude. To that end, we found great actors who hadn't done much TV, and gave them an innate air of reality. Further, as time went on, we only used celebrities, like Ted Danson, Rosie O'Donnell, Ricky Gervais, and Julia, Jason, Michael, and Jerry, as some dark id-like version of themselves. Which they all enjoyed immensely.

One of the key lessons I learned from *Curb* was to let go of control. Magic can't happen if you try to control it. You want to guide it, harness it somewhat, but be allowed to unleash the magic and let it flourish. If that happens in front of the camera, you establish that one-of-a-kind, one-time, lightning-in-a-bottle intimacy with the audience. And the audience responds.

Larry's impact on me cannot be overstated. Even more than Bob Dylan, he has had a profound influence over me. Though he himself didn't care about such things, he had deeply influenced my sensibility and visual style. *Curb* was simplicity and it was exactly what I needed in my life. Later, like everything else, it would become more complicated. Reality always does. But for now, I was a director! And Larry was still to have at least one more massive inadvertently oracular direction for me. And I didn't know it was coming.

CHAPTER 8

"YOU'VE BEEN A GALLANT CAPTAIN." (BOB DYLAN)

O ne of the first things Bob ever said to me was, "I'll never see this movie."

But let's back up.

I was on a plane to New York with Larry David. The first *Curb* season had ended. Larry wasn't even sure he'd do more. And HBO at that time was very willing to wait. But no matter what was to come, I had directed an episode. Though I had even been accepted into the DGA, I still couldn't quite utter the words "I'm a director."

Once in the air, we were joined by another comedy writer, Eddie Gorodetsky, whom I had never met but was a longtime acquaintance of Larry's. After some pleasantries, I could see Larry becoming restless. Finally unable to stay seated, Larry rose and said, "You guys should sit together. You both like music." And with that, Larry found another seat and left us together.

Eddie proceeded to pull out a large CD case and zipped it open. It must've held fifty discs. Indeed, we did seem to share musical tastes. Among the most represented artists in his traveling case was Bob Dylan. And I remarked as much. As we talked about Bob, his music, his unique musical and cultural phases, Eddie quickly shared with me that Bob's manager happened to be his best friend.

I thought, that was weird, and shared with him that I had always heard from my family that my cousin was Bob's manager. A cousin I hadn't spoken to since I was about seven or eight years old due to the falling-out between his grandmother, Sara, and her brother, my grandfather, Joe Wish, siblings who carried a grudge for decades despite living next door to each other. Eddie asked my cousin's name. Jeff Rosen. That was him.

We got off the plane with a plan to all meet up.

I will always be eternally grateful to Eddie, who went on from there to great success as an executive producer on some of the twenty-first century's biggest sitcom hits from prolific creator Chuck Lorre, like *The Big Bang Theory*, *Two and a Half Men*, and *Mom* (which he co-created).

The three of us had dinner, and Jeff and I stayed in touch thereafter, seeing each other when we were in the other's city, but more often in long phone calls. There was so much to discuss from the past weirdness and dysfunction of our family history, which led to our grandparents living next door to each other but not speaking to each other, to our present madness, marriage problems, children, music and movies and literature. But only when he brought it up, Bob. I make a pledge to myself never to bring up Bob. But Jeff and I had much in common apart from Bob, and we got very close. I enjoyed my friendship, my reconnection with my cousin. And continue to. And so did our mothers, Arlene and Phoebe, who grew up next to each other and were first cousins, but were not allowed to talk to each other.

Though Jeff has purposely carved out a life outside of Bob, there really is no escaping him. As Jeff has explained, Bob will call him in the middle of the night while on tour in Norway just to bullshit for a few hours. That's part of Jeff's job. And of course, much of Bob's bullshit is pure gold. So though it's a burden, it also gives Jeff exclusive exposure to one of the most important and original minds in the history of civilization. And I'm not exaggerating.

And it takes a certain brilliance to absorb all that, which Jeff possesses.

I, like most of Jeff's good friends, maintained a close relationship with Jeff himself without ever mentioning Bob. Not that my curiosity wasn't always on high alert. Then one day Jeff called.

Bob was in the midst of what is known as "The Never Ending Tour." Bob Dylan is a wandering minstrel who goes from town to town, country to country, venue to venue playing his songs. His humbleness and unpretentiousness about his task of sharing the songs are part of his profundity.

When touring in North America, he uses a souped-up bus, which at that time was equipped not just with sleeping quarters but a TV and VCR. Bob was an incessant movie watcher, and as Jeff explained on the call rather incongruously, Bob had become obsessed with Jerry Lewis movies. He was watching them back to back the way I'd eventually watch him light one cigarette from another.

Okay. Bob has developed an obsession with Jerry Lewis. Not Jerry Lee Lewis but Jerry Lewis. *The Errand Boy*, *The Bellboy*, *The Patsy*, *Cinderfella*. This was an interesting, if seemingly random, anecdote. But Jeff continued.

It seems that Bob would like to do a TV series...a what? I'm listening really hard because I'm having trouble believing what I'm hearing...he wants to do a half-hour comedy...although Jeff is a funny guy, he's not a prankster. I'm sure he's not joking around. In fact, he's as baffled as I am. And as we know from Bob's history, he will do exactly what you don't expect and possibly don't even want. And that's your problem.

I ponder this ultimately weird juxtaposition. A TV comedy starring Bob Dylan inspired by Jerry Lewis? I wasn't sure whether to yell "NO!" or "YES!"

Then Jeff said, almost apologetically, knowing the weirdness of the request, "Would you be interested in meeting with Bob and talking about it?"

You must keep in mind that, at this moment, nothing being said to me seemed real, which was probably good. I've met with too many people who "want to do TV" but are not ready to make the sacrifice or sacrifice everything else they're doing.

In my mind, the only substantial reality to this is meeting Bob Dylan. To me, that's the triumph. And I would be completely satisfied. I'd have one meeting with Bob Dylan and have a story I could tell for a lifetime. That was the extent of it. I had no fantasy that Bob and I would ever actually make something together.

Jeff explained the one rule about addressing Bob. Addressing him as Bob. Don't call him Mr. Dylan or anything else. He's Bob. Dylan is some construct. Dylan is the persona. The mask. Dylan is your problem. Not his. He's Bob.

We were to meet at a coffee shop Bob owned in Santa Monica. In the same building behind the coffee shop was a boxing gym, where he often worked out as well. I came to learn he owned the building, in fact, owned the entire block.

It was a cool unprepossessing coffeehouse. Young people made coffee drinks and served pastries. People sat together or alone with their computers. I wondered if the patrons knew this was Bob's place. Was that why they were there? Or was it just for the coffee?

When I discreetly announced myself to someone behind the counter, they offered me a table. I felt detached from my body as the words "I'm here to see . . . Bob . . . " stumbled out of my mouth.

This was a request the staff was used to. Quietly, the woman disappeared into the back while I sat and waited.

Could I have been wearing pajamas to this meeting? Maybe so.

Soon, Bob entered, wearing his "uniform," aged khakis and combat boots, a worn hoodie pulled up over and black beanie haphazardly and unevenly pulled down on his iconic head, and joined me. I imagine if he didn't own the place, he and I, dressed like two deranged hoboes, might be asked to leave.

His assistant approached the table and asked us if we wanted anything to drink. I requested an iced coffee. Bob said, "I want something hot. A hot beverage . . . "

With that, his assistant headed behind the counter as we spoke.

When she returned, she placed the iced coffee and the "hot beverage" on the table. Almost immediately, Bob took the iced coffee and began to drink it. This was a tough one. My first encounter with

Bob Dylan and he's stolen my drink. Do I say anything? Or just let it go? I choose to deny that this happened, leaving the hot beverage untouched while we talk until finally Bob said to me, "Why don't you have your drink?" And I said, "Because you're drinking it." He realized the mistake. Or did he? Was it a test? Either way, we both laughed. We never exchanged pleasantries. We never had an ice-breaker conversation. We had an iced coffee–breaker conversation, I suppose. But right then and there, we just began to work.

After that, I began to see him regularly, coming through the coffeehouse into the boxing gym, where there was an airless cubicle that we'd sit in for many months, and while he chain-smoked for a good twelve hours, we'd work on this surreal television series virtually every day. Or at least every day that he was in town. He would still drift off for a leg of "The Never Ending Tour."

As it happened, before Bob, I had developed a deepening interest in the blues, and besides being a collector of music, I actually took harmonica lessons at Boulevard Music in Culver City with master harpist Dave McKelvy.

At a certain point I had become semi-proficient, at least to the point that I might even go onstage occasionally at local venues and do some sort of monologue and accompany myself with the harmonica. I learned the harp solos of many songs, not well, mind you, but recognizable, which was thrilling to me. I performed both "Folsom Prison Blues" and "Goin' Down Slow" at different shows.

But once I knew I was working with Bob, I quit. It felt silly to learn how to play harmonica when you are with the Miles Davis of harmonica. Not that he would teach me, but that it was an embarrassment to hold a harmonica with the master. I never played again.

Bob had a box. It was a beautiful ornate box. One day, he opened it for me. Inside were dozens and dozens of scraps of paper. Piles of them. And on each was something handwritten by Bob.

He dumped the contents of the box onto the desk and said, "I don't know what to do with this." I began to sort through the scraps. They were mainly remnants of hotel stationery from around the world.

The notes scribbled on them, though seemingly random and incongruous and arbitrary, formed the basis for our project.

Some were aphorisms. Some were non sequiturs. Some simply had a name scribbled on them, like "Uncle Sweetheart." I would pick up one scrap and say, "Well, the character can be named Uncle Sweetheart," and I'd pick up another and say, "And he can say this."

Bob seemed amazed. "You can do that?" "Why not?" I responded. Though he seemed surprised that you could apply these techniques to screenwriting, he had clearly been practicing this craft in his song-writing for decades. Juxtaposing and merging thoughts, ideas, lines, and seeing what it produced. This synthesis created new meaning where there was none before. This technique had been pioneered by William Burroughs and Brion Gysin in their prose writing and, like all beat literature from Ginsberg to Kerouac, was an influence on Bob. But only one influence. Bob drew from an eclectic reservoir of influence. And had solved the problem of what Harold Bloom called the "Anxiety of Influence" that most artists suffer from. He not only got out from under his predecessors' and influencers' shadow. Bob created his own shadow that others stand under now.

I wasn't allowed to keep or take home any scraps he had scrawled or scribbled on. I had to transcribe them all and then return them to the box.

And so we worked for quite a few months conceiving this con-coction. A deadpan surreal stream-of-consciousness psychedelic Buster Keaton short with Bob as a Buñuelian Buster. A comedy.

If we were really going to do this, this was what we were going to do.

Feelers were put out, and HBO immediately wanted first dibs, at least on the pitch. It was decided among myself, Jeff, and my agent at the time, Gavin Polone, that it would be a slam dunk if Bob came to the meeting. Our strategy was simple. No one would have the balls to say no to Bob's face. Having Bob in the meeting was tantamount to getting a pickup.

But as a general rule, it was clear that Bob didn't attend meetings, so it was left to me to try to get him to relent and attend this one. I explained to him my logic. That they wouldn't dare turn him down. If the idea was to actually get this strange concept produced, then this was the guaranteed way to do it.

He agreed.

We were to meet in the courtyard of the Century Plaza Towers, where HBO was headquartered at that time, soon to be demolished. For Bob to show up in public involved knowing drop-off points and exits and egress for security and privacy purposes. I respected this, of course, and was thrilled he was coming.

I waited in the courtyard. Wearing pajamas. My hair and beard as long as they've ever been. I began to feel self-conscious standing in this massive courtyard in my pajamas as men and women, properly dressed in business attire, avoided me. It began to feel like a weird dream when a car pulled up and Bob got out dressed like a Western villain in black hat, black floor-length leather duster, black pants, and black boots. Boots of Spanish leather, of course.

I felt a little bit better. He may have looked weirder than me.

Together we strode into HBO.

I'll never forget the two of us marching down the hallway to the stunned bemused gawking of the rows of assistants on each side of us.

We finally came up to Chris Albrecht's corner office, in front of which sat his assistant, who happened to be my friend Richard's wife, Ronni. She had heard all about this meeting, had seen me wearing pajamas before, wasn't a massive Bob Dylan fan, and so wasn't thrown by any of this, in fact was anticipating it, and smiled knowingly as we strode past her into Chris's office.

Chris himself stopped us at the door. Just inside the door, expensively framed, hanging on the wall, were two original tickets to Woodstock. Chris was effusive and genuine in his excitement at being in the presence of Bob Dylan. And to demonstrate his unbridled enthusiasm, he proudly displayed these tickets for Bob.

"Bob, Bob, I'm such a big fan. Going all the way back, man. Look. Look at these. These are original tickets to Woodstock."

Without missing a beat, Bob walked past him and quietly snarled, "I didn't play Woodstock."

With that, he crossed the cavernous office to the floor-to-ceiling picture windows that overlooked Los Angeles and gazed out the window, back to us, silent through the rest of the meeting.

During my pitch, which now didn't seem as surreal as the dynamics of the meeting itself, I would occasionally have a Señor Wences moment with Bob. I might explain an idea and then say, "Isn't that right, Bob?" And he'd grunt in assent.

Nevertheless, despite the awkwardness, the weirdness, the alienation, not to mention the project being a Bob Dylan comedy, as predicted, Chris Albrecht bought it on the spot.

Jeff, Gavin, and I left Chris's office elated, congratulating each other and laughing about the meeting as we arrived at the elevator. However, standing apart from us, Bob was conspicuous in his sourness in the face of this good news, and impossible to ignore.

It would have to be asked so I did.

"Bob, what's wrong?"

"I don't want to do it anymore."

"What? Wait? Why?"

The elevator doors opened and Bob strode past me. "It's too slap-sticky."

We rode down quietly in the elevator. By the time we reached the ground floor, it was over. We hadn't even gotten out of the building.

On the street, I asked Bob if we could talk at some point and see if there was anything we could do to modify it. Once again, I received a grunt of assent.

As soon as Bob and Jeff left, Gavin, usually pretty stoic and jaundiced, pleaded with me.

"Get out. Get out now."

But this wasn't about economics or career. My decision had been made that first day when stealing my drink led to us working.

I knew that whatever twists and turns this journey would take, I couldn't think of a better path. I was collaborating with Bob Dylan. On whatever! I said to Gavin, "I'm on the Bob Dylan Train, and I'm not getting off till the last stop." And he looked at me like I was crazy. Maybe even shook his head in disbelief. And indeed he may have been very right.

Amazingly, with occasional interruptions for touring or recording, we continued working and the half-hour Bob Dylan HBO comedy morphed into *Masked and Anonymous*. Bob never tried to explain it or label it, and it wasn't until it was finished that I began calling it a sci-fi spaghetti western musical comedy. That was the best I could do.

It contained many of the elements of the original project but now expanded and layered with biblical, Civil War, and autobiographical language and imagery.

One of the great pleasures of my life, which I didn't dare feel at the time, was writing with Bob Dylan. Sometimes he would walk in with an amazing monologue he had written the night before. It might not even be connected to anything we were working on. But it was the nature of this writing process. Use whatever enters the psyche in the moment and let its subconscious meaning emerge.

But I would still need to turn it into dialogue for the script. So often I'd have to decide who said what, was it completed in its present form or did it need to be adjusted for the scene, what else was being said and what else was happening. Many questions. One of my methods for writing with Bob is something I call channeling. It's incorporating someone else's voice and writing through that voice. To write great parody language in sketches, you had to channel the old movies and TV shows they originated from. It was something I did when I worked with people who had a unique voice, like Larry David.

And though it's pretty seamless and hard to tell at times, much of *Masked and Anonymous* was written that way.

I had been thinking of a title, leaning toward something Dylanesque but hoped Bob himself would lay something down that would blow my mind as he has done so many times. So one day Bob came in and said he had the title. Now, Bob is a great titlist, from *Blonde on Blonde* through the album he was working on at that time, *Love and Theft*, and I was excited to hear his title for our magnum opus.

And then he said it: "*Masked and Anonymous.*"

"*Masked and Anonymous?* What? Are you sure? I can't even pronounce that. Your last two albums were *Time Out of Mind* and *Love and Theft*. Are you sure it can't be something shorter and simpler like that?"

But Bob was convinced this was the title, and so it was. And I was a believer. Bob was conjuring spirits from another realm. He was pure instinct. No second-guessing. Fearless as an artist. And he taught me to take that final step and be the same. Trust your instincts. That's all you have. Everything else is bullshit and illusion. Hey, wait a minute. How about *Bullshit and Illusion*?

And even if you're wrong, so what?

The next issue was credit. He didn't want any. I explained that I couldn't take sole credit for this script. We finally agreed to both take credit but use pseudonyms. He immediately had his pseudonym ready. Rene Fontaine. I was forced to come up with something on the spot and blurted out Sergei Petrov for some reason. Where did that come from? Again, from the depths of the subconscious. Was I Sergei Petrov in a previous life?

We got special permission from the Writers Guild, and that became the credit.

•••

One day we were writing. And I get to say this like it is a mundane experience: One day when Bob Dylan and I were writing. It's still unbelievable, we wrote almost every day, often for twelve hours a day without breaks. Often without food or beverage. But always with a cloud of cigarette smoke. The intensity of that situation created its own high. But that's what I wanted. I wanted to immerse myself in his head. And manifest that on the page and on film.

But one day we were writing and he suggested a line. "I'm not a pig without a wig." It was an incongruous line even for this script. It just didn't make any sense in any context, even in the dream logic and secret structures of this script. And by now, having worked together for months, I felt strangely okay about telling him so.

"Bob, I have to tell you, even in this script, even in this movie, that line doesn't make any sense. No one is going to understand that line."

And Bob, inscrutable and unconvinced, says, "What's so bad about being misunderstood?"

Was this a song? Did my head crack open? This was Bob the guru. Asking a question that had never been asked. That was counterintuitive yet right. That question took things to a metaphysical level that transcended the line and was a layer very present in the movie. What is so bad about being misunderstood? You see, Bob's been understood. Too understood. So understood, it creates misunderstanding. He's interested in what it's like to be misunderstood.

I had a moment of "Satori." But the line didn't make it into the movie.

But in typical Bob fashion, it found its way onto *Love and Theft* in his epic saga, "High Water."

Bob would have certain notions that I felt compelled to dissuade him from. One was to make the movie all dance. Every character would have their own dance. He had already called the choreographer Toni Basil to discuss it. When I spoke to Toni, I respectfully informed her that it simply wasn't even a possibility. Working out the choreography would take longer than the whole shooting schedule.

He also seriously considered using a very artificial accent. Once again, he did not cling to these notions.

But considering the vitriol and bile directed at him and the movie, maybe he wasn't wrong.

At a certain point the question of directing entered into my head. I had only directed one *Curb Your Enthusiasm* at this point. That was the extent of my directing experience. I knew this was a project that could have its choice of director, but no one would have the unique understanding of this material that I have.

I agonized for many weeks. Trying to summon the courage to

simply ask Bob. It was just too hard to visualize him saying yes. But finally I knew if I was serious, I had to cross that Rubicon.

One day, quite abruptly, I haltingly began: "You know, Bob, I was thinking about it, and I'm sure there are a lot of amazing people who would like to and could direct this movie, but I actually think I'm the most qualified. I really think I should direct this movie if that's cool with you . . ." and Bob, sounding like a patron in a diner who doesn't really want more coffee but accepts it anyway, says, "Okay . . ."

And just like that, I was the director of *Masked and Anonymous*. It was an awesome responsibility. To make sure I was prepared, I hand-drew storyboards for the entire movie. I still have them.

It seemed that, despite Bob's name, we'd still need some stars to finance the movie. As you can imagine, every name in show business was raised as a possibility. For many, it was true. The idea of working or hanging out with Bob was an enticement in and of itself.

The first two names that I was absolutely guaranteed wanted to be in the movie were Jack Nicholson and Johnny Depp. At that time they were the first two names mentioned for any movie. But I learned that massive stars of that magnitude circled many projects, and often landed where the money was.

Masked and Anonymous was budgeted at $4 million.

But the reality was, this could not be viewed as an indulgence, but as a commitment. And many actors opted out for a variety of reasons, not the least of which was money. But the actors who wanted to do it, did it.

What was amazing was how much they were like the characters before they even knew who the characters were.

Luke Wilson was the first to commit. And was ready, willing, and able to do anything asked for Bob. Just like his character, Bobby Cupid.

John Goodman drove nonstop in his Cadillac from New Orleans, just like his character, Uncle Sweetheart, would.

I met Jessica Lange at the Chateau Marmont. Jessica had a history with Bob as did her longtime partner, and one of Bob's other few collaborators, Sam Shepard, so she had no illusions about him but was intrigued more than cynical, despite her experiences, and up for the adventure, like her character, Nina Veronica.

I met Penélope Cruz at L'Ermitage in Beverly Hills. She told me about her OCD and how she obsesses on the number 3. And she was very much devoted to her boyfriend, Tom. These were the elements of her character, Pagan Lace, in the movie down to her boyfriend in the movie being named Tom Friend. I discovered during the shoot that the real-life Tom that she was devoted to was Tom Cruise.

Perhaps the two most difficult parts were essentially the antagonists to Bob's Jack Fate. Tom Friend, the journalist with an ax to grind like so many who want Bob to fit into their box and are angered when he can't and won't. And Edmund, Jack Fate's half brother, the Machiavellian son of Jack's dying father, the leader of this Third World America, who intends to brutally inherit the mantle of tyranny.

We thought Mickey Rourke, so intense in so many movies, would make a great Tom Friend, the bitter self-destructive journalist getting in Jack Fate's face about his history and his expectations.

This was when I learned a show business secret that I'd never known before. There is a book. Yes, a book. And in that book are the names of virtually every actor who has starred in a movie. Also every director who has ever directed a movie. And beside each name are a series of numbers. How many movies have they starred in/directed? What were the budgets? What was the box office? From this equation, another number was derived. That was the number above which says this is someone who has made profitable things on a fairly consistent basis. Below that would be the list of those who haven't.

Remember, we still didn't have the money to make the film.

My first sobering experience was that Bob Dylan himself meant nothing to film investors. Despite who he was, he was never a successful star in movies. But once I got over that, it was explained that none of these other award-winning major movie actors were enough in themselves to secure the financing for the film.

A film that was budgeted at $4 million and a twenty-day shoot.

It was explained to me in no uncertain terms that you cannot get investors—even, and in fact particularly, in a low-budget indie film like this—to put their money into a vehicle starring Bob Dylan, who isn't even in the book, and unfortunately, Mickey Rourke, who at that time had starred in a string of relatively unsuccessful films.

Mickey had fallen just below the line. Jeff Bridges had snuck in just above the line. If Jeff Bridges was Tom Friend, we could secure the financing. But Jeff had already said no.

I went to Mickey Rourke and offered him the role of Edmund. Edmund was a juicy role. He had some wicked monologues and really drove the climax of the movie.

I'll never forget spending a day following Mickey Rourke around town, always with his dog, Loki, to custom tailors to make him suits for his part and custom wig makers for a potentially exorbitant wig. But it was fun. We were creating the character through his clothes and hair.

I did this with each actor, getting inside their characters from the outside. Their costume would be them. Would define them. The story took place out of time. Sometime in the future that looked like a past. So synthesizing looks from different eras contributed to that quality.

And they were costumes because this was also a theatrical presentation on a certain level. A pageant with colorful costumes at the end of the world.

Further, if this was some sort of post-apocalyptic Third World America, where were people getting their clothes cleaned? This always bugs me in science fiction films. So each actor had to choose a look. In the case of John Goodman and Luke Wilson, they wore the same costumes throughout. Uncle Sweetheart wore a dingy powder blue tuxedo. Bobby Cupid wore the snakeskin leather jacket that Marlon Brando wore in *The Fugitive Kind*.

Jessica convinced me that Nina would have a change or two of clothing. She cared about her appearance and her hygiene and was trying to live a semi-normal life, which of course was a delusion.

Same with Bob. When Jack Fate was released from jail and picked up his things, it made sense that he had a couple of changes. After all, he had been a performer.

In the meantime, this actually happened. Jeff Bridges called my house one day and said he'd been thinking about the script and how would I feel driving up to his place in Montecito to discuss it? I told him I was on my way, and I drive fast.

On the dizzying drive up, I was fantasizing about the potential coolness of having two of my favorite actors, Jeff Bridges and John Goodman, and two of my favorite characters, the Dude and Walter Sobchak, together in this movie.

I decided I couldn't arrive at the Dude's house empty-handed so I brought a few joints with me. The very heady idea of smoking with Jeff Lebowski was already getting me stoned. But I also pledged to myself that I wouldn't just whip them out. I mean, I didn't really know if the real Jeff smoked. I would look for a sign.

Jeff's place was as cool and warm and comfortable as Jeff himself. Here was a movie star who was exactly as you imagined and hoped. We wandered for a while as we talked and I saw ashtrays planted throughout the property. Should I offer? But the ashtrays were empty. Maybe not.

We spent the rest of the day moving through virtually every room of the house. Jeff was an accomplished artist and musician as well as a celebrated actor. And in every room was an ashtray. Empty. Not a remnant of a roach.

But the conversation, the bonding, the hang was going great, and I knew that he had just committed to the movie when we started talking about wardrobe.

We thought it would be a cool layer, no pun intended, if when we met Tom Friend at the broken-down newspaper office with Bruce Dern as the editor, Tom would be dressed like Bob today. Gray hoodie, khaki pants, and army boots. But when he came to confront Jack Fate, he dressed like Bob circa 1966—black leather jacket, black pants, white shirt, and shades.

Jeff gave me a small figurine he had sculpted. It was a bust with a black mask on it. I still display it proudly on a bookshelf in my office. But most important, it was a symbolic ritual sealing of the deal.

Jeff Bridges was going to be in the movie.

I left elated. I drove home but was somewhat delirious and so I pulled out a joint that had been sitting in my pocket through the entire day and started smoking it. Stoned, I decided to take the scenic route along the coast rather than rush back on the 101 so I got off at the next exit. Two hours later I had no idea where I was. The roads in Oxnard were like a Borgesian short story. They seemed to head west, but when they ended, I was right back where I started. Circling. Getting no closer. I finally wended my way back on track and enjoyed the ride, savored the moment, something I rarely allow myself to do, knowing that this movie I wrote with Bob Dylan would be made and I would direct it and Jeff Bridges had agreed to star in it.

Bob and I spent a lot of time talking about the music for the movie. His band at the time happened to be tight, and he wanted to capture this era on film. He wanted to specifically perform five songs live with the band:

"Down in the Flood"
"Cold Irons Bound"
"Drifter's Escape"
"Standing in the Doorway"
"All Along the Watchtower"

He had in his mind the way old '50s and early '60s TV music was filmed. Generally, the technology was limited, but it created its own unique intense beauty. Often accomplished with one single moving shot. I loved the idea of trying to make an entire song work on one shot. It had a certain elegance and economy.

Scouting this movie with the mission of creating a sort of futuristic Third World America on a shoestring budget was one of the most creative endeavors of preproduction. Los Angeles is to some degree a futuristic Third World America. So it wasn't that hard to find. But along the way, we were privy to locations long hidden from view like the original Griffith Park Zoo, which became the prison Bob was released from at the beginning of the movie. Or the graffiti-festooned abandoned train station where Bob bantered with Cheech Marin and then caught a bus called Destiny. They've since blocked up that tunnel. We used abandoned buildings and flop-house hotels, which are now expensive lofts and trendy boutique hotels. We used the abandoned Masonic Temple that loomed over Wilshire Boulevard.

Finally, we had a shooting schedule, and everything was coalescing. Then someone noticed that Bob's tour was scheduled to begin the day the movie wrapped. Not having ever really made a movie before or had this much responsibility, and obviously neither had I, Bob and his team didn't realize that you had to leave a two-week padding once filming ends for any reshoots that might arise. It is a contingency built into all films essentially for insurance purposes. But the tour had no flexibility. Venues had been booked.

We were forced to postpone the movie. Many times during that month or two, I despaired that the movie after all that would never get off the ground. But it did.

Everyone's wardrobe was approved and photographed and doubled prior to shooting. Except Bob's. It was being custom tailored, and I literally wouldn't see it until he emerged from the trailer with his stylist for the very first shot of the very first day of the movie. Like so much with Bob, it was a leap of faith and one I was always willing to take.

This is the story of the jacket.

Finally the cheap trailer door swung open, and Bob descended the rickety stairs, accompanied by his stylist. His outfit was quite magnificent. Visually the whole movie felt like a Mexican Western to me, and I wanted Bob's clothes to be inspired by that and indeed this outfit was.

It was kind of a Nudie-style embroidered silk hand-crafted suit.

It wasn't quite brown or beige or tan. It was almost flesh colored. The patterns on the lapels of the jacket were handmade and woven.

I was very impressed. I told both Bob and the stylist that I thought the suit was awesome. Well worth waiting for. And in keeping with age-old requirements, it would need to be doubled in case something happened.

The stylist looked at me like I was an idiot and explained that this garment couldn't be doubled. It was made from one-of-a-kind vintage fabric, and there was no more of it.

Somehow during this conversation, Bob sidled back into the trailer.

But in the movie, Bob gets into scrapes and scuffles. He has an actual fight at the end. If something happens to the jacket, we won't be able to finish the movie.

But that's what he wanted to wear, and it was time to make a movie.

From that moment until the movie wrapped, the jacket became my obsession.

As much and as hard as I had to work on Bob's performance, I never took my eyes completely off the jacket. When crew members walked by with heavy dirty equipment, I would subtly place myself between them and Bob.

At lunch, if Bob ate fried chicken, I was ready with a napkin to lap up any grease.

If he smoked a cigar, I would be casually holding an ashtray.

I went in to visit with him for a minute before we officially began. Mainly to thank him for the opportunity. I had only one request: "Since this is a tight schedule and people are here not for money or career advancement but out of devotion for you, if instead of before a scene or after a scene going back to your trailer, and I know how private you are, but if we got you a nice comfortable chair and you stayed on the set so when someone walked by, they could say, 'Hi, Bob,' and you might say, 'Hi' back, and it would mean nothing to you, you'd forget it almost instantly, but it would be a significant moment in their life like it is in mine. That would mean much more to everyone than money."

Like so many other decisions I watched him make, without hesitation, he agreed.

Bob was amazing with people. He didn't really avoid anything. But never invited anything either. If people asked him not so much inane questions as questions that have been asked of him a million times, he would simply reply, "I don't remember...," and keep moving.

Often when people have the opportunity to encounter Bob, they want to ask him a question. Why did you do this? How did you feel about this? And he would usually respond, "How did you feel?" People would be tongue-tied. "How did I feel?" And he would saunter away.

The very first shot of the first day of shooting was an elaborate crane shot in an abandoned bank building that we had converted into a post-apocalyptic bus station.

I sat at the top of the crane like I knew what the fuck I was doing. I watched Bob and the Lady in Red, played by Laura Harring from *Mulholland Drive*, stand at a counter together below. But as we readied the shot, I heard music through my headset.

"What is that?"

I wasn't the only one. A search began to track down the source of the music. It turned up nothing.

I had someone run outside and see if anyone was blasting a boom box.

It was quiet outside yet the music persisted in my headset.

Meanwhile I saw Bob getting antsy down below. I thought, *Great, first day, first shot, and there's some weird inexplicable delay*, and now Bob is standing there thinking, *What the fuck is going on?* I had them lower me to the ground.

I walked toward Bob and the strangest thing occurred. The music was getting louder. How weird. By the time I was next to him, the music volume had grown the way a Geiger counter clicks wildly as it approaches something radioactive.

That's when I realized the music was emanating from Bob him-self. My first thought was shit, this guy is more than a genius. He's like some sort of shaman. Music is actually coming out of him. Like an uncontrollable force.

Then I saw the little earpiece in his ear.

I said, "What's that?"

He said, "What?"

He actually couldn't hear me over the music.

I repeated, "What's that?"

He said, "'Mona.'"

I said, "No, in your ear."

He said again, "'Mona.' Bo Diddley."

"No, Bob, that thing in your ear."

He explained that there was a guy outside in the parking lot, in a tent, a DJ recommended by Johnny Depp, who would essentially provide music for him throughout the day to get him in the proper state of mind for his scenes.

I said quite brazenly that there was no way Johnny Depp told you to play music during the scene. Maybe before the scene but not during the scene. You can't even hear yourself speak. And it was bleeding into everything we were recording. And even if Johnny Depp did tell you to play music through the scene, we can't afford to pay for Bo Diddley's "Mona."

I then ran into the parking lot. Sure enough, somehow between the time I arrived and went inside to shoot, a teepee was erected and a DJ stood within it spinning music for Bob. I told him to stop. Then I ran back inside and told Bob he had to take the thing out of his ear. He wasn't happy.

I was so thrown by this story about Johnny Depp that, for years after, I tried to track down the true story about the music. After decades I did. And it was true. Johnny Depp often had music piped into his ears during scenes.

There was no room for indulgence, and everybody came ready to work. Bob set the example. He was always there and always ready.

Nevertheless we had written a 159-page script and Bob insisted on shooting all of it. And I agreed.

The problem was we couldn't shoot a 159-page script on this budget and schedule. But Bob would not change his mind.

The producers reluctantly relented. On one condition. I had to kick back my salary, which was DGA minimum. Which I did. My agent almost killed me, but no one else protested. I made zero money on *Masked and Anonymous*. Good thing it was a labor of love, huh?

But I saw myself entrusted with this awesome responsibility. I was the captain of the ship, and I would go down with the ship because that's what a captain does.

On Jessica Lange's first day, she got into wardrobe and her wig, had her makeup done, and in quick succession I greeted her, led her onto the stage, put her in position, and said "action" and filmed her first scene. When it was over, she was dizzy, like what happened? I told her I wanted to capture that nervous energy she was exuding, which gave the scene urgency. The next day, she begged me to let her do the scene again. And I did. And it was great. She was never not great. But I used that first take.

In the scene, she harangues two network functionaries about the state of the world. The two functionaries were played by my former comedy-writing colleague Bruce Kirschbaum, who had given Barbara and me every Bob Dylan album up until that time as a wedding present, and Eddie Gorodetsky, who had inadvertently started this crazy train ride.

On breaks or at lunch, Bob would often change back into his civilian uniform—gray hoodie, khaki pants, and army boots—and wander the neighborhood we were shooting in. One day a neighbor called the police and said there was a homeless man wandering around the neighborhood. The cops picked Bob up. He told them he was Bob Dylan, and he was shooting a movie a couple of blocks away. They said, "Sure." They threw him in the patrol car. But finally they let him call Jeff Rosen, who went to retrieve him.

Bob didn't really have acting experience, and though Jeff Bridges was literally being his acting coach during scenes, it wasn't a process Bob adapted to quickly. And there was no time.

Sometimes, Bob would be in a scene and was enjoying watching the other actors so much, he forgot to say his lines.

I had to figure out a way to show Bob how to cross a set and hit a mark and say the line. So I had his stand-in, Brad, walk through every scene with the actors while Bob watched. Then Bob would step onto the set and imitate him. Bob imitated Brad, who was imitating Bob.

The death of Jack Fate's father, the dictator of this Third World America, took place on a stage in an abandoned auditorium. His bedroom was essentially the raised stage, and his followers camped out below. Jack would enter and try to say goodbye but there were no words. As we blocked out the scene, Bob turned to me and said quietly, "I want to cry." I was like, "What?" And he was like, "I want to cry in this scene."

Richard Sarafian, the great and underrated director of the original classic *Vanishing Point*, played the father. He lay in bed and looked at me like, "Whatever."

I conferred with the makeup person. In her kit, she carried a sort of menthol straw for just such requests. She would blow a gentle waft of menthol into your eyes, and you would tear up. It was pretty much a standard procedure in those days and before.

She approached Bob with the straw as he sat on the deathbed. She leaned over and gently blew. And Bob went blind.

He couldn't see a thing. He wasn't panicked. It was almost like he was expecting it. Like this would be a new persona. Blind Bob Dylan. But he was blinded, and hopefully not blind. Bob was rushed to the emergency room, where they flushed out his eyes. He came back, the trouper that he is perhaps above all, like he famously said, a song and dance man, and then he cried in the scene.

Bob hears things we don't hear and sees things we don't see. At one point in the movie a ten-year-old African-American girl (Tinashe, who would go on to R & B stardom) is brought in to sing an a cappella version of "The Times They Are A-Changin'." It was so rousing and stirring that it drew everyone on the soundstage that day closer to the stage to hear it, experience it. It was a mesmerizing performance. When it was over, there was a spontaneous explosion of applause. Most were weeping. While this outburst was occurring, Bob got up from the drum riser where he had sat rapt and listening. Without a hint of emotion he walked past me and said, "She said 'a' instead of 'the.'" And walked off.

Our official shooting ended with a 24-hour day. It was grueling. But weirdly it sort of worked for the scene. It was the dreaded fight scene between Jeff Bridges, Bob Dylan, and "the jacket." Jeff was scheduled to start another movie, and the producers had a plane waiting for him to whisk him to that location. But he had to be killed first.

Jeff is an intense actor, and he had to shove Bob. This would lead to Bob breaking a bottle to use as a weapon. And this would lead to Luke, as Bobby Cupid, stepping in to rescue Bob and murdering Jeff as Bob and John Goodman and Penélope Cruz and Jessica Lange looked on from various vantage points.

Although there had been some preparation for the scene—after all, there was violence and blood and death—and there was a stunt coordinator, there were no substitutions or stunt doubles. Just the actors and the jacket.

And I didn't want to rehearse it, I wanted to shoot it. I like capturing the intensity and spontaneity and even the mistakes. Shooting *Masked and Anonymous* was like shooting *Curb Your Enthusiasm* in many ways, trying to capture a moment, only with a sacred text instead of improv.

So in take one, Jeff shoved Bob. It had been a long day and, though a short shoot, an extremely arduous and grueling one. And Jeff was at least six-one or more and solid. Bob was smaller and far more diminutive and not a young man even though he was in great shape. So when Jeff shoved Bob, he launched him in the air. For me, everything became slow motion like a Peckinpah movie. Bob flying backward through the air. I watched with utter panic as he soared, his jacket like a wind sail.

I knew what went up must come down, and I shuddered in anticipation of that treacherous landing. Yes, of course I was concerned in that split second if Bob would be hurt. But somehow I knew Bob would survive. I knew Jack Fate would survive. It was the jacket's fate I wasn't so certain of.

Bob landed hard, and I rushed up to him. I asked him if he was okay, and to those watching, it looked like I was making sure he hadn't broken anything. But I was also checking the jacket. Any rips or tears, blood or other stains that would never come out.

But the jacket was all right. And oh yeah, so was Bob. And so we were able to finish.

We had actually made it through the movie and reserved the last day to film Bob and the band doing "All Along the Watchtower" as promised, plus whatever else he felt like.

Everyone who had worked on the movie, cast and crew, crowded in to experience this unique, intimate, yet intense concert. It was a celebration. Of the movie. Of its completion. And of Bob.

He and the band launched into an introduction of sorts to "All Along the Watchtower." It was actually quite great. It seemed to go on quite a while. I was really enjoying it. It reminded me of an instrumental version if it were done by the Allman Brothers. His band was masterful. And all cool guys. Loved hanging around with them. And loved watching them watch Bob to see what he would do. One never quite knew, but they had developed a sixth sense and intuition that allowed them to enter into his mind and musical world. Charlie Sexton and Larry Campbell on guitars. Tony Garnier on bass. George Receli on drums. But this stirring instrumental version of "All Along the Watchtower" continued long past the point that a vocal should've begun even in this elongated version, and the AD approached me wondering what he should do. I told him to wait and we continued shooting. I had been in "Bob World" long enough to let go of expectations and just let it happen, and I did.

After a few minutes more, Bob stopped. The band, caught by surprise, stopped too, though hardly in sync. Bob put his guitar down and exited the soundstage and returned virtually for the first time in the entire shoot to his trailer. I called for a break and headed out there to see what was up.

I entered the trailer and asked if everything was okay. He said he didn't want to play "All Along the Watchtower." I asked why, which was not a great question. He said he just didn't feel it. I don't know why, but I persisted.

"Bob," I said, "this was one of the five songs you wanted to film for the movie. We've filmed the other four plus a lot more. Now here we are on the last day, with a crowd of people who have shown up just to hear you play 'All Along the Watchtower.'"

Bob wasn't big for eye contact, but he paused and looked me in the eye.

"I've done everything you've asked on this movie without question, haven't I?" Bob posed this question with the same equanimity he applies to everything. I was humbled and chastened.

"Of course you have. I'm sorry. You're right. If you don't want to play 'All Along the Watchtower,' it's not a problem. I'll just go out there and call a wrap and that will be that."

There was a nano moment of silence. Then:

"I could play 'Knockin' on Heaven's Door.'"

I was floored. Muttered some, "Yeah, sure's," and, "That would be great's," and stumbled back onto the soundstage to get set up. He came out and played "Knockin' on Heaven's Door." It was one of the best versions I'd ever heard, and it left the crowd in tears as we wrapped.

Later, he would give me what remains my favorite compliment: "You've been a gallant captain."

Essentially that was the last time I ever spoke to Bob.

The first editor I hired wanted to shape the movie into something more traditionally structured, and so we parted ways. Instead, I promoted the assistant editor, Luis Alvarez y Alvarez, to edit the movie with me. And we made the movie I imagined. A three-and-a-half-hour extravaganza. A pageant. A comedy. A tragedy. Biblical, Shakespearean, and vaudevillian. As messy as the apocalypse. And as epic. I began to describe it to others as I had described it to myself: a sci-fi spaghetti western musical comedy.

The producers were understandably nervous. About everything. The movie was purposely dense with layers. And like the movies that mesmerized me in the '70s, justified its extended length.

They did not agree.

They decided to screen the movie to gauge some initial reaction. Unfortunately the producers didn't choose a college audience to be the first to witness this opus. Instead they choose three or four dozen agents, in their suits, after a long day's work, to squeeze into an old un-air-conditioned screening room for three-and-a-half hours. Needless to say, it was met with a hushed and respectful tone befitting a funeral. The agents told the producers in no uncertain terms that, in its present form, this movie was unsellable.

When the producers told me that no one understood it, I replied, "What's so bad about being misunderstood?"

In turn, they demanded that I cut the movie down to 110 minutes. When I refused, they pointed out a very specific but overlooked clause in my contract that demanded I turn in a 110-minute cut.

I had kicked back my salary and still didn't have final cut.

To try to make the new cut elegant and stand up on its own, they brought in the Academy Award–winning editor Pietro Scalia to recut it with me. He was a sweet and obviously talented man who had worked with Bertolucci, Stone, and Ridley Scott among others and had won two Oscars and had bartered his editing skills with the producers in return for directing a future movie, which never happened.

Together we cut the movie down. And indeed he was a master craftsman. Pietro had techniques to make large amputations seem seamless. At the same time, the anarchic unwieldy energy of the long cut, the humor, the spectacle, even the spectacular confusion, the picaresque, was very much lost. In its place was a more stately, symbolic, somber, portentous tale.

Yet it was another version of the movie. And I learned like music or poetry or painting, there can be many versions of a single work. Certainly Bob's music proved that. There are so many versions of Bob's songs, no two are the same. This movie had enough density to support other versions, and this would be one of them. Pietro was thoughtful and artistic in his editing choices. I was grateful for his delicacy and artistry.

And it would be sold that way as well. As an important picture instead of a picture that made fun of its own importance. That layer of context was gone. Along with a certain wild, out-of-control quality.

I had shared with the marketing department colorful pulpy images from Mexican Western posters, but they were ignored and replaced with a somber two-tone poster that I never embraced. Later when I saw posters for the movie from other countries, utilizing the colors and graphics and composition much closer to my own vision, it reminded me how much they had missed here.

But the movie was immediately accepted at Sundance. Not just accepted, but to be its Centerpiece Premiere.

It was a heady experience. It felt like everything could change in a way I wanted it to. Like *Fridays*, like *Seinfeld*, this movie could completely change my trajectory. And I was strapped in and ready.

But I discovered that Sundance can be a cold place in more ways than one.

The entire star-studded cast came to Sundance for the premiere. I was ecstatic. It was one of the most exciting nights of my life. At least that's how it started.

Bob came too. Somewhat inexplicably, wearing a wig. Not a good wig. A cheap wig. A drugstore chemo wig sloppily thrown on his head with a beanie pulled over that. Keep in mind Bob has a full head of hair.

He wears a wig, a fake beard too, in the opening scene in the movie, where he is abruptly released from prison after a long stint. He liked the look and decided to imitate it this night at the premiere of the movie at Sundance.

We all gathered backstage before the screening. I was told that Roger Ebert was here. He would be writing the very first review of the movie directly from this first screening at Sundance. He was sort of the pope of Sundance, and now before the movie, he had come backstage to bless the event. But also to get photographs of himself with all the celebrities. I was entrusted with escorting him through the backstage area, stopping cast members to have them say hello and take a photo with Roger.

When we were done with everyone else, I noticed that Bob had made himself scarce. For Roger, the photo with Bob was the jewel in the crown. The whole point would be lost without the photo with Bob. I scrambled to retrieve him.

I found him somewhere off chain-smoking cigarettes in the cold. I said, "Roger Ebert wants to take a picture with you." And he said, "I don't want to take a picture." I said, "Are you sure?" His silence said, *I wouldn't have said it if I wasn't sure.*

I went back to Roger and made an excuse for Bob. But Roger was visibly and verbally unhappy. The pope had been rebuffed by God himself.

Indignant and petulant, Roger headed off to his seat, the best seat in the house, to review the movie starring and co-written by the guy who wouldn't take his picture with him.

He hated it. Now maybe he hated it legitimately, but I could never fully shake the notion that the review might've been glowing had Bob taken that picture. Oh well.

In fairness, much of the massive insider audience seemed to hate it as well. There was a fair share of walkouts. I looked at that as a badge of honor. I would've been pleased with an all-out revolt.

I remember what Bob had said to me early in the process. "The critics will hate this movie. But the audience will like it, if they ever get a chance to see it."

They never did.

By every objective measurement, the movie was a failure. It never recovered from the bad word of mouth led by Roger Ebert's review. I would hope that someday the three-and-a-half-hour cut can be released. By the same token, the 110-minute version has been reassessed almost from the day after the Sundance reaction, much of it exactly the glowing open responsive reaction I had hoped for.

I remain extremely proud of this project. And like much of my stuff, it has, gratefully, continued to resonate, and perhaps increased its resonance with the audience. And I appreciate it. It wasn't just the triumph of the movie or the making of the movie or the fate of the movie. It was the impact it had on my life's journey. On my fate. Like after taking acid, I was never the same. In a good way. In a great way. And like Bob said, *Don't look back*. I try, and yet there would be no book without looking back. But it's about non-attachment. We can't change the past. We can only truthfully and honestly report it. Witness to our life.

Bob's wisdom continues to guide me to this day. Every step along the way, I felt that this gamble was going to pay off. The irony is, it did. Just not in ways I expected.

People ask if I'm still friends with Bob. It's the wrong question. You don't get friendly with Bob. Bob has no friends. If you look at most of his collaborations from Sam Shepard to Jacques Levy, they are one-term projects. And like them, our collaboration actually produced results. So when people ask me if I'm still friends with Bob, my answer is always, Bob has no friends but I amused him for a short time.

CHAPTER 9

MY LIFE IS PERFECT, EXCEPT I'M IN IT (ENTOURAGE)

I really didn't have any dreams, or at least my dreams had been surpassed by reality a long time ago, so to me, my experience with Bob was a completely successful experience on so many untold levels except one. The most superficial one. Box office.

As a result, my career as a film director, which in my delusions of grandeur would flourish and send me on a new adventure, instead was dead in the water. Publicly. Suddenly the road I was on collapsed, caved in, gave out. But I had failed before. And learned to embrace failure as part of the success equation. And knew that failure, like success, came in many unexpected forms. Not that failure didn't hurt and leave lingering wounds, but if you choose this path, you have no choice. There's a price you pay for everything. So I thought about my own failures. And I remembered that Bob had failed. Larry had failed. I went on.

I returned to *Curb Your Enthusiasm*, which allowed me to regain a footing in the commercial world of television. The show was cool, legitimately funny and original, and highly respected right from the beginning. And now I was fortunate enough to be part of it.

But *Curb*, based on Larry David's whims, was on the first of what would be many irregular hiatuses. After Season 3, he stopped with no concrete plan to continue. Hard to imagine now. Of course, this left the crew and the actors out of work without any promises or guarantees that they would ever return. And Larry wasn't even sure at that early juncture if he wanted to do more. It was that close to being over. It would be predicated on him having an idea that excited him enough to do another season.

I was unemployed, but I personally didn't feel adrift. I saw it as an opportunity to pursue other opportunities. I never thought of *Curb* as a long-term thing, and at a certain point, Larry had expressed his desire to end it and we almost did numerous times. It amazes me that, after those many almost finales, it was still going strong twenty years later. But as I've explained my MO, I've never had any interest and didn't get into show business for long-term job security. Though I completely understand that for Larry, it was, and maybe more so as time went on, a perfect vehicle.

But Ari Emanuel, my agent at the time, wanted me to meet another of his clients, Mark Wahlberg. Mark and his partner, Steve Levinson, and Steve's childhood friend, writer Doug Ellin, had a pilot they had made for HBO that had hit a snag, and HBO let it be known to all involved that if I agreed to work on the show, including going back and reshooting some of the pilot, they would pick up the show. The show was called *Entourage*.

There was also the promise of directing dangled before me as it often was to lure me in for what they really wanted, my writing and show-running abilities. I've said it before. I was hopelessly naive to the Machiavellian reality of Ari Emanuel and show business. It took me years to realize that he would say anything, do anything, to accomplish his larger agenda. He made the empty promise that would never be fulfilled on this show in order to make sure his far more valuable client, Mark, would get his show picked up.

I needed an agent to negotiate with my own agent.

And again I was a highly paid hired hand, with nothing to gain but my weekly paycheck, while others, many others (not the creative people involved in these endeavors), with less to do with its success, would reap the whirlwind of this and other shows and movies I would do under Ari's aegis.

It wasn't the first time Ari had used me this way, playing fast and loose with the truth, taking advantage of my skills, and it wouldn't be the last. Even long after he was no longer my agent.

And I couldn't deny that there was a symbiosis. I did gain a lot of cachet by doing *Entourage*, even if I didn't direct. And my directing career was certainly furthered by *Curb*, *Brüno*, and *The Dictator*. But because I wanted those gigs, because I was desirous, with pressure from Ari, I settled for vastly less than I should've received.

But I was into the show. This was often the problem. I loved *Curb*. And *Entourage*. Thought they were great shows. I wanted to contribute to great things, and it made me vulnerable to the unscrupulous behavior of the Hollywood manipulators. But I couldn't turn my back on them because of money or the conscienceless behavior that drove so much in show business.

●●●

I immediately connected with Mark, Steve, and Doug. Mark was from South Boston, which had many parallels with my part of Brooklyn as a tough old-school working-class ethnic enclave. Steve and Doug were from Long Island, which was like being from Brooklyn, only your father was more successful and smart enough to buy a house in the suburbs.

And indeed, Mark had an entourage. Including the real Drama and Turtle and E.

The idea of taking characters from those backgrounds, friends, a pack, and transposing them to Hollywood? And knowing most of what I was being told was real with the real characters now being portrayed on the show, I was even more excited. I could see it immediately. Of course people will love this. It is *Curb* with cool young guys and *Sopranos* with less violence. Guys who show their love and fierce loyalty with each other, not with platitudes, but with the most cutting vicious insults they can hurl at each other. It is their dialogue. Their code. Their dynamic. Their love. I knew exactly what this show needed to be a success.

The pilot had a cameo by Jessica Alba. But it was the traditional cameo use of a celebrity. You'd seen celebrities used this way before elsewhere.

In my mind, and what I expressed to them was, it needed to truly blur the lines of reality. Not just by bumping into celebrities but intertwining celebrities into the story. The *Entourage* characters, which were all based on real people anyway, needed to have relationships with real people. The *Entourage* characters should not exist in a separate parallel unreal world but inhabit and share the same real world, the same universe of the celebrities in the show. They sparked to this idea, and I started to give them examples of how this might be done in terms of stories.

In a weird way, I felt this immersion in the real world, even in the surreal world of Hollywood, made the regular characters more relatable. They were involved like we would be and have the same issues as we would.

So Drama has a beef with Jimmy Kimmel that gets settled live on his show. They run afoul of Gary Busey at an art exhibit. Or Luke Wilson tells them where they can procure hot, as in "fell off the truck" home entertainment systems. Luke was one of the actors from *Masked and Anonymous* that I remained and remain friends with. In fact, we had a blast traveling together to support the movie. It was like a barnstorming tour. I'd also remained friends with Val Kilmer, who rattled off one of the best monologues in the movie with wit and ease and spontaneity. He agreed to play the Sherpa on *Entourage*, a pot-dealing guru whom Vince and the boys visit, unrecognizable and uncredited in long beard and shades. This was a pop the show needed.

And perhaps more important, by embracing the reality of show business, it transcended show business. This show, the dynamic between the characters, the friendship, the rivalries, the conflicts could be anywhere, but it just happened to be show business. And as long as those themes were handled honestly, it wouldn't keep the audience out of an inside world but invite them in.

The other blurring of this reality was ironically centered on the portrayal of the man who had brought us together. Ari Emanuel. On the show he was called Ari Gold, and he was played inimitably by Jeremy Piven. HBO, for all their wisdom and insight about so many things I worked on, were not initially enamored of Ari Gold. Now, in fairness, not many people are initially enamored of Ari Emanuel. And it was usually downhill from there. Ari Gold, though based on Ari and many other aggressive alpha agents, was very much not Ari Emanuel. And I felt strongly that he was a crucial lynchpin of the show. His hunger, his drive, his yearning, his ambition, his outsider status both within *Entourage* and show business itself and his vulnerability as filtered through the ferocious intensity of Jeremy Piven made Ari Gold the potential breakout star of the show.

At that time, none of that was clear to HBO, who left him off the original poster, only to reinsert him later, and were afraid that Ari took the show too far into the realm of inside show business, which the show wasn't really about. Well, it was and wasn't, right? It's about outsiders inside the system. And Ari was the system, always in danger of exploding at any time. His volatility made him a compelling character. And fun to write.

In fact, the dominant tone on the show, which was true and authentic to its roots, was aggression as expression. This was true in the writers' room too, where tempers would flare and bodies and fists might come flying across the desk. I was often stepping in between these conflicts and finding solutions so we'd stay productive. I was able to help Doug and the writers channel some of that aggression into the show, and that's when the show took off. The language had a muscularity that was almost politically incorrect but so achingly honest too, it had to be respected.

I played the role of a sort of elder on the show, a shaman, trying to guide the show from this plane of existence to the next. This manifested in many forms.

I would often settle arguments by taking the scene in question and going into my office and locking the doors and hammering out a new version the way the shaman would go off and then return with some wisdom from the other plane.

In truth, the writers were much more volatile than the actors, who were by and large a mellow, extremely sweet group. The flinty intimacy and history of the lifelong friendships of Doug, the creator and main writer; and Steve, his best friend, Mark Wahlberg's manager, the executive producer; and Rob Weiss, who had made a splash as a writer-director with his first movie, *Amongst Friends*, and then crashed and burned before his resurrection on this show, made it easy and natural for them to slip into vein-bulging histrionics.

Meanwhile the actors—Jerry Ferrara, Kevin Connolly, Kevin Dillon, and Adrian Grenier—were thrilled to be there, happy to be working, and easygoing low-key guys who knew how to turn it on when the cameras rolled. It's true, Jeremy stood apart. His strength was his intensity, and he created his own energy, which was our job to harness. But he always owned his scenes.

Season 1 became one of the most explosive successes I've ever been involved with. It was immediately loved and immediately a mega hit. Although I thought the show was great and distinctive, that's all I usually have any control or influence over. The rest—the commercial success or viability of one project or another—always comes as some sort of surprise.

And the *Entourage* guys, the actors and Doug and Steve, enjoyed and relished it just like the characters on the show.

•••

Whoever or whatever I am, I was not able to enjoy the success of *Entourage* on that unabashed level. I felt I was being stretched too thin. I felt like the energy I needed to devote to the show was assuring that I would be drifting farther and farther away from projects of my own, which I wanted to do. But what did I want to do? Dream about abstract "other projects" while I was here in the midst of one of the greatest successes I'd ever been associated with? And was proud of too. And perhaps most profoundly, I felt guilty about my marriage and my kids. Barbara and I were going through the motions. The family was like a corporation, and we took care of business. But beyond that, there was very little emotional sustenance for either of us. Whatever successes I was having professionally, personally there was a failure looming at home that I couldn't face.

So rather than relishing this moment of great triumph, I was delusional and self-destructive. And it was in that state of mind that I entered into a series of extramarital affairs that each had their own unique earmarks of disaster. At first, I turned a blind eye to them. I just didn't care what the price was. It was a cowardly way to destroy myself and my life and the lives of others.

At the messy conclusion of each tryst, I would tell myself I no longer wanted to play this game. After each encounter I would pledge to myself that I'd be faithful going forward. I would accept and embrace my life as it was. Accept my reality. Love my family. Be a good husband and dad. Deal with it. And stop putting my selfish emotional needs first.

How long would that last?

I used to say, everything about my life was perfect, except I was in it. I didn't feel like I belonged in my own life. I would think of Tony Soprano, who remained married to Carmela and yet with the uneasy understanding or acceptance that he would never be faithful and that was the price they paid to keep their life intact. I could do that. And I think Barbara, like Carmela from an old-school Italian Catholic family, would've gone along with that scenario.

But it was me. Restless and angry. At what? There might be a million reasons, and none of them mattered. I didn't think I could continue this way and yet knew I hadn't the courage to face the truth. So Barbara and I soldiered on. Our kids thrived. We went through the paces of a relationship, a social life. But underneath that enviable facade lay desperation and loneliness.

And of course, it was around this time that Larry decided to return for another season of *Curb*.

And of course, the second season of *Entourage* was scheduled to be produced virtually concurrently with the fourth season of *Curb*. And I was expected to work on both.

Not only was I personally in a bad place, but I now had that compounded by being placed between the proverbial rock and hard place. There was no place for me.

So I spent a good part of both seasons, the second season of *Entourage* and the fourth season of *Curb*, splitting my time between *Curb*, whose offices were in Santa Monica, and *Entourage*, headquartered in Hollywood. The commute alone was torturous. But worse was splitting my time. I felt I was cheating myself and the shows.

As an executive producer for both, I felt a lot of responsibilities, and both shows were counting on me. So my life was basically the two shows for that year. My home life, already in serious decline, fell even farther faster.

It became clear I would have to make a decision. *Entourage* was just in its ascension, and as with *Seinfeld*, Doug, Steve, and everyone would've been happy to have me stay. And I would've likely reaped benefits if I had.

But one thing became clear: I would not be directing *Entourage* episodes. There was simply too much work to do—writing, casting, and editing plus the troubleshooting variations that would emerge spontaneously—so that being on a set directing a single scene seemed irresponsible for me. I was afraid, with *Entourage*, it would always be that way. Thus, *Entourage* could simply not be my future.

On *Curb*, I would be directing. I had to weigh that if I was serious about continuing to pursue that course. And I was being recognized for my directing work, eventually garnering two Emmy and three DGA nominations. Plus, *Curb* was fun, and I felt a duty to Larry even though the show really didn't need me. And I felt a duty to myself to take any opportunity to continue to establish myself as a director.

So for a while I refocused on *Curb*. I was free of the madness and dysfunction that I had brought upon myself, and while not happy or creatively fulfilled, I felt safe for a moment. In a safe place I knew. People I knew. A routine I knew. Lunches picked up for me. A parking space with my name. I did my work. I went home. And was for the moment at least, fully accepting of my reality.

I wasn't looking for anything. I didn't want for anything. I had what I needed. And didn't have the need to need or want more. I stopped worrying about the future and the past. At least that's what I told myself. I knew inside that emptiness was still there. But I increasingly had to admit that the emptiness was just a void, a dark chasm with no treasure, no answer, no solution, no end. And I just began to believe, to know, it would never be filled. And I had to be okay with that to survive.

Then one day, while sitting in my comfortable *Curb* office with all my talismans around me, my tokens of a superficial spiritual quest like the worry beads I constantly carried and needed and kneaded with me throughout the day, I had the mundane task of having to make a phone call. I have no idea today who that call was to. But the phone didn't work. Now, I was a technophobe, a modern luddite, unable to navigate devices, still writing longhand. So first I tried the phone again. And again. Soon I became frustrated. I was the executive producer of two hit HBO shows. My phone should work.

I thought about literally breaking the phone to release my anger—it was broken anyway—but this time I didn't act so rashly. Instead, I asked Linda Balaban, an associate producer on the show, to find someone to help me, which she did.

She brought back a young woman wearing a gray sweater and slacks. She had long, flowing blond hair. She didn't say much, but when she spoke, she had a voice like Glinda the good witch in *Wizard of Oz*. She seemed the epitome of goodness and sweetness and beauty. And she had a serious knife tucked into her slacks. I was more than intrigued. I was more than mesmerized. And as she explained that the phone simply wasn't plugged in, she met my gaze with her blue eyes, which sparkled like jewels, like blue diamonds. But the exchange of glances lasted far longer than any verbal information that was being transmitted. Her name was Keely, and in that moment, we both knew we were in love.

Oh shit.

And not just in love, but I can honestly say, I'd never really known love until that moment, and suddenly I did. It was love as epiphany. It was love as revelation. Nothing else needed to be said or done in that moment. It had happened. And nothing would ever be the same.

If Linda was still in the room, she had faded away, and if she spoke, it was muffled to me. Just sounds from another place.

Keely fixed my phone, and little did I know, she would fix my life.

CHAPTER 10

"I REFUSE TO ACCEPT YOUR APOLOGY ..." (CURB, PART 2)

I had gone from directing one episode of *Curb Your Enthusiasm* to directing Bob Dylan and an all-star cast in *Masked and Anonymous*. But as I returned to the set of *Curb*, I wondered if that really happened or was it some sort of a dream? How did I do that?

Curb was the perfect place to land. Almost no one gave a shit about the movie. Every star lives in a bubble. And *Curb* was Larry's bubble, and if you lived within it, there was no outside world.

Don't get me wrong. It wasn't complete ignorance and apathy. There was curiosity. But more like I had visited a weird country and returned or had a terrible accident and recovered. Jeff Garlin had a rock and roll heart and wanted to hear all about it. Richard Lewis was a rock and roll comedian and worshipped Bob. But the movie's failure and quick disappearance before it had a chance to register made it that much easier to ignore for most.

And if I learned anything from Bob, it was, *Don't look back.* I didn't want to be someone sitting around telling tales of the past, waxing nostalgic. I wanted, and more importantly needed, to look forward.

Though here I sit, writing a memoir. And so did Bob!

In a number of ways, *Curb* was a good thing. It brought me back to earth. It woke me up. It got my ego straightened out. It let my wounds heal. It gave me a new focus.

And after two years without making money, it was nice to be someplace where they didn't ask me to kick back my salary. Although again, in Ari Emanuel's world, I was still a salary man, a temp worker, while others profited mightily from my work.

And I was in love, which was a complication in itself. I had met Keely in the fall of 2004 soon after her thirtieth birthday. We needed to see each other, but we were both being very seen. We would "bump into" each other in the hallway, or stepping outside for a cigarette. We were only talking, but our talk flowed freely. I felt myself, like "this is me," and I think she did too.

We were "appropriate" yet pretty obvious. But beyond the obvious attraction and passing encounters, we had crossed no lines. Until Thanksgiving. She came into work that day in a red gown. She looked like a princess. I was overwhelmed. She carried a tray of cookies she had baked. She came into my office, and I closed the door. She offered me a cookie, but I placed the plate down on my desk and began to kiss her. She reciprocated. Quickly, she said, "I have to tell you something, I have a kid." And I said, "That's okay, I'm married." We continued to make out against that closed door, knowing we were about to make a life-changing choice.

I think, for our own personal reasons, we were both naturally excited but wary too. On the surface, there were a lot of reasons for both of us to call a halt to this. Instead, we proceed cautiously. She wouldn't let me come back to her place for a couple of months. So we cut a swath across the numerous area motels. It was great on every level except when we parted.

We spent weekends at the office. Working, writing, hanging out, and making love.

Soon, I would show up at her house on my way home, just to kiss her good night.

Yet somehow, it seemed weirdly balanced. Yes, of course we both wanted more. She continued to demonstrate through deeds and actions how much she loved me, and I knew she was the one. But that was still a far cry from being together. The emotion was pure and powerful, but that would require far more thought. It couldn't, it wouldn't go on this idyllic way forever, even though I tried to ignore that. I knew, if this was to be more than an affair, if this was to be the new life, it would require a great deal more pain and sacrifice.

•••

At one of the *Curb* wrap parties, Gina Gershon, who had played an orthodox Jewish woman that Larry lusted after in an episode I directed, brought along as her "date," record producer Rick Rubin. He was one of the godfathers of rap music, as the founder of Def Jam recordings and his work with the Beastie Boys, Public Enemy, and Run-D.M.C., among many others. He broadened his range into many other areas, producing seminal heavy metals bands like Slayer and Danzig and bands that were fusing and synthesizing many of the new forms in music like System of a Down and perhaps most notably the Red Hot Chili Peppers, before turning his attention to Johnny Cash, supervising his powerful series of swan songs, *American Recordings*. Gina brought Rick over to me and said quite matter-of-factly, "You two should be friends."

And by the end of the night, we were.

At that time, the prevalent social media technology was the BlackBerry. I scoffed at the new reliance on this communication tool. It seemed absurd and indicative of some sort of breakdown in society. But Rick had a way around that. As he did with all his friends, he bought me one so he and I could converse constantly. Suddenly I was in conversations with Owen Wilson and Ben Stiller, Tom Morello and Brad Wilk of Rage Against the Machine, and Flea of the Red Hot Chili Peppers and director James Gray. I was sucked in.

At that time, Rick had a large, almost Gothic mansion with a stuffed polar bear looming as you entered, overlooking the Sunset Strip in Hollywood. I spent a lot of time there. As I got to know him, I realized he had cultivated a more Buddha-like demeanor to the outside world, but in his heart, he was still the anarchic, rude rule breaker reflected more in his earlier work than his more contemplative recent work. Our sense of humor and ambivalence about those two sides of our personality synced well, and we spent a lot of time laughing while we watched *Abbott and Costello* and other older politically incorrect humor. We would often be joined by the late Ric Menello, a Rick crony who directed the original video for the Beastie Boys, "(You Gotta) Fight for Your Right (to Party!)."

They had been working for years on a project about an obscure racist, sexist *Abbott and Costello*–type vaudeville act called "Burt and Dickie." Owen Wilson was also involved at one time. We tried to strike the right tone but never quite could. It was simply too extreme.

Rick was a social animal and often had dinner parties. I started to get invited, but like most social gatherings, even though they involved important cultural figures, I found them boring and awkward.

Rick had a place in Malibu as well, and he offered to host a small screening of *Masked and Anonymous*. It was attended by such luminaries as director Wes Anderson, comedian Chris Rock, and actors Kate Hudson and Owen, who were a couple at that time.

Well, it didn't go well. There was stunned silence when it was over. I felt like a pariah, and when I was able, I made my escape back home. But I was surprised and disappointed they didn't get it.

Rick and I had some fun adventures. We were both into a woman from India known as the Hugging Saint. Amma. She would tour the world and people would line up to receive her special hug, which bestowed some sort of blessing upon you. It seemed very spiritual and yet culturally fascinating.

She was appearing at a hotel down by the airport, and we went. When we got there, I was shocked. The place was overrun. The lobby was jammed with people. It reminded me of the parking lot of a Grateful Dead concert. People selling everything from food to apparel and souvenirs.

The doors to the main ballroom were open, and there in the middle sat Amma with rows of people radiating from her like rays from the sun, waiting for the hug.

It was so crowded, they actually gave out numbers like a bakery.

Except we were number 900. That meant we wouldn't get hugged till morning. Amazingly she sat there without a break and hugged people until every single person got hugged. Her stamina was prodigious. But it was so crowded, I was ready and satisfied to check out the scene and bypass the hug.

Rick wouldn't hear of it. He looked around and spotted someone he knew. He always knew somebody. Or somebody knew him. In this case, an aspiring musician who was also part of Amma's retinue. They exchanged glances, and Rick had a few words with him. Within minutes of the musician handing Rick a cassette of his music, we were shoved up to the front of the line. Even in Amma's world, there was a way to grease a palm and get preferential treatment.

Everyone had to be on their knees as they inched up closer to her on the raised podium. In a moment, there I was. When I was next, two handlers grabbed me brusquely and threw me into her starched white robe. She grabbed me and hugged me hard and whispered a mantra in my ear. I was given a Hershey's Kiss and essentially spit out by the handlers. It was like a spiritual amusement park ride. Intense, weird, unforgettable. And over very quickly.

Rick asked me to attend all kinds of cool events, always in VIP fashion. We saw Neil Young perform his conceptual musical, *Greendale*, and a private performance by Brian Wilson, and went to Coachella in a helicopter with Anthony and Flea of the Chili Peppers and sat backstage.

•••

Rick would often text me on the BlackBerry he had bought me, to come over and hang, or to take a ride. We would often hop in the back of one of his Rolls-Royces (yes, one of; he had a couple as well as a driver) and get lunch, usually at Real Food Daily or Koi on La Cienega, or Mr. Chow in Beverly Hills or Giorgio Baldi in Santa Monica. Celebrity-laden places where he felt at home (but I never did) and could get food customized to his almost eating-disorder-like needs.

But we didn't always eat. One day, we drove from his dark Gothic mansion in Hollywood to a nondescript section of Olympic

Boulevard in West LA. In an anonymous two-story apartment building, we walked up to a door and knocked. It was opened by Leonard Cohen. He welcomed us with his one-of-a-kind dark deep gravelly voice: "Hello, my friends." And beckoned us in to his modest abode. Initially, I was in cognitive dissonance. Next to Bob Dylan, Leonard Cohen was as revered a writer and singer and poet and nothing less than a bard of our times and journeys with dozens of classic songs like "Suzanne," "Bird on the Wire," "Sisters of Mercy," "Dance Me to the End of Love," and "Hallelujah." I had heard he had devoted himself to Zen Buddhism and lived in a monastery on Mount Baldy outside of Los Angeles. But here he was, in a small but elegant apartment, not very different than the kind my grandmother or aunts might live in with the exception of an electric piano and his beautiful exotic girlfriend and collaborator, Anjani.

He had been successful for much of his long career and even had a few hits, yet here he was in a walk-up rental in a less-than-fashionable part of Los Angeles. It seemed wildly incongruous until he explained that his business manager had ripped him off for virtually everything he had, and financially at least, in his senior years, he was forced to start over.

Nevertheless, he was a most gracious host, culminating with him preparing absinthe for us. Rick, who never touched drugs or alcohol, of course demurred, but I was not going to pass up the opportunity to drink absinthe with Leonard. He prepared the green liquid, high in alcohol content with a hallucinogenic mythology surrounding it, in an elaborate glass vessel right out of the nineteenth century. Although we certainly got buzzed, its mind-expanding properties were indeed "highly" exaggerated.

He and Anjani played some music, we hung out, and it was quite a splendid afternoon. I guess Leonard felt the same way because he began writing me in the wake of our visit. I enjoyed our occasional correspondence (via BlackBerry, of course), but as it turned out, he had rediscovered his Judaism, and I most definitely had not. He began to ask me to accompany him to a local synagogue, and I was forced to continually demur, wondering to myself each time if there was any part of going to a synagogue, even a cool one, that I could justify, given my strong feelings about organized religion, and as a fallen bar-mitzvah boy, Judaism in particular. It was simply too hypocritical to rationalize even with enticement of accompanying Leonard Cohen. Inevitably, our communication faded and then ceased. But I still enjoyed his music and was happy to see his late-in-life career and creative resurgence and resumption of his rightful place in the pantheon of great and beloved musicians.

•••

I genuinely liked Rick, but at a certain point I started to feel the limitations of our friendship. I think that, despite all the rock stars, movie stars, and important people Rick knew, he was still lonely and liked to have somebody to actually talk to. But it had become too one-sided. I wasn't really getting much out of it. I was listening but didn't feel I was being heard. I had my own ambitions and needs and concerns, and for whatever the reason, he didn't seem to give much of a shit.

Although he had the healthiest diet of anyone I knew, Rick consumed a lot and his health was deteriorating. He began to focus on that with a very successful but strict diet and exercise routine, and he met a woman. I was glad for him. But our priorities shifted, and soon we drifted apart.

•••

Although I had directed only four episodes during the first three seasons, Larry was very happy with the particular results of those episodes and recognized our unique chemistry and trusted my instincts and sensibility enough to ask me to become an executive producer as well as direct almost half the episodes for Season 4.

Bob Weide, who had won an Oscar for his documentary about Lenny Bruce and won the only directing Emmy for *Curb*, had done most of the episodes up until that time. David Steinberg and Bryan Gordon, one of my other *Fridays* mentors, also directed episodes. And you couldn't complain about the results. Almost every episode was a classic. In fact, if the show was working, you shouldn't even be able to tell who directed what. And to some degree, that's what Larry was looking to change.

Larry trusted his instincts, and as the show went on, he knew he needed a different speed as well. To tap into a different level. And he knew me well. Knew I had a writer's sense of structure and a ferocity and intensity to my comedy that the more demure and genteel and tasteful Weide, Steinberg, and Gordon perhaps lacked. Larry knew I would push everything as hard and as far as I could. I would push that Sisyphean comedy rock to the top of the hill and then let it come crashing down, taking with it everything in its path.

Executive producing the show was fun and challenging. Aside from my directorial duties, I was performing many of the same tasks as I had on *Seinfeld* or as a show runner on other shows. Attending all casting and editing sessions and providing a sounding board for Larry's story ideas.

This was a golden time on *Curb*. We were doing great original episodes. Like nothing else on TV. And we had found that thin line between reality and farce and danced on it merrily. It was hilariously funny yet completely believable. And I felt creative, charged, and engaged. I felt I was making a crucial contribution to those episodes. Even the ones I didn't direct.

During the 2004 season of *Curb*, the concept was, Larry was cast in the Broadway version of *The Producers* by Mel Brooks. Larry's co-star in the show within the show was Ben Stiller.

The brilliance of this season, among other things, was how we'd deftly managed the magic trick of mirroring the plot of the movie and Broadway show without anyone noticing it until the end. I still marvel at that accomplishment.

I also got to work with some great people who raised the game that season, my game particularly.

Paul Mazursky was one. A bold filmmaker who had frighteningly reached a point where he simply couldn't get movies made anymore. If he couldn't get a movie made after *Bob & Carol & Ted & Alice, Alex in Wonderland, An Unmarried Woman, Moscow on the Hudson, Down and*

Out in Beverly Hills, Next Stop, Greenwich Village, Enemies, A Love Story, and so many other classics, what chance did I have?

But he was like Mel, super cool and generous and one of the few people I would try to prod into sharing his experiences.

Ben Stiller was another one. I admired his body of work. And his sensibility. Ben was not afraid in his own comedy to explore the dark side and depths of his own personality and human nature and mine it fearlessly for humor.

And he was Jerry Stiller's son, which always endeared him to me. I grew up watching his mom, Anne Meara, and his dad on *Ed Sullivan* performing their unique brand of comedy. There was Nichols and May, but besides them, I can't think of another comedy couple, which afforded them the chance to take on subjects and material that two guys, the normal comedy duo dynamic, could never express as honestly.

His conflicts with Larry provided some of the most memorable scenes of the season and even in the series. In the story, he finally can't deal with Larry anymore and leaves "The Producers' Revival," only to be replaced by David Schwimmer.

David was a skilled and underrated performer. Yes, of course he couldn't have been more successful and popular than he was as a cast member of the phenomenon known as *Friends*. But he was not at all satisfied to rest on his laurels. He was interested in pushing. In all directions. He had opened a theater in Chicago. He was directing. And he was taking off-beat unexpected roles. Perhaps none more so than "himself" on *Curb*.

His energy was different than Ben's. Ben and Larry were aggressive like two dogs on tight leashes. David derived much humor from a more passive-aggressive approach, and the different dynamic worked splendidly. He was fun to work with and loved taking risks with his persona.

Of course, that season, I had the pleasure and honor of working with Mel Brooks again. Much more closely than we even had on *Mad About You*. Now I was directing him, and in the *Curb* process, that meant working on scene structure and improvisation.

I would often reflect on how lucky I was to be in his orbit in any way. It was a dream I had never dared dream. And now it was my job. And whether he knew it or not, he was a paternal influence on me as well. Yes, an inadvertent oracle and mentor. He had a nurturing quality that you could imagine he naturally put to good uses as a director himself.

Mel was loved. It was that simple. And Mel, like most performers, loved being loved. It led to one of the most *Curb*-like surreal incidents in my professional life and certainly on the show.

One of the myriad plots that season was that Larry inadvertently insults Mel's lesbian assistant, played by Rachael Harris. As he tries to squirm out of it, in *Curb* fashion he gets in deeper.

This episode, which I had directed, had been shot earlier in the season. But when the show was actually broadcast, quite a long time after that, Mel gave me a call. It seemed his actual assistant was a very religious young woman who was seriously offended by her portrayal as a lesbian. I didn't have to explain to Mel that we knew nothing of his actual assistant and this was a strictly completely fictional character. He told me it didn't matter. She was deeply offended, and to make things right with her, we had to apologize. Otherwise his life would be a living hell.

As I said, I loved Mel and I figured it would be no problem for me to apologize. Apologizing was a big part of *Curb*'s comedy, and this seemed like no big deal, so even though I wasn't really all that sorry, as executive producer and director of the offending episode, I was happy to do it.

But when I called her up, and explained the misunderstanding and apologized profusely with as much sincerity as I could muster, she actually refused to accept my apology. I couldn't remember when someone had refused to accept my apology. I was taken aback. She sternly rebuked me. Said it brought embarrassment and shame to her and her family. And an apology would not suffice. We ended the call quite unsatisfactorily.

Now I was forced to do something I hadn't wanted to. Go to Larry. I told him what was going on, and he was surprised. But

Larry was an expert apologist and felt supremely confident that his apology would succeed where mine had failed.

Not only was he wrong, but after she rejected his apology, the conversation even got heated. It became something of an argument with Larry explaining again that it had nothing to do with her and her adamant about the shame it brought to her and her religious extended family. And with that, they hung up, and the matter was never truly resolved.

My main thought in the aftermath was how did Mel Brooks of all people hire someone with no discernible sense of humor? She must've been a great assistant.

•••

I was now an executive producer and director of *Curb*, by all descriptions a well-groomed show; everyone was extremely clean cut, shaved, and hair styled, with nicely pressed fresh clothes. I had abandoned the pajamas but still dressed as my father would say, "like a bum."

One day we were shooting in Venice, which since I've lived in Los Angeles, has always been a dicey homeless enclave. We were shooting at a trendy restaurant, the James' Beach, on one of the small side streets that led to the beach, where it ended at what is called the speedway, where people wander and walk and roller-skate and ride bicycles and street vendors sell their wares and street musicians jam and street people hassle the tourists.

This was where craft services were set up for the show. Craft services consisted of a series of tables with coffee and refreshments, snacks and more substantial food overseen by usually one or two people who had a little trailer that might have a refrigerator or hot plate.

In between takes, I was craving a snack of some kind and headed over there. I was wearing a ragged old army coat, torn sweatpants, and a worn T-shirt so old, the insignia on the front was barely discernible. My hair and beard were a long tangle, and I wore my ever-present sunglasses. This was my mask. My disguise. And indicative of how cool Larry and everyone on the show was, I was completely accepted without question. If you knew me, you knew what I looked like and it was never an issue or problem. Now, if you didn't know me . . .

So I wandered out to craft services. And as I examined the bountiful choices on the craft services table barely discernible from the street people all around me, the dutiful security guard spotted me and assumed I didn't belong. He approached me somewhat aggressively, although I felt he was just doing his job and made what seemed to him an accurate observation. When I told him I was the director, he didn't find that amusing or credible and began to hustle me down the street. I made my case more vociferously, which any street person would do, which only solidified his position. His job was to get rid of me. As he yanked me away, it was time to shoot again, and fortunately my trusty AD, Dale, came to my rescue, not for the first time or the last, and explained everything to the diligent security guard. He was still skeptical, but as Dale pulled me back on the set, I remembered Bob Dylan being stopped by the police for a similar offense.

When I think back to that time, it was obvious I was in conflict. On many fronts. Mainly my identity. Who was I? Was I some sort of rebel doing subversive radical work or was I just a high-level high-paid hack? Was I a married man with a family or a hopeless philanderer? Was I grounded in reality, or was I a deluded dreamer? Was I in love with Keely, or did I just think I was in love, desperately wanted to be in love? Was I willing to pay the price for love and face the consequences? Was I a Comedy Samurai, a comedy bodhisattva, putting off my creative enlightenment in order to help others fulfill their vision and reach theirs? Or was I a fraud, in over my head? Of course, I was all of those things and more. Much more. And much less. And it was my responsibility to reconcile those many sides if I ever wanted to know peace. And as I knew, the tranquility and serenity of peace might be the ultimate goal, but it would take war to achieve.

CHAPTER 11

"IT'S REAL. JUST NOT THE REALITY YOU THINK IT IS." (BORAT)

M y only steady employment was as one of HBO's most valuable workhorses. Emmy-nominated multiple times as both director and executive producer of *Curb* and at the same time executive producing their nascent hit, *Entourage*, on the surface I was on a roll, but underneath I remained restless, looking, seeking something, and I wasn't even sure what. I just hoped I'd recognize it when I found it.

As part of the perks of that position, HBO was often willing to give Larry and me VIP treatment to HBO sporting events, which at that time mostly consisted of boxing. Usually in Vegas. We'd be flown up, hang out backstage, have ringside seats, be announced as dignitaries in the crowd, hang out for the party after, see an exciting and brutal boxing match, and fly home that very night.

Larry and I had often watched live championship boxing going back to *Fridays*. But it wasn't like this. In those days, we'd hear about someone in the valley who was getting the fight on PPV and finagle an invitation to a crowded sweaty apartment filled with screaming strangers. Everyone brought beer, and so there was always an assortment to soothe your throat after yelling nonstop for sometimes twelve full rounds.

It was funky and fun and egalitarian. A far cry from being treated like royalty by HBO.

It was unusual for there to be a big fight in LA, but finally there was a heavyweight championship fight (Klitschko-Lewis) being held at the Staples Center, and once again, minus the plane, we attended.

Hanging out backstage, bullshitting and hobnobbing with the usual assortment of luminaries, stars, and personalities, was our agent at the time, the ubiquitous Ari Emanuel, who unknowingly was on the verge of becoming an icon through Jeremy Piven's indelible, thinly veiled portrayal of him named Ari Gold. With Ari was an anonymous, tall, gangly, and shy Brit. Though he towered over everybody and wore a cap tightly pulled down on his head, I immediately recognized him. Sacha Baron Cohen. Most people there didn't recognize him, even if they knew *Da Ali G Show*, which had recently been playing on HBO. But I was a massive fan of his groundbreaking and mind-blowing British series and knew who he was right away. And was excited when Ari introduced us. As it turned out, he was a fan of my work as well.

I had worked with Andy Kaufman on *Fridays* and, as a kid, enjoyed *Candid Camera* and even the super-hip conceptual prankster of the '60s, Alan Abel. Comedy that pioneeringly blurred the boundaries between fiction and reality. And I myself was forced to invent many alternate realities to stay alive in Brooklyn. But without being aware of any of that, Sacha had created a new form of comedy obliterating the line between fiction and reality in a brand-new way. It was the next step, and I could feel it and was excited and inspired by it.

Although I laughed heartily at the ignorance of Ali G and the rude bitchiness of Brüno, Borat was my favorite character, and I could see that wonder and innocence in Sacha.

We must've spoken for fifteen or twenty minutes before the fight, about comedy theory and process and life, before we were separated and were ushered to our seats. I barely remember the fight. But I didn't forget the conversation. However, I had no ambitions or aspirations to work with Sacha. It seemed that our worlds collided for a minute backstage at the fight, we acknowledged our mutual admiration, and then I imagined he would spiral back to his world and I to mine and that would be cool. I was just exhilarated by our dialogue.

Honestly, I didn't think much more about it.

But a couple of years later, in 2003, deep into a *Curb* season, I received a call from Ari. Would I be interested in meeting with Sacha? I said of course. At that meeting besides Sacha, was his brain trust: three hard-core British comedy writers who couldn't have been more different from each other. The hard-living post-punk Ant Hines; the affable Welshman Peter Baynham, who'd once served in the Merchant Navy; and the effete, bone-dry schoolmate of Sacha's, Dan Mazer. The three were relatively short men, and Sacha towered over them so they formed a strange quartet. At this meeting, Sacha asked me if I'd be interested in directing the movie version of *Borat*. I responded with an enthusiastic yes. He looked at my appearance. Torn sweats, a beat-up army surplus jacket, hair down to the middle of my back, and a very long straggly beard. As I said, I was often mistaken for a homeless person even in those post-pajama days. Sacha looked at me for a minute, then said, "Would you ever consider...," and rather than finish the sentence, he gingerly pantomimed a very slow dramatic cutting of my beard. I didn't hesitate. Of course I would. It will grow back. I'm not Samson. It's not sacred to me. I'm just a lazy groomer. Which was true. I hated going to the barbershop or shopping for clothes. My answer heartened them tremendously. I wondered if it had been a stumbling block since I had first met him at the Staples Center.

Before my final answer, however, I felt obligated to talk to Larry. First of all, we were still in the middle of the *Curb* season. I had been unfailingly loyal to him through the years and didn't want to simply announce the news. And I didn't just want his permission. I wanted his blessing.

I was nervous about speaking to him about this. Would he feel I was being disloyal? That I was abandoning him? And if he did, what would I do?

But he never hesitated. He absolutely felt very strongly that not only should I do it, I had to do it.

Again, this was an example of Larry's oracular guidance and generosity. Just as he encouraged me to experiment when I left *Seinfeld*, and encouraged me to direct, so now, he was pushing me out of that comfortable *Curb* nest. Once again, in one deft offhanded stroke, he had changed my life.

After that, things moved fast. I was called in to meet Debbie Liebling. I believe Jay Roach, the director of *Meet the Parents* and the *Austin Powers* movies, who was producing the movie version of *Borat*, was there too. Debbie was about the coolest executive I've ever dealt with, before or since. Her reputation rested on her being the Comedy Central exec who nurtured *South Park*. That's the kind of credit that will give an executive credibility in the creative community. They laid out the reality of the situation, which like everything I've ever done, wasn't nearly as clean as I'd hoped. There had been another director on the movie. Actually the driving force behind it. His name was Todd Phillips. I wasn't that familiar with Todd at that time. He had made a documentary I admired about the most notoriously transgressive rock musician of his time, GG Allin, and hadn't yet directed *The Hangover*. Todd and Sacha had actually shot two weeks' worth of material before they started having unresolvable conflicts. They told me that Todd had been mean to Sacha, domineering and controlling. Even making him cry.

They gave me the two weeks' worth of scenes to take home and watch, and give my impressions.

Amazingly, despite all the conflict, the footage was great. I was quickly doubled over in laughter. But there was a problem. Todd had really cast himself as the star of the movie, and Borat was essentially his protégé, the sidekick, the co-star. When Borat was doing his thing, there was very little else I'd ever seen that was as funny, but when Todd was on camera, the film sank like a stone. The whole dynamic was wrong. Borat is not a supporting player. He is a star. Borat has to be the star of *Borat*. Any scene with Todd in it would have to go and be done over. As it turned out, this was what all of them wanted to hear. I soon learned Sacha and the writers loved doing scenes again and again to see if they could tweak and even top the versions that preceded. This was a challenge. It took me a while to get into that mindset, but once we were on the road, I began to appreciate that sensibility. Let's do it again! We had one thing in common, and we openly stated it. We wanted to make the funniest movie ever.

We discarded everything Todd had shot with one exception:

There was only one scene of Todd's I felt we'd never be able to re-create or top because of the spontaneous events that took place during the filming. That was Borat at the rodeo. I felt that Sacha could at least equal his performance, and by doing it a couple of times, we'd probably get great crowd reactions. But I was astonished by the timing of the horse that comes riding out behind him and suddenly collapses. I didn't think we could get that lucky again. So we decided to save that scene. The only issue was that Todd himself was very prominent in that scene, during the backstage banter with the rodeo participants. He didn't contribute much but he was there. Quickly I was assured that he could be digitally removed, which we did, and I'm glad we made it work. The scene was a classic. And my hat's off to Todd for that one.

By that time, it was spring 2005, and all the footage had been shot in the fall and wouldn't match well either. And the story itself, though obviously never finished, seemed lacking in structure, something I thought would aid the narrative so that it didn't feel like simply a loosely connected mélange of sketches. Further, with Borat up front, I felt he would benefit from a foil and the character of his "producer." Azamat was created. On paper.

Of course, casting Azamat would prove to be a challenge. I asked Allison Jones, who had cast *Curb* and was perhaps the premier comedy-casting person in Hollywood. Allison was such a great casting director that her assistant, Phyllis Smith, who often sat in the back of the room keeping track of the actors on *Curb*, became a regular on *The Office*. If anyone could find Azamat, she could.

But we stumbled out of the gate. A series of well-meaning earnest actors doing vague Eastern European accents. Perfectly acceptable in a sitcom or typical movie in which they would be interacting with other actors. But this was the real world, and they had to create a completely believable facade so like, with Borat, our targets would never suspect that this wasn't reality. We saw none who fit that criteria.

Finally Allison brought in a man who spoke very little English. She told us this would be a long shot. He was short but extremely rotund and uniquely strangely misshapen in a way that was fascinating. His bad hair transplant was dyed jet-black, and he wore a worn threadbare suit that hung loosely even on his large body. He was complaining in some foreign language from the time he came in and seemed clueless to the whole process. I remember so well, all of us suppressing our laughter so as not to make him feel bad. I asked him if he had ever improvised, and in badly broken English he asked what "improvise" meant. Oh boy.

Nevertheless, he sat with Sacha and tried to keep up. We were all laughing hard and feeling quite guilty about it, and in my head, and I'm sure everyone else's, we wondered if we could get him through the process of an arduous shoot on the road in the real world. I immediately felt protective of him.

We couldn't suppress our laughter any longer and stopped the "improv." We thanked him profusely and gave him very grateful and encouraging words. With that he turned to us, and in perfect English said, "You want anything else?" We were stunned. He had fooled us. Our jaws dropped. He was Ken Davitian, an out-of-work and virtually out-of-the-business Armenian-American actor. And a fucking genius. And he was Azamat.

Usually with movies, you have a month or two to prep. There are a lot of details. Here we had two weeks. And I was still doing *Curb*. In fact, the last episode of the season, in which Larry thinks he's adopted. Thinking he's a gentile, he is able to donate a kidney to Richard Lewis, but dies in the process and goes to heaven. Pretty ambitious.

Heaven required more art direction and preparation than I had done on a *Curb* previously. We worked on images from heaven, trying to keep it classic so as not to completely reinvent it. For comedy purposes, I felt it had to be somewhat familiar.

In heaven, Larry would meet his two guardian angels. Larry had asked Dustin Hoffman to play one of the angels, and he said, "Yes." That was exciting. We also asked Bea Arthur to play his mother, who berates him like old times when they meet again. This may have been one of her last roles, but she was amazing and got everything out of her scene.

Without knowing that I was now working with Sacha on *Borat*, Dustin without asking Larry or me, had asked Sacha to play the other guardian angel. Although it was slightly out of line—I mean, what if he'd asked someone we didn't want?—it happened that Sacha, of course, was brilliant, and further, it would give him and me and Peter, Ant, and Dan a chance to work on the script while we were shooting the episode. It turned out to be a mitzvah in disguise.

In between takes, Sacha and I would run into a small makeshift tent that had been set up offstage to confer with the writers. Back and forth, back and forth. It was a creative tornado that I was in the middle of and loving.

Although I was willing to shave my beard and even my head if it was called for, Sacha, in his wisdom, felt I would be more effective if I simply trimmed it all, and traded in my homeless attire for something more academic-looking, suits instead of sweats, shoes instead of sneakers, the effect being that I had some sort of professorial authority. Wow, was he right. Instead of always being questioned about why I belonged somewhere I did, I was welcome everywhere I didn't belong. This was part of the psychology of shooting *Borat*.

But I almost immediately realized that this wasn't a regular directing gig. There was no "action." There was no "cut." There was no "take two." Everything in front and behind the camera was the movie. Including me. Everyone was. I adopted a nom de guerre, Larry Carlson. A freelance documentary maker who had just met Borat that day, or the day before. I would spend a lot of time with the targets before setting the scene. Borat came from a country far, far away. Kazakhstan. Did you know it? No one did. This understandable ignorance was key. If you knew nothing about Kazakhstan, then we could make it anything we wanted, no matter how outlandish. I would explain that he knew nothing of Western or American ways or rituals, and his English was shaky, so please be kind and patient with him and not be offended even if he says the wrong thing. I would sometimes tell people that he didn't even know what a chair was, and shockingly, people always believed me.

Once I was doing it, I realized that this was what I had been groomed to do since childhood. I was a natural at these off-camera scenes. Intuitively understanding vanity and ego and playing into it to soften people up. Or get us out of trouble. Or even save our asses. I might say to the unwitting target, as I explained who Borat was, explained the imaginary Kazakhstan and what we would be shooting, that I felt the target had real charisma, wondered if they'd done much in front of the camera, talked about getting in touch with them after the scene to maybe do a pilot together. Buttering them up for Borat.

Two other important and crucial aspects of a successful scene were that no one in our small crew could ever laugh. It would just have to wait until we escaped. And perhaps most important, we never revealed that it was a prank. Just when things got excruciatingly uncomfortable, even sometimes physical, that was when the scene often took off. When Sacha was feeling confident, he would push and push, taking the scene too far but always in a great and unprecedented way. Even as I was shooting, I often couldn't believe what I was seeing.

But never, though it would've relieved tension but defused comedy, never did we say at any point whether a scene went well or broke down halfway through, "Oh, it's just a movie," or "It's just a joke."

In the story, Borat has two children, a son with an enormous cock, which Borat is quite proud of, and a ten-year-old daughter, who is incestuously pregnant with Borat's baby. Among my first responsibilities was to find those kids and take Polaroids of them. Our office was off Santa Monica Boulevard in a seedier area near

La Brea where male prostitutes loitered on the street and much gay pornography was on display. For the son, I sent someone down onto Santa Monica Boulevard to find someone who was willing to whip their dick out on camera for money. Within minutes we had someone.

He found it all amusing if a little confusing but happily took his photos, got paid, and went back downstairs. When Borat would brag about his son to strangers, they would invariably ask to see pictures and he would show them these.

My eldest daughter, Sophie, was already working as a researcher on the movie. Why not keep it all in the family?

So for the daughter, I volunteered my own ten-year-old, Zelda. She was fitted with a peasant wardrobe and pregnant stomach and looks very unhappy next to a stern-looking Borat.

BORAT IN DC

Our first stop was Washington DC, and right off the bat, the first night covered Borat celebrating Gay Pride at DC's rally and then inviting young men back to his hotel room to wrestle.

So much of both Borat and Brüno took place in motels and hotels. It was like satiric voyeurism.

It was a bizarre spectacle to be waiting in an adjoining room or loitering in the hallway as wrestling aspirants turned up to grapple with Borat, in their underwear. But this would only be the first experience of not believing what I was seeing. It would only be the first in a series of bizarre spectacles that I witnessed and recorded.

The next morning we caught two Republican conservative politicians. First, Alan Keyes, a conservative African-American, sort of the Herman Cain of his time, who had been running for president. Second was Bob Barr, a notoriously outspoken reactionary Republican congressman.

After priming the interviewee for meeting this journalist from Kazakhstan, Borat would enter with Azamat, speaking a foreign language, which of course people assumed was the Kazakhstani language, but was actually Sacha's Hebrew and Ken's Armenian with some Polish and an occasional Yiddishism from both. They would feed off each other until it sounded like one coherent language and no one ever caught on. This was the first step in softening participants up, conditioning them that this was authentic and far out of their comfort zone but it would be okay, though hopefully it wouldn't be. When it worked, before they knew it, before they had a chance to react, they were ensnared in the bear trap and every squirm made it tighter and tighter, until it would be too late for them to extricate themselves. And we never freed them. They would often go off not very sure what had just occurred to them until, months later, when someone they knew saw the movie.

And we were always better prepared than anyone could imagine. That often meant taking my *Curb* AD, Dale, who I knew has a sense of adventure and would revel in this experience, on furtive stealthy scouts in the middle of the night to the proposed locations, not merely to figure out camera angles but also escape routes. I didn't just draw shot lists, I drew maps. Where can the van meet Sacha? Where can the crew run and hide?

We didn't "scout" a location, we "cased" it.

I was amazed at the preparation that Sacha underwent to get into character and stay in character. He had to wear certain underwear and certain socks and have certain monogrammed handkerchiefs in his pocket. He also needed to come out of the hotel in the morning in character and essentially not break character all day. Slipping would be the end of the scene, and sometimes through sign language, I'd have to remind him that he had to keep smiling or that he was losing the accent.

There was no margin for error, and he did it for months at a time, breaking only when the day was officially and safely over, which might even be after we'd stopped shooting but were being hassled or threatened by the police.

In my mind, his performance took the concept of acting to another level. Well beyond the groundbreaking styles of Laurence Olivier and even Marlon Brando. No one was doing what Sacha did.

No one had ever done what he did. And no one has done it since. He should've been nominated for an Oscar for *Borat*. Neither Peter Sellers nor Jim Carrey nor Christian Bale nor Joaquin Phoenix nor Daniel Day-Lewis ever even attempted anything like this. It broke all the rules with "great success."

Our first encounters with the police began in Washington DC, the most policed city in the country. Who were we? A gangly obviously foreign man with dark mustache, eyebrows, and hair incongruously driving a nonfunctioning ice cream truck with five strange men crouched in the back holding equipment that could be mistaken easily for weapons slowly cruising past some of America's most sacred monuments and institutions. Each falling within the jurisdiction of a different law enforcement agency, ranging from the Capitol Police to the Secret Service to the FBI.

And we were stopped by them all. Every day. And I would try to film as many as we could. So much so that our assistant cameraman, now an accomplished DP in his own right, Mark Schwartzbard, began keeping a list. By the time we were done with the movie, he'd tracked over 150 times we had been stopped by various police agencies around the country during the making of the movie.

This was what the movie was about as much as anything. Americans either completely arrogant and ignorant of anything outside their borders or a smug condescension about it. Americans thought America was the world but found out the hard way, the very hard way, it isn't.

After Borat and Azamat would confer, the next step was for Borat to ingratiate himself with the guest he would be interviewing for Kazakhstani television. If the guest was male, when they went to shake hands with him, he would instead lean in to kiss them on both cheeks. Once again, catching them off guard. We knew if they accepted the kisses that they were pliable.

Of course, it was the opposite with women. He was often rude and condescending to them as men from the masculine-dominated Kazakhstani society, where men kissed and held hands and women were only useful for raping and procreating, was the custom.

Next, Borat would offer them little gifts from Kazakhstan. A lapel pin with the flag, some candies. Again, they would accept them graciously though patronizingly, which lulled them into a false sense of superiority and thus trust.

It was usually with the next gift that things got interesting. In the case of Alan Keyes, Borat presented him with a bone brought from Kazakhstan. Keyes accepted it graciously, and once it was firmly in his hand, Borat explained that this was the bone of a Jew. The color almost drained from Keyes's face as he realized he had accepted the bone of a Jew on camera and he freaked out, stopping the interview. I tried to assure him it was a mistake but he wouldn't hear about it. It was just completely unacceptable for him to be part of that.

We retreated to various corners of the hotel suite. Sacha told me in no uncertain terms, as Borat by the way, that I needed to get Keyes back in the scene. In my mind this seemed like an impossibility. But by accepting Keyes's wrath and apologizing profusely and explaining that it was merely a language issue, of course Borat didn't mean a Jew's bone. Who would ever say that? And it's not a Jew's bone. It's the bone of a doe. A deer. It was just a big misunderstanding, and eventually Keyes actually returned to the scene. I did it. I had in real time just talked somebody out of their reality and back into ours. It was the first time, but it would certainly not be the last.

The scene is in the movie.

On the heels of that, we went to Congressman Bob Barr's office housed in a beautiful old federal-style brownstone. We went through the rituals again: my preamble, "I don't really know him at all. I just met him this morning. My crew and I were only hired for two days…" Borat enters and kisses the congressman. Then the gifts. In this case, Borat pulls out a bundled cheesecloth with fresh cheese from Kazakhstan. He offers it to Bob Barr as a token. Barr, attempting to be polite, takes a too large piece and pops it in his mouth. As he chewed, Borat explained that, "This was cheese from Kazakhstan…" Barr with mouth full, "Uh-huh…" "My mother make that cheese…" "Hmm-mmm…" "She make it…from her tit." Barr, realizing he's eating tit cheese, almost chokes. He can't spit it out on camera. So instead he is forced to continue masticating with eyes bulging until he can force it down.

That's in the movie.

One of the most amazing and unique aspects of the movie experience for me as the director was to not believe my eyes even though I knew it was real. When I felt that, I knew the scene had entered another level of hyper-reality.

In improv directing, like *Curb*, you encourage the unknown, for the actors and for yourself. Nothing pleases me more than being surprised. In capturing a moment that could only happen once. But Borat took that idea into the real world where "surprised" could mean failure, disaster, injury, arrest, or death.

It was exhilarating. And for some reason, perhaps my own sociopathy or my Brooklyn conditioning, these confrontations never freaked me out. Instead a sense of calm came over me where I could see everything clearly like when a batter sees a home run pitch.

Often people would stop after a particularly impertinent Borat question and turn to me off camera during the scene that they didn't realize they were in and say, "Is this real? Is this real?" And I would say, "Yes, of course it's real...," and then in my head, *It's just not the reality you think it is.*

Sacha had many techniques to manipulate the conversation and get the desired reactions and results. Often his question was so rude, that people would laugh it off to his naivety and innocence. But he would keep a straight face as if the laughter hadn't occurred and simply ask the question again and again until he got the answer he sought. These served as our "takes" since shooting this was essentially one-take filmmaking, and if something went wrong, we couldn't simply yell "Cut!" and do it again. We would literally have to leave the city and do it again somewhere else.

Another beautiful thing about making *Borat* was allowing inspiration to strike. Fox, the studio financing it, had made us sign a waiver in case we got caught or arrested that disavowed any knowledge or involvement in the movie, taking absolutely no responsibility for anything, even anything violent that happened to us. It was a complete risk. But complete freedom is a complete risk. And we didn't think twice about it.

Our crew was minimal. No one came along on the shoots unless they played an essential role. That would mean, in the ice cream truck: me; Dale the AD; Anthony and Luke, the co-DPs, who also manned the two cameras; Mark Schwartzbard, the assistant cameraman; and Scott Harber, the soundman. In a van that parked far away from the scene of the impending crime were Jason Alper, Sacha's costume designer, and Thomas Kolarek, who tended to Sacha's hair. We had a headquarters in a conference room at the out-of-the-way outskirts-of-town hotels and motels we stayed at, where Monica, the line producer, and the other writers and various office personnel would gather. One writer was allowed to tag along with us per day. But not always. We were in constant need of material and revising and readjusting material, and again in that pursuit of the funniest movie, simply trying to top what was there, and the writers were forced to constantly generate pages to reflect all those needs. For movies where all the participants, but one, have no idea what they are going to say next, these "scripts" often ballooned into the hundreds of pages to cover every eventuality.

Shooting this way meant if we felt inspired by something we saw out the window, we could stop, shoot, and get back in the vans. That led to brief cinematic interludes where we saw the character and the stakes and the emotion underneath them. This gave the film feeling and focus and shape.

But things could change at a minute's notice too—an interview is canceled, or the people don't show up, or it's a scene that ends abruptly with someone pulling off their mic and storming off and suddenly we'd be left with nothing to do.

BORAT IN NEW YORK

Our next stop was New York. Surprisingly, New York provided much of the emotional ballast early in the movie for us to root for Borat and sympathize with him as a three-dimensional character.

This is some of Sacha's best stuff. Not designed for hilarity but deepening the connection with the audience so hilarity could ensue. Not until later in the movie would we feel the depths or poignance of his despair. We had many inspired days in New York, shooting planned sequences but also improvised material that portrayed him as a foreign person lost in New York. In Central Park, Borat washes his clothes in Turtle Pond and thinks that the mass of joggers running in one direction are running away from some sort of attack. In Times Square, he simply tries to cross the vast endless boulevard and is then overwhelmed by the neon lights. And of course, squatting and taking a shit in front of the Trump Hotel.

Another challenge in *Borat* was manipulating targets to help us push the story forward. In New York, we did an interview with a group of middle-aged fairly humorless feminists. Of course, Borat insulted them ceaselessly, questioning their intelligence and pissing them off. But being told to be patient with a naive foreigner kept them in the scene. Borat needed to head to California to find Pamela Anderson, and we needed the feminists to tell him that's where she was located. After much banter, Borat zeroed in on Pamela Anderson. The feminists were offended that he was so obsessed. But Borat couldn't let go. We needed that exposition. One of the most tolerant feminists finally volunteered that she believed Pamela Anderson lived in California, at which point Borat abruptly ended the conversation and hurried out on his quest, leaving the women baffled.

It's in the movie.

There were so many different types of humor operating in *Borat*. Sometimes all at the same time. There were the mind-fuck, one-of-a-kind satiric interviews Borat conducted with self-important, self-righteous, closed-minded, hypocritical people, leading them into a trap they never saw. But there was also classic physical comedy that exploded out of the frame of a movie into the real world, which was unprecedented.

The chicken on the subway was a great example of this. A conceptually audacious sequence in which Borat has entered the subway with a suitcase with air holes that contained his live pet chicken, which he had taken with him on the trip. Borat enters a very crowded subway car and quickly the suitcase opens, releasing the chicken, who leaps and flaps around the crowded enclosed subway car to the horror of the passengers. The cameramen and myself wore hidden cameras so we could be on top of the action.

We had permission to be in the subway. But not permission to bring the chicken.

Within a stop or two, the police had been alerted and were trying to track us (no pun intended) down on the platforms, but we conducted an elegant and elaborate pas de deux worthy of Fernando Rey's eluding of Gene Hackman in *The French Connection* as we shuttled between cars and subways, heading in many different directions and thus staying one step ahead of the police while we garnered enough footage to edit the sequence. Once we were sufficiently done, we hurried upstairs and iced down the chicken.

We were thereafter officially banned from the subways.

The shooting of the scene was as exhilarating as the scene itself, and I believe one of the X factors of *Borat* is that you feel that verve, that exhilaration, that excitement oozing out of the pores of the movie because we were always so excited. We managed to capture that elusive vibe.

But being willing to relinquish control to fate and seeing what happens didn't always elicit the same results.

While filming a scene in Manhattan at the old Hotel Pennsylvania, the premise was that Borat had never stayed in a hotel, ridden in an elevator, sat in a chair, or slept in a bed. Beyond that, the concept, which was a bit pushed, was that Borat had the mistaken idea that the room furniture was his to keep, and he tried to bring a mattress and chair from the room down to the lobby. Where he would take it from there had not really been addressed.

The desk clerk, who was a ringer for Eugene Levy but not as funny, slowly lost patience with Borat. He attempted to obstruct Borat as he tried to exit the lobby with the mattress and chair and drag them out into the street.

In New York, unlike most places, especially the rural areas we would subsequently visit, there were cops everywhere, and unlike almost every situation I'd been in with Sacha, the cops were right there.

This was an unusual night in many respects. The furniture being taken from the room wasn't actually from the room. They were from the motel we were staying at in New Jersey. So technically we weren't stealing anything from the New York hotel. However, we had "borrowed" the furniture from the motel in Jersey without permission.

Also unusual and never to be repeated, we had more personnel than usual on the "set." Monica was rightfully concerned that there would be a misunderstanding about the furniture and wanted to make sure it was returned to Jersey safely. But when she explained that the furniture was not stolen from the Hotel Pennsylvania, only borrowed from this motel in Jersey, she was placed under arrest. And so was our AD Dale.

It was a misunderstanding that was easily resolved, but it meant they had to spend a night in jail. And although there would be detainments and handcuffing and questioning and threatening, those were our only official arrests. Not bad.

Much of what we did skirted around the legalities of the First Amendment. If we didn't understand the parameters of that law, it could result in arrests, and in Sacha's case, even deportation.

Our First Amendment lawyer, Russell, lived incongruously on an ashram in India. When we would have First Amendment discussions, which was often, we'd call him in India and he'd advise us from the ashram. And he was always right. He was like a First Amendment guru.

Sacha's method acting extended into areas that most actors would not delve. Sacha stopped bathing and didn't wash his limited wardrobe. Ken followed suit. And as a result, they both stank.

If people could or would tolerate Sacha's pungent stench, it was a sign that they would be accepting of Borat's subsequent and more extreme transactions. So in a sense, though it is unseen, it was an integral part of the performance and part of the scene.

But those on the crew asked me how I could take being so close to them both in that unhygienic condition all the time. And that's when I realized I had lost my sense of smell. It was clearly my body, my brain, protecting me so I could survive in this environment. I did not regain my sense of smell until sometime after the movie wrapped.

But losing my sense of smell was more than compensated by my other senses becoming heightened and honed.

That's why comparing *Borat* to any other movie, fiction or non-fiction, is a pointless exercise. We were doing something on film that simply had not been done.

BORAT IN THE SOUTH

Scenes like the Southern Dinner illustrate the one-of-a-kind process that goes into a successful sequence. The Southern Dinner was always meant to erupt at some point. But there were so many offenses committed along the way, you never knew how long it would last.

Failure would often give us a chance to rethink the scene. Why didn't it work? What needed to be changed or added? And then move on to another city and try it again.

The Southern Dinner was done three times in three different cities and states. Each scene was different, and each scene was fascinating if not always as hilarious as hoped. They were at the very least anthropological spectacles and still a scene that no one has ever shot in the history of cinema.

There were always numerous X factors that affected the outcome of the scene. How long would they tolerate Borat's behavior? How long before they called the police? How offended would they be? Would this be enough to push them, or too much and push them over the edge?

By the time of the last dinner scene, the one in the movie, the process and projected outcomes had been revised and honed and amped up and, after the previous failed attempts, worked masterfully.

It begins with my ingratiating myself with the hostess and the guests of the dinner party. And then I explain the whys of the scene to them. Who Borat is. Why he's here. Why he's interested in observing Southern hospitality and Southern culture. And his own ignorance of such customs. But finally, I assure them that if anything goes awry, I'll be right here, and they should just say, "Larry," and I'll take care of it. This gives them an illusion of security, which allows complacency to seep in. They could never really imagine what "awry" really means. Complacency, cognitive dissonance, these psychological states would all be experienced in one form or another by every subject in the movie. All of those states provided extra time to film before the targets would come to their senses, snap out of the trance, and return to reality, but by that time it was too late.

The next thing that happened was the placement of the shit. Well, the first thing was the procuring of the human shit. And it had to be human shit. It had to be real and believable and it was. It was one thing for the diners to think it was shit. But it was another to smell it and know it was real. But who would volunteer for such a task? Without hesitating, Jason Alper, Sacha's longtime intrepid wardrobe designer, casually said he'd do it.

We were all impressed. He could shit on cue. He said it would be no problem. And lo and behold, he shit in a plastic bag and snuck it into a drawer in a small table near the toilet for Borat to retrieve later. Another piece of ultimately good luck was that the bathroom he'd be using was upstairs, which gave us separation as one camera followed him upstairs and one stayed down with the dinner guests.

When Borat descends the stairs holding the baggie of shit, it's hilarious but there is no anger from the participants. Shock, yes. But there is much more sympathy, patience, and yes, condescension. The situation is hilarious, yes, but their reactions are completely uncontrived and honest. In fact, as crazy as it is, the woman teaching Borat how to flush a toilet could only be described as sweet. A sweet racist. This is another aspect of what made *Borat* unique.

But after a series of harsh but again hilarious insults directed at the guests in the context of a Kazakh man not really knowing the niceties of Southern etiquette and then the appearance of the

African-American hooker and future wife of Borat, Luenell, the line is crossed and our hostess begins to shriek my name.

What I neglected to tell them was, as soon as the scene begins, I will disappear, and all the screaming for me will not bring order to the chaos you have unleashed. Further, the cameramen, Luke and Anthony, are instructed not to respond to any comments or questions or complaints directed at them.

In many of the unedited versions of scenes from the movie, you will hear people yell "Larry!" helplessly with no response.

We spent a lot of time that summer in the South, headquartered in a motel on the outskirts of Jackson, Mississippi.

We had a very high success rate, but sometimes we chased things that didn't pan out, and I never liked to waste time when we could be shooting things. Mississippi presented a lot of great opportunities.

One night we were heading back to the motel after a long but not particularly fruitful day. We passed a sign that said MOUND BAYOU and further explained that it was the first independent black community, started by ex-slaves back in 1887.

We had no agenda, no script, no scene, but I felt that this was a one-time unique environment Borat could interact with. It would be a welcome relief to see him bond with African-Americans when part of the concept of his character was that he didn't realize the American Civil War was over. So we went into the pool hall, and he and Azamat started playing pool with the regulars and everyone was very cool.

I loved filming stuff like this, and there is hours of it. I found it endlessly fascinating on a completely different level. Many times in a scene like this, Borat gave us glimpses at old, weird, out-of-the-way, dying, fading America and its many subcultures, which didn't produce laughs but illumination. Mega-churches, Civil War reenactors, plantation re-creators, illegal exotic animal zookeepers. Sometimes I was amazed by what we were filming. Sometimes I could only absorb the weirdness of the situation.

In the end, most of this didn't make it into the movie but would provide on its own a unique cinéma vérité ethnographic situationist nonfiction film.

But that didn't mean every day was successful, and even when we got fascinating footage from a place like Mound Bayou, I knew the items on our actual agenda, our needs, were not accomplished today.

I would take this very personally. I felt the pressure to deliver. To succeed. To achieve. I wasn't sleeping. Would often simply sleep in my clothes, too exhausted to do anything else, and this was after all in the spirit of the film. It was tough to eat, too. It wasn't like we were sampling the best of Southern cuisine. We were eating at a string of fast-food and chain restaurants.

Sometimes I would get too pent up and not realize it until it was too late...

When we came out of the pool hall, it was night. And it was hot. As we prepared to climb back into the van, Dale looked over at me. My back was turned. He thought to himself: *Wasn't Larry wearing a white shirt? Now it's black.*

As he approached, he saw that the blackness that had enshrouded me was a halo of flies. They completely covered my back in the few seconds outside.

Suddenly we all realized we were being attacked by marauding aggressive flies. We began to fight them off as we hurled ourselves back in the van and took off. But the flies swarmed the inside of the van, so as we sped away, the attack continued.

I was in the front passenger seat. Sacha, Dale, and the rest of the crew were behind me.

I was very stressed and hungry, and adding to my anxiety, everyone had rolled up their script sides and were now using them to swat at flies. Every "thwap" of the rolled-up scripts made me more uncomfortable. There was fly blood everywhere, and the buzzing was deafening.

Feeling very jittery and starving, I almost unconsciously took a piece of beef jerky from an opened package on the dashboard.

I threw a piece down my mouth and, without bothering to chew, swallowed it.

It immediately lodged in my throat. No one knew. I didn't want anyone to know. When you realize you're choking, one of the thoughts you have is that you're too embarrassed to signal for help and it might be better to just die. But I began to pitch forward, saliva drooling out of my mouth, and emitting an involuntary and otherworldly moan.

Dale—he always kept a good eye on me—noticed something was wrong. He asked if I was okay, but he already knew I wasn't.

Dale was ex-military and had famously performed an emergency tracheotomy on a stranger on a bus with a Bic pen. Was it true? Shit, man, at this moment I sure as shit hoped so.

My response was a guttural noise. That was all I could muster. Dale had the driver pull the van over. He whipped open the side door, jumped out, whipped open the passenger seat door, grabbed me like a rag doll, and pulled me out of the car. Just as I was giving up on life, he Heimliched me and dislodged the jerky.

Working with Sacha, I would come to expect threats, physical assaults, weapons being brandished. But this was the closest I got to death.

We spent a lot of time on the legendary Highway 61. It was filled with colorful small towns like Clarksdale, Greenville, Vicksburg, and so many more, where essentially the blues was invented and first recorded.

On Highway 61 in Tunica stands a venerable diner. The Blue and White. Built in 1924. And characterized by its blue and white tile inside and out. One night with nothing to do, we pulled in there with the intention of shooting Borat and Azamat at a table eating pie and discussing their dubious futures in their concocted native tongue.

Again, just seeing these two incongruous characters sitting in a Southern diner was surreal enough for me. I loved these juxtapositions. But it's what happened in the parking lot that became even more fascinating.

Sacha was paranoid about getting recognized. In truth, most people, especially in the Deep South, had never experienced Sacha and his characters, so it was rarely if ever a problem. Even in LA and New York, he was able to do his thing, with cameras recording and most people not really paying attention. Which was great and emboldened us to push further.

But while we loitered in the parking lot of the Blue and White, a large bus roared in beside us. A window opened and another incongruous character, a middle-aged man with flowing blond locks, stuck his head out the window.

"Sacha!" he shouted. And even more incongruously, in a British accent.

Sacha quickly turned his back on the man, and in a very weak and unconvincing American accent, said, "You got the wrong guy."

But the man in the window would not be deterred. "C'mon, Sacha. I recognize you. It's okay."

Ant Hines and I, who had been watching this exchange, looked closely at the man in the bus window.

Oh shit, it was Robert Plant!

We immediately told Sacha, and though he appreciated it, I didn't get the sense that he was a big Led Zeppelin fan. I was. Their performance at Madison Square Garden in 1972 was the first concert I'd ever been to. And Ant had a similar affinity for the band.

Plant and his band were doing a gig in Memphis, about an hour north, and after exchanging some laughter and pleasantries, he rode off.

Even when things went off the rails, it resulted in memorable one-of-a-kind moments, some of which were filmed, that bonded the crew. We were like the Dirty Dozen with that same sense of high stakes solidifying the camaraderie. And I encouraged that feeling because again I believed that if that sense of verve and spontaneity and exhilaration could be added to the proceedings, it would translate to the audience. And it did.

Although one of the conceits of Borat was that he wasn't aware that the American Civil War was over, in the South it was not hard even for those who knew better to believe it had never ended. The Confederacy reared its ugly head everywhere we went. And quite blatantly. We met antisemites and neo-Nazis and secessionists.

Among the weirdest off-shoots of this still-active Confederate culture were the plantation reenactors. Everyone by now has heard about Civil War reenactors. But few know that down in the South, there are hundreds if not thousands of plantations, where the mistress of the house in hoop skirt and imperious yet somehow nostalgic racism presided over modern African-Americans portraying faux slaves tending to the cotton fields, still intact, celebrating that way of life. The tours and the souvenirs also pay for the maintenance on a massive estate. The people who own them, often the descendants of the original owners, not only offer tours of their property, but "perform" a re-creation of plantation life, including slaves, for the price of admission.

The idea was that Borat and one camera guy would stay about a quarter of a mile back in the ice cream truck, while the rest of the crew and I set things up at the plantation. On a cue, unbeknownst to those in charge, Borat was to come riding onto the property and try to free the slaves.

It was an audacious scene, if it could be pulled off. That day, the weather didn't cooperate. It was raining off and on, and this entire scene was outside and would be adversely affected by heavy precipitation.

It forced us to hold off on cueing Sacha, hoping that we'd get a clear patch and we could go. Because once we went, we'd go until we couldn't go any more.

But now we were waiting.

While waiting, I wandered out into the cotton fields, where a young African-American man stood waiting as well. He would eventually be portraying a slave in the reenactment.

This was so bizarre, it was hard to process.

I asked him almost facetiously, but with genuine curiosity, if he made enough money as a slave to live on. He said, no, he had a second job at McDonald's.

These were the one-of-a-kind ironies that could only be experienced on this project and that changed and expanded me every day.

The lady of the house, the mistress of the plantation, the owner, replete in vintage pre–Civil War garb, escorted us around the property, but while we waited for that break in the weather, you could feel her uneasiness and suspicion begin to rise. Fuck the weather. It was time.

Sacha came bounding down the road in the ice cream truck and right onto the plantation property. He jumped out and approached the plantation mistress, who seemed stunned and confused.

The various elements that were needed to create a successful scene were not quite meshing.

Because of her reticence, Sacha became slightly more aggressive. The goal was to get to the cotton fields, but they were quite a ways in the distance. So now we were crossing this expansive field near the paddock. Outside the paddock stood a life-size plastic replica of a horse. Sacha seized on this.

"What have you done to this horse, Gypsy?" He often accused women of being gypsies.

The woman was completely confused. "You have put curse on this horse, Gypsy?" The woman must have felt at this point like she was tripping on acid. "Do not put curse on me, Gypsy."

I don't know, but to me, it was hilarious. Sacha was relentless. But the woman became almost frightened, and then angry, and then before we got close to the cotton fields, she called for her husband, who came running out of the house on the phone with the police, chasing after us as we all spread across the field, back to our vehicles.

Sacha was in this country on a temporary visa, so if he got arrested, he risked deportation, which would be the end of the movie obviously, so the first order of business was to get Sacha safely away. Often across state lines for extra security.

He and Jason and Thomas and the driver took off immediately and got across the nearby state line.

We had to load our equipment into the truck, but we beat as hasty a retreat as we could. We pulled out into the road and took off, only to be intercepted by four police cars, who made us turn around and escorted us back to the plantation.

Shit, I thought, *this is it.* We are fucked. This plantation woman is friends with the cops here. And they're all Good Ol' Boys. She is a large property owner. She has sway. It doesn't matter if we have all the signed paperwork, and we haven't done anything illegal. In fact, everything was done with her permission, for which she was paid a fee, which makes it binding. But none of that would matter. It's a Friday. We'll be arrested. Thrown in jail for the weekend. Then maybe released on Monday, but still, a weekend in jail seems pretty fucking awful.

So if we were going to jail, it would be with as much resistance as I could muster. I pulled out my paperwork and approached the cops, who were already in conversation with the mistress.

I explained that we had done nothing wrong, we had entered into an agreement, and if anything, she was the one who had violated the agreement. She should be arrested. She and her husband argued vainly, but it didn't matter because these good old boy cops were going to arrest us anyway as far as I was concerned.

But I had at least thrown a monkey wrench into their plans. The cops perused the paperwork and handed it off to each other. Then they conferred. Finally, they admitted they were a tad uncertain as to how to proceed and they were going to call their lieutenant to come to the scene and sort it out.

The lieutenant? Well, I had done my best, but once the lieutenant arrived, the jig would be up and we'd be off to the slammer.

The lieutenant arrived. Much to my pleasant surprise, he was African-American. I didn't know what the reality would be, but I instinctively felt better. I felt if we had any shot of getting a fair hearing, it would be with this guy. He was younger and in better shape than the white cops who answered to him. He surveyed the situation. Then he looked at me and said. "What's going on here?"

I looked up at the gray and ominous sky. I inhaled the thick humid air. And then I said it:

"She's got slaves, man. She's got slaves..."

He took one more look around, at the plantation, the plantation mistress, the young African-Americans playing slaves for slave wages, and thought for a moment, then looked back at me.

"Get out of here."

I expressed our gratitude as we climbed in the van and sped off for the state line to catch up with Sacha.

I got good at this.

BORAT AND THE BEAR

If you saw Borat, then you know that another character in the film is the bear. At first, working with a bear was taken very seriously. There were two bears, who like the twins who played O.J., Brüno's dubiously adopted baby in *Brüno*, switched off on camera. Although ultimately one bear, like one twin, wound up doing the bulk of the work. There were two handlers as well. They seemed very strict. Anyone who might come in contact with the bear had to attend bear camp. This was a sort of hastily thrown together penned-in area where the bear could become familiar with you without swiping off your face.

The trainers were very adamant about following protocol. At first. But their standards slackened precipitously during the shoot.

Sacha was very brave. He swam in the pool with the bear. He slept with the bear's paw on his genitalia. If he sneezed and the bear castrated him, how would I explain that? To his family? To Fox? To lawyers? Why would I have allowed that? For the movie? Yes. These were the kind of thoughts that drifted through my mind as I filmed this movie.

But soon enough, the trainers were lying back, drinking beer, while we went around with the bear doing our thing.

Often Anthony, Luke, Scott, and I rode in the back of the ice cream truck with the bear while Dale drove us to the next location.

In Dallas, we were going to shoot a scene where Borat would pull up to a park in the ice cream truck, and when the kids would come rushing to the window for ice cream, the bear would lunge out and send them all screaming and racing away. Pretty simple. Except death and disfigurement of children looms over the whole scene. Which is why I loved it.

The trainers had found a cozy spot in the shade dozens of yards away to get their buzz. Parents of the kids were congregating but far enough away to not be able to get there in time to stop the scene. By the same token, they wouldn't get there in time to save their child either. Action!

The kids were specifically instructed to run, run, run. Not to linger by the truck. Both for the comedy of the scene, but also safety.

And the first two takes were great. The bear was on his marks and roared with intensity. The children all screamed and ran away on cue. All except one. One kid. One kid who was mesmerized by the bear. One kid who stood there paralyzed staring at the bear that was close enough to behead him.

I told the kid in no uncertain terms that he had to run or be killed. He wouldn't listen. He did it again. After the second time, I had no choice. I had to fire him. It was painful. But it was either that or sacrifice his future. Someday he'll thank me.

THE NAKED FIGHT

Perhaps the most notorious scene in the movie, and perhaps one of the most notorious scenes in movie history, was the Naked Fight. For it to appear spontaneous and real required some challenging logistics. The scene, from Borat emerging from the bath to discovering Azamat masturbating to images of Pam Anderson, to the hotel room fight to the chase down the hallway and into the elevator, with unsuspecting passengers, across the lobby of the hotel and then bursting into the mortgage brokers convention for the climax required multiple locations. Each time we filmed a section, we'd be kicked out of the respective hotel.

When we were filming on location, I would often get overly intense. We weren't just filming scenes, but situations. And I lived and died with each success and failure. I rarely backed down from law enforcement or angry participants. I felt confident that I could fix it. In fact, I wound up relishing these confrontations.

But even during the staged scenes, I would go overboard sometimes. The movie, the comedy had to be intense and hard, and I was determined to make the staged scenes as real and in your face as the so-called unstaged ones.

One example was during the climax of the hotel room portion of the Naked Fight. We had worked out the choreography for the corpulent Azamat to wind up sitting on Borat's face and trying to smother him.

There was a lot of nakedness in that room. And many discussions of what body part would go where and how that was to be accomplished. For instance, ball placement had to be accounted for.

Sacha was understandably concerned about hygiene. Specifically the hygiene of Azamat's ass. So there were abundant wet wipes on the scene. Sacha also realized that a wipe simply wouldn't be sufficient. We came up with a way to place a surgical mask over Sacha's face and then lower Azamat onto him so Sacha's facial orifices would be protected.

Further, we worked out a signal for when Sacha could no longer breathe. He would essentially tap out. If he tapped three times, we were to yank Azamat off his face immediately.

But I was looking to capture that magic, that X factor, that lightning in a bottle. And once the mask was on and Azamat was lowered on to him, the cameras and I were right on top of them, capturing the action like a live sporting event. We were all on the bed bouncing up and down. And I was screaming to keep going, keep going.

Somewhere during this, I saw Sacha tap out. But I knew he wouldn't want to do it again and I would have to agree. But that meant I had to be sure we had enough footage. I knew this would be an important one-of-a-kind moment. So I ignored the tap-out. Sacha began to tap more furiously. He was suffocating.

I knew Sacha wouldn't die, and further, I knew he'd be happy to have this great version of the scene. After a few more seconds of mayhem, we pulled Azamat off Sacha's face.

Sacha was upset that I had ignored the tap-out, but as he berated me, we realized he was no longer wearing the mask. Where was it? We searched the bed and sheets. It was nowhere to be found. Was it up Azamat's ass?

While doing the next take, my worst fear was realized, as the mask appeared, oozed out of a fold somewhere in Azamat's lower torso. We threw away the mask, Sacha sanitized vigorously, and we moved on.

I've already spoken of my feelings about Sacha's performance. It ranks with anything and I might argue transcends anything by Laurence Olivier or Marlon Brando. And I think they'd agree. Sacha created twenty-first-century acting.

After Azamat's post-fight departure, Sacha once again demonstrates the unexpected range of this character as Borat falls from grace and becomes a lost soul wandering the bleak American landscape.

Sacha committed to this as much as he committed to the comedy. It was essential to me to lean into the emotion of this phase of the movie. Without this section, the movie was always at risk of being a series of sketches. And I knew it could be so much more. This gave the audience a chance to think, to feel, to breathe. To invest and fall in love with this character.

By the time we got to the mega-church, where I had to explain to the church leaders who Borat was, what had happened to him, how lost he was spiritually, and how ready he could be to accept Jesus, and then these people being generous, if not somewhat deluded, but fully committed to helping him get to that place, only to watch a broken Borat enter the church and be led to the stage, where he was healed in a wave of frenzied, ecstatic glossolalia and prayer, we had entered yet another dimension, of the movie, yes, but also reality.

This hitting bottom gave Borat a chance for redemption and epiphany, but of course, in comic fashion, the redemption and epiphany may not quite be interpreted correctly. We don't want our archetypal comedy characters to change or learn too much. The Tramp doesn't. Inspector Clouseau doesn't. Neither does Borat.

BORAT'S ALTERNATIVE ENDINGS

Comedy endings are hard. There are very few perfect endings in comedy like Billy Wilder's *Some Like It Hot*, when Jack Lemmon in drag tells Joe E. Brown that he's really a man, and Joe E. Brown deadpans, "Well, nobody's perfect."

Unfortunately, *Borat* didn't possess a clean ending like that. Of course, in many ways it couldn't. Billy Wilder followed his script, and that perfect ending naturally emanated from it. But the *Borat* "script" was really some scenes, some dialogue, some jokes, and some suggestions. We didn't really know how it would turn out. We couldn't know. And in fact, we didn't even agree on how it should turn out.

The first ending struck me immediately as wrong. Convoluted, contrived, cumbersome, and far from the anarchic hilarity or even the grounded emotion of the rest of the movie.

In that ending, Borat becomes aware that Pamela Anderson is getting married in the backyard of her Malibu estate overlooking the Pacific. He decides to arrive at the wedding via raft. How he was able to secure a raft is never really established, which damages the credibility of the scene right off the top. It also required at least four scuba divers to guide the raft but remain unseen through the entire scene. On the raft is a large boom box, and blasting on the boom box is an original song called "You Be My Wife." He disrupts the wedding, only to find out that it's not Pamela Anderson getting married. It's her dog.

We knew as we were shooting it, it sucked. And I couldn't allow the movie to end on such an unsatisfying note when there was so much fodder for a potentially great ending.

Sacha's British writers had been working nonstop through the entire production, and they really didn't have much new to offer. I suggested we bring in Alec Berg, Jeff Schaffer, and Dave Mandel, formerly of *Seinfeld* and *Curb*, among others. I also asked another writing team from *Seinfeld* and old friends of mine by now, Tom Gammill and Max Pross.

Together with Sacha and the British writers, we sat around and pitched ideas for the ending.

It was important to me that the ending connected the dots of the movie. That it wouldn't be just some arbitrary scene that happened to be the last scene of the movie. This movie deserved a boffo finish. Maybe we wouldn't have a "nobody's perfect" moment, but we should try to get close and at least, like that ending, make sense.

We started to talk about what would really happen at this point in the movie. The idea arose that Borat could track Pamela Anderson down at a book signing and attempt to kidnap her. This was in keeping with the spirit of the movie. It would be raw and real. And no one would know except Pamela, who had been cool and patient through this whole process.

We secured a Virgin Records store in Orange County. We had cameramen inside makeshift shelving and used stationary security cameras as well. Anthony and Luke's handheld and visible coverage made it seem like they were there to cover the book-signing event.

This was similar to a tactic used elsewhere, like the mortgage brokers convention for the culmination of the Naked Fight. Make it seem like the cameramen were there to cover one thing when they were actually, of course, there to cover our scene. That made them seem as innocent as the rest of the bystanders.

Borat disrupts the signing and kidnaps Pamela with a burlap sack. He runs through the store, closely pursued by security and Anthony and me, into the parking lot, where Pamela is freed and Borat is roughly tackled.

This leads naturally to Borat's epiphany. He isn't in love with Pamela Anderson. He's in love with Luenell the prostitute. It sounds crazy and it is. But I knew it could be strangely sweet and innocent too.

BORAT IN ROMANIA

In the end, Borat returned to Kazakhstan, with the slightly misinterpreted cultural lessons that he brought back from America. One example was adopting Christianity, which provided the opportunity for my cameo. Hung from a cross as a crucified Jew.

We had explored many countries and even back lots here in Los Angeles to find Borat's village. We chose the village of Glod somewhere in the Bucegi Mountains of Romania. We stayed about an hour away in the city of Bucharest.

Bucharest was a strange and fascinating city. Wild packs of dogs roamed the streets. The overabundance of statuesque Eastern European women meant seeing these aspiring supermodels doing all kinds of menial labor like dumping the grease at a fast-food restaurant. And of course, there were signs of its ignoble past like the absurdly massive edifice, the People's Palace, built by the dictator Ceaușescu and where he was chased and gunned down in a courtyard to end his murderous regime.

It wasn't a Western European country like England or France with its deep connections to the States. It was Eastern Europe. A truly foreign country to me from its history, its government, its customs. I was truly a stranger in a strange land, and I loved it. I thought, *This is what I've wanted to do all my life, and now I'm doing it.*

And what was it? Making movies with impact. With audacity. Making movies that were singular. Shooting a movie guerrilla-style that couldn't be easily classified, a new genre all to itself. And traveling the world making trouble and getting away with it. I felt invincible. Usually a dangerous delusion but in this case necessary to make the movie.

Filming in the village was the perfect synthesis of the nonfiction documentary quality of *Borat*, on par with straight documentaries, and its overlay of fabrication. We pretended it was Borat's hometown without ever really explaining it to the villagers. They wound up being unknowingly cast as friends, family, and neighbors.

I would literally audition people on the road or in front of their modest domiciles to play roles in the movie. It was instantaneous filmmaking at its best and lent an air of verisimilitude and spontaneity even to the planned material that I'd never seen another American film attempt.

In another town in the area we had scouted for Borat's village, I spotted a kid smoking cigarettes. And by kid, I mean twelve or thirteen. He seemed wise beyond his years. His name was Elvis. I instructed our Romanian AD to ask him to accompany us to Glod to play the driver of the car that Borat takes to start his journey. He agreed but skillfully negotiated a nice payday for his toils.

In fact, we paid him so much that when the local man employed as Borat's double found out, he was miffed and quit.

But when it came time for the scene, of course, Elvis couldn't drive. We got enough shots of Elvis behind the wheel smoking a cigarette, but when it came time to actually drive Borat out of town, there were no volunteers. In fairness, the car seemed like a death trap. What could I do? I was the director. I got behind the wheel with Sacha in the back and we drove down the steep hill that led out of town. The brakes and steering had long outlived their usefulness, and I only hoped we'd outlive this scene.

It was another instance where I could have easily killed Sacha, and these thoughts haunted me, yet nothing could stop me from going for broke on this movie. Death would not stand in my way.

There was much meticulous planning that went into the setup for any scene that Borat would enter. Essentially, we would create a trance state, an alternate reality, but you could only hold people in that state for so long, and one thing that had emerged after a couple of months of filming was that Sacha would be chronically late to enter. Sometimes very late. Sometimes extremely late.

The excuse was always the same. He was taking a shit.

Having the target snap out of it could be devastating to the scene and never give Sacha a chance to establish himself. So after much curiosity about Sacha's tardiness, I felt compelled to ask him, "Why the lateness? What's with the shitting just before the scene?" And he told me how scared he would get before the scene. That he would get so freaked out in the moments leading up to the scene that he was literally scared shitless. He had to shit. And once he did, he could face the dark unknown of the scene before him.

I finally understood. It made perfect sense. It was almost impossible to put myself in Sacha's shoes, particularly in that moment, just before he entered a scene. It was a high-stakes performance. Failure could mean injury, arrest, or death. Once he was on the roller coaster, he, like the target, couldn't get off until it was over, and it was impossible to know when it was over beforehand. It was one X factor that couldn't be controlled. It was scary. But it was also a peak adrenaline-rushing, one-of-a-kind exhilaration that was comparable to the addiction of a war correspondent. It was the action. The action was intoxicating. I got it. I had it. The addiction. The action. And there has never been a movie with this much action, real-world action with real-world consequences, and in a comedy no less.

Success, and yes, survival, bonds people, and when the movie became not only a hit but a global and cultural phenomenon, to this day still referenced and revered, Sacha, the crew, and I felt like we had gotten away with murder and had also collected the reward. We had shared a once-in-a-lifetime adventure. We were war buddies in a war we won, except we may have made the funniest fucking movie ever.

CHAPTER 12

AN ATHEIST THANKS GOD
(RELIGULOUS)

Fox, like any movie company with a success, wanted a sequel. A sequel to *Borat*. We were all uncomfortable with the idea. Especially Sacha. It felt like it would taint this magical experience to go back to the well. But we decided to do our due diligence and at least discuss it.

Sacha, the writers, and myself sat down and kicked around some ideas. They were all funny, but none felt inspired. I had suggested a premise where Borat must roam the world to bring Kazakhstan a new religion. It would satirize religions of all kinds and give us a chance to apply these methods and techniques in strange and exotic and very, very foreign locations.

Sacha wasn't buying any of it. He was protective of what we had accomplished and didn't feel like there would ever be an idea that could justify a sequel. We all agreed, and any discussion of a *Borat* sequel died, seemingly forever.

So, once the idea of a sequel for *Borat* was quickly dismissed, I tried to ignore the predictable seductions of money and fame and use my leverage as the director of a hit movie to do *something impactful and iconoclastic.*

The idea of a movie that explored religion but used the endless kitschy Hollywood imagery to make these satiric points seemed like a sharp satire as well as a surprisingly entertaining movie. And as close as *Borat* came to documentary, it ultimately wasn't. In many ways it was more. A meta documentary. But with the exception of *Borat*, the only movie I'd ever seen, and it has stuck with me since then, that could be considered a comic documentary was *Millhouse*, by the great documentarian Emile de Antonio, who before this had had many hard-hitting documentaries including *Rush to Judgment*, about the Kennedy assassination; *Point of Order!*, about the Joseph McCarthy hearings; and *In the Year of the Pig*, about Vietnam. But *Millhouse*, made in '71, chronicled the all-American, weird, corrupt criminal rise of Richard Nixon to president using clips and popular music and fast pacing. This wasn't the objective observer documentaries of the Maysles brothers. This was a "Can You Believe This Shit?" documentary. That was what I wanted to do.

My agents then told me that Bill Maher was thinking about making some sort of movie about religion also.

Would I be interested in meeting him? Despite being close to the same age and having a large group of friends in common, Bill and I had never met. But after a few seconds of talking, it was as if we'd been friends all that time. We were laughing at the same reference points, old TV shows, comedians. We had recounted all the people we both knew for many years, including a female comedian we had both slept with back in the '70s, and we were shocked our paths had never crossed. I was very happy we found each other this way.

We met in the offices of Palmer West and Jonah Smith's company, Thousand Words. I don't think I've ever said this to them, but I've worked with many, many producers, people putting money into projects, and these guys were the best. You could see them get excited as Bill and I riffed on ideas, and they immediately put their money where their enthusiasm was.

That enthusiasm carried over to the making of the movie. It is possible to have fun making a movie, and this was a prime example.

All we had was an outline, basically a rough merging of all of

Bill's and my bits and pieces and sequences. And then we'd go out and shoot those and anything else we could gather or felt like while we were in these unique holy locations like Rome, Jerusalem, Salt Lake City, and the Holy Land Experience in Orlando, where Jesus is crucified for tourists four times a day. With kitschy Broadway-style music.

Then I would take all that material and use my deep memory of hypocritical corny religious sagas from Hollywood and around the world to create a mosaic, something that we were familiar with but, in a new context, would elicit howls of knowing laughter. Our goal, to shine a light on the absurdity of religion. What could be more impactful and iconoclastic?

Sacha had shown me a new way of approaching the idea of making a movie, and now I would have a chance to expand on the methods we'd used in *Borat*. I call it the "whoever could fit in the van" theory of filmmaking. The fewer people, the better. The fewer people, the deeper we could penetrate. The fewer people, the more anonymous we could be. The fewer people, the fewer questions. I believed philosophically in this lean, mean, almost primitive but powerful form of filmmaking and have remained committed to it as the closest version for me of honest filmmaking. No glamour or indulgence or waste. Everything on the screen. And everything on the screen would hopefully be something you've never seen before.

And it resembled *Borat* in one other important aspect. If you were a fool, you would be portrayed as a fool on camera. One simple and sometimes rude question from Borat or Bill would reveal your true self.

Our first stop was Israel. I've been to Israel on a few occasions and Palestine too, as well as a number of other Middle East countries, including Jordan, and have had the privilege to not experience these places like a controlled tourist. And I would say to anybody who has strong opinions about the Middle East to go there, and step off the tourist bus and talk to people.

That was my job whether it was for *Brüno* or *Borat* or *Religulous* or perhaps especially later for *Larry Charles' Dangerous World of Comedy*.

In Israel, we began in Tel Aviv. Israel is a country with a certain siege mentality. They are ready for war and violence. Expect it, really. When you are stopped at customs, they ask two or three seemingly unrelated mundane questions, but they are designed psychologically to reveal your behavior and perhaps your true intentions. The questions are simple enough: Where are you coming from? Why are you here? Where are you staying? But then they might throw you a question like, What school did you attend? Your reactions to the questions were as important as the answers. Perhaps more so. We arrived at night, and as soon as I got in the car to the hotel, we were pulled over by Israeli law enforcement. I wasn't sure whom. But once I had explained my presence in their country, they let us proceed.

Our first interview, that first night of arrival, incongruously, was not with a Jew, or a Christian or a Muslim but a Raëlian. Raëlianism is a religion founded by Claude Vorilhon, a sports car journalist, in the '70s that essentially believes that God is an alien, actually an alien species called the Elohim, which is a Hebrew name for God, who came to earth and created humanity using their advanced technology.

They draw on many aspects of Judaism, which was why we met one of their leaders in Israel, where they are lobbying to build their version of the second temple, in essence a landing pad for the Elohim spaceships to return to earth.

Their logo combines the Jewish star and a swastika. Covering all their bases.

Religulous, indeed. We were off to a great start.

The next day we headed to Jerusalem. The nexus and the birthplace of the three Abrahamic religions, and filled as much with delusion and insanity as faith and spirituality. And of course, violent historical conflict.

In Jerusalem, I scouted locations like the Via Dolorosa, where Jesus supposedly walked and now tourists walked, purchasing souvenir T-shirts and magnets. A happy memento of the crucifixion.

We walked through the various gates of the ancient walled city,

Damascus Gate, Lions' Gate. Lionsgate eventually distributed the movie. Seemed worth noting.

I guess I looked suspicious because I would routinely be given the once-over by groups of female soldiers carrying Uzis, who would pull me out of a crowd to ask what I was up to. Were they flirting or just fucking with me or were they legitimately suspicious? No way to know and that's how they wanted it. And almost every spot where I'd be stopped had also been the scene of a horrific deathly explosion that had killed many. So I got it.

This is how people in Israel must live. On guard. Waiting for the next horror. Exactly as the Palestinians do.

It was a historical problem. We would drive on roads where battles had taken place not long before. You could see remnants of the 1967 war and the 1973 war. But you could also see rubble and relics from when the Romans conquered Jerusalem.

We went to Megiddo, the biblically prophesied site of the future Armageddon. It was a fairly deserted tourist destination. A small hill off the highway with plaques explaining its significance and a walking path to the top.

We walked among the caves where the Dead Sea Scrolls were discovered.

These moments were filled with awe but also laughter for Bill and me. It was impossible to separate the seriousness and significance of these locations with their inherent silliness. Megiddo, the site of the apocalypse, was a small unimpressive nondescript hill. In the desert, there was a rock that was supposed to be Lot's wife after she turned to salt. The Dead Sea Scrolls were discovered in caves, but subsequent forgeries made it impossible to know what was authentic.

Everywhere we looked, we saw *Religulous*.

Our fixers, the people who help crews like ours navigate the intricacies of a foreign country and facilitate our access to various places, were both Palestinian and Israeli. Thanks to that synergy, we were able to gain entry to places that were often off-limits to others, like the Al-Aqsa Mosque and the Dome of the Rock, both part of the holy and controversial Temple Mount, which is venerated by Islam and patrolled by Israeli security forces.

We visited Jesus's burial sites. That's right. There's more than one. The Garden Tomb. The Talpiot Tomb. And the Church of the Holy Sepulchre, where you get not only Jesus's empty tomb but also the location of his crucifixion in Golgotha or Calvary. It's all confusing and, despite the age and the beauty, all pretty clearly fake but tourist friendly.

We met street beggars named God. Rabbis trying to invent contraptions to trick God on the Sabbath. The desperate prayers people would scrawl on a scrap of paper and insert into the holes of the Wailing Wall, hoping for an answer from God, and then witnessing a cleaning crew yanking them all out and sweeping them away to some anonymous garbage dump.

It was a holy place all right. But sometimes more "holy shit."

It seemed a natural transition to Rome.

Rome, like Jerusalem, is an overwhelming and surreal city. One of the cradles of civilization. Full of antiquities and history and reminders of a once great empire. And like Jerusalem, cashing it all in for a tourist buck. And as proof, within its city limits lies a country of its own. The Vatican. Technically a city-state.

But before we entered the grounds of the gilded palace of Roman Catholicism to get a dose of that madness, ancient madness but madness nevertheless, we spoke to some other more modern madmen.

First, we had managed to arrange a visit with the leader of Raëlianism himself, Claude Vorilhon, now known as Raël.

We met in his opulent Roman hotel suite. He entered. A slight man with his hair pulled up into a sparse top knot, wearing what I could only describe as a kitschy 1950s sci-fi-movie-style alien uniform. All white adorned with gold and symbols and winged shoulders. He was accompanied by a bevy of attractive female acolytes in sexier cuts of the spacesuit, who lounged around the room as we filmed Bill in conversation with him.

Like many people we met along the way on this journey, despite the getup, he seemed like a rational, reasonable man. Cool, even.

But once he expressed his beliefs, the spaceships, the human cloning, the lifestyle, it was clear something was off.

We had this experience again and again. Rational people in every way, except in their belief in some crazy myth about their God, be it Jewish, Christian, Catholic, Muslim, Scientologist, Mormon, or Raëlian. It's a disconnect that seems ingrained in the human mind. But if you listen and think about it, it's all fucking nuts.

Sunday morning seems like a good time to be at the Vatican. It's the day the pope gives his iconic blessing from a window above to the adoring and immense crowds below.

The Swiss Guard, in their harlequin outfits, didn't seem up to the task of defending this small city. You could sense their defensive attitude as you walked past them. "Yeah, I know I look like a playing card, but I am a playing card that will kill you if you try anything funny."

Bill had an essay he was to do on camera. We stood before the large, almost absurdly ornate palace of the pope, St. Peter's Basilica. You know, where he stands at the window and gives his blessing. For the best shot, we walked Bill onto the grounds of St. Peter's Square, so he could stand right before the building as he delivered his anti-religious screed. But we were quickly escorted off the grounds because filming is not permitted. We managed to pull the camera back to an acceptable place and shoot the piece.

Our next guest, in very non–Roman Catholic fashion, was the charismatic conspiracy theorist David Icke. He and Bill walked around the grounds of St. Peter's Square as crowds began to gather for the pope's blessing, talking of power and bloodlines and an elite class of reptiles disguised as humans, including the royal family and George Bush and the pope himself, that ruled the world. Honestly, after some of the shit we'd been fed on this journey so far, it didn't seem that implausible. Or at least no more implausible than the rest.

After that, we were to meet the Vatican Latinist. A Milwaukee-born priest named Reginald Foster.

The most enlightened people we met on our journey by far, and perhaps most ironically, were the Vatican priests. Why? They were well educated. In fact, they were PhDs. They understand the difference between the value of myth as representative and metaphorical for truth versus reality. They had no illusions about God, Jesus, religion. But they had to continue selling the message to the masses. Somebody had to make payments on the house.

But it seemed like Father Foster would be a no-show. We weren't exactly sure what he looked like and the crowd had thickened, making it even more difficult to identify him. Bill grew impatient and was getting ready to head back to the hotel while we would go off and shoot B-roll of the Vatican and Rome itself.

But just as we were about to give up, Father Foster ambled over to us. He was a smiling, affable, razor-sharp senior citizen, who wore no collar or gave any sign that he lived on the same floor as the pope.

He died just recently, but I'll never forget his interview, which we were fortunate enough to record for posterity. In it, he said such iconoclastic things as "December twenty-fifth wasn't Jesus's birthday." He would dismiss much of the stories about Jesus as "nice stories." He looked back at the grandeur of the buildings behind him as he told us in no uncertain terms that Jesus would never live in the Vatican. He would've lived in a tent in the hills of Rome, if anything.

And then he invited us upstairs. Upstairs where the pope lived? Yes.

We followed him, past the guards, and up to the floor where both he and the pope lived. It was like the oldest apartment building you could imagine. But it was beautiful, the hallways adorned with frescos. Views of the city. It was spectacular.

We were in disbelief, which was ironic since this was a movie about belief and disbelief. But think of it. There had already been a famous assassination attempt on the pope. Now here we were, being led by a doddering but spirited old man, carrying our bulky black bags of equipment, which weren't even searched. Father Foster pointed just down the hallway from his door. That was the pope's place. Really, I'm not saying we would've gotten away with it or escaped, but if we had been assassins, we were there.

Instead Father Foster pulled out a bottle of plum brandy and shared it with us. In a journey with many outrageous unforgettable moments, this one might've been at the top.

Later in North Carolina, where he was teaching at a university, the Vatican astronomer, Guy Consolmagno, another American and another PhD, sat with us and explained the crucial difference between science and religion. Science wasn't even invented until five hundred years after religion, so of course, religion couldn't ever reconcile scientific evidence with faith. Religion is not, nor was it meant to be, nor could it ever be, science. That simple timeline explained so many misconceptions. If more people realized that, instead of clinging to the magic and fantasy of religion, we'd probably be a saner world.

They were happy to tell us these things if we asked. But it seems the great majority of people in the world don't. So it goes largely unspoken.

While in the Carolinas, the small group of us shoved into a van after shooting all day, it seemed like we were done. There was nothing more on today's agenda. So a joint was lit up. We all relaxed and laughed and that led to the beginning of great conversation with Bill. Before it went too far, I asked the DP Anthony Hardwick, who had done *Borat* with me, to pick up a camera and film it. And Bill riffing off my off-camera questions came out great and became the connective tissue for the movie.

I asked Bill off-the-cuff questions about what we had experienced, so he could deepen his commentary, but also autobiographical questions about his upbringing. His mother Jewish, his father Catholic, but neither religious. Later we interviewed his mother and sister, who confirmed these memories. He talked about deals that he made with God, like if he successfully quit cigarettes. The kind of wagers with God we all make. All this happened in the van during our end-of-the-day rides. And it revealed not just what Bill believed and why but who Bill was.

In England, we drove past Stonehenge, which was fenced off and under repairs. But we interviewed Richard Dawkins at Avebury, yet another Neolithic henge, and even stopped at the massive pictograph of the Cerne Abbas giant with the massive cock and wound up in London, where we met a man, Benjamin Crème, who told us the messiah, or Maitreya, was already here. Apparently he was a Pakistani man living in East London and he would emerge when the time was right. We tried to get a name but he wouldn't divulge it. In the meantime, Crème has died, and we're still waiting.

Speakers' Corner in Hyde Park is a popular spot for people of all points of view, who can stand on a box and rant and rave at the passing crowd about any subject they're obsessed with.

We dressed Bill up as a sort of street person, gave him a box and some talking points from Scientology to spew. Out of context, it sounded like the ravings of a lunatic. But instead, it was the foundation for one of the fastest-growing religions in the world.

Amsterdam, particularly at that time, was a city much misunderstood, especially by tourists hoping to smoke pot anywhere anytime in public. It wasn't like that at all. It was a city in the midst of a difficult transition. As in most of Europe, the influx of Muslim refugees created new tensions in cities that had been doing things the same way for thousands of years.

We stood on the spot where Theo van Gogh, the filmmaker who had made a film critical of Islam, had been murdered by a Muslim extremist.

We talked to Muslim politicians and Christian politicians. We interviewed charismatic and popular, but also virulently anti-Muslim, right-wing politician Geert Wilders at the Hague.

Though you could still smoke pot in designated cafés, the city was evolving away from its reputation as a stoner's paradise.

One exception was the Church of Cannibas, which celebrated the herb as a sacrament. We sat with the "high" priest. To create some atmosphere, we lit candles around Bill and the priest as they smoked and talked, and within minutes, we smelled something familiar. The priest's hair had caught fire. We put him out and went on.

Bill liked to do his thing, the interview, the essay, and head back to the hotel. He would be the first to tell you that the traveling was his least favorite part of the experience. He tried to eat healthy but wound up craving burgers and tuna sandwiches, which reminded him of home. And he conceded there is no substitute for conducting an interview or performing an essay before the Vatican or Anne Frank's house or standing in the setting of the Book of Revelation or the amusement park Jerusalem of the Holy Land Experience.

Back in America, we met Jews for Jesus in Boston, Jews who don't believe in the existence of Israel in Upstate New York, and a Satanist in Coney Island. The Satanist was perhaps the sanest person we met. They should consider changing their name to Sanists. In the South, we met gay converters who themselves were clearly closeted gays. In Washington DC, we stood outside the Jefferson Memorial on a freezing day, after being kicked out by park rangers, and we spoke with my high school colleague and now esteemed journalist Ray Suarez about the Jefferson Bible, a version of the Bible that Jefferson himself wrote, which omits any reference to miracles or the supernatural. How many religious patriotic Americans realize that? Also in DC, inside the halls of Congress, Bill used the same logic to expose the hollow belief system of the then–Arkansas Senator Mark Pryor, who argued extremely half-heartedly for the literalness of the Bible. It was one of the squirmiest interviews we did. Pryor eventually lost to Tom Cotton, who believes the same false bullshit but defends it more vociferously. We also met then-Senator Joe Biden in the hallway but he wouldn't stop for an interview. I thought he was scared of Bill.

At the Creation Museum in Kentucky, we saw quasi-scientific exhibits that set out to prove the earth was only six thousand years old, and all of science and archaeology was wrong. It reached its height of silliness when we walked past the animatronic dinosaurs being ridden by cave children and presented as fact. The Flintstones as documentary. The founder and curator of the museum, Ken Ham, an Old Testament Charlton Heston type, sparred weakly with Bill's unassailable reason and rationality but simply dug in his heels even deeper.

In Salt Lake City, essentially the Vatican City of America, the capital of Mormonism, we were denied access to the Mormon temple and their genealogy library, where they secretly convert dead non-Mormons, from Jews murdered in the Holocaust to Adolf Hitler, to Mormonism, without them ever knowing it. We were unceremoniously escorted off the grounds.

At the Holy Land Experience in Orlando, where they do four shows a day with song and dance depicting the crucifixion, we talked to the man playing Jesus, who came off more like Jesus Lebowski. Wherever we went, we found hypocrisy and absurdities. But even as these people would be caught in their own absurdities, they clung tenaciously to their beliefs. And though people are abandoning organized religion in droves, it's still holding its own with an unprecedented historical brainwashing PR campaign.

Editing this movie was a blast. We created the structure in the editing room. We all could feel as we inserted the hilarious clips from Hollywood religious epics to the wild range of interviews and locations that we had something special.

We had a very special group of editors, all of whom went on to greater successes. Jeff Werner, who edited the masterful *The Kids Are All Right* as well as Emmy-winning work on *Olive Kitteridge*; Christian Kinnard, who has edited *Insecure* and *Superstore* as well as my Nic Cage movie, *Army of One*. And Jeff Groth. Suffice it to say that he was nominated for an Oscar for *Joker*. I got very lucky with those three.

We needed a title song, and as you can imagine, there were a lot of candidates. But the song that continued to ring in my head was "The Seeker," by The Who. We cut an opening title sequence with it, and I became addicted. The only problem was that Pete Townshend very politely declined our request to use it. But over the next few weeks, Pete Townshend, without any prompting that I know of, had a change of heart and granted us access to the song. Everything was in place.

I'm a fan of the portmanteau. Taking two words and combining them into a brand-new word. It was during the editing that I started to experiment with titles and portmanteaus and arrived at *Religulous*, which said it all, religion and ridiculousness, even if some people had trouble pronouncing it. (Note: The "g" in *Religulous* is pronounced "juh," not with a hard "guh" sound.) And even though many people today still pronounce it wrong, they also still remember it well. Plus, as I'm told so often by unsolicited fans, the movie has had a lasting effect on so many who've seen it. That's the impact and iconoclasm I seek. To open minds. To change minds? Maybe.

I wanted to market *Religulous* as a nonfiction comedy because I knew that, as an entertaining and enlightening documentary that used comedy to make its point, it would never get taken seriously by the earnest and often humorless people who sat on these awards committees. And though that prediction came true, we were shut out of any awards, a reminder of how bullshit awards are, the movie continues to reverberate with the audience in ways that no awards could match and remains one of the most successful "documentaries" of all time. And as ironic as it sounds, I have no one to thank more than God.

CHAPTER 13

A COMEDY ABOUT HATE (BRÜNO)

S acha had introduced two other brilliant creations on *Da Ali G Show*. The eponymous Ali G. And the gay fashionista, Brüno.

But a scripted version of the *Ali G* movie had been made years before *Borat* and didn't work. It was too bad because *Ali G* could've worked the way we filmed *Borat*. Ali G, like Borat, had that lovable innocence that buffered his rudeness and ignorance and impudence and allowed him to skewer self-serving pompous people as he did so memorably on the TV show.

That left Brüno. For me, Brüno was a much tougher character. More complex. Not so easily lovable. And very gay. What made Brüno funny was his offensiveness to straight people and his narcissistic bitchiness, which worked great in *Da Ali G Show* sketches when he was pitted against testosterone-fueled but insecure straight men.

Sacha had taken years to develop these characters, down to their nuances and idiosyncrasies and even their underwear, so the idea of Sacha taking a few years to create and experiment with a new character just didn't seem realistic.

Brüno was what was left. Could Brüno be expanded? Could he possess the layers that became so readily apparent in Borat? Or was he forever to be relegated to a sketch character? No one was sure if it should be pulled off, but everyone was skeptical it could be pulled off.

Plus, who wouldn't recognize Sacha at this point? Thanks to *Borat*, he had become instantly world famous.

These were a lot of issues to grapple with. So we agreed that we would sort of just try the character out at first. Wearing a store-bought wig and a little makeup and a lot of attitude and using phone cameras, we had Sacha sashay down Melrose, interacting with unsuspecting pedestrians and store owners, and much to our shock, he didn't get recognized once. It was on.

The first order of business was casting Lutz, the Azamat of this movie, Brüno's assistant and eventual lover.

One thing that was important to me was to use as much of the foreign language as possible even as in *Borat*, it was an amalgam of Hebrew, Yiddish, Polish, and Armenian. It was all about the illusion, and when Borat and Azamat spoke, you believed they were speaking the Kazakhstani language. We needed to create that level of credibility here. It was essential to creating the alternate reality trance state necessary to make people believe that what they were seeing, hearing, witnessing, experiencing, was real.

Although Ken Davitian was not a particularly funny person (he wondered what was so funny about him being naked in the Naked Fight, and I just told him, "Trust me"), it's easy to see why he would be funny. His version of "real" was hilarious and one of a kind. He was the perfect comic foil for Sacha.

Sacha appreciated this, though in real life they had no rapport, and Sacha wanted Ken to be kept away from him at all times except when shooting. I didn't think much of it at the time. I wanted Sacha to be happy and clear-minded for the dangerous tasks he had to endure.

Gustaf Hammarsten, a truly fine Swedish actor who spoke fluent German and had been in a couple of Lukas Moodysson's very cool Swedish movies, was suggested. Although he was an experienced actor, he was virtually unknown outside of his home country.

Gustaf was a very subtle and low-key actor. Further, he was asked to play a sort of sad sack character. The dynamic between Sacha and Gustaf, like the dynamic between the characters, was problematic at best. An issue for a comedy.

I had watched Sacha be dismissive of Ken, forcing him to travel in a different vehicle, keeping his distance, I felt he was doing it for his character and the movie. So I supported it and spent much time tending to Ken. He was a primitive in the best sense of the word, and I wanted him to perform with abandon. I didn't want him to become self-conscious.

But as I watched a similar thing happen with Gustaf, I saw a pattern emerge. Sacha was used to being a solo act and was not comfortable sharing. So we cast somebody who would not be able to compete comedically. Unfortunately for a trained actor like Gustaf, it led to confusion. I was often having to explain Sacha's rude behavior to him in the best light in order to keep the movie moving. And Gustaf was, as they say, a trouper, who never gave it less than his all.

Gustaf made Lutz real and believable and credible, which made Brüno more real and credible too, which was great. But he was rarely given any comedy to play. The chemistry was never there.

But as we began filming, it was clear this was not going to be *Borat*. Not because conceptually it wasn't funny. In many ways it was funnier. But the world we entered with a flamboyantly gay character was a far darker one than the world Borat experienced.

Where people would be patient with Borat, which often helped the comedy, the opposite was true with Brüno. People felt no compunction about quickly getting physically and verbally abusive with him or being disgusted by him. Or being really angry. And we didn't shy away from that. We stepped right into it and were shocked ourselves of the portrait of America and the world we were capturing.

BRÜNO IN BERLIN

But first we had to film Brüno's fall from grace in Europe.

I've grown to love Berlin. It reminds me of Brooklyn today.

Surprisingly cool and funky and diverse. But this was the first time I was there, and since I was a Jew, even a completely Godless non-practicing Jew, it was impossible not to be struck by all the remnants of Nazi culture; Nazi architecture, like the Soviet graffiti scrawled on the ruins of the Reichstag or the imposing Templehof Airport; Nazi consequences, like the Kaiser Wilhelm Memorial Church, which stands bombed out, destroyed in the middle of the city; or the still very fresh examples of the Cold War that followed like the Brandenburg Gate and Checkpoint Charlie.

As we scouted, it wasn't unusual to see buildings now repurposed for more benign applications still carrying faded Nazi signage.

I know it sounds strange, but the Germans themselves seem defeated and embarrassed and ashamed by their Nazi history. You could see what defeat looked like in their eyes and demeanors.

And under the surface, Berlin still had a certain decadence that easily reminded me of movies like Cavani's *The Night Porter* or Visconti's *The Damned*, or of course, *Ilsa, She Wolf of the SS*. All films I saw in Manhattan as a teenager.

Sacha, the writers, and I scouted the infamous Kit Kat Club, where you could only gain admittance by getting undressed. Though I was in Berlin to direct *Brüno* and I was standing in perhaps the most decadent location in the city, I was still in many ways that kid from Brooklyn who was prudish and very shocked, so when we reached the check-in for the club and we were told we could not go in without disrobing, I was caught by surprise and extremely reluctant.

We were only there to scout and observe. Not participate.

The proprietor did not recognize Sacha, but when he saw me, beard, hat, black coat, looking like a rabbi who was there to check the flesh for kosher inspection, he surprisingly relented and let us wander about fully clothed.

Our first encounter, before you could really enter the bowels of the building, was with a naked old man, in great shape, dancing nonstop like a frenzied dervish. It set the tone. We stood mesmerized before moving on.

The club such as it was, was a large formerly abandoned industrial space with many floors and hallways and rooms with exposed plumbing. It was essentially pitch black except for the occasional colored light illuminating something you didn't want to see.

It was like a fascinating nightmare. We were like tourists on a guided tour of Dante's Hell. People in all sorts of combinations, fucking, every which way they could, everywhere you turned. I had accidentally walked into the first meeting of Plato's Retreat in New York and was stunned then, I literally couldn't believe what was going on, but that was like day camp compared to this. I kept my clothes at that time too.

In order for Brüno to be out, he had to create a scandal in the fashion world; he had to commit a fashion faux pas that would brand him a pariah. We knew this would ostensibly involve disrupting a runway show. We shot runway shows in Berlin and Paris, where we got a lot of funny interviews, oblivious and arrogant and rude behavior, and our share of confrontations and forced ejections.

BRÜNO IN MILAN

And then we hit Milan's legendary fashion week.

And when it was decided to put Brüno in what he thought would be a cutting-edge fashion statement that would turn out to be a career-ending disaster, the idea of the Velcro suit came up.

Designing it, though amazing and iconic, like all of Jason Alper's costumes for Sacha, would prove to be the easy part. Somehow inserting Sacha in the suit onto a runway show unannounced would prove to be trickier. It involved a number of solutions. Done in different ways while the camera crew and myself would record the event not surreptitiously but as anonymously as possible. And only accomplished like many of Borat and Brüno's most outrageous stunts, Borat's Naked Fight, Brüno's cage fight, on different days and locations, only to be edited together in a cohesive sequence, hopefully, later.

With all the media attention directed on fashion week, it still wasn't hard to get Sacha or the crew inside the venue. We had some-how gotten media passes so we could roam relatively freely once inside and be indistinguishable from the rest of the onslaught of paparazzi.

But by the same token, it was equally important for Sacha, and particularly the Velcro suit, to remain under the radar so the sur-prise could be maintained until people were watching it "unfold" on the movie screen.

We got backstage at a major fashion show during the frenzied last-minute fittings and activity before the runway show began. Brüno was there to do interviews and was barely noticed as he posed impertinent questions to the distracted designers and staff even while wearing the Velcro suit.

But as hoped for, once the suit got stuck to a large curtain hung on a rack and Sacha began to whip around in what we hoped would be a spectacularly unsuccessful attempt to free himself, chaos, also as hoped for, quickly reigned.

That's in the movie.

The fashion shows, like the Cannes Film Festival, struck me as grim affairs. They lacked humor but had an overabundance of pre-tension and elitism. It was a hermetically sealed world oblivious to the world around it, except to mindlessly exploit it.

Like the hate we would encounter in America, it was fascinating, but not hilariously funny.

We had considered a concentration camp fashion ensemble for Brüno as a guarantee to offend, until we found out someone had beat us to it for real. That's how fashion worked. Offense, bad taste, exploitation, and profit. That was when we turned to the Velcro suit.

We now had the setup scenes, but having caused such violent eruptions and disruptions to achieve them, we had gotten ourselves firmly placed on the police radar. Indeed, it would prove to be even more difficult to infiltrate the runway. And if we did, it would be in front of the global paparazzi. We started to get kicked out of various venues. Plus we didn't want anyone to know what we were doing. Yet we were still missing the key component of the scene.

Because of our behavior, we lost our original credentials. We managed to get another set of much more limited credentials. In theory, we'd be able to get back inside. Then it was about placing the camera crew strategically around the runway to capture the events. This itself would not be easy, as the paparazzi were a desperate bunch. Their livelihoods depended on getting a sellable shot, and they would stop at nothing to achieve their goal of establishing a favored position, including using their cameras as weapons to move upstarts out of the way. It was brutal. But my camera guys were used to it. And jostling among the paparazzi was an acceptable part of these occasions.

Plus, we had worked out an elaborate bait and switch to get Sacha, in the Velcro suit, wrapped up in the curtain from the previous scene, staggering down the runway.

Sacha had a stunt double, Oliver. He would be snuck backstage, wearing a mock-up of the Velcro suit but covered in the stuck curtain from what would seem in the movie like the previous scene, and then literally thrust out onstage in front of the audience, where he would stumble around blindly until he could make it backstage, at which time Sacha as Brüno, fully visible but disheveled and cloaked in the massive curtain, could gather himself enough to sashay down the runway.

But Sacha wasn't satisfied with the plan. He had one more request:

Sacha had asked me if I was willing to shave off my beard. This was before *Borat*. And I said yes, of course, but it never came up.

But now Sacha seemed to think one of the issues with successfully infiltrating fashion week was that I was getting recognized. With all the flamboyant and truly famous people loitering around these things and desperately seeking media attention, I really didn't agree. But nevertheless, in the interest of giving Sacha the security he needed to perform his monumental task, I willingly, even excitedly, agreed to shave my beard. Ironically, most people wear fake beards to disguise themselves. I shaved mine off to accomplish the same thing.

Case in point, when I returned home, my own children didn't recognize me.

Thomas did the honors, and it was covered with cameras by everyone in our little office in a nondescript building in Milan. I hadn't seen my own face for many years, perhaps since I'd been a bellhop, and I hardly recognized myself. It was liberating.

Now we were ready.

As planned, the camera crew and I set up at various places inside the hall, poised to capture whatever action took place on the runway. Oliver was simultaneously snuck inside and backstage, ready to stumble onto the stage while Sacha waited in a bathroom until his cue.

At a certain opportune moment, everything was set in motion and indeed worked like clockwork. Suddenly Brüno was onstage, disheveled and disoriented, wrapped in the folds of the curtain attached to his Velcro suit. Realizing where he was, he seized the moment and sashayed down the catwalk, disrupting the actual show to the accompanying boos and catcalls of the crowd. He relished it, however. This was, at least in Brüno's mind, Brüno's moment. It was a singular and audacious moment, and there was a great sense of triumph.

One semi-brave soul sitting at the lip of the stage made a half-hearted attempt to stop him, but Sacha easily swatted him away and made it look like he was simply trying to free himself from the unwieldy curtain.

Once we had what we needed, we all began our multidirectional retreat. But as we all tried to egress from our various positions in different directions, often our exit strategy in these situations, we were quickly surrounded by the Milan police.

Sacha was taken into custody by the Milan police, and we were lined up and stripped of our credentials, literally ripped off our necks in a public display like a court martial.

But we had the scene and the tape, and truly in those days, that's all that was important to me.

Although Sacha was ultimately released and we were not charged, in some ways it was worse. We were banned from the venue and the authorities were on the lookout for us to infiltrate again.

BRÜNO IN THE MIDDLE EAST

In Israel and Jordan, we were under siege almost the entire time. The stakes seemed considerably higher than at any fashion show. Just getting from one country to another was tricky and treacherous. We took a bus across the vast desert and wound up at some arid existential way station straight out of Antonioni's *The Passenger*, or Camus, or Paul Bowles, where visas were bought simply to cross the border. The setting would make a great play as people of all backgrounds sat and waited for permission to cross, from Arab families to mercenaries and drunken journalists. And us.

We stayed in Amman. And it seemed unlike most locations we visited, we'd stay in a nice hotel. It was a nice hotel. What was concealed from us was that it had been the site of a massive bombing, leaving much death and destruction, and in the aftermath of the violence, an especially large gaping, many-storied hole remained in the hotel itself. For whatever reason, it was decided not to repair it. So pulling up was a bit of a shock. Now I understood why we were staying in a nice hotel.

This was also the first time I encountered the kind of security that has now become the norm and that I encountered everywhere on every subsequent project in every country except here. There were spike strips laid across the carriage entrance to prevent a fast-moving vehicle from either entering or leaving. Heavily armed military guards stood at the front doors. And a metal-detecting machine made sure no piece of luggage got inside the lobby without being x-rayed for weapons and bombs. Enjoy your stay.

A couple of days later, Sacha, Monica Levinson, the producer, and myself were invited to dinner at the home of the brother of King Abdullah II, Prince Hussein. This was also revelatory, as Prince Hussein, his wife, family, and friends were essentially more Western than we were. Ivy League educated, wearing jeans. It was not what I had expected.

Although it was an interesting, cordial, memorable evening, I couldn't help thinking the entire night: "Do they know why we're here?"

The very next day we illustrated my point. One of Brüno's signature moves, very akin to Borat's presentation of small gifts and candies to potential targets, was to bring a sumptuous gift basket of frankly feminine beauty products to the interview. And our first interview was with the then–prime minister of Jordan.

So much can go wrong in these situations, and it's often something you could never anticipate. While Brüno and the camera guys filmed the interview in the prime minister's office, I sat discreetly on a couch in the ornate waiting room, headphones on, watching the action on my monitor, the LC5000.

All began smoothly. The prime minister's bodyguard, armed, hovered near me but couldn't see or hear the action inside. If he did notice something amiss, not only might the interview have abruptly ended but so might our freedom, and I can't stress this enough, even our lives. So when overcome by curiosity, he plopped himself down next to me on the couch, I had an ominous sense that trouble might ensue.

At first I tried to keep the monitor from his view the best I could, but he was insistent on watching. As I felt his suspicions grow, I decided to take a different tack. As the bodyguard began to pepper me with questions, I noticed him twirling a beautiful set of ivory and sterling silver worry beads between his fingers.

I had taken to carrying worry beads a couple of years before. Men in the Middle East would sit at cafés and hookah bars each with a set that they would rhythmically manipulate around their fingers. It seemed like a calming and simple ritual. And the beads were often quite beautiful. But I had never seen a set like this.

I was so hyped up and intense that when I twirled the beads, usually on a set, it became somewhat maniacal, almost like an act of OCD that would often lead to the beads exploding in my hand and flying all over the place. People would scramble to retrieve them, but I would stop them. This was the fate of the beads, I explained, and I would find another set. As I had in my pocket at that moment.

As I watched him deftly swing the beads, I expressed my admiration for their beauty and distinction. To show him I understood, I reached into my pocket and pulled out my far less impressive set. He was flattered by my compliments, and in an act of generosity that I would witness again and again all over the world, he insisted I take his set as a token.

I was caught by surprise. I hadn't expected him to offer me the beads. Only to distract him enough until the interview was completed. I was torn. If I took the beads and then the shit hit the fan, he would be even more pissed for getting played. But I knew I would offend him if I didn't accept his very personal act of largess.

I took the beads graciously, and he relaxed. The prime minister seemed more confused than angry, and we were able to extricate ourselves from the building without incident.

Because we were literally the only Jews in Jordan (they didn't seem aware that there were a few other Jews on the staff and crew), Sacha and I were assigned heavy security. While Sacha was able to pretty much stay out of sight until it would be time to film, I needed to wander the streets, scout locations, and be visible, so I was assigned the recently retired chief of police of Amman as my security. He was a warm man and took good care of me. He took me to the legendary Hashem restaurant, where he was welcomed like royalty for an authentic Middle Eastern street food experience. Some of the best I've ever had.

As we walked the crowded streets, I took in the sights. I couldn't help but notice the preponderance of street vendors selling their wares, mostly books and bootleg DVDs, on blankets one after the other. And there were three items on virtually every vendor's blanket: bootleg DVDs of *Borat* and *Seinfeld* always next to copies of *Mein Kampf*.

Our security detail was never consistent. Some days, some cities, some countries, they were amazing. Other places we seemed to have picked security people from mental hospitals and rehab facilities.

In Jordan, besides the former chief of police, we had a couple of cool English gentlemen. Quiet and efficient. Very Bondian. The kind of security you wouldn't notice until they were needed, which often was never.

Sometimes the dangers faced in these situations weren't from the authorities, the military, or the government. One day we were filming in an open-air market in town. Brüno moved through the stalls improvising encounters, asking rude oblivious questions to sellers and buyers, most of whom didn't understand the language. It was funny but would mostly be used for one funny moment or even just as B-roll between scenes.

Nevertheless, I was, as usual, crouched anonymously, surreptitiously, in an obscure corner behind an ancient wall, seemingly unconnected from the goings-on, watching on my monitor and listening on my headset to observe the action, moving the cameras when necessary. I spent much of *Brüno* and *Borat* in that position, crouched in corners, sprawled on a floor. There were no director's chairs. There was no anything. And that was the way I wanted it. Being comfortable was the opposite of the vibe we were creating, and as long as Sacha was putting it all on the line, asking for any kind of creature comfort seemed obscene and oblivious and obtuse.

But that meant I was often isolated, out of sight so as not to rouse attention yet be able to communicate to the camera guys during the action. But this day, behind one of the old buildings that ringed the market, sitting on a stone step, completely immersed in the scene just beyond me, I found myself surrounded by a group of youths whose agenda was not clear. I am an intuitive person, especially when it comes to danger, something that was essential to Sacha's survival and my own. And I felt these kids weren't merely curious but perhaps deviously opportunistic. Isolated, they squatted down around me and spoke quickly in their native tongue. I didn't know what they were saying, of course, but I didn't trust the tone. I tried to be welcoming, allowing them to look at the monitor, and some were indeed fascinated by that. But when a couple of them pulled knives and began stabbing the stone steps between my fingers, I felt I might be in some danger, and frankly I wasn't sure what to do since I didn't want to draw attention to myself or put the scene in jeopardy, or get stabbed.

As I've said, I would do anything for the scene when I worked with Sacha. I looked at each scene as the only time we might be able to do it, and therefore, it needed to be successful. So I was loath to get up, interrupt the proceeding, call out for help, and potentially ruin the scene.

I was feeling the pressure of these kids either planning to steal my stuff or stab me, or perhaps both. And if they did, there would be very little that could be done about it. Since I was looking down at the monitor on the ground next to me and could only feel the kids working themselves into a frenzy that I believed would result in me getting attacked, my purview was limited as well.

But the knife was getting closer. When it seemed like the next drop of the knife would be more of a push, and rather than landing perilously close to my hand, that it would land *in* my hand, an adult hand reached in and grabbed the knife-wielding child's hand. I looked up. It was one of our English gentleman James Bondian security people, who had been watching this from a discreet location.

The kid and his friends looked up at this imposing figure. He didn't say anything. He didn't even gesture anything. He just stared into their eyes, and they knew. They quickly got up and scurried away. I was grateful. And the scene was never interrupted.

BRÜNO GETS STONED

For a production that often needed quick exits from our locations, Jerusalem's inner city was not well suited. The ancient hilly cobblestone streets were not designed for modern traffic as we would discover almost fatally while shooting what we thought would be a relatively quick scene of Brüno, dressed obliviously and inappropriately in Hasidic-themed hot pants and sleeveless cropped jacket with a Hasidic-styled hat cocked jauntily to one side, strutting down an ultra-religious street. He was literally to be dropped off on one corner and picked up on the next. But it didn't go quite as planned. It went more dangerously, but also much better, than we could have anticipated.

Our fixers, whom I had recommended from my experience on *Religulous*, were a mix of Palestinians and Jews. All cool guys, old friends, journalists, former military (all Israelis are required to do military service). After the *Religulous* experience, they were a bit taken aback by the stunts we intended to pull on *Brüno*. But they were cognizant of the reality of Jerusalem and the environs, and after warning us and trying to deter us, they would be left with no choice but to refuse to accompany us to certain parts of the city. We were essentially left on our own. This was one of those times.

I had pushed to have Sacha do this flouncing strut in the skimpy Hasidic costume on a street in the most heavily ultra-orthodox neighborhood in Jerusalem, Mea Sharim. Immediately our fixers said, *No way*. We would never make it out alive, and they couldn't condone that kind of reckless risk for a gag.

It didn't seem like a big problem to me. I thought they were exaggerating. The scene, such as it was, would be so quick, I wondered if anyone would even notice. After discussions with the fixers, however, we compromised and chose what was perhaps the second most ultra-religious neighborhood in Jerusalem.

We had two DPs again on *Brüno*, but since there was no other camera crew, both were responsible for shooting. Sacha seemed to sadistically relish pitting the two guys against each other. It became uncomfortable. And he would often put me on the spot. On *Borat*, it was Luke Geissbuhler and Anthony Hardwick. Sacha would ride Anthony constantly about his height. He felt Anthony was too short to get eye level shots of him, which of course was absurd but I'm sure Anthony had been hearing snide remarks about his height all his life and did not take kindly to it. I loved and appreciated both Anthony and Luke, but Anthony was based on the West Coast and so I wound up working with him on many other projects including *Religulous*, *Army of One*, and numerous pilots as well. Both of them were fearless in the face of much risk and abuse and even danger.

On *Brüno*, to accommodate Sacha's incessant complaining about Anthony's height, we paired him with a tall Berlin-to-Brooklyn transplant named Wolfgang Held. Wolfgang looked like Peter Graves in Billy Wilder's *Stalag 17* (he played a Nazi spy pretending to be an American POW), but in reality Wolfgang was a cool, laid-back bohemian.

Unlike Anthony, who had hardcore experience with this style of shooting, thanks to *Borat*, Wolfgang, though an experienced and skilled documentary maker, had never done anything like this, and so was a bit tentative at times when he was needed to be assertive. That would change on this day.

As promised, the van with Sacha inside parked at one end of a busy commercial street, waiting for the cue. I tried to optimally position Wolfgang and Anthony to get the best angles without being too conspicuous. Anthony crossed the street to get a wide shot with the option of pushing in or tracking Sacha. I was at the top of the hill at the other end of the street with a good clear perspective of the street as Sacha in theory would come walking toward us and the waiting van. I had Wolfgang take a position there by me. I held my monitor and prayed.

At the cue, Sacha stepped gingerly out of the van, made sure his outfit was intact, cocked his Hasidic hat at a rakish angle, and began his saunter. At first no one noticed. But then, within seconds, people began piling out of their stores, shopkeepers and customers, screaming bloody murder at the top of their lungs in Hebrew. Threateningly, wagging fists, they came at Sacha, who was forced to alter his course to avoid physical confrontation. To his courageous credit, he kept on, despite the slight detour and maintained his Brüno attitude.

But swiftly after that, people began to swarm from all directions. They were chasing him now, and he had to abandon Brüno and, fighting for his survival, run. Fortunately his long legs allowed him to stay ahead of the pack. As was my philosophy, we kept shooting.

Desperate, Sacha shouted out in Hebrew that he was a Jew, but rather than placating the mob, it further incensed them. Rocks began flying. Meanwhile I noticed that the van had never made it to the other corner. The serpentine cobblestone streets, filled with obstacles, had stopped the van from circling to the agreed-upon spot. Oh shit.

There was a van parked near us. A van for myself and the crew, but now we commandeered it for Sacha, who literally dove in while it was still moving as they absconded away. Great. Sacha was safe.

But what about us? Simultaneous to all the action taking place before the camera, an angry, frenzied mob on the cusp of violence was surrounding us behind the camera. The scene was done, and possibly, so were we. That scene was over, but this scene was just getting started. But there was no van. There was no security. There was nothing. Everyone grabbed their gear and took off in different directions. Quite alone, I backed up on the hill as the mob encircled me, young yarmulke-clad men with jagged stones in their fists. I had nothing to protect myself with except my handheld monitor, the LC5000, which was encased in metal with a strap that allowed me to hold it, and perhaps my greatest weapon, my mouth.

I stopped and cocked the monitor like a weapon, which took the angry young men surrounding me by surprise. Without waiting, I angrily, aggressively told them that if any of them made any kind of move with their rock, I'd crack their skull open with this sharp, heavy piece of metal. I cocked it back a few times to emphasize my point. Then continued to back away. They bought it. They didn't follow.

I backed up the street, never taking my eyes off them or lowering the LC5000. Eventually the van that had managed to arrive and gather the rest of the crew caught up with me, and again without stopping, someone reached out and pulled me inside.

I wasn't happy. Not because I'd almost been attacked but because I assumed the scene hadn't been recorded. One of my last memories before the shit hit the van was Wolfgang pulling up his tripod and moving out of the way of the oncoming tide of angry Jews. I didn't blame him but couldn't imagine he'd captured the crux of the action. That meant somehow we'd have to do it again, and our options in Jerusalem would be severely limited.

Almost as an afterthought, as we regained our bearings, and certain I knew the answer, I asked Wolfgang if he had gotten any of that. Uncharacteristically, he smiled broadly. He had gotten it all. Yes, he had picked up his tripod but sidestepped the mob and just repositioned himself. I gleefully, ecstatically patted him on the back and thanked him profusely. We had the scene. I was happy.

BRÜNO AND THE "TERRORIST"

Perhaps the scariest and most notorious scene in the movie, at least until we got to Arkansas, was Brüno's interview with a "terrorist."

As you can imagine, interviewing a "terrorist" requires a unique set of logistics.

The first time we tried to pull off this scene, we had secured a stone shack in the middle of the desert to meet "The Terrorist." The location provided good sight lines into the distance so we could see any group of armed men who would drive up to the shack and shoot us all from virtually all directions. We wouldn't be able to do anything, but at least we'd see who was going to kill us far in advance. And despite the Israelis' pride in their defense, they refused to accompany us, and so we really had no defense. We were sitting ducks should the worst-case scenario unfold.

When we saw the lone vehicle coming toward us in the distance, we were at once relieved and also suspicious. Was this a setup, or had he essentially come alone? When he entered the shack, he was immediately suspicious. He looked at us, myself and the crew, and knew something wasn't kosher or halal. He peppered us with questions, and before we could answer, he walked out, stepped back in the vehicle, and was whisked off. Smart man. At least from his point of view.

From ours it meant, improbably, doing it again. Somehow. Somewhere. With another "terrorist"? That part wouldn't be easy.

Researching a Brüno interview with a "terrorist" was no easy task, and we had relied on an outside person who was sincere and knowledgeable, but we hadn't much experience with, to make that connection. So when he told us he had lined up a "terrorist," an actual member of the notorious al-Aqsa Martyrs' Brigade, who had served time for an infamous bombing, willing to be interviewed, with documentation and research, we knew if we were going to do this scene, this might be our best shot, no pun intended.

Having now met a few "terrorists," imprisoned ISIS members, former al-Shabaab soldiers, I have come to realize the murky nature of these limited definitions. One man's terrorist is another man's freedom fighter. A terrorist today may very well be a world leader tomorrow. There are always fanatics and psychopaths who can play out their pathologies through these organizations, but it seemed to me that most were not like that. Instead, they went along, because they believed in the cause, but just as often were coerced into joining.

Brüno, in his desperation to be globally famous, is cynically but disastrously experimenting with different methods to achieve his goal. He goes to the Middle East to bring peace to the region, but in a summit with a Mossad agent, Yossi Alpher, and a Palestinian official, Ghassan Khatib, he mistakes Hamas for hummus and then awkwardly sings his self-aggrandizing paean to himself, "Dove of Peace," to the two incredibly uncomfortable men. Needless to say, it does not go well.

As another aspect of Brüno's attempt to acquire fame at any cost while in the Middle East, he pretends to be kidnapped by terrorists and forced to make a hostage video. However, the video is more gay sex tape than plea for help with well-muscled and oiled Islamic "terrorists" (really, extremely uncomfortable extras) engaging in erotic behavior with him. The plan was to have a "terrorist" critique the video.

It's hard to describe the tension surrounding "executing" (no pun intended) a scene like "The Interview with a Terrorist." Brüno through his obliviousness and ignorance would insult the terrorist from his personal appearance to disparaging his leader. And if we were still going, to show him the hostage video, which would likely deeply offend him.

Some scenes in *Borat* and *Brüno*, you see exactly as they went down. But some scenes require tricky editing of very disparate parts to provide the illusion of narrative cohesion. Sometimes these scenes were filmed in different cities, or even countries, and usually at different times in the shoot. The hope was the kidnapping and hostage video, both of which were staged and controlled by us, and the interview with the terrorist, in which much control had to be ceded due to its unpredictable nature and outcome, mainly we would not be killed, could somehow be cobbled together to seem that it all took place in relatively real time.

Of course, the audacity and the risk of these scenes were a big part of the point of them. And the high stakes of scenes such as these contributed to that, even if at times it required the illusion of verisimilitude, if not the real thing. A lot of this scene's success, at least on the surface, would be getting out of there alive.

Sometimes creating a reality was a necessity.

And by the very nature of *Brüno* as opposed to *Borat*, almost all scenes carried that high-risk ratio.

The Everest Hotel on the West Bank was our mutually agreed-upon meeting place. Though not geographically far from Jerusalem, it required crossing through the imposing newly constructed wall the Israelis had erected to separate the Palestinians even farther from Israel and many Israeli checkpoints to enter. The wall, very tall and monolithic, resembled nothing so much as the kind that surrounds a prison, and with armed Israeli soldiers, that feeling was not a coincidence. It was clearly intended to keep the Palestinians in their still disputed home and not easily cross over into Israeli territory proper.

Later on, in *Larry Charles' Dangerous World of Comedy*, I would spend more in-depth time on the West Bank, where these kind, gentle people, not terrorists, not criminals, not militants, but hard-working, peace-loving Palestinians, were literally "imprisoned" by the Israeli military, unable to move about freely and subject to their capriciousness of how the law was applied.

Another aspect of this location was that the Israeli security and fixers assigned to us once again refused to accompany us. If they thought it was too dangerous to take the risk, how would we possibly fare?

When we arrived, I felt even less secure. The Everest is a small quaint hotel in many ways. But it is five narrow steep stories straight up with one way in and one way out. We were scheduled to meet in a room on the top floor, accessible only by a narrow staircase. Once we were up there, it was clear if we were attacked, if this was any kind of a setup, there was no way out.

When we reached the top, there were two small rooms separated by a door, which opened directly onto the rickety stairs. We tried to keep our group as small as possible. Sacha as Brüno and Anthony the cameraman in one room. Our stalwart one-man sound department, Scott Harber, and I behind a closed door in the other.

We set up an unmanned camera to capture the two-shot, including the TV where the video would play between them, and Anthony would be responsible for the crucial coverage, the pans, the singles, the zoom-ins, etc. I had been through a lot with Anthony, and I knew he had balls of steel and great instincts.

We set up the hostage tape on a small TV, made sure everything was working, and then waited silently.

The room I was in had a window, which overlooked the front of the hotel. I noticed a couple of unidentified cars slowly, suspiciously circling the building. I also looked closely at the hotel's awning. I thought to myself, if we are ambushed, could I jump from here and land on the awning to break my fall? Maybe I'd break a leg but also be spared?

Soon enough, "the terrorist" arrived, accompanied by a translator. When you think someone is a "terrorist," it really colors your perception, but he had a name, Ayman Abu Aita, and he seemed to be armed only with his car keys, which he held throughout the interview.

Because of being surreptitiously sequestered behind the closed door, able only to hear what was being said on my headphones and seeing what Anthony pointed his camera at on my small monitor, I never saw the other man but heard his off-camera voice translating and perhaps even editorializing a bit.

Although, as I said, colored by our perceptions, the "terrorist" had a certain sinister mien, but in truth, he seemed more confused and befuddled than angry. The language barrier didn't help. Sacha recited elaborately worded jokes for which there really were no translations.

The "terrorist" was not effusive either in voice or expression and so hard to read. When he watched the video, he was likely offended but tried to be polite. Perhaps the most important aspect of the scene, Sacha's performance as Brüno and his ability to get through his prepared material, miraculously went off without a hitch.

But to a large degree, this scene was concocted in the editing room. Things that the "terrorist" said, expressions he had, were moved to opportune moments for maximum tension and laughs. In the scene as edited, he didn't always say what was said when it was said. We felt carte blanche to rearrange the elements of the scene for utmost impact. Although it was manipulated, in truth, it was no more manipulated than many scenes in both movies. To a large degree, that's how these scenes are made. Although the translator's off-camera voice is heard, the last line, "Get out. Get out now," was said not by him, but by an actor back in Los Angeles.

With that, we headed back to America. Little did we know that the darkness and hate we'd experienced abroad would be dwarfed, eclipsed by our own virulent homegrown version.

BRÜNO IN AMERICA

In Europe, especially within the fashion industry, the homophobia didn't seem as big an issue. It seemed like Brüno was dismissed more as Euro trash than for being gay. But in the United States, it was quite different.

America had been going through a long-overdue reckoning about gay rights. What is credited with beginning with the Stonewall riots in Greenwich Village in 1969, and staggered through the much-ignored AIDS crisis, the gay rights movement had not only never caught on with mainstream America, but had left simmering resentments, anger, and even hatred among those who felt threatened by any minority in this society declaring and demanding their equality.

And no matter what we did, no matter how funny, no matter how brilliantly conceptual, it cast a deep dark hue over the proceedings.

Add to it the blatant racism that emerged simultaneously with the rise of Barack Obama, and you could feel the hate oozing from America's pores and honestly, to a large degree, you can still feel it today.

Rather than the exhilaration we often felt upon completion of a great *Borat* scene, our mood was rather somber in the wake of shooting equally if not more brilliantly inspired scenes for *Brüno*.

We weren't enthusiastic about a lot that we had filmed. It was ugly and distressing and disturbing more than funny. Where *Borat* was strangely about love, *Brüno* was turning out to be about hate. A novel theme for a comedy.

Here are some examples.

On the night of Obama's victory in the 2008 election, we filmed *Brüno* having his ass waxed on Ventura Boulevard.

But a couple of nights later, in a series of San Bernardino bars, while trying to film a lonely, self-pitying, recently dumped Brüno lamenting his lot in life and trying to pick up a cowboy or a redneck to assuage those feelings, he had the following exchange with a drunken bar patron. And this is verbatim:

> **Brüno:** This is the worst day of my life.
>
> **Bar patron:** You? This is the worst day of *my* life. They just put a nigger in the White House.

For me, this was America distilled in one sentence. A singular cinematic moment. Even Sacha was visibly taken aback by the comment and didn't want it in the movie.

And that hate extended beyond the predictable, though overabundant homophobia, to some members of the gay community themselves, who saw a farce made by a group of straight men not politically appropriate at all.

As I've said, the movie was extreme in its concepts. And I always wanted to push, push, push to take it even beyond that. But sometimes I pushed too hard.

To play Brüno's unfaithful gold-digging boyfriend, Diesel, we had cast a sweet and very game young actor of Filipino descent, Clifford Bañagale. He was thrown into some situations that were beyond his imagination and experience.

The opening sequence in the movie was set in Brüno's Vienna

apartment but actually filmed on a soundstage at The Lot in West Hollywood. The writers had come up with a device, the pedal-powered fucking machine. An exercycle that powered a large thrusting dildo at the end. Our prop person was able to brilliantly execute a working version of the machine. It was decided that Clifford/Diesel would do the fucking and Brüno on his hands and knees would be getting fucked. But it was an illusion, of course. Sacha understandably wasn't about to take anything up the ass involuntarily.

But the rest of the sequence was a series of sight gags involving extreme gay sex. One involved the insertion of a fire extinguisher up Diesel's ass and turning it on. But as we did this again and again, deeper and deeper, and releasing the foam, we finally went too far and Clifford blacked out.

My paternal instinct, which was often in conflict with my comedic and directorial instinct, came out in situations like that, and as with Ken Davitian and Gustaf, I wound up being very protective of Clifford, without ever compromising the comedy, sometimes a difficult trick to pull off, and tried to make sure they didn't get hurt.

But Clifford was fearless and always game for a challenge. And he would have one on the rural outskirts of Kansas City.

The Midwest was having biblical floods that summer. Driving along the highways, trees, light and power poles were submerged in water almost to their very top.

There was something about this apocalyptic weather that colored what we did as well. On this day, we were to meet a white supremacist at his house. The concept of the scene was that Brüno was to meet him and begin to flirt with him. Brüno would then spill something on his own pants, which forced him to take them off, leaving Brüno wearing only very revealing and flamboyant thong underwear. As Brüno's pantless flirting grew more frenzied, Diesel was to burst in and "catch them" and accuse the white supremacist of trying to steal his boyfriend.

At least that was the idea.

Tension was high even before we entered the house. As we got ready to go in, standing in the teeming Midwest monsoon, Sacha stopped me. "You can't go in." "Why?" "You look too Jewish." "Me? *You* look too Jewish." We argued about who looked more Jewish while standing in front of this white supremacist's house. Of course, Sacha had to go in and naturally I understood that. And I often stayed outside, especially once I'd introduced myself as the authority figure, and the "marks" were seeking order in the chaos that was erupting from me and I'd be nowhere to be found, but I saw no reason to keep me out of this scene. The closer I was to the action, the more I could impact it. I was often able to keep things going even as they were in imminent danger of falling apart. And honestly, I thrived on the action.

But alas, I was destined to lose that argument, and Sacha and the crew entered while I stayed outside watching on the monitor and talking to Anthony and Wolfgang through my headset.

But even on the monitor, I could feel a weird ominousness. This guy proudly and blatantly displayed Nazi memorabilia throughout his house. This was only the second time I'd seen this. The first was in *Borat* when we unsuccessfully attempted a scene in an antisemitic veterinarian's house in South Carolina. In both cases it wasn't just a book on a shelf, it was many books, and art and flags, etc. This dingy modest farmhouse was a veritable mini museum of Nazi memorabilia.

Even as I was repulsed, I loved it too. This was our job, our mission, to root out these hateful racists and show them for what they were. I don't think America realized that in a country that celebrates the defeat of the Nazis there were people, and as it turned out many of them, who celebrated Hitler and the Third Reich and its eventual, and for them, inevitable return to power.

One of our security guys pretended to be a boom operator. This gave Sacha a false sense of security. But as I often told Sacha, if an angry target wanted to punch Sacha in the face, or even, God forbid, shoot Sacha with a concealed weapon, there would be no way that the security guard would ever be able to stop that. Yes, if it got more out of control than that, then sure, he would be expected to intervene. But myself, Dale, Anthony, and our AC Tim were, if not all big guys, always ready and willing to plunge in to save Sacha. In fact, Sacha's fate and safety were more important to me than anybody else's. I felt responsible for everyone's safety, but none more than Sacha, even though I did more to risk it.

The scene, despite the distraction of the Nazi keepsakes, was actually unfolding as planned. Sacha had spilled his drink, staining his pants and had gone to the bathroom to change and had emerged in his underwear. Though the white supremacist seemed nonplussed, he was still barely tolerating this blatantly flamboyantly gay man parading around and flirting with him. And barely tolerating was all we needed.

I learned how to read Sacha even from afar and knew that when he senses a safe response from the target, his instinct is to begin pushing to make the scene cross a line. This was a risky gambit but was often necessary if the scene was to have the magic moment that would force it without dispute into the movie. Otherwise it would either have to compete with the many scenes that didn't quite reach that level, though still unique and funny, or find another white supremacist in another city and do it all over again. In the wake of those moments, we'd dissect what went wrong and amp up the conflict, tension, and comedy for the next attempt.

The question would always be: Will we ever get to the next part of the scene? But as the white supremacist grew more enraged, it would be my responsibility at just the right moment before the white supremacist completely lost it to cue the abrupt arrival of Diesel. Sacha was blatantly flirting with the white supremacist and his attitude shifted from barely tolerant to almost murderous. I cued Diesel.

Diesel entered the scene. The white supremacist was confused. What the fuck is this? Diesel stayed in character and accused the white supremacist of cheating with his boyfriend. The white supremacist lost it and swung a creaky roundhouse kick at Diesel's head. At that moment, while still filming, the security guy jumped in, there was a momentary melee, and then everyone was thrown out.

Later, we would discover this wasn't your run-of-the-mill white supremacist or antisemite. This was Frazier Glenn Miller, one of the most infamous and notorious white supremacists in America. That modest dingy house held a massive cache of weapons. And when he became murderous, he followed through, and indeed just a few years later opened fire at a Jewish Center in the very suburb of Kansas City where we were staying, and murdered three people in cold blood, for which he was sentenced to death. He was not fucking around. His level of hatred was pretty unprecedented. As it turned out, none of his victims were actually even Jewish.

This was the culmination of a lifetime of hate crimes, many of which he was convicted of. He died in prison.

Other than some great barbecue, the flooded plains of Kansas City represented some of the most depressing times in my life and in the production of the movie. Besides the relentless rain, there was the relentless reign of hate. Virtually everywhere you turned.

To illustrate, the next sequence, which was filmed in the opposite order of how it occurs in the film, for reasons that will be apparent, was Brüno's confrontation with the Westboro Baptist Church. In fairness to the more conventional Baptists, they disowned the church and have never acknowledged them. You might remember them as the hate-filled "church" that protests at military and celebrity funerals with signs reading, GOD HATES FAGS and THANK GOD FOR DEAD SOLDIERS.

What can you say? They were completely insane. The problem is their hatred of African-Americans, Jews, homosexuals, and any aspect of society that tolerates those groups and other minorities hasn't dissipated, but instead proliferates, even today.

What happened to us? How did we get so fucked up?

The premise of the scene was rather simple. Brüno and Lutz, shackled together in their S & M gear, including a toilet brush in Lutz's mouth, find themselves on the street unable to free themselves. As they lumber along the road, they bump into, or perhaps crash into, a Westboro Baptist protest march. Of what? For what? No one, even they were never sure.

Not knowing who these people are, Brüno and Lutz march along with them, Brüno pleading for their help in unshackling his companion and himself.

Once again, we set the cameras with long lenses far enough from the action as to be inconspicuous. We might have been news crews giving them the publicity they constantly crave.

They weren't in a very altruistic mood. But rather than striking Brüno, which would not have surprised me, they tried to ignore the bound-and-chained couple. But Sacha, a comic opportunist in the best way, would never let this moment pass. Especially since he felt emboldened by the lack of violence that could be inflicted upon him, he intruded even deeper into the protest march, eventually getting himself and Lutz entangled with a placard-carrying church member until they all tumbled to the ground.

The scene that preceded this one in the movie was actually shot after.

The preceding scene would need to take place in a hotel room. The crew and I scouted a number of hotels in the Kansas City area. I remember repeatedly dismissing Sacha's concerns about my recognizability, but when coming out of one of the hotels and climbing back into the van, the valet who held the door open said, "Here you go, Mr. Charles..." I was mystified, but couldn't deny that he had a point. Needless to say, we didn't use that hotel.

Instead we chose the venerable Hotel Phillips, in downtown Kansas City. Once the tallest building in Kansas City, the Art Deco masterpiece had seen better days. They couldn't be too picky. We booked a suite.

The lobby was dark and dingy, looking and feeling more like a forgotten retirement home than a bustling hotel lobby. Our suite was yellowed with age like an old newspaper. It would be perfect.

The premise of this scene is that after a long absence, an acutely lonely Brüno reconnects with Lutz after committing "carbicide" by eating too many pies at the local Village Inn, and caught up in the moment, they have sex. It seems pointless to call any sex scene in this movie "making love" or "sleeping together." Far too polite for what we depict.

The sex in question is a night of debauchery worthy of Pasolini's *Salo*, Fellini's *Satyricon*, or Bob Guccione's *Caligula*. Those were my personal inspirations.

Though it starts innocently and even romantically enough, by the time they wake up in the morning, we see how far they have taken it. There is shit splattered and flung against the walls (in this case, amazingly, not real shit though we had used the real thing many times), like some sort of bas-relief sculpture or variation on a Jackson Pollock painting. We had put up large plastic sheets to protect the actual walls of the hotel and to make cleanup and escaping easy.

There are remnants of their bizarre sexual practices strewn around the room. Somewhere in the middle of this session they inadvertently ordered *Mr. Magorium's Wonder Emporium* by getting the remote stuck in Lutz's rectum.

And they're now trapped in the bed, shackled in chains, one end attached to a choke collar around Lutz's neck, a toilet brush acting as a gag inside his mouth, both in the aforementioned S & M gear.

Once we had shot the shit out of the setup, so to speak, we were ready for phase two of the scene.

They needed help.

As per the script, we called maintenance.

When the maintenance man arrived, to find Brüno and Lutz in their compromised positions and a camera crew recording the whole thing, he was undoubtedly stunned but surprisingly sanguine. Despite Brüno's pleas and his complaint about being charged unfairly for *Dr. Magorium's Wonder Emporium* because of shoving the remote up Lutz's ass, the maintenance man didn't think he could, should, or would do anything and instead stepped out into the corridor and called the manager in the lobby, trying to explain what he had stumbled into while the cameras recorded the conversation.

When the manager came up, the mood changed. He was almost perfectly cast. Fastidious and impatient and indignant like Franklin Pangborn stumbling into Laurel and Hardy in the same position. After a few minutes of banter in which he made no progress with

Brüno, who continued his pleas and complaints, the manager left to call the police.

Now, at this point I had shot about a movie and a half of Sacha's shenanigans and we'd had our share of run-ins with the police. I was no longer intimidated by those threats, knowing that we had actually not broken any laws and, in fact, had a signed-and-paid-for agreement with the hotel management, which in the past had proven to be ironclad, and I felt confident after quite a bit of practice in eloquently pleading our case. Because of that, I felt no need to rush or run or panic. I was prepared to deal with the police and explain the legality of what we were doing.

I instructed the crew to pack up and wrap the location as they would from any scene, and we would calmly take the elevator down and walk through the lobby and out the front doors of the hotel to the van, which was waiting below.

I also knew from experience that the police did not rush to these scenes, and chances are we'd be long gone before we even heard sirens, let alone when they arrived.

As I have stated before, some of our security guys on various continents were extremely cool guys, exercising admirable restraint and discretion and good judgment.

But there were some glaring exceptions. Like the security guy who sat in the back of our van watching graphic kill videos from Iraq and sadistically subjecting the crew to them. I would sit in the passenger seat and hear gunfire and screaming from the back. He didn't make it more than a day or two before being dismissed.

And then there was another overly intense British ex-soldier turned "security guy." Sacha had been enamored of the British security guys, and indeed as I've described, the guys who accompanied us in Jordan and elsewhere were among the coolest cats I'd encountered. They kept us out of trouble and danger often without anyone noticing. Even us.

But this one was different. He was British. And highly decorated. But he was a bit too gung ho and exceedingly, absurdly zealous.

Despite my assurances that there was no reason to run or rush or panic, without asking permission he completely ignored me and immediately swept up Sacha and Gustaf, still trapped in their S & M gear, and raced out of the room and down the hallway, not to the normal elevators but to an obscure service elevator far beyond those where the hallway ended. Although racing might be the wrong word when two men are attached by the neck and feet by taut thick chains.

As we continued packing up and wrapping, he threw the two actors, the star and co-star of the movie, think about that, into the service elevator and headed down.

We had more than enough time to get them out of their gear and into normal clothes before they left, but he chose to abscond with them in their constraining and frankly dangerous costumes. This gear was not made for quick escapes.

Meanwhile, we had cleaned up the scene and wheeled our stuff to the elevator bank, entered the elevator, and ridden down to the lobby. We strode through the lobby. No one stopped us. No one said a word. And indeed we exited the lobby to our waiting van, put our stuff in the back, and climbed in.

I expected that Sacha, as usual, had already made his safe escape and was ahead of us, but I was informed that they had never emerged from the hotel. Hmmm? What happened?

Of course no one knew.

Still assuming they were right behind us, or were long gone, I had our van wait just to make sure.

But what had actually occurred was far from that. Once in the service elevator going down, literally and figuratively, this security guy, who will remain nameless, perhaps in the midst of some sort of flashback, realized the elevator did not go to the lobby but ended its downward journey on the ninth floor. They were forced to get out. Still believing they were being pursued, he chose not to take them to the normal elevators. He made the ill-fated decision to force them to climb out the window at the end of the hallway and take the fire escape. For nine stories.

Having no choice, Sacha and Lutz clanked and clomped down the rickety metal stairs barely affixed to the side of the building. But that wasn't the end of it. The bottom had not been reached, literally and figuratively.

The fire escape ended on a roof too high for even an experienced jumper to attempt. But this maniac forced Sacha and Gustaf, still attached, to make the leap to the ground below. Remember, Gustaf was wearing a tight choke chain around his neck, a toilet brush in his mouth, and both wore large Kiss-like platform boots.

Unhappy with this choice but having no other, after a moment they jumped. They hit the ground, and upon impact, Sacha broke his foot.

They lurched to the van, which was around the corner of the building because they had no idea where Sacha and Gustaf had landed. Literally.

But the damage was done. We left Kansas City and headed for Kentucky, where we were informed that Sacha's fracture was serious. We had to shut down the movie.

BRÜNO'S BROKEN FOOT

Shutting down in Kentucky might've been the end of the movie. We weren't enthusiastic about a lot that we had filmed. Although endlessly anthropologically and sociologically fascinating and compelling, it was also ugly and distressing and disturbing more than funny.

But instead of shutting down, we spent the five or so weeks of Sacha's rehabilitation and recovery giving everyone a chance to recharge and redoubling our efforts to make this movie great.

Many new brilliantly unique and potentially hilarious conceptual scenes were formulated. All to underscore the increasingly absurd lengths that Brüno was willing to go in his insatiable quest for fame.

Brüno essentially swapping an iPod for a black baby in Africa, lampooning the weird trend at the time of white privileged elitists adopting children of color from impoverished countries. We shot at the baggage claim at LAX as unsuspecting travelers waited for their luggage. Brüno had returned from Africa. And among the luggage that circled the carousel was a fairly flimsy cardboard box. When Brüno and Lutz pulled it off the carousel and opened it to reveal a black baby, people around them were stunned.

We then staged a talk show hosted by then-popular Jerry Springer–like Richard Bey with at least two or maybe even three unsuspecting audiences bussed in as they do on those shows, in which Brüno proudly and shamelessly displayed the baby like a prop. The audience's outrage increased as the show went on, culminating in Brüno announcing he had given the baby a proper African name: O.J. Soon afterward, a legitimate representative of Child Protective Services came onto the show and took possession of the baby, who by now had fallen asleep. The crowds were excited that Brüno had lost his ill-gotten baby, but the result was a deep sadness for Brüno, which became hard to laugh at or with, despite its patented absurdity.

The two or three audiences were seamlessly edited together to look like one, but if you look closely, you will see elements of all three in the cut as we were concerned with the best and funniest responses in that tabloid talk show vein.

The baby was one of a set of twins that we switched out throughout the shoot, per child labor law regulations, though in reality we had very little supervision in terms of protecting the baby ourselves. We were left to our own devices and tried to be responsible. But I noticed that the babies would fall asleep even in the loudest, brightest chaotic environments like the airport and the talk show. Although the parents were really nice and cooperative, I was informed that the mom was a nurse, and I came to believe that the babies were being drugged. I never got confirmation of this, but since I'd had four children who rarely slept through anything, this was my strong suspicion.

I doubt they remember much of it and hope they are doing well today and can laugh at their participation in the movie. But if they felt differently, if they felt they were exploited, either by us or their parents or both, I would have to understand.

Besides the talk show, Brüno wanted to do a photo shoot to

introduce himself and his latest accessory, O.J., to the world. But the photo shoot was conceived as hilariously dangerous and offensive. In one photo, an exposed O.J. is being held by Brüno, who wears a beekeeper's costume while bees swarmed around them. In another, O.J. is crucified on a cross while other babies dressed as Roman soldiers surround him. In yet another, O.J. and the other babies reenact a tableau from the Nazi Holocaust.

Most of these were carefully staged and even photoshopped, although the bees were real.

In order to cast the babies, Brüno holds an audition, where young parents are so eager to get their newborns and infants into show business, they're willing to entertain thoughts of putting their eight-week-olds on crash diets or even undergo liposuction, and they have no issues with putting them in dangerous situations, like explosions, or dressing them as little Nazi soldiers.

While conceptually funny, it couldn't help also being jaw dropping and harrowing even to us. This line would be continuously and bravely blurred and become characteristic of the movie itself.

In LA, we rented a swanky house in the hills to shoot *Brüno's* pilot, in another desperate attempt to capture the elusive fame, which included a montage of Brüno in provocative poses and close-ups of his flaccid dick (a double's) flopping around in time to some pulsating dance music. It was then shown to a series of unsuspecting focus groups, all of whom unanimously hated it.

While there, we also staged the infamous Mexican chair people scene. Luring quasi-celebrities to be interviewed for his pilot, Brüno realized that the expensive chairs he ordered would not be arriving, and forced to hastily improvise, he enlisted the gardening crew outside to crouch on all fours and serve as chairs. This was crazy enough. But what was far crazier, and of course the point, was that almost no celebrity who attended thought it was weird and gladly sat on the obviously straining men.

Among the celebrities who bragged of her humanitarian pursuits while sitting on the men was Paula Abdul, who after some hesitation, seemed to find the concept rather chic and trendy.

Perhaps the most fascinating to the American crew members was scandal-plagued baseball great Pete Rose, who didn't mind sitting on the men very much but was deeply offended by Brüno himself. He threatened to punch Brüno out before his abrupt departure.

And then there was La Toya Jackson. She sat quite willingly on the men as Brüno rather blatantly tried to wheedle information about Michael Jackson out of her, including his personal phone number.

This led to one of the most surreal moments in the movie. Well, not really in the movie, but at the premiere.

But in the meantime, we were shooting scenes that were unquestionably audacious and one of a kind. And the comedy could not be denied.

BRÜNO'S SEX TAPE

It was decided that Brüno would conclude that a sex tape with a famous person would be his ticket to fame, or at least infamy. He really didn't care which.

This led us to Washington DC. I think it was only for a day. But it was a momentous day. We booked a suite in a DC hotel with the premise being that we would lure politicians to the room under the guise of doing an interview for European youth TV. At a certain opportune moment mid-interview, the power would go out, which was literally just me holding a plug in my hand and pulling it, and Brüno and the "guest" would have to take a break while it was fixed. The only room not in a manufactured frenzy of activity as we "rushed" to address the problem was conveniently the bedroom, where they would retreat and where hidden cameras had been planted, totally legal by the way in DC, and Brüno would flirt, first innocently, then mercilessly, leading to Brüno's disrobing. At this point, who knew what would happen. Perhaps one would cross a line and forever compromise themselves.

We did the scene four times in one day. With Christian activist Gary Bauer; with America's first Secretary of Homeland Security, former Pennsylvania governor Tom Ridge; with John Bolton, who had worked in numerous Republican administrations, though he became much more famous during his stormy tenure with Trump; and finally with Ron Paul, who ran for president three times and was running at the time.

We'd gotten the first part of the scene pretty well down. The plug would be pulled, Brüno and guest would retreat to the bedroom, but the bedroom also had a door, and Bauer, the first guest, beat a hasty retreat before anything untoward could happen.

I realized that the second door made it too easy for the "guests" to bail so we moved all our luggage and created a labyrinthine path that led to a dead end so the guest could not simply exit the bedroom door, but would have to retrace his steps back through the bedroom and through the front room to the main door.

For Tom Ridge, this was unnecessary. Seriously or not, he seemed quite unfazed and nonchalant in the face of Brüno's blatant flirtations.

Of the four, Ridge was a dashing guy with a thick black Elvis-like pompadour with charm to match and seemed to thoroughly enjoy himself. But his time ran out and he had to leave.

We still didn't have the scene.

Bolton was next. All went well, the power went out, they retreated to the bedroom, but Bolton quickly got uncomfortable. He saw the bedroom door in the distance but didn't notice the insurmountable obstacles to get there, so he headed desperately to the door and then was stopped in his tracks by the mountain of luggage. But he had no intention of staying one more minute and pushed his way back into the front room and out the door.

It was pretty funny, but it still wasn't the scene.

Finally, there was Ron Paul. The power went out. They retreated to the bedroom. But as Brüno upped the ante on his flirtations with champagne and strawberries, Ron Paul tried to ignore him. Paul sat on the bed thumbing through a magazine waiting to resume the interview. But it allowed Sacha to hit all the beats we had aspired to in the scene.

Although Paul tried to ignore him, that was impossible with Brüno. And finally when Brüno de-pantsed, Ron Paul had enough and pushed past Brüno and made a hasty exit. As he entered the front room, where we were pretending to fix the power, I asked what was wrong and he uttered the phrase that's in the movie, "He's queer as blazes."

Indeed he was. But we had the scene.

Recently I saw Ron Paul get caught doing a Zoom meeting in his underwear and thought how close we were to some deeper truth.

BRÜNO IN LA

Brüno was shot during the controversy over Prop 8 in California, which was part of a larger national discussion about gay marriage. Los Angeles, which has one of the largest gay communities in the world and is one of the two or three most progressive cities in the United States, had managed to garner enough support to get this proposition, to ban gay marriage, on the ballot. It was outrageous and absurd. And it passed.

In its wake, people took to the streets. We headed downtown to perhaps the biggest rally of its kind. It was typical of Los Angeles. All sides, including the fringe, the extreme, and the downright insane, were represented, which in typical Los Angeles fashion, resulted in complete chaos.

Brüno would stealthily infiltrate a Prop 8 support protest and sort of take over, eventually in theory, leading the easily manipulated homophobic crowd in an inadvertent chant in support of not merely gay rights, but a blatant graphic celebration of homosexuality before they realized it.

But as Sacha successfully worked his way into the crowd, with Anthony and me trailing him to record the proceedings, I noticed another cameraman also shooting Sacha. I quickly realized he was some sort of freelance stringer who had recognized Sacha. And clearly his intention was to unmask him for his own profit. I got it. We are all doing our jobs, right. But his "job" was interfering with ours. And I simply couldn't allow that.

He and Anthony were jostling for position amid the crowd. I

came up behind the stringer and stated calmly that I knew and understood what he was doing but could he please back off as he was ruining our scene. He not only refused but pushed deeper and more aggressively into the scene until he and Anthony, cameras on their shoulders, were essentially fighting. I had to jump in. For Anthony, yes, though I knew from experience that he could take care of himself, but for the sake of the scene, which I felt was crucial in blurring that line between reality and alternate reality that was the hallmark of this movie.

I gave the dude one more chance, less polite this time, to get out of the way, and much less politely, he refused, at which point I grabbed him by the hood of his hoodie and whipped him around and into the ground. Before it went any further, Dale jumped in as he often had to and quickly spirited me away. But the stringer called over the mounted police trying to keep order and immediately filed a complaint.

In the wake of this incident, the stringer edited together his footage to favor his very self-serving rendition of the events, which he posted quickly on YouTube, which in turn led to the police opening an investigation into my behavior. This went on for six months.

Finally, we put together our version of the events with our footage, which showed conclusively that he was the aggressor with Anthony and was intruding where he didn't belong and my actions were focused on defending both Anthony, and Sacha, and of course, the most important thing, the scene.

The investigation was finally dropped.

Part of Brüno's backstory was that he had been the lover of Rob Pilatus, one of the original members of the notorious lip-synching R & B duo Milli Vanilli, who had died tragically of a drug overdose in 1998.

By this time in the story, Brüno was lost and looking for guidance and decided to seek help from a psychic whom he hoped could get him in touch with the spirit of Rob.

We found a willing psychic on Ventura Boulevard and in a darkened room he conjured for Brüno the invisible presence of the late lip-syncher. "He's here," he kept insisting, and with little more prompting than that, Brüno's longing for his long-lost love quickly turned semi-pornographic.

For me, this was one of Sacha's tour de force moments. Of course, there were many. The bravery of Sacha's performance as Brüno, the risk, the stakes, the levels, far exceed even that of Borat, which had easily been the most audacious performance I had ever witnessed up until that point, let alone be directing.

But here he was, pulling down the invisible Rob's pants, performing a graphic fellatio upon him, turning him around, licking his ass, and generally and intensely pleasuring the unseen specter of Rob Pilatus. It became more and more frenzied, licking, blowing, flicking, fingering, as the psychic looked on with increasing chagrin.

By the end, Brüno was grateful. He had the answers he was looking for and knew how to proceed on his journey. But the psychic, who had been exposed as a fraud, was pissed.

I tried to assuage him somewhat, but he knew he had signed a release and accepted payment, and thus like so many people in our travels who regretted their encounters with Borat and Brüno, he had completely lost control of his fate.

It remains, purely as a performance piece, one of my favorite scenes in the movie.

But Sacha would keep topping himself in sequence after sequence.

BRÜNO AND THE SWINGERS' PARTY

One of the conceits presented during the course of the movie was Brüno's ignorant and slightly naive yet cynical epiphany that all the famous men in Hollywood were actually straight. He cites a number of Hollywood's leading men whose actual sexual preference has always been questioned. But his conclusion is that he must be straight to achieve his dream of stardom at any cost.

To this end, he decides to attend a swingers' party, where he pretends to be straight in hopes to pick up some tips on heterosexual sex. This led to a series of encounters with the men in various swinging couples. While fully clothed on a patio, Brüno and another man run through some positions, and although some of them can be considered "straight," the way they do it suggests anything but.

Fully clothed Brüno enters a room where a naked man and woman are fucking. The woman gets very annoyed quickly. And appropriately. But the man just wants to keep going. While they try to continue, Brüno offers encouragement, which quickly shifts from verbal to physical, putting his hands on the naked man's body, which eventually becomes too distracting. The man tries to be patient but eventually gets angry and Brüno leaves.

For the final scene in the sequence, we hired a dominatrix who was tasked with taking Brüno's heterosexual virginity. Although she was an intimidating-looking woman, tall, especially in the boots, with large obviously fake boobs, in reality she seemed like a gentle person who saw this as a gig.

Sure enough, she is extremely patient with Brüno, trying to ease him into disrobing and having sex. But Brüno does everything he can, makes every excuse to squirm out of it.

The scene wasn't working. Sacha's will was far stronger than hers, and if his job was to avoid sex, he was succeeding too well.

He had said to me before we began to stop the scene if it seemed like they were actually about to have sex. He was controlling the scene and the situation too much, and she was far too cooperative and understanding and sex did not seem to be on the horizon. I asked her to come out into the hallway.

Once out there, I reminded her of what she had been hired for, and if she didn't perform as promised, she wouldn't be paid. Yes, I threatened to withhold her pay if she didn't successfully complete the task of taking Bruno's heterosexual virginity. She was not to take no for an answer, she was to push brusquely past any resistance, she was to do her job and not to leave the room until that job was done. It wasn't true, but it was some of my best direction in the movie, and it motivated her.

She stepped back into the room. She was now the dominatrix. I think she even caught Sacha by surprise with her newfound aggression. She forced him to take off his clothes, down to the last layer of his many pairs of underwear. Then she removed his belt and began whipping him with it to submit. I could hear the thwack and see Sacha wince and knew it was real.

She chased him around the room. This was the scene. I wondered if it was going too far, but I've wondered that a lot and didn't want to stop it, didn't think Sacha would want me to stop it unless sex was imminent, which I knew it wasn't.

Eventually, Brüno could take no more and literally jumped through the window, smashing it to shards around his barefoot almost naked body. Thank goodness he didn't get cut. We hadn't really considered the possibility. We got lucky. The cameras followed him as he ran away into the woods. The dominatrix earned her money.

BRÜNO IN THE SOUTH

This was actually Brüno's last appearance as himself before he transformed into his new heterosexual alter ego, Straight Dave. But in the South, we shot three more seminal (you should pardon the expression) scenes of him trying to adopt a straight lifestyle.

The first was at Fort McClellan in Alabama, now a National Guard training facility, where he would be put through some basic training by a couple of willing drill instructors.

My first observation was how easy it was to access the grounds. We weren't really asked for any identification before we were waved through, despite being two strange white unmarked vans filled with black bags with obvious equipment tucked inside.

I've mentioned this phenomenon before, both when getting stopped by the Secret Service in Washington during *Borat*, and when we accompanied Father Foster up to his apartment next to the pope in Rome on *Religulous*.

No one asked us shit.

But here we were on a military base. Hundreds of recruits are going through training right in front of us as we walked in carrying these bulky black bags with "stuff" inside. What if they contained explosives or automatic weapons? There would be no way any soldier on the base would be able to defend themselves.

This reminded me again about the lie of national security. Since 9/11, we were told we were safe, but everything I saw doing these movies, particularly that day, illustrated that not only wasn't that true, but even the military themselves weren't safe from attack.

The scene, Brüno being put through the paces by two seemingly tough but very sympathetic drill sergeants, was undoubtedly funny in an almost classic fish-out-of-water way. It was a slightly more innocent and likable Brüno.

But soon enough, word spread on the base that there were interlopers there. Us. It was time to beat a hasty retreat. And as if to finalize my observation about national security, as we climbed into our vans and sped just past the slowly closing gates intended to stop us and to a nearby shopping center parking lot to immediately ship the tapes back to Los Angeles, I wondered how we were so easily able to gain access and especially gain egress from an American military base, only to be informed that because of steep cuts in the budget, much of the infrastructure of American military bases had been outsourced to independent private companies who have no direct contact with the base leadership. That meant we were able to easily escape before the military was able to communicate to the gate to stop us.

Lucky for us. Unlucky for the country?

Perhaps the most arduous scene we shot was the infamous hunting scene. This scene took hours to set up and even more hours to execute. It's hard for an audience to realize that a scene that might be only a couple of minutes on-screen may have taken over seven or eight hours to shoot in real time without breaks, and that means cameramen carrying equipment and especially Sacha staying in character. In this case, with armed and hostile and homophobic men surrounding him.

We hung out with these three hunters for a couple of hours, getting them comfortable with the idea of taking this effeminate Austrian out to hunt with them. They weren't necessarily bad guys; after all, they didn't shoot anybody. And they weren't even particularly unreasonable guys. They tolerated Brüno's strange behavior. But they had their line in the sand. And that included, despite numerous pleas, to have their loaded weapons with them at all times.

This was one of the most complicated scenes to set up. It verged on convolution though the premise itself was relatively simple. After many hours of stalking and shooting game, all of which needed to be covered even though it only takes up less than a minute of the actual scene, the hunters and Brüno, after sitting around a campfire, are to retreat to their tents for the night, where Brüno, ostensibly frightened of the dark, shits in his tent and, completely naked, tries to share a tent with one of the obviously unwilling hunters.

I said "relatively simple."

So, sometimes it is necessary to create not only alternate realities, but multiple alternate realities in order to achieve one reality. In this case, Sacha couldn't spontaneously shit in the tent in real time, so in the midst of all that was going on, someone else, it might've been Jason Alper, who seems to have the circus-freak-like ability to shit on cue, took a shit, a very real one, and secreted it in the tent. Then in front of the hunters, it would be "revealed" that one of our PAs, a young German-speaking woman whose job it was primarily to speak to Brüno in German before scenes to lend credibility to his identity, had out of nervousness and fear, taken the shit herself. At that point, playing the "director," I became irate that she would do such an indiscreet thing. She began to cry. This was all performance, mind you, without cameras, for the benefit of the hunters, who rather than being pissed that somebody had shit in a tent, defended the honor of the PA. This loosened them up, no pun intended, for what was to come and allowed there to already be a shit planted when it was time for Brüno to go to sleep in his tent.

It was already pitch black when this occurred, and now it was time for the infamous campfire scene. Brüno sat amid the hunters, the fire raging before them. I remember asking them once again before this began if they would consider putting down their guns. Again, they refused and did the entire scene holding their loaded weapons, growing increasingly angry as Brüno made barely disguised gay sexual innuendo, compared them to the *Sex and the City* girls, and looked up at the star-filled sky and remarked how it reminded him of all the hot guys in the world. This led to one of the longest and most awkward silences in sound movies. You could almost hear the hunters saying to themselves, *"I'm going to kill this motherfucker."*

Although the fire is lighting up their immediate area, it was ink black darkness all around them. We stood in that darkness filming. As the scene, such as it was, ended, the hunters' anger grew and there was much movement in the dark, but it was too dark to distinguish crew from hostile armed hunter. It was a recipe for disaster that fortunately was averted. But we still had the tent scene.

If I'm not mistaken, at least two of the three hunters bailed after the campfire scene, leaving perhaps only one hunter left to participate in the sleep-out. He slept in one tent, Brüno in the other. Then with infrared cameras, we shot Brüno's numerous attempts to wheedle his way into the hunter's tent, leading eventually to him trying to get in while naked, explaining that a bear had eaten all his clothes but had left these condoms, etc., until the hunter, ready to explode or shoot, had had enough and stormed out of the tent at us.

But miraculously we had a one-of-a-kind scene, and no one had been hurt. Always the goal.

THE CAGE FIGHT

"Luck is the residue of design." But sometimes luck is just luck too. A strange mystery based on numerous variables that no planning can ever anticipate.

Much of what was shot with Sacha was based on that mystical truth. Beyond our comprehension. No amount of control imposed on any situation could truly control the situation. Control, to a large degree, is an illusion. Luck occurs in that nonrational realm between complete control and complete letting go. For a director, that is a valuable lesson to learn. One I learned over and over again. And not always willingly.

Case in point, the cage fight. So much of the story of the cage fight has been well chronicled:

How we set it up originally in Texarkana, Arkansas. How we built the cage. How we offered cheap beer to the audience. How we were assured by our security team (one guy) that no one would be able to breach the cage. And then once the scene started and Sacha as Brüno as Straight Dave challenged the audience, but before the scene proper could take place, how an angry aggressive cage fighter came out of the audience and scaled the cage in three seconds and challenged Sacha/Brüno/Straight Dave, and how Sacha had to be swiftly removed from the scene before he got the living shit beat out of him.

For that first night, Sacha had wanted some sort of tunnel attached to a trap door built into the ring so that he could make an easy escape in case something went wrong. But based on the expert security man's assessment, it was deemed unnecessary. I had resisted the idea based on aesthetic reasons. I wanted to do the scene once because I felt it would be tough to stage such an event easily again. Sacha went along as well, but very reluctantly. But after the incident the first night in Texarkana, I couldn't argue with him. He needed a quick escape valve or someone might really kill him.

So the next day in a completely different town, Fort Smith, most famous as the corporate headquarters of Walmart, at some expense, we had a crew build a trap door attached to a tunnel that led outside, where a waiting van would whisk Sacha to safety. I hoped it wouldn't have to be used, or at least not used until we had the scene in its entirety.

Although the setup from the beer to Straight Dave's preamble would be the same, there was now a tunnel at the end of which a van would be waiting. Further, unlike the night before, the chairs were zip-tied together so no one could simply pick one up and fling it into the ring.

The elements were in place as best as they could be to get all the way to the end of the scene.

As was the case the night before, I had cameras placed around the venue, some manned and some affixed in position. We often hired local cameramen, whether it was Paris or Fort Smith, to help us out. Plus, once again, Anthony would be inside the cage with Sacha getting various closer coverage. I stood behind a curtain on the other side of the cage with eleven monitors and tried to track the action, treating it like a live sporting event, which it was. A blood sporting event.

And this time, the variables worked in our favor and we completed the scene that serves as the climax of the movie. But not without the chaos being barely kept at bay. By the time Lutz got into the ring, the crowd was in a frenzy of blood lust and were not prepared when Straight Dave and Lutz's wrestling match turned into a homosexual love fest. At first, they were stunned virtually into silence as they processed what they were seeing. For many, it was probably the first time they saw two men kissing, let alone graphically making out. It was a case of mass cognitive dissonance. It took a moment to process that what they were seeing was what they were seeing. No one took it as a joke. But soon everyone believed it was real. And then the silence turned to violence.

As they began to scream and shout and throw their beer and anything else they could grab into the ring, Sacha knew that he had something and kept going as the beer and detritus rained down upon them. A courageous Gustaf stayed in it as well. But the crowd had lost control. And so had we. And once someone had finally figured out how to get the chairs loose and the first one flew into the ring just barely missed their heads, it was time to wrap it up.

Sacha headed into the tunnel. Lutz and Anthony had been left behind. Somehow they finally made their way into the tunnel. Waiting in the van were Dale and the security detail, and they quickly sped away. Meanwhile I was still behind the curtain making sure we had close-ups and reactions of the angry and stunned crowd. But soon the crowd pushed through the curtain and confronted me, followed quickly by an angry cadre of police, who didn't appreciate us causing a riot in their town.

In situations like this, I don't fear as much for my safety, though perhaps I should. My primary concern is that the tapes are safe. I made sure I had possession of them as the mob and the cops descended upon me. But I stopped them in their tracks, as if I was holding a bomb, and loudly announced that I didn't care what they did to me, I wasn't giving up these tapes. I told them that I knew my rights, that we had every legal permission to be here and I would be leaving with these tapes, so if they wanted them, they'd have to kill me. I admit it was overkill, but overkill was the theme of the night, and I knew I couldn't live with myself if the tapes had been confiscated and possibly destroyed after all that. And in that moment, that seemed like a distinct possibility. After an excruciatingly long wait, a van appeared, and I and whoever was left behind climbed in and were sprinted away.

We had the scene. We had the climax of the movie. We had the tapes. It's in the movie.

•••

Like *Borat*, *Brüno* was a hard movie to edit. There was so much footage, and much of it was great. And some of it was hilarious, and some of it was harrowing, and some of it was hateful. And sometimes all at the same time. Could it be synthesized into a coherent movie? But this time, unlike *Borat*, we had six editors often working on multiple versions of the same scene. The chaos we had created on camera was now spilling over to the editing room. Editors were brought on and let go.

Sacha and I had clashed at various times during the movie. Those tensions had escalated quite a bit since the phenomenal success of *Borat*. It became clear to me that Sacha, who was the star, co-writer, and producer, wanted control and didn't seem to be interested any longer in collaboration. Only for us, the writers, the editors, myself, to do what he said. Some people were confused. Some people were happy to go along. I wasn't. It wasn't me. I felt like my voice was being drowned out by this groupthink and the movie would suffer as a result. I understood what Sacha wanted, but I vehemently disagreed. And I felt it was my job to continue to present my alternative point of view on scenes, themes, and the movie as a whole. I wasn't about to come this far and just walk away. I would have to be pushed away at this point. But I was made to feel like an outsider as people curried favor with Sacha, who held all the power. I transcended that, and my mantra remained as it does today: "What's best for the movie."

It was a tough movie with a tough tone to achieve. And I think, considering all that had happened during the shoot, we arrived at a version of the movie we all felt represented what we shot and experienced and felt.

I knew it could never have the universal appeal of *Borat*. The lead character was a narcissistic solipsistic homosexual. The world and the America it portrayed were not places of tolerance and acceptance as in *Borat*, but more of the true America. The America that Americans themselves don't want to face, especially in a comedy. A dark, angry, hateful, violent place filled with deeply held prejudices and simmering resentment. All of which we've now seen come to the surface with the success of Donald Trump.

But in that sense, the movie was a one-of-a-kind event.

So, though I was thoroughly alienated by the postproduction of the movie, I was also extremely proud of it. Everyone had worked hard and put it all on the line. And as the premiere approached, my emotions were a mixture of excitement and anxiety.

I assumed I would never work with Sacha again, but I felt we had made two classic films together that presented the two sides of the coin of America and the world. Two unique documents that could never be replicated. What more could I ask for? So though I myself had much lingering simmering resentment, I was also grateful to Sacha for giving me the opportunity.

Again, on a certain level, I sympathized and supported Sacha's bitchiness. After spending sixteen to eighteen hours in character, you can take off the wig but you can't simply shut off your mind.

Which brings us to the premiere.

Having painfully separated from Barbara and my kids but wanting to stay close, I was living in a high-rise on the Wilshire Corridor in Westwood. My apartment on a high floor had a terrace that faced north toward Bel Air.

On the day of the premiere, set to take place at Grauman's Chinese Theatre on Hollywood Boulevard, I sat nervously on the terrace, as I often do when my work is about to be exposed to the public, when I saw a helicopter rising from the stately hills of Bel Air and heading to and then landing at the UCLA Medical Center, also within my view. I don't know why, but I had an instinct about who was in the helicopter and what had happened. I flipped on the news and had it confirmed. Michael Jackson was dead. On the day of the premiere. And I watched the whole thing unfold live in front of me.

There was a mad scramble. The editors were rushed to the theater and literally physically removed the La Toya scene from the print that would show that night. And at the premiere that night, already tainted by the death of Michael Jackson, the red carpet laid out for Brüno's arrival wound up covering up Michael Jackson's star right in front of the theater.

Brüno could never escape that vibe. Gloom and sadness and darkness and, as I have mentioned, hate hung over the movie like a persistent cloud, which made the comedy that much harder to be enjoyed.

If Sacha deserved an Oscar for *Borat*, he deserved to have the award name changed to the Sacha for *Brüno*. It's hard to act when you secretly fear you are about to be injured or killed, and that was a virtual daily reality, which makes his unprecedented singular performance that much more astonishing.

In many ways, *Brüno* is a braver, bolder, and more radical film. I often compared the two movies to the Beastie Boys' first two albums. *Licensed to Ill* was a good-time raucous American party record. Their second, *Paul's Boutique*, was more jagged, post-modern, complicated, and complex. Borat was *Licensed to Ill*. Brüno was *Paul's Boutique*. Which also explains why *Brüno* was far less popular than *Borat*. Guy Debord would've been proud. *Brüno* was truly a spectacle.

CHAPTER 14

WHEN YOU REACH THE TOP OF THE HILL, YOU CAN SEE THE END OF THE ROAD (SHIVA)

By nature, I am a private person. I am reluctant to share personal details about my family. To protect them. And protect myself. From what? Embarrassment? Shame? Yes. So while there is a noble intention, there is also a selfish one.

Here goes.

I never really gave a thought to being a husband or a father. I never thought about love. As vivid as my imagination was, those scenarios never entered the picture.

My father had seemed really into fatherhood when I was a young boy. We did everything together. If he needed to drive somewhere, to see his siblings, or to go clothes shopping, he would take me along. And there was a lot of singing and joking in the car. On Sundays, we'd get up early and walk on Brighton Beach Avenue, picking up the Sunday *Times* and bagels and lox. Or in the summer, walk over to the beach and have it to ourselves for a little while.

But by the time my brother was born, my father was bored

and resentful and offered virtually nothing that resembled fatherly behavior, except absence and infidelity.

I wanted to be an artist. I wanted to be successful. I didn't want to be him.

I considered myself a good person. Compassionate and sympathetic. Decent and ethical and honorable. But how? What was the proof? Just me thinking it without corresponding actions didn't seem sufficient. If I was a good person, with all those altruistic characteristics, what had I ever done for anybody that could be perceived as a kindness? I racked my brains, but other than holding a door, or giving up a seat on the subway, I was hard pressed to make my case.

Yes, as I think back, those were lies, or if not lies, half truths I told myself. The "whole" truths were much less wholesome.

I was involved with crimes, even though I told myself I wasn't.

I was unfaithful to virtually every woman I was ever with. I hurt a lot of people.

And I can honestly say, none of them deserved it.

But was I in love with any of these women? Did I ever love anyone? I submit that I really had no clue what love is.

It's taken me a selfish lifetime to feel love, to give love, to be self-sacrificing, putting others before myself. It's taken me a lifetime to get past the definitions of compassion and empathy and honor and ethics and actually start to practice them. And I'm still not that good.

I felt guilt and remorse and self-pity, a lot, but beyond that, I didn't think about it that much. And based on my patterns of behavior, those thoughts and feelings never lingered long either, allowing me, justifying myself, in continuing down this self-destructive path.

Here I was, in the 1990s, on some level, a successful husband and father. A successful writer and director. But who was I? I increasingly had no idea. I never contemplated the significance and consequences of these events. I was moving through my life like I was wading into the ocean. Pushing past the vast water, the waves, pushing past life.

My whole life was on a spaceship, but I was outside the ship on a spacewalk, and my tether was quickly fraying.

Ironically, though I had been in various therapies, my introspection was purely superficial. I was too smart for my own good. I could talk the talk. I could talk any talk. But they were words as armor. Even I didn't understand how true that was. I was pushing outward when I needed to be looking inward. And nobody can make you do that. And it's a scary place to go. And though I gave it lip service, in truth, I was suppressing my fears, my rage, my dread, until they began to permanently manifest themselves in my dreams.

My greatest fear was facing my greatest fears.

But instead, I was piling my plate from the buffet of life till it was overflowing. And we know how disgusting buffets are. This was life without a sneeze guard. Overlapping jobs, affairs, trying to maintain a "normal" family life with four children, in constant motion, and being fucking miserable.

I was no better, no different than my father. I stood in his dark shadow. I was a selfish bastard, I'd tell myself, and perhaps even romanticize it as the curse of my father. Like Bruce Springsteen said, "Adam Raised a Cain." To not appreciate what you have, but only to want something else. It was a good definition of both doom and failure.

I was entering the highest summits of success. A higher place to fall from. But I kept climbing.

But when you reach the top of the hill, you can see the end of the road. Based on everything in my life up till that moment, I didn't like what I saw.

I wasn't taking drugs, shockingly. Though my problems, like most people, likely had some chemical component. I was experiencing a very raw version of my reality. This was my attempt to see clearly. To not delude myself.

But I became good at dismissing the side of myself that was trying to help.

And instead, continued to up the ante on my behavior. It's the serial killer who wants to get caught because he can't stop. Maybe that's a bit melodramatic, but you get the idea.

I was moving through jobs, writing, directing, producing, telling myself this one will get you where you want to go. But I had lost sight of where that destination was. Or even what the point of the journey was.

Is the Samurai, fearless in battle, frightened by the threat of mundanity, serenity, peace, and harmony? Of life without conflict? Of love? Does he move on to the next village to avoid exposing his feelings, his emotions, his vulnerability? Is it easier to move on, armor and legend and maybe even the lie he tells them and himself, intact? Is it easier to not allow those around him to ever truly know who he is? And is it easier still for him not to know who he truly is because that truth is too painful?

Rather than helping me, these jobs were keeping me from facing my fate.

At the same time, I had gone from a frustrated but faithful husband in the first years of our marriage to emotional affairs that I told myself were not the same as physical affairs, and were ultimately unsatisfying because the emotion wasn't real, to a series of actual relationships with women, from many backgrounds and places in my life. Each one, I allowed to get close to me, maybe even loving me, knowing at some point on some level, it would never work out.

Sometimes, it sort of worked out okay. But sometimes, it didn't. And sometimes it was disastrous in every way possible. And though I had set these actions in motion, I had no idea how to deal with them.

It was cruel and irresponsible, really reprehensible, but I had proven that no matter how high the ideals I set for myself, I could violate them without a second thought. Well, maybe a second thought, but clearly not a third.

When I would emerge, I would swear to myself I was done, until I naturally drifted yet again. It was pathetic. But impossible to cease without the key to understanding the "why" in the first place.

But now I was at a crucial crossroads. Keely and I had gone from a torrid affair to a full-blown extramarital relationship. And it had been years like this. But now, we had reached a breaking point. A breaking-up point. She wanted something real. Something open. Not hidden in the shadows. But I was okay with it enough to let it remain status quo while not being aware that I was chipping away the faith that she had shown in me. I was breaking her and still did nothing. I knew she loved me, and if I let her go, I was sentencing myself to a life of loneliness and unhappiness. But committing to her, as much as it was what I thought I wanted, seemed too daunting. Too daunting to face Barbara or the kids. Something had to give. And that something was me.

As nauseous as it made me, it was time to tell Barbara it was over. Zanini, the Italian-Jewish Zen Buddhist Jungian psychiatrist but really shaman, would help me walk through this minefield. And mind field. I would return from the wild ride of *Brüno* and end my marriage. But in keeping with my patterns, I did it the most cowardly way possible.

Zanini had helped me to see the patterns that formed me. It was a slow elevator down to the basement of my mind, but at least, I was finally on it.

When the doors to the elevator opened, through the dusty darkness, past the detritus of forgotten ideas, half-baked concepts, and fading memories, I could see one item all alone, way in the back of that shadowy basement that had been completely neglected: love.

Understanding how that hole formed and how, rather than letting it heal, I kept covering it up so it would never heal, ensuring it would remain an open wound. Forever infected.

Zanini thought I deserved love. Why not? Doesn't everyone deserve love? Doesn't everyone need love? I hadn't been sure about any of that.

Yes, Keely had many attributes that were easy to see, easy to experience. Yes, we could talk about anything. Laugh about anything. And be silent and telepathic about anything. Yet somehow, I had never experienced those things before with anyone else. Unwavering support and loyalty and trust. Unconditional love. She was a fierce warrior in the name of love, a single mother struggling nobly and honorably to get by. Her love was formidable. Her love was a superpower. And when I felt that love, truly felt it, it washed away all my resistance. Keely's love was like a hallucinogenic drug; she was my ayahuasca. She broke through me. She broke me open. I saw myself differently. As a being who could love. As a person who had the capability to love and be loved.

She had been the key that unlocked that.

Yes, it was wrong. There is no denying it. And Keely continued to persuade me that declaring this relationship in the open, being honest, not avoiding it, not hiding it would be the only path. I knew she was right.

And wasn't a dishonest irretrievably broken marriage wrong? It was time to reckon with that.

And though Keely and I broke up and got back together, each time it was more obvious that being apart was a mistake. I would think, if everything I've done up until now was self-destructive, what was letting go of somebody who loved me like Keely?

I knew if I let her pass, that my fate would be sealed. This tunnel of love would seal itself closed with me on the wrong side.

And yet, and yet, years passed. And I remained married.

And Keely's disappointment began to take its rightful place next to her love.

I would say to myself, I had no interest in being Tony Soprano, staying in a marriage for all the wrong reasons, having relationships on the side and slowly being eaten up by self-loathing.

Yet here I was floating again, avoiding, while fucking everyone in my life over. Maybe ultimately, most of all, me.

Keely wasn't just my girlfriend. She was my everything. She had eased into the role of muse, someone whom I had needed and desired for so long without even knowing it. Somebody whose opinions and sensibilities I respected and trusted. Somebody who pushed me beyond my artistic barriers without concern for economics.

We often got in the car and went, exploring the far reaches of Los Angeles County, getting lost like I used to when I first moved here, and then finding our way back, almost disappointed that we couldn't stay lost forever. We took longer trips for research on my various projects. We'd exchange ideas, and she'd be a sounding board for whatever I was working on whatever the stage of it might be, from writing to editing, to navigating the soap opera of making a movie.

It was romantic. It was loving. She was immediately my partner, in "crime," in life.

She took care of me. She had my back. But more than that, she had my mind. She protected that like a hawk.

I remember watching all the dailies for *Religulous* with her in her apartment, huddled together in front of her small old Apple computer while she took all my notes and feeling so lucky. In fact, she has watched and taken notes on virtually all the dailies for all projects I've done since then. She would excitedly type and proofread and offer her thoughts on my rewrite of *A Walk in the Woods* and then feel the same blind-sided devastation when I was fired.

And she has done the same on virtually everything I've written almost since we met (including this book). That's how she is.

So, what did I want, what was I looking for, if not this? Was I simply full of shit? The way people get when they lie to themselves for so long it becomes the truth?

I had found what I was looking for, yet risked losing it, losing her forever, if I didn't act.

And you can't go back and fix what was. There is only one direction.

Stasis is a powerful force, but no longer an excuse. I'd stood on this cliff too long. Either I stepped up, stepped past, stepped over my emotional cowardice and fear and faced the truth, or I would relegate myself to a world without love.

I had never been able to imagine the conversation I would have to have with Barbara. I would have to hurt her. There was no getting around it. And it was time to end the facade. No healing could ever begin without this. But I dreaded it.

I would have to think she had known at least on some intuitive level all along for many years, yet she had somehow reconciled herself to that dynamic and was willing, as so many suffering spouses do, to look the other way as long as her world remained intact. I was afraid of Barbara's reaction. She had deep feelings that she did not express. This would all explode or implode, shattering her existence, even if it was built on a false premise, once presented with the news, no matter how delicate, that the marriage was over.

And even more difficult, telling my kids.

•••

The day my father told me my parents' marriage was over had been traumatic and haunted me all my life, and now here I was about to haunt others. Like a living ghost.

But my psychiatrist, Dr. Zanini, had been so instrumental in supporting me on this path that I felt, as horrific as the prospect was, I was ready.

I was scheduled to see him at my usual time, Monday at 8:00 p.m., and my agenda for that session was to review what I would say to Barbara, how I would tell her our twenty-three-year marriage was over.

I arrived at the building at 26th and Wilshire and headed up to the fifth floor. As usual, the hallways were quite quiet, everyone who worked there having gone home hours before. I went up to the office door as I had done for years. I turned the doorknob to gain entrance, but it was locked. That was weird. I tried again. Definitely locked. I looked around at nothing in particular as people do when they're confused. I checked the date and time. Everything seemed right. But nothing was.

I pulled out my phone, but before I could call the doctor, I saw a message. My phone was always on silent so I never heard anything. I played the message. It was Dr. Zanini.

"Larry, this is Dino Zanini. You are probably trying to enter the office right now and finding the door locked. I'm sorry you have to find out this way but I have been diagnosed with a very serious cancer. It will require a long hospitalization, a bone marrow transplant and a long period of treatment and hopefully recovery. But as a result I will not be returning to the office again. I will have to cease my practice effective immediately. I wish you the best of luck. Dino . . ."

Tears welled up in my eyes. This man had been my savior, my salvation, my shaman, and now he was gone. Like that. I left a message on his machine expressing my sorrow, my understanding, and my fervent wish for his full recovery. I then staggered to the elevator and into the parking lot to my car.

I was on my own.

And like I said, though I finally broached the subject, I did so in a less honorable fashion, to everyone. I told Barbara some of the truth. That I was unhappy and wanted out. She was stunned, even unaccepting. But though I didn't relent on this main point, I weaseled out of the deeper truths. I softened it and, in doing so, obscured the truth rather than made it more palatable. I told her there was no one else. That was an obvious lie. And I told her that maybe it would be temporary. Also a blatant lie.

I did the same with the kids. I made it sound temporary, hoping that it would naturally spill over into some sort of permanence. I swore to always be around, nearby, that maybe things would be better. And indeed the kids had experienced our late-stage marital dissolution close-up. The screaming and fights and disruption and fear for them. They knew things weren't good. But ending it? It wasn't something they had conceived of.

Sophie was in college at USC, and Pearl was a high schooler, and although they were hurt deeply, they had enough life experience and friends going through or having gone through the same thing, to at least intellectually understand. Emotionally, I still see the remnants of that pain I inflicted on them today.

Zelda and Francesco were too young. I imagined I had scared Zelda and traumatized her. She didn't seem interested in maintaining or cultivating a relationship with me, and though I tried, I had to reluctantly understand and respect it. I'm not sure our relationship ever truly recovered.

Francesco was even younger and I think was just confused. Is this how it works? Plus he was willing to spend time with me, and we were able to build a relationship as a result.

There is no pain I've experienced or forced others to experience more than the dissolution of my marriage. And though I felt a heavy burden of guilt and responsibility, I never regretted my decision. I had considered it for many years, maybe spent more time thinking about this than anything else, that I knew it was the right decision. For all I have felt, I have never regretted that.

But I will never forgive myself for the pain I caused. How do people do it? How do people do it more than once?

Once I was out, I wasn't going back. Once I was out, Keely and I would be together full-time. So Barbara was shattered, but my lies and obfuscations and tentativeness shattered Keely as well.

It would still be years before we were married, and the damage done would never fully heal.

I quickly moved into a vast and anonymous apartment complex in Westwood just a few minutes from the house in Bel Air. I got an extra bedroom so my son, Francesco, could stay over. He was too young to have any preconceived judgments and thus was more accepting of the reality. We'd watch artsy Japanese horror and sci-fi films, old Hollywood classics, and binge on *Lost*. We'd go to movies and walk around Westwood, get breakfast. It was good amid that sadness.

From there, I moved into a far better place on the Wilshire Corridor called Crown Towers. It had parking valets, a doorman, services of various kinds. It was a two-bedroom on a high floor with a great terrace facing north opposite the heavily trafficked Wilshire Boulevard and overlooking bucolic landscapes leading from Holmby Hills into Bel Air, where I told you, I watched in stunned silence as Michael Jackson's lifeless body was transported by helicopter from his Bel Air estate to UCLA Medical Center on the day of the premiere of *Brüno*.

•••

Keely's son, McLain, was really no more than a baby at that time, and she was still sharing custody with McLain's father although even by the time of the birth, they were no longer together. When McLain was with his dad, Keely might stay with me or I might stay at her place down in Santa Monica.

But this arrangement would be very much temporary. McLain's father was upping the ante on their conflict rather than defusing it.

Calling the police without cause on Keely numerous times. Taking McLain, then just a very young child, into dangerous situations like mountain biking in the pitch blackness of night. And stalking us, and even me alone. It kept us on edge and lasted for years.

And certainly took its toll on an unsuspecting child.

Keely and certainly I would've been happy with a co-parenting situation with McLain's dad, but it was not to be. After getting caught up in the system, Keely had no alternative but to defend herself and try to protect McLain. Following a protracted legal battle and many visits to the children's court just east of downtown, Keely—who represented herself and McLain with a series of indisputable recorded facts and evidence against Mclain's dad's high-powered attorney and his phony rhetoric, paid for by his parents—finally prevailed and was awarded sole custody.

Although the aberrant behavior and even the stalking continued for some time after that, even after we moved years later, McLain's biological father eventually completely disappeared from the scene.

•••

Although I had met Keely in 2004 and didn't separate from Barbara until 2008 and didn't get legally divorced until 2013, and remarried in 2017, I was oblivious to the damage this could cause a relationship over the long haul. Broken promises, delayed commitments, avoidance as the path of least resistance.

Barbara and I had thrown millions of dollars away to maintain the trappings of our married life, and now as we divorced, there was very little left. What I thought would be a painless divorce—I'm always looking for the painless route and failing to find it—turned into a tense, volatile, perhaps even clichéd battle between exes. Lawyers came and went; demands were made. But agreements seemed hard to reach.

My business manager had even abandoned us and, further, frozen our assets so I couldn't even use a credit card or ATM. I was broke and desperate. And in disbelief. Where would I turn?

After Larry having asked me to write on *Seinfeld* and direct *Curb*, I finally had to ask something of him. Help.

He responded without hesitation. In 2010, Larry offered me a job on the New York section of *Curb*, Season 8, and I took it. It was always a safe harbor, and I needed one.

I was a producer on all the New York episodes but directed only one episode of that New York section, an ambitious and densely packed episode and one of my favorites. It was called "Mister Softee" because of Larry's Pavlovian sexual failure upon hearing the music emanating from the eponymous ice cream truck, which leads to a flashback to young Larry getting caught in the back of the truck with the driver's daughter and getting tossed out into the street naked and humiliated. He visits a therapist, who violates all kinds of confidentiality by inappropriately mentioning other clients and their issues. It also involves Larry's car problems, which turn it into a motorized vibrator, and Larry's softball team, which pays the price when Larry hears the Mister Softee theme in the distance. Finally it is about former Red Sox great Bill Buckner, known not for his many accomplishments but for one very public fielding gaffe, who gets a chance to redeem himself by saving a baby from a burning building.

Both Francesco and Keely and even my youngest daughter, Zelda, stayed at various times with me in New York. Keely brought McLain once, and we celebrated his birthday in Manhattan. I got to see my father and brother. But in typical fashion, we never discussed my personal life. Although my brother was an occasional confidante, my father did not want to know how much my spiral was paralleling his. Even my gracious, charming, and always accepting mother visited and bonded with Keely. And though my personal enthusiasm for living and working in New York had steadily waned over the years, this was a burst of positive energy. The city healed me and gave me hope for the future. And I had a few bucks again.

I moved in with Keely shortly after returning to Los Angeles.

It was a one-bedroom on Hill Street, just off Lincoln Boulevard, in Santa Monica. If Keely had McLain that week, he would have the bedroom, and Keely and I would sleep out in the living room on a futon on the floor. And if McLain's father had him, we'd have the bedroom.

I loved it. I loved living with Keely. I loved *being* with Keely.

It might sound ridiculous, and I understand. But you can't underestimate the role of fate, of luck, of synchronicity in all our life decisions and choices. We don't understand that force, but it is real.

As idyllic as Hill Street was in its own way, we felt like we needed to find a place together for all three of us. We found one in Topanga. Soon after, Keely gained full custody of McLain.

I went back to Bel Air and retrieved one of the original dogs still left from the pack. And one of my two favorites. A black Lab mix named Shiva after the destroyer deity of Hinduism, and I took her to our new home with me. My other favorite, an ornery golden shepherd chow mix named Kai, had died recently.

Kai died after I had broken up with Barbara. They called me when he was sick, and I got to see him a few times. He was a regal dog, and it pained me to see his decline. When it came time for the end, Francesco and I took him to the vet to be put to sleep. The death of people had always seemed abstract, though that was rapidly changing for me. The death of Kai destroyed me. I was a wreck, and I think about him often.

And I've often felt that his death was my fault. I had broken his heart too.

Shiva was luckier. She was given special treatment, being the only dog for the first time in her life. She got adequate exercise and space. And Keely loved her as if she had raised her from a puppy. After many more years of Shiva, her health declined. She eventually lost the ability to get up or walk and our doctor, Dr. Lupo, advised a merciful ending.

By this time, we were living in Malibu. He came to our house and administered the lethal dose while I held her. I could see and feel the life pass out of her. McLain, Keely, and I all wept. I couldn't stop. Shiva had been named after the destroyer, but she was a creator of love of life. Her ashes sit on my desk.

We liked living in Topanga. It was verdant. Very mystical and magical and mythical. Often nestled in the mist and the fog and the rain sometimes regardless of the season.

Topanga had its weirdness. A lot of loose and not very friendly and often confrontational dogs. And some sour neighbors too. But occasionally we'd see Cloris Leachman smiling, beaming really, as she engaged with a neighbor or a stranger in front of her modest rustic and eccentric home. We embraced the weirdness.

When I thought about coming to Los Angeles in the '70s, and even as I lived in Los Angeles, Malibu was not a goal of mine. I lived in Venice and Marina Del Rey and Santa Monica and now Topanga. Malibu struck me as elitist and unnecessary. And far.

And even if it was something to aspire to, it was far out of my reach. After my divorce, the idea of buying something or spending inordinate amounts of money on rent was equally out of the question. I would likely never be in that position due to the path I had taken. And taken proudly. And again this was the Keely X factor, with her unwavering support. She simply wouldn't let me sell my soul when the lure was hard to resist. But I didn't and I'm glad I didn't and am eternally grateful to Keely for that. I've accepted who and what I am, whoever and whatever that may be, including the illusion of self, itself.

But things change. And it often has nothing to do with your dreams or desires. It often has nothing to do with you. And sometimes those things are disastrous. And sometimes surprisingly, once in a while, things work out.

As an example, or perhaps reward, or perhaps karma, we found ourselves in Malibu.

CHAPTER 15

"IT DEPENDS WHO'S DOING THE FUCKING AND WHO'S GETTING FUCKED." (THE DICTATOR)

*T*here were many things wrong with *The Dictator* right from the start. But many things right too.

It was clear from the first draft that *The Dictator* wouldn't be the funniest movie ever made, but neither was *Dr. Strangelove* or *Sullivan's Travels,* and yet they are considered among the greatest classic comedies ever made. I felt *The Dictator* could rightfully aspire to those heights. Comedy can't always be defined by laugh ratios. This script had great comic conceits, great comic concepts, great comic sequences, great comic characters and dialogues. It had a surfeit of twists and turns and surprises and a fresh satiric take on the global political landscape, too.

Most of all, it was an ensemble comedy, like *Strangelove,* where Peter Sellers was the undeniable star, but he was supported by normally dramatic actors doing unforgettable comic star turns themselves like George C. Scott, Slim Pickens, and Sterling Hayden.

What *The Dictator* script had, which is in such deficit today, was structure. The intricate surprising structure characterized not by the formless recent American comedy movies, but by the movies of Billy Wilder and Preston Sturges and still carried on today by *Seinfeld* and *Curb*.

But much of that intricate clever work was to be thrown away by Sacha himself for cheaper gags designed to make *The Dictator* as much of a one-man show as *Borat* and *Brüno*. I felt strongly that this was a fatal mistake, but it was characteristic of my status on this movie that I was summarily ignored.

•••

My relationship with Sacha had shifted quite a bit, from the giddy post-*Borat* brotherhood to a tense power struggle during *Brüno*, after which I was sure our collaboration had come to an end.

In the wake of *Borat*, Sacha showered me with gifts. I remember him giving me a large humidor of Cuban cigars. He seemed to truly and deeply appreciate my role in the staggering success of *Borat*. Moreover, he seemed to understand how I had snatched victory from the jaws of defeat when I stepped in to rescue a movie that was on the brink of cancellation and delivered the goods in unprecedented fashion.

But the power and wealth that Sacha accrued as a result of that one film certainly had an impact on his demeanor, toward everyone, but especially toward me. As time went on, he seemed more reluctant to acknowledge my essential contribution to this unprecedented success and, in fact, seemed to resent it and revise it in his own mind with the encouragement of the inevitable entourage that he had gathered around him. It resulted in a less-than-gracious, sometimes insufferable version of Sacha. At best.

I don't want to give the impression that Sacha was some sort of ogre, although on occasion he was, or that I was a naive innocent, though occasionally I was.

More often in life, there are no heroes or villains. Only flawed humans. And reality.

And I was never my best advocate. For instance:

Sometime after *Borat*, while Sacha and I were still basking in the glow of success, he invited me to a birthday party being thrown for him by Courteney Cox at her house in Malibu. I had decided long ago that I was uncomfortable and self-conscious at these gatherings, massive amounts of people crowded together, making awkward small talk, most of whom knew each other but didn't know themselves and certainly didn't know me.

So the idea of this party did not excite me. It wasn't Sacha or his birthday or Courteney Cox. It was me. Yet I knew I should attend, and so I began the process of psyching myself for the experience.

An hour or two before I would leave for the party, I received a call from my friend Adam, comedian, crackhead, criminal, and Fagin to my Oliver Twist during our wild teen years.

At this point in Adam's life, he had reached new depths of desperation, depravity, and despair. He was living on the streets, hopelessly addicted to crack, but too old to really be living that life. He was breaking down. He now had publicly threatened suicide in order to be placed in a 72-hour hold at a mental health facility.

Adam wasn't exactly suicidal, although he flirted with death until death took him up on the proposition. No, it was more that he had run out of places to run. Places to land. Crash land. He had crashed with me at numerous addresses, had his own places where he couldn't make the rent, even for one month, managed to get admitted to various rehab facilities around town. But he had used all that up and was nowhere with nowhere to go.

He had been told by one of his cronies about the 72-hour watch. If you publicly threatened suicide, the authorities were obligated to stick you in a mental health facility for a mandatory 72 hours. For Adam, that meant 72 hours with room and board. A bed and meals. A full stomach. A good night's sleep. Shelter. And drugs. Things he was not able to procure on his own anymore, even for a 24-hour period, let alone longer.

So, somehow, he got a hold of a gun. He certainly didn't buy it. He might've stolen it. Or found it, which was usually the same as stealing except what you told the cops. Or traded for it. Or stolen something else and traded for it.

He walked into a local mall and began waving the gun around, threatening suicide. Swiftly the authorities were summoned, and Adam was taken to a county mental health facility downtown for the mandatory 72-hour hold. For Adam, this was what success looked like now.

But the night of the party, the 72 hours were up. He was to be released and once again had no place to go. I couldn't put him up with me any longer. He had destroyed two different places and had even scared my kids, who had always loved him and enjoyed his company.

He was finally able to convince his old friend from the Catskills, Bobby, to allow him to crash with her in the Bay Area, where she was now living. But he didn't have money for the bus fare or a ride to the station.

I saw this, if not an emergency, as an urgent situation that needed to be addressed for Adam's survival. If he didn't get on that bus and get up to Bobby's, his fate seemed quite grim. So I told him I was on my way.

All the while thinking I could take care of this and still attend the party.

But it took much longer than anticipated to get him released. Then we drove to the bus station, where I bought him a ticket, gave him some cash for food and cigarettes, and waited with him until it was time to board.

We didn't talk about much. There wasn't much to talk about. Here we were after all this time. Pathetic. And then he boarded the bus.

When I started heading west again, it was late, but not too late for a party. In my mind, I imagined throngs of people crowded together, drinking and smoking, and I thought, *Who's even going to notice that I'm there or not?* What were the chances that I'd even be missed? And I couldn't be the only person who wouldn't show. I would just call Sacha tomorrow and explain to him what happened. It certainly wouldn't be the end of the world.

I got home, and soon after, the phone rang:

"Where are you?"

Oh shit.

"What do you mean?"

"We're sitting here waiting for you."

In my haste, I had dismissed the party as just another big gathering of anonymous people, where I wouldn't be noticed or missed. It never occurred to me that assumption might be woefully wrong.

It never occurred to me that it was a small intimate dinner party. And that there were ten people sitting around a table with empty plates in front of them and the food getting cold, waiting for me.

Wow. I really fucked up.

I tried to explain to Sacha what I had been doing, but understandably he wasn't interested and never heard my explanation.

Although I had done what I had to do, what I felt compelled to do out of my last vestiges of love and loyalty and friendship for Adam, who would never ever be able to truly feel that or repay it in any way, I also damaged my nascent relationship with Sacha.

After Bobby threw him out, Adam made his way to Vegas, which was the perfect town for him. Filled with delusions, false hopes, pipe dreams, yet endless possibilities.

He had somehow gotten himself hooked up with an old friend who was running a nude variety revue at one of the hotels on the Strip, with music, dancing, and yes, nudity. He asked Adam if he could keep it together enough to be the MC. Introduce the numbers and do a little comedy in between. Suddenly Adam had a job.

He invited Keely and me to come visit him. He was renting a nice house in one of the many developments in one of the many suburbs that surround Vegas. In a generous mood, I had also given him my old Jaguar, which he displayed proudly in his driveway.

But within a couple of short months of getting himself back to a respectable existence, the loneliness, and the ceaseless desire to fill an ever-widening hole, coupled with the money to finance his self-ruin, led Adam back to crack.

He missed a number of shows until he was unceremoniously fired. The only work he could get was passing out flyers on the streets for the show. And that was an act of charity by his boss and former acquaintance. But he fucked that up, too, and was quickly begging his former colleagues, literally borrowing clothes and sleeping under the maître d's desk at the club where he'd been fired. But Adam knew no bottom.

He had crack dealers coming and going from his house, robbing him and often slapping him around if not downright beating him.

And then he lost the house. And then he wrecked the Jaguar.

When he called me and left a message that he was going to kill himself, that he had an elaborate pain-free plan that involved a hibachi grill, I was seized by the desire to record him, his surreal one-of-a-kind adventures, many of which we'd shared, many of which I knew and remembered better than he did, before he successfully did himself in.

At that time, he worked phone sales in a boiler room. His charm had been eclipsed by his desperation many years before, and he had lost the knack of taking advantage of suckers. No one bit. He lived off one Happy Meal a day and was still overweight.

But as was so often the case with this cat of nine lives, a friend from the Tropicana called him. Would he like to do a week at their comedy club before it closed?

I hired a local Vegas freelance news crew, Keely and I got rooms for us and Adam at the Tropicana, and I spent the weekend interviewing, prompting him with stories, filming him from morning till night, in the hotel room, on and backstage at the club, and in and around the downtown Vegas neighborhood that doesn't attract tourists unless they want to score crack. It was a desolate neighborhood far from the Strip, very unglamorous, lined with crack motels posting their hourly rates. We shot inside one room and in front of others, each with a harrowing story attached.

I edited the footage back in Los Angeles with Christian, whom I had worked with on *Religulous*, and it came out pretty great. The select few that I showed it to really loved it. Even, or maybe especially, if they didn't know Adam. Although it was very real and raw, I had also restored Adam's mythology. He admired Bukowski and Tom Waits above all. And his story could've been told by either one.

I called it *I Can't Go On*, after the first half of Beckett's famous line, "I can't go on, I'll go on." Many of Adam's stories ended with, "I can't go on."

The Tropicana gig sadly served only as a temporary respite from Adam's descent. A way station before his final stop.

This time the call didn't come from him but from his brother John. He was weeping and I knew what he was going to say before he spoke. I was in the car with Keely taking one of our numerous midnight drives to uncharted parts of Los Angeles. Adam was dead. He had OD'd in one of those motel rooms. Accidentally or on purpose, no one would ever know for sure. Yet we did. He only hoped the decision would be made for him and it wouldn't hurt. And that he'd be in an air-conditioned room. When they found him, it was freezing.

•••

I was surprised when I was asked to direct *The Dictator*. I had no illusions and simply assumed I wasn't the first person asked. And I did some serious soul searching before reaching a decision. Did I want or need to go through an unpleasant experience again and, worse, to have the finished product compromised and worsened by forces beyond my control? No. Definitely not.

But then I read the script, and I had that feeling. This could be a great movie. In fact, a classic. All I had to do was ignore all the noise inside my head and say "Yes."

The original script was written by Alec Berg, Jeff Schaffer, and Dave Mandel. They had worked on *Seinfeld* after I left, but *Seinfeld* writers are always part of that club. I really enjoyed their minds, and we had then had the opportunity to collaborate on *Curb*. Sometimes one of us directed, with the others sat on set "producing" but really amping up the scenes from take to take. We collaborated well. No egos. Only strong opinions. And my mantra was theirs: "What's best for the movie?"

When the original *Borat* ending failed as I feared it would, being so convoluted and complicated and cluttered, covering up its lack of inventiveness or inspiration as to render it almost incomprehensible and so far from funny unlike the rest of the movie, I suggested Alec, Jeff, and Dave come in and sit with Sacha, the British writers, and myself, and help come up with an ending that worked. That led to the ending that worked. The attempted kidnapping of Pamela Anderson at her book signing. It had everything the other ending didn't, a sense of reality, of spontaneity, the threat of violence, inappropriateness, and most of all: an honest execution of what would really happen in this situation. It was a great payoff to that movie.

Their important contribution to the success of that movie, the comedy cavalry charging in, in the nick of time, led to some tension on *Brüno*. Alec and Dave were unavailable, as it turned out, but Jeff was essentially given the job of writer/producer along with Ant, Peter, and Dan. They had been trying to pull away from Sacha for years but, with their own projects failing, were always drawn back. And Sacha didn't really like being dependent on them either. Resentments began to build. These began to manifest during *The Dictator*. Much of it expressed to me. Sacha was done with Anthony, Peter, and Dan, and they with him, yet here they all were on *The Dictator*, unhappy and uninspired. Alec, Jeff, and Dave were Sacha's fair-haired boys, at first. But soon, he would turn on them as well. And they, him. During a writing session, Dave Mandel could hold his anger no longer and exploded at Sacha's obstinacy, and Sacha asked, really demanded, that he leave. I didn't blame Dave, but uncharacteristically at some point, he returned too. How happy could he have been?

I was excited but it seemed like no one else really wanted to be there.

My first sign of trouble came from what would be an uncharacteristic straight, direct phone call from, of all people, Scott Rudin. Although I would speak to him many times after this, this was the one and only time it could be considered straight and direct.

Scott was a temperamental, tempestuous, volatile producer, who liked to verbally abuse his employees and anyone else he could get away with. He was known for throwing phones and other "tantrumy" behavior, which was more than tolerated, it was rewarded continually by an amoral Hollywood because Scott had exquisite tastes and made hit movies.

In this call, Scott asked me if I would consider co-directing the movie with Sacha. Remember, I'd already agreed to direct the movie. That was done. But as I've learned again and again, it's never done until it's really done and things often seem done when they're not. That is the nature of power. Undoing what is already done.

Wow, I thought, Sacha had managed to get Scott Rudin to do his bidding. This was indicative of the leverage Sacha would have and abuse. I said, "No."

After that, for weeks after, Scott would call my house. Initially I treated these calls like any other. But they weren't. I'd pick it up after the second, third, fourth ring, only to be told that Scott was no longer available and he'd have to call back. Really? I'd literally just picked up the phone. Then I started picking up before even the first ring was done, and amazingly, I'd be told the same thing. Scott's no longer available, he'll have to call back. Often I wouldn't hear back for days, only to go through the same routine. I got it. But what was I to do? He was not only Scott Rudin, but the producer of the movie. And you could hear the wincing anguish in his assistants' voices. They were reading from a script for a role that they loathed playing.

I felt all this unnecessary game playing was a bad portent of what was to come, but I must admit I really wanted to direct this movie and I didn't want anybody else to; thus I was vulnerable. I needed to play these games to be in the game.

And remember: Desire leads to suffering.

So I received calls from Scott regularly, yet almost never actually spoke to him. He called but he didn't call. It seemed silly, absurd, comical after a while.

Ironically, I was finally flown to New York to meet and have dinner with Scott. I wondered if he'd show up. That would've been a real topper to the phone bit. Fly across the country to have dinner with Scott Rudin, only to have his assistant waiting and telling me Scott couldn't make it.

But I did it. Flew to New York, went to the restaurant, and

indeed Scott was there. And weirdly, dinner was delightful. Quite unlike everything I'd heard and had experienced, I really liked the real Scott. We hit it off. He was smart and funny, was openly gay, and had obviously displayed great taste in his projects. I had faith that, games aside, he would protect the movie.

I imagine this was the experience for many filmmakers. A smart, creative producer who would be ferocious on your behalf. It's no excuse, but it made it easier to ignore the abuse.

However, in the end this, like so many assumptions I made about this movie, turned out to be wrong.

Once I was hired, the next weird thing happened. Sacha insisted on hiring Larry Sher as our DP. Insisted on it. Wasn't interested in talking about or seeing anybody else. He had never loved Anthony Hardwick, even though Anthony had done yeoman's work on both *Borat* and *Brüno* as well as *Religulous* and other projects of mine.

What made this so weird was that Larry Sher was primarily known as Todd Phillips's DP. I asked Sacha why, of all the DPs in the world, would he want to work with Todd's? It seemed like another weird choice. You want to work with the DP of the person you hate perhaps more than anyone in the world, who is faithfully loyal to that person? Why?

Sacha never provided me with an adequate answer. This was part of his new power trip. He didn't have to explain. He wanted it, and that was enough.

Another irony: Larry Sher and I became great friends and collaborators while shooting *The Dictator*. He was an excellent DP, who has gone on to an Oscar nomination for his work on *Joker*. Directed by Todd Phillips. But by the end of this shoot for no good reason and certainly through no fault of Larry's, Sacha grew to resent him and Larry lost respect for Sacha. This would be yet another creative relationship I would have to mediate over the course of the movie to get things done.

Sacha's next demand struck me as equally weird. He wanted Joe Reidy as the AD for the movie, unceremoniously throwing over Dale, who I had brought onto *Borat* and *Brüno* and was one of the all-time great ADs, especially for me and Sacha. None of that seemed to matter to Sacha now, who was obsessed with Joe's status. Joe was most renowned for being Martin Scorsese's AD.

Now I'm a massive fan of Scorsese. He is unquestionably one of the greatest and most influential American filmmakers of our time, and I have only the deepest respect and admiration for his body of work, going back to his student films from the '60s, like *The Big Shave* and *It's Not Just You, Murray!*, which I had watched in the '70s during my short time at NYU film school.

And Joe Reidy was a legendary AD because of that association. But Sacha couldn't help repeating again and again, as if trying to either impress me or intimidate me, "He's Martin Scorsese's AD."

By the way, Joe had worked with other great directors as well, like Darren Aronofsky and Oliver Stone.

And ironically, once again, I loved Joe. He was nothing like Sacha's buildup. Instead he was a humble, die-hard New Yorker. If you wanted the best coffee or best steak or best Chinese food, he knew where to go. He was kind and patient. I grew to like him very much, though I'm sure by the end of the shoot, he was sick of me.

But before I met Joe and experienced the three-dimensional person beyond Sacha's hype I thought, *I don't really think of Scorsese as a comedy person.*

Sacha had developed the habit at previews of the previous movies of marking each laugh with a grade based purely on audience reaction, and those gags with lower grades would be dropped. It seemed quite clear to me that he had lost his instinct and was no longer confident to stay ahead of the audience and was satisfied with them telling him what to do. The audience was now telling Sacha what was funny, and that could be lethal.

Although it is well known that the Marx Brothers wrote and edited their movies that way, most of them after *A Night at the Opera*, though filled with jokes, were less and less satisfying to the audience they kowtowed to, as opposed to trusting themselves and their brilliant writers.

The more reliance on the audience to guide the performers, the weaker and weaker the product.

I saw this mentality take hold of Sacha somewhere between
Borat and *Brüno*. My unmistakable impression was that he went
from trusting me, trusting the writers, mostly trusting himself,
to trusting an audience of anonymous people not invested in this
process at all. And letting them dictate the course of the movie. He
would have a handful of production assistants, all nice people but
not to be entrusted with the fate of the movie, sit at various junc-
tures around the audience during these screenings with a clipboard
and pencil. On the clipboard was a list of the jokes in the movie.
And these young inexperienced people were to gauge and judge
their portion of the audience's reaction to each of the listed jokes
and assign that joke a grade. Like a joke is like an athletic event.
These jokes were separated as if they were one-liners. When many
of them were part of a scene or sequence or exchange and virtually
none of them were one-liners and therefore immediately a flawed
premise and a flawed system. You cannot judge a joke in isolation.
It doesn't exist in a vacuum. Its success is not just attributable to
the joke, but to the context it's placed in. When a joke fails, it's usually for a variety of reasons. Yes, it may be the wording or phrasing.
Sometimes rearranging the thought to deliver a better payoff will
rectify that. But there are many mitigating factors: Is the character
compelling? Not likable necessarily. That concept is a product of this
market-driven, audience-driven decision making. I believe what an
audience responds to is a compelling character, good or bad. From
Larry David to Tony Soprano to Walter White, from the Bible and
Shakespeare to Patrick Bateman and beyond and before, we decide
what and who is likable and we don't need anyone's "help." So yes,
we need to care about the character and his plight. Be invested in his
fate. But we don't have to pander to achieve that goal. The audience
acts as a mass and looks to us to offer them what we think is funny.
And of course, once they've broken apart and returned to their status
as individuals at the conclusion of the screening, their opinions will
vary. They all might believe it was funny, hilarious even, but will
disagree about the funniest parts, their favorite parts. Or what they
didn't like. And that's great. That's okay. That's to be expected. That's

organic human behavior. You learn nothing by contriving that. You can't reverse engineer that process. Another important factor that Sacha's report card overlooked was the situation. Do we care about the situation? Is it plausible or farcical and absurd, and if so, is that tone clear? There is no quick description of that subtle and nuanced and elusive aspect of the success of any single joke to grade.

Structural questions regarding jokes and laughs can be broken down into micro-structure and macro-structure. An example of macro-structure is: Is the premise that this whole scene rests on even funny? And if not, why not? The micro might be, the payoff might be perfect, but the setup is wrong and is stopping the joke from reaching its maximum laugh potential. And what if an audience is laughing so hard from the previous "joke," they laugh over the joke in question? How do you accurately grade that? Indeed, this is an example of junk science applied to this process in a delusional and futile attempt to quantify creativity. And sadly, *The Dictator* was its poster boy. But the problems with *The Dictator* began early, almost immediately. And they were like a toxic oil spill in the Gulf. They spread quickly and poisoned the waters and the life within it. And ruined everything for many years to come.

One of the most important factors to me in the success of a comedy is essentially the cinematic equivalent of an icebreaker joke, much the same as a live performer might do. In *Borat*, the logo for the Kazakhstani television station served that purpose beyond our wildest dreams. Something to relax the audience so they can feel excited about joining you on this journey. That is an X factor that can't be graded. That sense of joie de vivre that bursts through the screen and makes your audience a partner in crime. But it was very hard to duplicate. So much of *Borat* is unique and inspired and singular and without precedent, the true definition of a phenomenon, it would prove to be hard? difficult? impossible? to replicate.

Larry David never worried about what the audience thought. And he never worried about jokes. In fact, he was anti-joke and pro-structure. If the character and the situation were well set up, then you didn't need jokes to make the scene funny. And indeed much of Sacha's funniest moments had nothing to do with jokes, but with the truth and the honesty of the situation and the release that the dialogue provided.

There are no jokes in the Naked Fight. There is instead a strong concept, a strong conflict, and then just following through on what might happen as a result. It is not all that different from drama. Character, conflict, situational honesty. But instead of those elements eliciting emotion, or tears, in a comedy, they elicit the catharsis of laughter.

I also draw on my obsession with the synthesis of comedy and horror. In the Naked Fight, the audience is brought to screams, rendered helpless, by the action literally unfolding before them. They are howling and writhing. And finally, the screams and writhing lead to laughs, waves of laughter.

There is ultimately no laugh greater than the laugh that is wrong, but you can't help it.

But Sacha was no longer listening to me. Instead he began to rely on the outside opinions of a coterie of celebrities whom he had been increasingly hobnobbing with. It's the danger of living in a bubble and insulating yourself from the real world.

The audience doesn't want to tell us what's funny. It's relying on us to tell them. That is the responsibility of a comedy.

Of course, I heard complaints from the writers. It was a natural outgrowth of making creative contributions without the sufficient power or leverage to enforce them. I'd never met a writer who didn't complain. Including myself.

But on *Brüno*, I began to hear Sacha vocalize more loudly about his unhappiness with the writers. And I knew if he was bad-mouthing them to me, then he was bad-mouthing me to somebody else.

On *Brüno*, that was a difficult balance to strike as I found myself mediating these conflicts far more than I should. On *The Dictator*, it became chaotic and unwieldy and out of hand. On *The Dictator*, it became impossible.

Ant and Peter indeed were sweethearts. Dan was a good guy too, quite brilliant, but he prided himself on his misanthropism and almost compulsive colonial version of Anglophilia, but I enjoyed the company of all of them.

Though my ideas had been used extensively in the rethinking of *Borat* that led to its success, increasingly my uncredited contributions were ignored and dismissed by the time of *Brüno*, and I had to filter my ideas through Jeff and the Brits, who, themselves, were scrambling simply to hold on to their tenuous status in Sacha World.

As I observed up close and firsthand, Sacha's innate innocence and buffoonishness and awkwardness and obliviousness manifested in the character of Borat, and his narcissism and bitchiness and self-ishness and ego manifested in the character of Brüno. But now I witnessed, as you could imagine, even darker aspects of Sacha's personality manifest themselves in the character of Aladeen, the Dictator.

Sacha had always pitted people against each other. Like the Borat DPs, Luke and Anthony, or the British and American writers. Why? He seemed to me to simply get off on the power trip. I could not see a constructive purpose. Why treat people who are devoted to you so poorly?

Another case in point was his loyal devotee, costume designer Jason Alper. Jason had been in sync with Sacha for many years and created the iconic costumes for Ali G, Borat, and Brüno. He had been a solo act and only occasionally needed someone to help with the mundane realities of getting costumes together. Things like sewing and ironing. But he had a vivid imagination, and you can easily see that in the costumes for Sacha's classic characters.

But even more than abandoning Anthony and Dale on his quest for some strange status that he didn't realize he already had transcended, Sacha decided that he wanted a higher-level person to be the wardrobe designer for *The Dictator.*

Now in fairness to Sacha, Scott Rudin was a shadowy figure, and he may have very well been a behind-the-scenes influence on these decisions. Sacha was vulnerable to the star trip, and I can sort of imagine him being seduced by Scott's promises of the best for every department.

In that context, it's really quite amazing I was hired to be the director. I imagine that many directors would have jumped at the chance or had perhaps been offered the job but for one reason or another said "no." So after desperately trying as with Anthony, Dale, and Jason to replace me, I was offered the job by default.

I know that Alex, Jeff, and Dave had hoped to tandem-direct the movie and were rebuffed, but as writer-producers, they formed yet another clique, though supportive of me, that had to be dealt with.

Albert Wolsky, a highly respected veteran costume designer who had won two Oscars and been nominated for five others, was hired. Albert was a sweet man, a low-key person, but also somebody who had developed a work process that had become somewhat set in stone. He also possessed a trait that was anathema to these movies—good taste. One essential aspect and key to the success of *Borat* and *Brüno* and *Ali G* was their utter contempt for good taste. Risking bad taste is an important component of great comedy. Good taste was a target of satire and derision in great comedy. Those sensibilities could not be reconciled. And Sacha, despite the status of having another Oscar winner running a department, soon tired of Albert's methodology. Albert had exquisitely good taste but utterly lacked humor. And his costumes for Aladeen reflected that.

Beyond that, he insisted on making everything, which meant a long slog through fabrics and patterns and manufacturing and resulted in less than stellar results. He really didn't get it. But he should never have been hired and should've been told honestly that it wasn't working out.

Jason, who had been completely frozen out initially, was now sort of brought on under the radar to help with at least Sacha's Aladeen wardrobe. This did not sit well with Albert. Understandably. He felt he was being undermined, and he was. Rather than parting ways, Sacha allowed Albert and Jason to work on parallel lines, which again was unproductive, expensive, and time wasting.

These parallel lines, explorations, in costumes, country insignias, and many other aspects of the production, were further examples of Sacha's expensive, wasteful, and unnecessary indulgence.

We were squandering money and time on frivolous decisions while important things, like the script, or rehearsals, or Sacha's desperately needed work on his character, were left to languish as the budget continued to balloon.

Jason got Sacha and knew what he wanted. Jason was a funky fellow, and he borrowed ideas from pop and alternative culture for his costume creations and quickly figured out that what Aladeen needed was not a good taste wardrobe, but a garish, vulgar, bad taste wardrobe.

I remember Jason going to Harlem and raiding those pimp-like clothing stores and, for a fraction of the cost of what Albert was still in the process of doing, came back to our production offices in SoHo with fully realized costumes, including accessories, that would become the foundation of Aladeen's Dictator wardrobe.

Jason had created another iconic costume, but Sacha's portrayal of Aladeen never fully had the confidence of his clothes.

Albert soon left. But rather than letting Jason step up, Jason was relegated to dealing with Sacha's wardrobe and another celebrated designer was brought in. Jeffrey Kurland had been Woody Allen's costume designer for eighteen films and had won numerous awards and been nominated for one Oscar.

Jeffrey was a born New Yorker and was not afraid of conflict. Although I doubt he had ever dealt with as dysfunctional a situation as this. But he found a way to incorporate Jason's unique creativity into an overall costume plan while maintaining a strict hierarchy.

I remember Jeffrey and Jason both complaining to me, and though I was sympathetic, with Sacha and Scott asserting themselves, I was also rendered powerless to do much about it.

Borat, Brüno, and Ali G were characters who had been developed by Sacha for literally years until he knew every nuance of them inside and out. He knew how they walked and talked and dressed, down to their underwear and socks and the flotsam and jetsam they kept in their pockets.

But Aladeen was a character in someone else's script. In an ideal world, Sacha would have spent a few years developing this character, bringing it to a three-dimensional life. But time waits for no man, and that just wasn't a realistic scenario. Now I believe that if he had plunged in and devoted the time allotted to crafting the unique details of the character, he could have approximated, in an accelerated fashion, that process. But it seemed quite obvious to me that instead, most likely out of some deep-seated, unexamined fear, he refused to bear down and get underneath Aladeen, allowing himself to get distracted by the bullshit and minutiae of the preproduction. This seriously marred the potential of his performance. From my vantage point, he was more concerned with being a boss, a dictator, in control, than in the very elements that would've made him a classic comic character. We spent weeks looking at flag color combinations. Trying out guns. To the point that he was still groping for the accent while we were shooting.

And shades of his hero, Peter Sellers, Sacha was scheduled to play two characters. There was Aladeen, but also the lookalike goatherd Efawadh, a simpleton who takes Aladeen's place à la *The Prince and the Pauper*. Sacha spent so little time on Efawadh that except for a few choice moments, in editing he was essentially thrown away and with it the intricate plot that accompanied the switch. Yet Sacha was willing to spend untold time and money to fly his teacher from the clown school he attended in France as a young man to help him choreograph and advise on the Dictator's physical comical movements. I would attend many of these sessions and thought they were absurd. I'm sure the clown teacher was a skilled man, but what he was teaching Sacha seemed contrived and, like most clowns, extremely unfunny. It also lacked any semblance of spontaneity, and despite the scripted and planned nature of the movie, the illusion of spontaneity would still be crucial to its comic success. Sacha knew all this too, and essentially, after far too long under his tutelage, the clown teacher was dispatched back to France.

Sacha's demands, coupled with his short attention span, had the whole production in a constant state of scramble that escalated the budget beyond its set amounts.

Perhaps the most egregious example of this overindulgence and overspending of a star to the detriment of the movie itself took the form of an intricate set piece involving Aladeen dangling from a wire across two Manhattan skyscrapers to get inside the hotel suite where he would switch places with the goatherd played by Sacha as well, with whom he had been replaced by Aladeen's evil scheming uncle, Tamir.

We knew it was unlikely at best, and more likely impossible, to ever get permission to shoot a scene with Sacha dangling one hundred feet or more above New York midday traffic. Nevertheless, despite all the evidence to the contrary, he insisted he absolutely wanted to do it for real, and he insisted we find two buildings on opposite sides of a street wide or narrow where he could be suspended and do this sequence live on camera.

Every day for what seemed like weeks, whatever other major unavoidable obligations we had to face in the preproduction of this movie, Joe Reidy; Larry Sher; our impossibly elegant production designer Victor Kempster, who had worked with Oliver Stone on *JFK* and *Natural Born Killers*; and a rotating group of location managers would pile into a van and drive around the city, trying to find these two magical buildings, knowing full well we'd never get permission to shoot there.

But we spent a lot of time getting spectacular roof's eye views of Manhattan. It was a one-of-a-kind scouting trip.

Two things became abundantly clear almost right off the bat. Joe, Larry, Victor, and I were bonding, which was great. We all enjoyed each other's company, the anecdotes, the coffees and lunches as we traveled around the city looking at buildings that fit this strange criteria. This would create a shorthand to maximize the movie. Sacha inadvertently caused that positive thing to happen, but he didn't recognize it and instead continued throwing unforeseen obstacles in the path of the film. His *own* film.

However, something else became much clearer virtually immediately. Even if we got permission, even if we figured out a safe way to do it, Sacha, understandably and rightfully so, would be scared shitless while being suspended between two skyscrapers. It was the kind of thing even the Wallendas would be scared to do.

Finally, with official word from the City that no such permission would ever be granted, the idea was shut down. Sacha was able to avoid the abject fear that would've accompanied such a stunt and spare his pride by blaming it on the bureaucracy.

Instead we created the illusion in a massive outdoor green screen space in Brooklyn, and if you look at the scene, it's pretty seamless. And even at thirty or forty feet, fully harnessed, with a thick pad underneath and surrounded by the crew, the stunt was still scarily high and dangerous.

One irony was that Joe, Larry, and I, in order to do this scene, had to take a scaffolding class. If you've been to New York in the last few years or even seen movies, TV, or still photographs, you know that scaffolding now surrounds almost every building. It was rumored to be an organized crime operation and the class was part of the scam. But we all passed and even got laminated scaffolding class graduation ID cards, which I still carry proudly. (Even though it expired ten years ago. Good photo.)

The next set of decisions with tremendous implications was the casting of the three main supporting players: the villain, Uncle Tamir; the sidekick, Nadal; and the romantic foil, Zoey.

We auditioned many able character actors for the role of Tamir. And they all acquitted themselves quite well, though none struck any of us as particularly comical enough. A villain with comic energy is hard to find. At one point, Academy Award winner F. Murray Abraham came in and was giving a good audition with Sacha as Alec Berg and I watched, but inexplicably at a certain moment in the scene, we couldn't help noticing that a pair of underwear had appeared on the floor. As Alec, Sacha, and I checked to make sure it wasn't ours, we realized that it had been stuffed into F. Murray Abraham's pocket and had fallen out during the course of the audition, or he was, unbeknownst to us, a quick change artist, or damn, this guy packed really lightly. It was distracting. Alec and I and Jennifer Euston, our New York casting director, couldn't stop staring at it and each other in befuddlement. Even Sacha in the midst of the scene was understandably distracted. F. Murray made no acknowledgment of it, even after we finished, until we said, "Ahem, your underwear is on the floor." At which point F. Murray picked it up like it was no big deal. Like, *What? Haven't you ever seen a pair of underwear on the floor during an audition?* I wondered if this was a trick he had pulled during the *Amadeus* auditions. He didn't get the part.

At this point, Sacha became very consumed and excited by the idea of Sir Ben Kingsley. He really began to push the idea. And he tried to get me to be inspired by the choice. And I was, to a degree. My issue was and always is in these situations, is he funny? I hadn't recalled any big laughs in *Gandhi*. But how could you say no to Sir Ben?

Oh yeah, that was another aspect of it. He had to be addressed as Sir Ben. Always. He insisted upon it. Being an American with little respect for the British monarchy, I found that weird. But Sir Ben, even at this point in his life, seemed to have a lot to prove. He not only had come from a poor immigrant background in East London, but had been shunned and ostracized as a youth by his own family and had achieved all his prodigious accomplishments purely on his own. That I respected. Deeply and profoundly. But I didn't feel it any more deeply because he insisted on being called Sir Ben.

Sacha didn't seem to care as much about Sir Ben's comic chops. He was Sir Ben Kingsley. What could go wrong?

Sacha and I had a fancy lunch with him. Fancy restaurant meals are something else that are anathema to me. I just don't dig the pretense. Plus being constantly reminded by everyone to address him as "Sir Ben." And sure enough, the first time I met him, I called him "Uncle Ben."

He struck me as a super-serious person. Almost humorless. But as he talked about himself, I began to realize that even playing Gandhi and winning an Oscar hadn't filled that hole within him. He was still seeking respect, but by the same token, like many of us, had accrued many expenses, and in the end, if we could meet his "quote," he would say "yes." And we did.

Casting Sir Ben gave gravitas to the role, but Sacha and I were both more concerned with laughs, and this would prove an issue later.

Nadal, the scientist whom Aladeen believes he executed back in Wadiya only to turn up alive in New York and become the exiled Aladeen's accomplice, quickly boiled down to two great comic actors, each with their own idiosyncratic style and energy. One was Fred Armisen, who from *SNL* to *Portlandia* and everything in between, had one of the most surprising and original comic sensibilities. And Jason Mantzoukas, whose work at the time I was less familiar with.

I had actually directed Jason in a pilot that we shot over a weekend written by Ant Hines sometime before this, and I really enjoyed his slightly more aggressive but also distinctive comic energy.

The creative team was divided into two camps, those in favor of Fred and those in favor of Jason. I was initially in favor of Fred, quite honestly. I had seen virtually the entire breadth of his work and knew how resourceful he was.

But to his credit, writer-producer Jeff Schaffer was a relentless one-man band for Jason, having had much more experience with him as part of the ensemble of Jeff's show, *The League*.

We had them both back numerous times, and while Fred was almost quiet and subtle while still managing to be hilarious, Jason kept transcending the auditions and really owning the character in the best way, until I and everyone else could not deny him the role. He earned it and deserved it.

Fred graciously accepted a smaller role in the movie and, of course, was wonderful as well.

Jason, with my encouragement, virtually stole the movie, in what I felt would be a star turn for him. His improv was relentlessly hilarious. He was the most present actor you could imagine. Happy to veer in any direction Sacha led him and happy to forge new paths of comedy himself. I think his high level of repartee both in his performance of the scripted material and his ferocity when winging it caught Sacha by surprise. Instead of rising to the occasion, Sacha felt threatened. So much so that Sacha actually asked me to tamp down his performance, which I felt was a fatal mistake and refused to do. Was Jason too funny? I knew Sacha would come off great in these scenes too; it was just that he couldn't see it. And this, too, would prove to be an issue later.

The final piece of the puzzle was Zoey, essentially the romantic lead of a very unromantic movie. It seemed like we had auditioned every young comic actress in Los Angeles and New York. In fact, the repeated auditions started to feel slightly abusive to me. We had seen a half-dozen women, maybe more, including the eponymous Zooey Deschanel, and the great comic actress who eventually got the part, Anna Faris. They were all great, but it didn't seem to be about that. What was Sacha looking for, I wondered and inquired many times.

I finally realized that, at least from my vantage point, he seemed embarrassed to have a romantic relationship in the movie. And I could only surmise that as a recently married and sometimes religious person, he was self-conscious about any onscreen sexuality that wasn't played purely for comedy.

Think of his "romantic leads" in *Borat* and *Brüno*. In *Borat*, his eventual partner was the lusty, bawdy African-American comedian Luenell, who plays a hooker in the movie. And in *Brüno*, he winds up with sad sack assistant Lutz, a purposely bland, mundane, unglamorous person played by Gustaf Hammarsten.

So after much discussion and debate, Anna was chosen. Anna was very attractive, and the first thing Sacha wanted to do was rewrite the character to "uglify" her and desexualize her and then make humor at her appearance and expense as much as possible, and as much as she was willing to tolerate. She was game and went along with it though it made their onscreen chemistry rather difficult, if not impossible, to decipher. This, too, would create issues later.

This, to me, was another of Sacha's strange self-sabotages. Undermining any chance of an actual human connection. It was possible that a comic dynamic could have been established, but instead her character was woefully underwritten, and the jokes at her expense were mean spirited and misogynistic and rarely achieved a funny enough tone to rise above that.

In another power play designed to reduce my autonomy, Sacha insisted we hire a storyboard artist to draw out every angle of every scene with me before we shot it, in order for Sacha to be able to change and veto any shot in the movie and also to remove any possibility of spontaneity. J. Todd Anderson, one of the most accomplished storyboard artists in movies, who had worked extensively with the Coen brothers, was hired.

Now, I'm a massive fan of the Coen brothers. All their movies. And their comedic touch and sensibility are very specific and unsurpassed. But their comedy is based on planning and control and intricate cinematography. They didn't rely on much improvisation or in capturing a spontaneous moment of lightning in a bottle, as had been our bailiwick in the previous two movies. At least as far as I could see. And that style had obviously served them well. But I was skeptical whether it would serve us in the same way.

Yet having been an aspiring cartoonist, I embraced the challenge. And J. Todd and I began spending our days together discussing the scenes as we'd trade sketches back and forth.

Of course, like Larry Sher, J. Todd became a friend and collaborator. We enjoyed each other's company, and the creation of a storyboard became a creative act unto itself. I even became excited by what we were coming up with.

But two things happened that marred this experience and that ultimately made this process, like so much of the decision making out of my control surrounding this movie, absurd. The first was Sacha's capricious undoing of any storyboard presented to him. Insisting, because he could, that this angle be changed to that angle, although when challenged with why, he never had an answer. It certainly had nothing to do with the comedy and obviously had everything to do with his almost obsessive need for control. These changes are often referred to as lateral changes because they don't move things forward, only sideways.

But considering it was all abstract at this point and would change dramatically once we were actually in locations which we had not even chosen yet, I felt if that had been the extent of it, it wouldn't have mattered.

What wound up not only being detrimental but a waste of time and money, as so much was in this movie, was the constant overhauling rewrites that would render days of J. Todd's brilliant storyboard work completely irrelevant. Although it was a source of frustration to me as I watched the script go through these arbitrary changes that were not making the movie anything but "gaggier" and rarely better or funnier or deeper, J. Todd also voiced a growing resentment of this chaotic disorderly process imposed on us by a growing dictator-like control freak who was blind to the destruction he would be causing himself by this assertion of power.

I wish we could've published the storyboards in graphic book form. As entities onto themselves, they were fascinating.

Yet despite all this, somehow, naively, I was still super excited and enthusiastic to shoot this movie.

But Sacha was extremely unprepared. He didn't know his lines, had never mastered any of the elements of Aladeen's personality, his walk, his accent, and further insisted on shooting every scene with alternate and different jokes and endings, which left us dangerously behind schedule right off the bat.

This was different than shooting *Brüno* or *Borat*, where we could essentially shoot for sixteen hours at the same cost as an eight-hour day. It was only Sacha and me, and the small crew.

But here, there were actors and extras, costumes and props, sets and vehicles, and a full camera crew and sound crew and lighting crew, drivers and catering and massive numbers of extras, all of which had to be maintained and adjusted during the course of each and every scene. And so much of what we were shooting was clearly superfluous, and done more to assuage Sacha's growing uneasiness and anxiety about the movie and especially about his performance. Yet it was easier for him to distract himself with these external matters than immerse himself, Peter Sellers–like, in the characters, which I knew he had the capacity to do, but he simply couldn't face the fact that he wasn't going to do it.

Although some scenes were undeniably funny and couldn't really be ruined by the constant meddling, there were many scenes that were uneasy mixtures of so many sensibilities, they made no sense and were unsatisfying and surprisingly flat, comedically and emotionally.

I had encouraged Sacha to trust his instincts, but it became clear that his instincts had been clouded beyond recognition by all the emphasis he placed on everything *but* his character and the content of the movie. He didn't seem to know what was funny. At least for this movie. And I was extremely sympathetic. I only wanted Sacha and the movie to be great. And I could see he was lost, and I tried to help him "get found," but he resisted my entreaties.

While we were in New York, we would all meet in Sacha's trailer before shooting began, to discuss and critique the day's upcoming scenes and see if there were solutions to each one's myriad problems. Although it was relatively civil, there was no consensus about anything. This left me with the task of shooting multiple versions of the same scene, draining and depleting energy from each one. It was a shitty system.

And Sacha's solution seemed to be to continue to expand the "too many cooks" syndrome to absurd lengths. At various times, Sacha brought in dozens of writers, literally, to sit around a large table and pitch jokes on upcoming scenes. Even on scenes that had been shot in order to improve them. Prestigious writers such as Armando Iannucci would be crowded in this room, elbow to elbow. Frankly it seemed embarrassing, and the results were less than stellar. I couldn't get him to see that this was the opposite of the solution to the problem. It had to do with characters, themes, story, something or somebody to care about. These elements were rapidly falling by the wayside, only to be glossed over with mostly weak jokes. Sacha would sit at the head of the table with his computer, and as writers shouted out joke ideas, he would choose what to write down out of view of everybody so no one ever knew what was being kept or discarded until the scenes appeared. It was dysfunction personified.

Sacha had the kind of trailer associated with big stars. It was a far cry from the back of a fifteen-passenger van on the first two movies. And we would pile into this luxurious mobile home parked in New York City every morning before shooting and debate. Besides Jeff, Dave, Alex, Dan, Ant, and Peter, Scott Rudin often joined us to provide his input. Like I said, I found Scott's instincts strong. He knew what this movie was missing and what it needed. And he was undeniably a strong personality. Furthermore, the American writers and I usually agreed with him. But Sacha never did, and this led to even further conflict. You could feel Scott's increasing frustration, and finally one day we were informed that Scott Rudin, the master of conflict, couldn't take it anymore and had quit the project.

I would shoot scenes with Sacha and Jason Mantzoukas and with people like Fred Armisen, John C. Reilly, and JB Smoove doing hilarious and potentially classic scenes with Sacha that crackled with the kind of comic energy the movie was starved for, only to see their roles wind up being cut down into straight men and foils for Sacha in editing. It was disheartening to witness this process.

Even if the scenes proved to be hilarious and one of a kind, Sacha would create unnecessary conflict to distract from the work. At a certain point, Sacha became disenchanted with Sir Ben and his somber, serious approach to the material and surreptitiously and relentlessly would demand, in stark contrast to his insistence that I "tamp down" Jason's funniness, that I somehow make Sir Ben funnier. Sacha's solution was to be rude and disrespectful toward Sir Ben and to treat him with the same disdain he had treated non–Oscar winner and non-knight Ken Davitian.

No matter what I said to Sir Ben, however, this was the performance he was able to give. We'd have to make the best of it.

Increasingly, Sacha and Larry Sher started to have a dysfunctional relationship. Larry was working hard to make the movie great and I would stand up for him, but Sacha had made up his mind that Larry was undermining him with the shots and angles and camera moves that we had all already agreed upon. This reached a head while we were in Harlem, shooting the scene with JB at a funeral home. Sacha demanded that Larry be removed from the set. Sacha then retreated to his trailer and refused to come out until that was done.

Joe Reidy and I looked at each other. There was no reasoning with Sacha. Larry got it and stepped away, and we were finally, after hours of negotiating, able to at least finish the scene. But there was no escaping the black rain from the dark cloud of bad vibes that soaked the entire production.

I had managed to keep my shit together and my composure

through the entire torturous, arduous shoot. But on the last day of shooting in Spain on a fairly insignificant scene, that all changed too.

We were shooting essentially a single elaborate joke about absurd things that Aladeen wanted his soldiers to destroy in a bonfire. We built an incredibly large fire, but you could feel the heat and the tension even before the flames were lit.

The logistics of the scene were not going well. The fire was waxing and waning, the soldiers, who spoke no English, were misinterpreting my directions, and we had to do the scene over and over again.

Joe Reidy, in his attempt to defuse the situation, kept taking the blame for the failure of the scene. This didn't mollify my increasing anger and frustration. And it wasn't true. It was a combination of factors, including perhaps the innate weakness of the scene itself. I wasn't interested in fault. I was only interested in getting the scene right.

Finally, after Joe once again masochistically took the hit for another bad take, I lost my shit and had, appropriately enough, a meltdown in front of the fire. I screamed at Joe, at everybody and everything. It was the uncoolest thing I had ever done on a set and was immediately embarrassed and ashamed. Mainly I was angry at myself.

Sacha came running over, but not to calm me or defuse the tension, but to remind me that paparazzi were watching.

I apologized profusely to Joe, who was of course the consummate professional about it, though my guess was that even the volatile Martin Scorsese had never had a temper tantrum of that magnitude.

My relationship with Joe was irreparably damaged, and it remains a major regret in a life filled with them.

But life, even with major regrets, must go on.

I had one last chance to fashion the movie into the epic comedy I still thought it deserved to be. On *Borat* and *Brüno*, I had deferred my right as the director to a first cut because I saw these projects as creative ensembles, and on *Borat*, Sacha and I had collaborated so well together. But on *Brüno*, it had clearly disintegrated with rooms of editors doing multiple versions of scenes. And so I had decided to assert my rights on this film and demanded my ten-week uninter-rupted director's cut. I did this in the vain hope that Sacha would see what the movie could be and relent.

But instead, it created further tension as Sacha waited impa-tiently for me to finish, and on the day I did, I was immediately ostracized and removed from the editing process and Sacha began his work to dismantle the cut.

Sacha was determined to turn the movie from an ensemble com-edy with an ingenious and topical plot in which he would shine in two tour de force roles, into a scripted, unspontaneous, uninspired version of the one-man shows of *Borat* and *Brüno*.

An epic comedy with the breadth and width and depth and wit and originality and funny characters and set pieces, and the great energy of a potential classic, was reduced to another eighty-three-minute gag fest. It was a fatal miscalculation.

That is not to say that there aren't brilliant sequences that remain. There are many original visual gags that rank with the best physi-cal comedy done anywhere. The scene with Jason Mantzoukas in the rocket factory (shot in a shuttered nuclear power plant on Long Island), with JB in the Harlem funeral home, and with John C. Reilly in the lobby of the New York hotel containing some uniquely hilarious wordplay were all painfully and needlessly truncated to their detri-ment, yet were so funny that their essence remained.

And perhaps the best moment is Aladeen's speech toward the end, in the hotel to the packed house of visiting and quite cor-rupt global government officials, when the now liberated Aladeen exposes the true and ironic nature of democracy. This speech, I believe written by Dave, Alec, and Jeff in some form, satirically skewered the shibboleths of our illusions of freedom. Though Sacha had doubts about it, I was able, in one of my last bits of leverage, to ease him into accepting the importance of the moment and perform it as only he could.

I felt it ranked up there with Chaplin's final speech at the end of *The Great Dictator*. I was very proud we did that.

My only option during this movie was to quit, and though there were many times I wanted to, and despite the poor decisions often being made, I don't quit; it's not my nature. More important, I still felt we could make a great movie, which as I've said, was my only purpose. This was what kept me going. A blind faith that it would still turn out as great as I hoped and be hailed as a classic that would join the other classic political satires in the pantheon. And I felt with the elements we had that it was still very possible. And I hoped optimistically that everyone would see it as I did instead of the way it was, factions divided and vying for power over the finished product.

But once I turned in my cut, it was ignored by Sacha, as was I. Not even a comment or critique, though much of that cut survived anyway because they were the right cuts of the scenes, even as the overall movie would get dismantled. But as a final blow, I was disinvited from any further participation with the movie.

It was hurtful, but it was made abundantly clear by Sacha that he was no longer interested in a synthesis, a dialectic, a dialogue with me, but in calling all the shots, even though he had no idea what those shots should be. He had become power mad, but like the tyrants Aladeen was based on, his abuse of power could only lead to self-destruction. Or in this case the destruction of the movie.

One crossroads moment really illustrates this point. There was a big set piece that had taken a while to both set up and execute. It involved one of Tamir's female assassins coming to America to assassinate Aladeen. The role was played by a woman with absurdly humongous breasts that the British writers had discovered online. These mammoth breasts and the stunts she performed with them were her calling card. We watched YouTube videos of her crushing cans and breaking bricks with her breasts. It was how she earned a living, and in actuality she was a very sweet middle-aged woman in a long-term marriage and this novelty was how they'd earned a living over the years. It wasn't sexy at all, except perhaps to those who fetishize such things. But it was grotesque and garish and shocking, which was in keeping with the type of humor we trafficked in.

We shot the scene, including her breasts getting caught in doors, as Aladeen tries to escape, batting away cans with her breasts as she stalked Aladeen, beating Aladeen senseless with her breasts but in the end drowning in a kiddie pool, weighed down by her enormous mammaries. She was a great sport, suffering injuries to her breasts, which were, you should pardon the expression, her bread and butter, and even almost drowning in the kiddie pool because we needed her to stay underwater so long. It was an arduous scene to shoot, yet undeniably one of a kind.

But Sacha was unhappy with the scene. Although it had been set up and paid off intricately through the movie, Sacha's wife, Isla Fisher, perhaps rightfully so, found the scene sexist. There was a certain level of exploitation that was unavoidable. And like the "uglifying" of Anna Faris's Zoey, Sacha had become, once it was shot, suddenly more "woke" or prudish, depending how you interpreted it, to those issues, even though Aladeen also fucks Megan Fox for money in the movie and Isla herself did a sexy turn in an extremely funny Aladeen music video that wound up mysteriously cut too.

But the replacement scene in my view was worse. Far worse. And wrong. An emergency birth delivered by Aladeen shot from inside Kathryn Hahn's vagina. For me it was crass, classless, and cringe-worthy. Worse in terms of humor, worse in terms of exploitation and sexism, dripping with misogyny, and ultimately much worse because it really connected to nothing else in the movie but was designed somehow weirdly to make Aladeen a "good guy." It felt contrived and cynical and decidedly unfunny, a sad uninspired attempt to create a scene that people would talk about. But they didn't. I realized that Sacha didn't really understand why the Naked Fight worked. It worked because we knew and cared about the characters of Borat and Azamat and were invested in their relationship, so that the Naked Fight arose organically out of the situation and characters, as extreme and radical as it was. I really felt this replacement scene bore no resemblance to that. As scripted, the scene was quite bad, well below our previous standards, though obviously new standards were being established in my view, without thought and in desperation.

I made my feelings very clear, but received no support. From *anybody*. I had finally become the odd man out.

Rather than trying to convince me to shoot this humorless, cynical scene or be open to discussing another alternative, Sacha used it as a pretext to replace me and had his friend, and a great director that I respect, Adam McKay of *Talladega Nights* and *Anchorman* and later of *The Big Short*, direct the scene instead.

I was devastated that it would end this way after all this. After all, my only goal, as I've stated from the beginning, was to make a great movie. And I felt like as much as I had devoted myself tirelessly to Sacha and protected him both from physical harm but perhaps more importantly creative harm, my heart was broken by this treatment.

When I began *Borat* and was told the horror stories by Sacha of working with Todd Phillips, I never dreamed that when this debacle ended, my sympathies would shift and I would understand what Todd went through and how Todd must have felt.

•••

At this point I was prepared to walk away. Really wanted to. Didn't need to be involved in the marketing or promotion. But my agents, answering to their boss, Ari Emanuel, who represented Sacha, but had demoted me to lesser agents in the agency hierarchy, wouldn't let me. Maybe my money would be withheld, maybe there was fear I'd bad-mouth the product, so my agents begged me to stay involved. They put a lot of pressure on me to eat shit, and against my better judgment and instincts, which had gotten me this far, I did. So I sucked it up and humiliated myself by shooting some promos and attending the London premiere, which gave my soon-to-be-wife, Keely, and me a luxurious weekend in a fancy hotel near the Thames.

But I don't recall exchanging any words with Sacha during the awkward premiere or after it, or essentially ever again, until years later when his dad, whom I had gotten to know, had passed away and I sent him a condolence note.

The movie was being produced by Paramount, and the president of the company, Adam Goodman, and the other Paramount executives hounded and harassed me by phone or in person on the set almost daily about Sacha's indulgences and bad behavior. They told me what a great job I was doing navigating all of it. In the end, of course, that was all bullshit. In the wake of the middling success of *The Dictator*, Sacha still signed a lucrative deal with Paramount, and I was shown the door.

I did have one more encounter with Sacha a few years later. Looking through some photographs, I found one of me lounging with a cup of coffee on the pedal-powered fucking machine from *Brüno*. I posted it.

Sacha sent me a short note, which read: *"Do you ever think we could do something like that again?"* I responded with what I thought was an innocent and conciliatory and completely appropriate joke: *"It depends who's doing the fucking and who's getting fucked."* Perhaps I was wrong. I never heard from Sacha again.

The Dictator would prove to be the worst moviemaking experience of my life bar none. And yet, inexplicably enough, I'm still proud.

CHAPTER 16

A (VERY, VERY SHORT) WALK IN THE WOODS

I was very broken and brokenhearted by the experience and aftermath of *The Dictator*. Sacha's hostility to me, my agent's abject abandonment, the broken promises of the big movie company, really soured me and made me question what the fuck I was doing and what the fuck I should be doing. And at least for a moment, I had no idea. Despite my own disappointment with the final product, I still wanted the movie to be a hit, and when the box office returns were also disappointing, I knew I'd find myself in a no-man's-land, wandering the comedy desert once again.

Failure is essential to creative growth. Even though I didn't want to have to live through it again. But there I was.

I knew one thing. I knew I never wanted to deal with the bullshit and hype and lies and waste and indulgences of a big-budget movie again. That much I was sure of. And I didn't want to commit to anything that took two years or more of my life, only to wind up regretting it either.

At least when Robert Redford fired me from *A Walk in the Woods*, it was before we made the movie.

Robert Redford, cinematic icon, wanted to make a version of the long-standing best seller *A Walk in the Woods*, by Bill Bryson, and I was asked if I'd be interested in directing. The chance to work with Redford was very seductive, and I found the book to be great source material for a potentially great movie.

Now Redford was at least twenty to thirty years older than the protagonist of the book, but shit, he was Redford and age was always a weird thing in movies. Guys going out with women half their age while women their own age play their mothers. This shit goes on constantly. So why not Redford, who was Redford after all, playing a much younger man? Somehow I convinced myself it would be okay. This was a story that could work for a guy Redford's age, especially a guy like Redford, still dashing and in great shape. I bought it.

The story of Bill Bryson's walk along the Appalachian Trail was nonfiction, but very much a dark, dark comedy filled with fear and weird characters and environments and surreal moments. And whatever modicum of romance would be age appropriate so that weirdness wasn't a concern.

Now, Redford in a comedy? That was another issue. But I thought back to *The Sting* and *Butch Cassidy and the Sundance Kid*. I thought about one of my favorites, *The Hot Rock*, and remembered he had a dryness that was comically quite original. Paired with the right actor to play his sidekick and foil, and we might have something. When Nick Nolte signed on, I thought it would be a winning and surprising combination. Both guys out of their comfort zones, literally, as actors and as the characters. Perfect. I started imagining the movie.

Both Redford and Nolte had not just been stars since their youth, but both were beautiful men. Literal matinee idols. And it illustrated the different paths stars, actors can take to retain or abandon their economic clout.

I'm not telling secrets or revealing agreed-upon confidentialities to say that Redford, like many actors, male and female of his vintage, had had work done. Not a lot, but it was noticeable in movies at that time. I don't even consider it vain. I consider it a tool, and Redford clearly felt, despite his rugged image, that he needed that tool to continue doing the things he wanted to do. And he was still

Redford, not some grotesque caricature of himself. And I had the deepest respect for him.

Nolte was a study in contrasts. His brushes with the law, and probably most famously his unkempt mug shot, were notorious. He still had a full head of hair, but he had gained weight and would be described by the casual observer as having "let himself go." And he didn't give a shit. And I loved him. He accepted who he was and fuck everybody else.

By the same token he was a sweet and easy man to get along with and hang out with.

They were both cool dudes. They were Redford and Nolte.

I was still smoking. Redford had quit a long time ago. But Redford and I got into the "habit" when we would meet of going out on the terrace of his office and furtively smoking cigarettes together. I found it very endearing.

We decided to do a three-person read-through. Me, Bob, and Nick. Nick ambled in completely toothless. He reminded me of one of my best friends, Barney, who had through his difficulties over the years become homeless but was still as affable and guileless as he was in high school. A good guy. Truly lovable. With a big toothless grin.

He promised he would have teeth by the time we shot.

I try to find the metaphor in all the work I do. In *Borat*, as the title said, it was about Cultural Learnings of America, and for me, it was even more than that. It was about the ignorance our cultural imperialism bred in our psyche, so that we didn't know shit, real shit, about the rest of the world, but the rest of the world was expected to know about us. And you see this played out through much of *Borat*. And that lesson was something that resonated so profoundly for me, I applied it as I began to conceive a couple of years later of *Larry Charles' Dangerous World of Comedy*.

A Walk in the Woods, too, was like a walk through the dark true history of America. An almost iconoclastic Howard Zinn–ish version of our country's trajectory and the lies that we tell ourselves.

Our casual read-through confirmed for me that the script was light. Safe. Heavy on the clichés, but underfed when it came to the darkness and potential comedy and unpredictability of their journey as told in the book. I found the book so much more satisfying than the script.

The script had already gone through so many people's hands, including Oscar-winner Michael Arndt's, who was one of the dozens of writers brought in to deepen the romantic relationship in *The Dictator*, only to have his stuff pretty much thrown out too. The current draft was credited to Bill Holderman, who worked in Redford's office, I assumed, as a production executive.

After our three-person read-through, I gave Bob my honest thoughts. This could be so much more than what it was. There was an untapped potential in this story that would make a much more fun and funny and fulfilling and challenging experience, which was truer to the spirit of the book. There was a scary quality to the book as the two unprepared men ventured forth into the ominous woods filled with unseen forces of both beauty and evil to face their fears and mortality that had tension and comedy intertwined.

Bob was extremely responsive. Extremely. He agreed completely. He encouraged me to go off and do a pass based on our discussion. I had been signed to direct the movie, but as was and is so often the case, I would never make a dime unless the movie actually got made. And I did these script passes for free, based on my obligation to the movie.

So I went off and did my pass. In the meantime a plan was made for us—me, Bob, and Anthony Hardwick, my *Borat* and *Brüno* DP collaborator, whose sense of adventure made him a natural pick to lens this movie—to all go to the Appalachian Trail for an extensive location scout. It was getting exciting.

I spent about seven to ten days intensely amping up the script, using the book rather than any previous draft as my guide, and felt I had captured the cinematic equivalent of the book. This was what had been missing from the previous drafts, and I was confident Bob would be exhilarated by reading it. After all, we had discussed these changes in specifics, and he couldn't have been more encouraging.

Then I handed it in. I felt like I was giving them a gift. A script that would work on all the levels, commercially and artistically, with more performance-oriented material for the actors, great opportunities for supporting characters, set pieces, and multilayer, multilevel, thematically rich, satisfying storytelling.

But instead of an immediate "Wow, Larry this is great," I heard nothing. Nothing. For days. Days stretching into weeks. *Oh no.* I had a nose, an instinct, for disaster, and for some reason, I suddenly found myself in the middle of one.

Finally Redford called, and in a voice, a tone I'd never heard while hanging out with him or for that matter in any film he'd ever been in, he said, "So, what do you have to say for yourself, Larry?"

Wow. Even when I was a child, my father didn't talk to me this way. I wasn't used to being called on the carpet, particularly for doing what I considered great work, alchemy really, turning the shit of the earlier draft into gold. How ungracious and ungrateful. And supremely uncool.

There wasn't much more to it. Redford didn't have any explanations or elaborations. He had no critique of the script. No notes. Just a shitty shut-down attitude. I thought we were buddies. I thought we were bonding.

Suddenly we were strangers. I was fired.

CHAPTER 17

NIC UNCAGED

I was on a roll. Unfortunately it was a rapid roll downhill. I kept putting my all, everything I had, into these projects, but instead of being rewarded, I was being punished.

I had a moment of "Why me?" But I'm not really a believer in that. There are too many billions of people suffering in the world for me to think I've been singled out for misfortune.

Oh yes, *A Walk in the Woods* got made with a different and more cooperative director, and like the earlier draft it adhered to, it was a forgettable mediocrity.

Regardless, I was lost again. Cast adrift. But before quickly sinking to the bottom I made *Army of One*.

When my agent gave me a small article in *GQ* about a charismatic but delusional handyman on dialysis from Colorado who became a self-styled mercenary tasked by none other than God himself to go to Pakistan, sword in hand, and capture, not kill, Osama Bin Laden, I thought I could turn this into a cool movie.

Gary Faulkner was an unforgettable, lovable, larger-than-life character, and his story was the stuff of fables and metaphors and cautionary tales. But not necessarily positive ones. At best, it was a poignant and absurd story. Comical and lyrical and real and not real. Interesting juxtapositions that provoked me and intrigued me in the best ways. I saw it as a dark metaphor about America's impe-rialistic delusions. How we believe we can justifiably destroy coun-tries and cultures as long as it's in the name of our God.

Gary was a great character. But in my mind, God and Osama Bin Laden would be characters too. I started to get excited. And that's always dangerous.

Because once you commit to a project, there are no guarantees. It can end badly as it has for me on occasion. Sometimes you have to make the entire movie to find out.

Condé Nast, the publisher of *GQ* as well as *Vanity Fair* and other magazines, owned the rights. It was interesting to watch Condé Nast, such an important and influential magazine publisher, have to pivot away from the dying print business. As someone who lived at newsstands before the internet, I lamented the loss.

But although technology changes and shifts and evolves right below our feet without realizing it, the people who ran the company were smart and saw the possibilities of bringing their business into the present, and hopefully the future.

One of their ways of achieving those goals was to package their memorable magazine pieces into source material for movies and television. *Army of One* would be one of their inaugural projects.

But as I've spoken about before, it's not like Condé Nast writes a check and the movie is paid for. That's only the first step. And the next steps often lead to trouble. Not only does the money still have to be raised from multiple sources with various degrees of lever-age over the project, but it then needs to find distribution, which is another deal with the devil. And in this case, I mean it quite literally.

This didn't seem to be a "too many cooks" proposition at first. But one cook too many can ruin everything too. And as new cooks introduce themselves, they can literally poison the broth. That's sort of what happened here.

Emile Gladstone was the first "cook." He was some sort of pro-ducer with no discernible role except to be an irritant. I'd dealt with many bad personalities in life and work, but Emile was near the top. The kind of kid who would get his ass kicked after school and actually deserve it. He was always there. But from the beginning, he seemed to be undermining me in so many ways and trying to impose his vision of the movie, which was literally the opposite of mine. He "saw" *Army of One* as a pro-America story. A positive story about the American dream. Weak. Lame. And wrong. The story of a self-righteous delusional prevaricating handyman with total ignorance of the world imposing himself on another country to do God's will, a pro-America story? We had a problem. And not at all what I was interested in, or what I pitched. But though he was a "producer," he didn't seem to be in charge, or even have any clout, or even to be taken very seriously. He just seemed to be there. Why, I never found out.

And once we got to Morocco, it only got worse. He became a fly in the ointment for everybody. We began to clash, which was an energy I didn't need with the pressure of making the movie. This all culminated one night during a dinner at a local gas station where the food was better than the hotel's, with me threatening to crack a plate over Emile's head, which admittedly was uncool, but no one was going to stop me. In fact, I believe the crew that accompanied us would have broken out in spontaneous applause. Instead, I restrained myself, regained my composure, and asked him to leave. Leave the set, leave Morocco. And he did. And I never saw him again.

Then there was Chef Jeremy. He was into everything! A very positive, upbeat, and easy-to-like guy, and I did. He was an aesthete, which was unusual for a producer. He was into the ideas, the reference points, the music. He loved it all, until it counted. On the set. Then he transformed into an automaton that I didn't even recognize. Emile, I had no expectations for from the beginning. I knew instinctively I would personally dislike him. But I'd hoped Jeremy would be a collaborator and even a friend, but he wound up being a chef who waited for the broth to almost be done and then threw some rancid spices in there, which left a foul taste in the film's mouth, if you'll pardon the "strained" no-pun-intended metaphor.

The third chef was a tall, lanky, easygoing multimillionaire named Jim Stern. Jim was also an affable fellow. I wasn't sure where his money had come from originally, whether it was a family inheritance or something else, but he was an unpretentious, modest person. I knew he had been an investor in some Broadway blockbusters such as *The Producers*, which I imagined enriched him further. He had produced a few movies as well. I saw him as a smart and supportive collaborator. What I didn't know was that he was also an aspiring director. Always dangerous when a producer really wants to direct. I started to feel the heat of that burning desire of his as he began looking over my shoulder once we were deep into production, then I found him leading the charge to take the movie away from me so he could refashion it in his own safer, less controversial fashion. Which I had told them from the beginning would be not just an artistic mistake, but a commercial one as well. They ignored my prescient words once I had done all the hard work of actually making the movie

Jim and Jeremy had really fooled me, coming off as good and supportive guys, but in the end being henchmen who, in order to protect their investment, kowtowed to the truly malevolent force behind the dismantling of *Army of One*, Bob Weinstein.

The movie would only be budgeted at a very modest eight million dollars. I enjoyed the challenge of trying to make this movie on that kind of budget, as my philosophy was no waste, no indulgences, lean and efficient productions, which this was.

I was aided in this by the line producer, Patrick Newall. He was a veteran line producer who worked mainly on cool low-budget action movies with great directors who had hit the skids through no fault of their own but merely the vagaries of the box office. I may have fallen into that category myself.

He knew production people around the world and knew how to stretch a buck or whatever the currency in any country. We would wind up shooting this movie in Morocco substituting for Pakistan and what has become my favorite and most livable city, Vancouver.

The exoticism of Marrakech was overwhelming, but its charm wore off. Ironically we had wanted to shoot there for *The Dictator*, but it was off limits at that time due to terrorist activities, including the bombing of a popular tourist shopping area inside the main square, Jemaa el-Fnaa.

Now we scouted there daily, walking past the bombed-out areas, which was something I had become strangely used to since staying in the fancy but bombed-out hotel in Amman, Jordan; seeing the bombed-out highways and marketplaces of Jerusalem; and viewing the remnants of World War II damage in places like Bucharest and especially Berlin, and realizing that most of the world has been bombed out at one time or another and how lucky we in America have been to mostly avoid such destruction and devastation, though I had sublet an apartment in lower Manhattan during *The Dictator* that overlooked the hole where the World Trade Center once stood.

We also don't honor our destruction like they do in many of these international destinations by letting them remain as reminders of what humans can do to each other. We cover ours up as quickly as possible with new construction and a plaque making it easier to forget the pain and trauma of the original event like in Pearl Harbor, or the site of the World Trade Center.

Two screenwriters had been hired to do a treatment for *Army of One*. They were good and talented guys. Scott Rothman and Rajiv Joseph. Their treatment was a great place to start. I felt that, with some adjustments of my own, like making God and Osama Bin Laden characters and mining some more of the absurdist humor, I could shoot this without a formal script, which would take months to prepare and be subject to notes that would water down the content.

I knew I could find actors who could roll with that seat-of-the-pants style of filmmaking and actually thrive on the spontaneity and urgency of shooting this way. And I managed to convince the producers that we could budget, cast, and make the movie simply based on that initial treatment.

We cast the great comic and improvisational actors Will Sasso and Paul Scheer and Wendi McClendon-Covey to play Gary's friends and long-suffering girlfriend. We also cast locals from Marrakech, which actually had a thriving comedy scene, even being the host of a stand-up festival, which again subconsciously influenced *Larry Charles' Dangerous World of Comedy*. Knowing that there was comedy even in an Islamic monarchy made an impression on me.

Casting comedy people in Vancouver was an embarrassment of riches. There are so many great actors whom we rarely see, it was a joy to be exposed to them and use them all in the movie.

Scott and Rajiv would be intermittently available to fill in the blanks. But mostly I found myself in Morocco and Vancouver writing scenes the night before or the day of when I needed more structure.

But we still had to cast Gary. And we still had to cast God.

One day, while still prepping the movie in Los Angeles, I was driving with my then-teenage son, Francesco, and I was telling him about the movie, and the character of Gary Faulkner, and we got into a conversation about who could play this larger-than-life character. Actually it was a short conversation because almost immediately he said, "Nicolas Cage," and I knew he was right.

The producers enthusiastically agreed, and so did Nic's representatives, and a meeting was arranged for Nic and me. It would take place in Las Vegas, where Nic was living at the time. We were to meet at the Golden Nugget steakhouse, an old-school-style place. I was excited and nervous. Nic is a legend, and I desperately wanted him to do this.

Keely and I drove up from Malibu.

● ● ●

I've always had mixed feelings about Vegas. My gambling days were behind me, and so the casinos, though fascinating places to walk through and people-watch, held little allure for me.

I had attended some great boxing matches there during my tenure at HBO and received VIP treatment, which made it vastly easier to navigate the traffic and crowds, both of which I tried to avoid assiduously in my everyday life.

In those days, I usually drove back to LA after the fight, but if I stayed over, it would be at the Four Seasons, which was a part of the

Mandalay Bay Resort, which was just on the edge of the Strip and allowed me to be there and not be there at the same time.

•••

At one point, I was to direct the film version of the best-selling book *The Dirt*, by Mötley Crüe and Neil Strauss, about the band's notorious exploits.

The script was written by Rich Wilkes, who had also written a great script about Sam Kinison, which I had been scheduled to direct before it fell apart.

I hung out a bit with Mötley Crüe, attended rehearsals for one of their perpetual farewell tours, and felt their growing internal tension at that time. But I believed their story had the narcissism, delusions, violence, death, surrealism, fatalism, and decadent self-indulgence that characterized the best rock and roll sagas. It didn't matter that they weren't the Beatles. Except they thought they were.

I was invited to see them perform at the MGM Grand in Vegas. Keely and I drove up, with the intention of seeing the show, spending the night, and driving back the next morning.

The show was scheduled to start at eight, and our hotel was about twenty minutes away. Keely was pressuring me to be punctual, but I scoffed. They're Mötley Crüe. They're rock and roll personified. There's no way they will start on time. We don't have to be there until nine o'clock at the earliest.

Finally, we took off for the MGM Grand. We seemed to get there in plenty of time for a 9:00 p.m. start. But parking in the MGM Grand was a challenge. Their parking lots were like three city blocks long and were super crowded on a Saturday night. We parked a long way from the hotel and then had to walk. When we finally got to the hotel, we discovered that the venue in which they were playing was clear on the other side of the hotel, through the massive casino. We picked up the pace.

We finally made it to the theater, presented our tickets, and walked in, only to hear Vince Neil, the lead vocalist, shouting, "Thank you very much!" as the band left the stage.

It was a portent. For a variety of reasons, mainly differing visions of who they were and what the movie should be, the project fell apart until it was resurrected a couple of years later with a different director.

That was the last time I was in Vegas.

•••

The Golden Nugget had survived the many permutations of an ever-reinventing Las Vegas and had managed to maintain its old-school cool and charm. The steakhouse, Vic & Anthony's, was highly regarded. Nic had picked it, and I assumed he knew what he was talking about.

When I arrived, he was already there, resplendent in an Elvis-like white tufted leather jacket with a shawl collar. It was Nic Cage, of course.

I was very hyped up and excited and sort of assumed we'd be having a cocktail. But Nic was having iced tea and so, like Jeff Bridges, whom I had assumed would be smoking pot like Jeff Lebowski but didn't, and so neither did I, I passed on the alcohol and ordered a Diet Coke and we got to talking.

Nic was immediately excited not just by the character but by my filmmaking methodology and philosophy. He hadn't been called on to improvise much in his illustrious career, and this would give him the opportunity.

How should I describe Nic besides prefacing whatever I say by first stating, I loved him. He was in the truest sense an aesthete, a true artist. As much as he is a creature of pure cinema, he is also, to some degree, out of time. He would not be out of place in the salons or stages of the nineteenth century. He could've been a silent film star too. He is downright Byronic. A poet. He follows his muse wherever she (I'm pretty sure it's a she) takes him. He is truly inspired and inspiring.

By the end of the meal, which was amazing by the way, he agreed to make the leap with me. I was ecstatic.

I returned to the hotel to share the news with Keely, and the next day we stopped at a large rock and mineral store in downtown Vegas and bought matching meteorite engagement rings before heading home.

The producers were as excited as I was and quickly a deal was struck for Nic to play Gary. Brilliant.

As much as Gary had made some of the talk show rounds to tell his improbable story, they were short segments that only hinted at his true personality and idiosyncrasies, so Nic and I agreed it would be invaluable to spend some actual unrestricted time with Gary.

For Nic's convenience, the meeting was arranged in Las Vegas. I would essentially interview Gary about all the details of his life, and Nic could chime in with questions or comments of his own. The producers arranged for a suite, and the whole thing would be filmed by multiple cameras. Gary, who was flown in from Colorado and put up at the hotel, was thrilled. If my relationship with the producers hadn't soured later, I would've edited this conversation and made it into a film of its own. A companion piece to the movie. But as it is, I have no idea where the footage is and will probably never find out.

Gary arrived with some of the props of his life, including the katana that he carried in a sheath on his side the entire time he was in Pakistan. And his first unabashed comment to us, including Nic, none of whom he'd ever met before, was that he had shit the bed the night before. Have a seat, Gary.

Gary was a garrulous and uncensored fellow. I took copious notes. This would be the basis, the foundation of the movie. He quickly let Nic know that he wasn't his favorite actor. It was Clint Eastwood. But he had no secrets, and for about three or four hours, he waxed rhapsodically about the events of his life, from the first signs that he was communicating with God to his life as a rather unreliable handyman in Colorado, to his weird but perhaps imaginary encounters with the Mexican cartels in Vegas to his kidney disease, which required dialysis, and despite that, his fearless but failed attempts to reach Pakistan eleven different times. He finally made it. This was followed by his unsuccessful attempt to capture, not kill, but capture Osama Bin Laden and return him to the States to face justice. I scribbled furiously.

Nic grew weary after about ninety minutes and left. But I couldn't, and though weary myself, I wanted the whole story before we finished. Gary never ran out of energy and clearly could've gone for hours longer. But at the end I was excited. This was more than I'd bargained for. I could see scenes, story, plot, characters, sequences, tone. I could see the movie.

I rewrote Rajiv and Scott's treatment, and we were off.

I added two main characters to the story, taking it into the blurry world of real vs. hyper real vs. unreal that reflected Gary's consciousness, and that in my view the movie needed to soar.

The first was Osama Bin Laden himself. This was easy. I had done a global Pringles campaign a couple of years before. It was a literal trip. From Prague to Uruguay to Bangkok. In Prague, we not only shot Czech Pringles commercials but also flew over talent from Germany and the UK to shoot commercials for those countries in the same apartment.

The British cast was, of course, the easiest to work with because of the shared language. They were also all skilled comic actors. One actor who stood out among the ensemble was a lanky British actor. Amar Chadha-Patel. He had a very original persona, smart yet a clown. I was immediately struck by him and quickly made him the centerpiece of the commercials we shot. The minute I thought of Osama Bin Laden as a comic character, I thought of Amar. He was game. We cast him.

There was still one major obstacle. One might say, it was the greatest obstacle of all. Casting God. I knew once I talked to Gary that God had to be a character in the movie. He spoke of endless dialogues with God, and so much of what he did was motivated by God's words, it seemed weirdly natural to make God a character in the movie. But who to play him?

I looked at God's relationship with Gary as one of frustration and annoyance. He asked Gary to do something, and he never quite did it right. Yet Gary wanted more than anything to please God, so God, without any other candidates to do this task, stuck it out with Gary. This would also give God an attitude that could be quite funny, I thought.

And so I thought, a comedian would be perfect to play God. This was God as a misanthrope. Tired of having his will thwarted. Reticent to pull a power trip on humanity, but rapidly losing his patience with the species and with Gary specifically.

Most of God's scenes would be filmed in Morocco with an additional few in Vancouver. Every comedian and comic actor I spoke to was into the material, but I also found that, as Americans, they were reluctant to travel to Morocco for a low-budget payday. I got it, though was disappointed that I kept coming up empty.

The producers and I continued making lists and finally a name came up that seemed so right. And though he was a comedian, he was decidedly not American. But he was one of a kind, and this was the role he'd been born to play: Russell Brand.

Russell was a world traveler and, coming from the UK, was intrigued rather than put off by the thought of working in Morocco.

Although Morocco is an Islamic monarchy, it is also a popular tourist Mecca, no pun intended, and so they walk a fine line between taking their religion and their royal family seriously and welcoming secular visitors from all over the world, particularly Europe. That said, the first thing I was told upon arrival in Marrakech was, don't make fun of or insult the king publicly in any way or you will be arrested. I guess they knew my sense of humor.

I had grown accustomed to traveling in Islamic countries, but was always taken somewhat by surprise when all activity stopped and people dropped to their knees wherever they were to do their five-times-a-day prayers. Sometimes in the middle of a take. But you adjust.

And like all religions, we get the impression that every Muslim or Jew or Christian is a zealous observer, but my observations have been that the casual convenient cultural believer in all religions is just as prevalent.

Patrick knew how to "work" Morocco, having shot there many

times before. So he knew the fixers and could arrange decent accommodations and stay on a budget.

Fixers are crucial in these countries, as I've stated before, and it is essential that they have a "can do" attitude because that's what's required to get things done. We need locations secured and crews and casting and equipment, and a great fixer has a bead on all those things in their home country.

Our fixers led us on wild exhilarating tours of the city, often to out-of-the-way places that the average Western tourist would never get to see. I'm always interested in where people actually live and we saw many houses and apartments in addition to more well-traveled areas.

But seeing this city behind the city this way revealed many of the issues of a country like Morocco. There were many wealthy people, often foreigners and exiles and artists who had settled there. But the Paul Bowles version of the city, the dark shadowy city, hostile to foreigners, poor, and without adequate services or resources, was part of what we saw as well. This tempered the charm of the architecture and the people.

Once we went into an apartment for a scout. It was dark. I took it upon myself to venture deeper into the apartment, leaving Adam, the AD, and Anthony, the DP, and the rest of the crew behind. I walked through a door into an even darker, bleaker room, and sitting on the bed was a teenager, who was curled up and howling like a wounded feral animal, and was clearly left there all day in the dark. I'm sure the parents felt burdened and also knew there were few options for a child like this. That memory continues to give me perspective.

After traipsing through the medinas and souks, lunches were fun too. Our exuberant charismatic fixers always took us to cool places where we could sample the local cuisine. These were probably the best meals I had in Marrakech.

But when we returned to the hotel at the end of the day, day after day, it became quickly unable to hide its strange flaws.

Two things in my travels I realized that we Americans take for granted here in America are clean water and paper products. This isn't the case virtually anywhere else in the world, where clean water and paper products are scarce commodities. The water in the shower didn't seem clean. Drinking water had to be from a bottle. And thin toilet paper was about the only paper you might see in a hotel room with equally thin napkins in restaurants. These things didn't bother me. I'd come to expect that.

Convenience is another thing Americans take for granted. Stocked 7-Elevens and supermarkets are the norm in the States. But in most places around the world, there are empty shelves and little choice.

But if that were the only issue at the hotel, I might've been happy there. There was much weirder shit. Like coming out of the shower to realize I was being stared at by a "security guy" who stood outside my ground-floor terrace. Or the fact that the hotel restaurant only served Indian food. I like Indian food, but I needed a break, and we were so isolated from town, the only other choice was a meat emporium in a gas station down the road—which, by the way, was great. But it wore me down quickly.

The highly touted room service would never arrive. The keys didn't work. The halls were essentially pitch black at night. And the lights in the room were so dim that when I started needing to rewrite scenes or write new scenes the night before filming, it was hard to see what I had written. Adam, the AD, did the typing, and we would struggle simply to see the words on paper.

Everyone was exceedingly polite, but it never translated into action. Sometimes it felt like a Peter Sellers movie, and early on, that was comical. But it soon turned into *The Sheltering Sky*.

But once I was out of the hotel for the day and shooting in these exotic, yet very real, locations with Nic and Russell and Rainn Wilson and Denis O'Hare and Amar Chadha-Patel and the abundance of local talent, I felt at home and in my element.

Besides the city and the environs, we were scheduled to shoot a number of crucial sequences in the spectacular Atlas Mountains, which ringed the city proper. It was about a two-hour ride to reach them, driving through small towns and narrow roads and farmland.

It was high enough in altitude and the right time of the year to be covered in snow during our initial scouts, and even some of our B-roll hang-gliding sequences. In fact, the area we shot in was a ski destination.

At one point, the weather got so bad that our rides on these narrow roads became treacherous as rain and snow fell in torrents, and large boulders, larger than our vehicles, literally rolled onto the road with no way to avoid them, get around them, or move them.

I had taken to wearing a suit, a tie, a fedora, and good sneakers during my time in Morocco, which was sort of silly but that's all the clothes I had brought. And I would return to the hotel muddy beyond repair.

•••

Marrakech was surreal. And there was no escaping it, so I embraced it and it is very much reflected in the movie I made. But not necessarily in the movie that was released. But I will get to that.

Nic and Russell, in fact all the actors, entrusted me with their performances. Nic had made some choices to capture the essence of Gary, which I encouraged and supported. I might write Russell's monologues but always gave them to him to "Russellize" or "Godify," and he would turn them into pure poetry.

After an out-there take that I loved, Nic would ask me if I felt this stuff, essentially his performance, would stay in the movie. I told him with complete sincerity that it was the centerpiece of the movie and I expected it to, and further, I would fight for it.

I had mentioned Nic was a Byronic figure, almost from another era. Russell was too. I had never met or been around anybody who was as casually brilliant as Russell. His mind was dazzling, and I often basked in his words, off-screen and on.

The surrealism of the movie was key. God shows up in unlikely places. The monitor at Gary's dialysis treatment. Driving a psychedelic truck, like you see in that part of the world. In various guises on TV as Gary tries to change the channel. Third eyes would show up in the oddest places too. On the arrival board at the airport. As

graffiti on a dilapidated wall. As the symbol for a home improve-
ment store.

This gave the movie the dreamlike and funny quality that I felt
could reflect Gary's mindset.

Nic's Gary was lovable. Good-natured, heroic, and fearless, but
sadly and dangerously delusional. It was the perfect metaphor for
America.

And Russell's God seemed more realistic, more grounded, than
Gary. Annoyed, impatient, frustrated, and angry with humans not
"getting it" and, like Gary, failing in the tasks he set before them.

I think I was split between the two characters. They were both
sides of me. It was becoming autobiographical, and not in a good
way. I was feeling producer pressure, and not reacting well. I was
getting the work done under arduous conditions but only getting
hassled about it. I could feel agitation rising, and there were no
outlets.

When we finished in Morocco and came to Vancouver, I breathed
a sigh of relief. Here was a city I understood. We stayed in an apartment hotel in a cool part of town. I could walk without security anywhere I wanted from Yaletown to Gastown.

Keely had come to visit me in Marrakech, and we had fun, but
when she left, she was ill and got caught in a bomb scare in Mar-
seilles. I tried to help but couldn't, and I started to lose my mind.

But I was happier when she came to Vancouver. We would go out
for oysters and Bloody Caesars. We had one of the best meals of our
lives down the street from my apartment at a place called the Blue
Water Cafe. We would want to see the city on my day off, taking
photographs and exploring. These were some of the best times of
our relationship. If I could've arranged to keep working in Vancouver, I think we'd have both been happy to move there permanently.

In Marrakech, it was clear that Nic's life and marriage were
both falling apart. By the time he got to Vancouver, he seemed more
relaxed as if perhaps his marriage had ended, except as usual in his
hectic life, his schedule was insane. He had just finished a couple of
movies in a row before this one and was scheduled to start another

one as soon as he wrapped. They all required different weights, different hair, different voices. Nic rarely repeated himself. He felt that pressure. He had so many relationships, it was hard for him to say "no" to anybody who asked. And each character he played was radically different from the last and the next. By design. It was a burden and an addiction, but mainly a passion. I could relate. And we connected without so many words over that shared madness.

I felt for him but really couldn't help him except to listen. It didn't seem like anyone was listening or looking out for him.

I had another last day meltdown. We had too much to shoot, and they were crucial scenes, and I didn't feel we had given ourselves enough time to do them. So once again, I embarrassed myself by losing my shit. When I'm in that state of mind, I feel the whole world is against me. It must go back to my childhood. The feeling of not being heard. All the trauma of my life was triggered by these pressurized moments, and they manifested in the worst way. It was born out of some deep profound primal fear. But still there was never an excuse for my behavior. It's only in retrospect I realize how destructive it's been to the stuff I work on, to my relationships, and to me.

I have sabotaged much in my life, professionally and personally, with that out-of-control behavior.

Naturally, that anger, that energy, wound up propelling me through that difficult day, and we wrapped with everything in the can. I did my usual round of apologies and thank-yous. The irony being that much of that stuff was simply carelessly cut out when I was ultimately removed from the project. Karma is a bitch.

For me. And for Bob Weinstein.

The producers had sold the movie to Bob Weinstein, who would distribute it. They seemed happy. I imagine they got their money back and then some. I was never privy to these conversations.

But Bob began calling me. At first he was excited. He kept comparing *Army of One* to *Borat*. I appreciated his enthusiasm but cautioned him that this was a very different movie. I'm not even sure he had seen it as this point.

Eventually the tone of these calls started to change. He didn't like Nic's take on the character, particularly his voice choice, which while peculiar, was very close to Gary's voice itself. Gary had a strange way of being, which included his voice and his syntax, and Nic had channeled that in his own unique way.

I told Bob respectfully that I liked, in fact loved, Nic's take on the character, and more practically, we'd almost finished the movie already. Yet he kept asking me to change it.

Uh-oh.

A few years before, I had met comedy manager Dave Becky of 3 Arts at some TV critics convention. He managed some of the biggest comedy talent in show business like Kevin Hart and Louis C.K. He had expressed deep admiration for my work and even singled out *Masked and Anonymous*.

I had never had a manager before, never felt I needed one. But feeling I was heading for an impending conflict over the fate of the movie with Bob and the producers, I called him and asked him to manage me. He said "yes." I was thrilled. I would finally have somebody on my side with some clout and leverage to fight these battles alongside me.

The producers seemed to recede as individuals and suddenly began acting like Bob's minions. Complaining about the movie. And trying to treat it like a typical commercial release.

I didn't agree with this approach and felt the movie, at least my version, should be handled a little more carefully. Maybe a film festival or two where Nic was due for a reappraisal. Get some critical mass before releasing it to a general audience.

I was ignored. Instead they subjected it to a typical preview like they would for a Marvel movie, or a franchise movie like *Fast and Furious*.

I spent the next few months editing *Army of One* with one of my most trusted longtime editors, Christian Kinnard.

We had an easy rapport from spending so many hours in the editing room, and I was really happy with our cut of the movie. We wound up being a minority.

When it came time for the preview, Dave Becky and the

producers all attended. As I said, I was against this sort of treatment for this movie.

The movie received a mixed reaction. I was not surprised.

Bob and the producers intended to use this reaction as an excuse to recut the movie as a happy-go-lucky fable. Changing all the music, adding an inappropriately patronizing narration, and most important, clumsily recutting scenes to make it an optimistic tale of an American dreamer rather than a blackly comic cautionary metaphor about America itself.

Crucially, they changed the ending so it seems like a positive love story instead of a poignant, and even sad, denouement of Gary's life, who not believing Osama Bin Laden was dead, leaves his long-suffering girlfriend and sets off again to find him. Which is true.

The cut was done poorly and clumsily, though I don't blame the anonymous editor but the producers with director aspirations, and it left the movie incoherent since the footage didn't exist to justify it. All its actual charm just seems forced and weird now as they tried to shoehorn their version of the movie into mine.

I pleaded my case to Dave Becky. At first he was sympathetic, but quickly he faded from view and I never heard from him again. That was a very quick foray into management. Never got an explanation, but really what could he have possibly said that would justify that? If you're willing to behave that way, you're willing to say anything to justify it.

I wrote letters to the producers. I talked to my agents at WME, Phil Raskind and Jeff Gorin. They were all afraid to take on Bob Weinstein in any sort of conflict. Their loyalties were clear. And they were not to me. How cowardly and shortsighted their decisions seem now.

I spoke to my lawyer, Melanie Cook, who promised to get into it but never made any headway that I knew about. It was clear everyone's relationship with the Weinsteins was far more lucrative than their relationship with me. It seemed forgotten as soon as I heard the click of the phone hanging up.

I even consulted with a litigator. An aggressive guy who likes taking people to court. But I couldn't afford the cost of a long court battle with the deep pockets of the Weinstein company.

But all these epiphanies and all the anger were quickly washed away by what would turn out to be my mother's fatal car accident.

My relationship with my mother over the last few years had been truly flowering. My mother would always come out to LA when I was married to Barbara. She loved the grandkids, and she was an ideal doting grandma. She and Barbara got along, but they were cut from a different cloth, so they never formed that strong bond, though they undoubtedly had a long history together.

But when Keely came along, she, a Leo like my mother, found a kindred soul. My mother had lost her closest friends—her mother and her sister. And Keely was estranged from her flinty mother. They filled the void in each other, and it was a joy to behold. We began to visit her down in Florida, and even got to explore parts of Florida I'd never been to.

I imagined we would enjoy each other's company for many years to come. My mother, the most alive, optimistic, generous, sweet person I knew, did not die immediately in the accident. She suffered in agony for a couple more months until my brother and I struggled to make the call to take her off life support.

But between the accident itself and her succumbing and letting go and surrendering to a void she was not the least bit interested in, there were many trips to Florida. Sometimes alone, sometimes to meet my brother, sometimes with Keely and my kids or Danny's wife and kids. And eventually all of us. In my mom's condo. My mother would have loved the company.

And on these trips, I would find myself sitting in my rented car, in the Florida heat, in the hospital parking lot, arguing with the producers and the agents and especially Bob Weinstein, who were all too glad to remind me that I had no power or leverage in the situation. They were referring to the movie's fate, but I understood ruefully on some deeper and larger level that it meant my mother's as well.

And we got caught up in the false optimism that the medical establishment sells. She might recover. She might recover but be compromised. And my brother and I and our entire families clung to any version of alive. Keely and I talked about coming down to Florida and driving her, in whatever condition she might be in, to my niece's wedding.

We visited with her ninety-year-old boyfriend, who was driving the car on that fateful night. And who miraculously was not hurt at all.

None of us were ever fond of her boyfriend. He was controlling. And jealous. With a bad temper. And possessive. He reminded me in the worst ways of my grandfather, my mother's father, and he ironically was named Joe Wish.

My mother seemed to like him so I tended to overlook his less-than-stellar traits. My brother wasn't fond of him long before me. He had refused to allow my mother to attend her granddaughter's wedding. This pissed my brother off. He was right.

And his version of events seemed at best suspicious. They'd had a glass of wine at dinner. He chose to drive. Someone had cut them off, and to avoid them, he swerved into a tree.

If you haven't been able to tell by now, I am a suspicious, skeptical, and paranoid person. My brother and I, when we heard the boyfriend's version of the event, like our entire families, simply didn't believe him. But my brother and I weren't satisfied. My brother and I drove past the fateful tree numerous times. It was a thick palm tree. Its trunk was gouged and almost severed. Was this swerving out of the way as he said, or ramming full speed into it? And with Keely and Danny's wife, Dafna, we headed to the junkyard where my mother's car sat in a crumpled heap. It told another chapter of the story. The driver's side of the car was completely intact. But the passenger side was mangled like it had been subjected to the car crusher at the salvage yard. We went to the police and retrieved the police report. There was no sign of another vehicle having been involved.

Now I'm not saying that this old man murdered my mother. Certainly not on purpose. But what I am saying is, what did seem likely was, that he was drunk, had words with my mother, which would be instigated by someone like him, especially in an inebriated position. Then due to his slowed reflexes, he reacted poorly to some surprise in the road and stepped on the gas instead of the brake and went full throttle into that tree. How "on purpose" any of it was, we'll never know.

But it resulted in my mother's premature death.

My mother was cremated per her wishes, and we held a small secular shiva or memorial service in her condo. Our entire families were there, and it was well attended by her many friends and acquaintances from the condo. Some were warm and consoling. Others were so frightened of their own death, they simply couldn't face it. And others could not get past their own petty selfish concerns.

Her boyfriend, in a last act of confirmation for us, did not attend.

That morning as we brought back the food from her favorite deli, Flakowitz on Boynton Beach Boulevard, for the memorial service, Keely, my sister-in-law, Dafna, my brother, and I and all the kids parked our cars in front of my mother's condo. And as we walked to the front door, we looked up, and written in the sky was the word "LOVE." A final message from her. It was Mother's Day.

The movie died. My mother died.

The true circumstances of my mother's death will always be mysterious. And we will always have our suspicions. And we all, my brother, our wives, and our kids, all miss her still every day. And my brother and I both carry the burden of knowing how much pain she was in and how powerless we were to do something about it.

The true circumstances of the movie's death are easier to understand. It was human nature at its worst. In the end, in a sense, this wasn't the case of too many cooks. But too many directors. None who had the actual balls to make the movie except me. But all who felt okay ruining it once I had done the hard work. I will never respect that or them.

When you are in my position, a filmmaker scraping by trying to make risky, challenging projects on low, and sometimes low, low budgets, you have to take certain leaps of faith. And if lucky, you find other less personal work while you toil for years on personal projects that may never produce any income, or even get produced at all.

Sometimes you make it all the way through the process, only to be screwed in the end. Like *Army of One*.

In the end, so many people let me down on *Army of One*. The producers, Bob Weinstein, my agents, my lawyers, my short-lived manager, Dave Becky.

Who rose to the occasion? Nic Cage, the entire cast and crew, the people of Marrakech and Vancouver.

And as others bailed and disappointed, there was one person with no stake in the results who actually helped me. Who gave me a "reason to live," even though I couldn't do anything to save my mother. He was David Dreyfus at the DGA. When all the supposedly powerful people in my life who were promptly collecting their fees from my work simply chickened out, David, because he saw a wrong and was willing to fight to right it, stepped into my corner and, on behalf of the DGA and myself, threatened Weinstein and the producers and got them to back down. To a degree. But on paper.

Since the producers and Weinstein blew any chance of this movie being a financial success, I am now liberated to show my cut, or multiple cuts, in exhibition or screening form, as long as I don't profit from it. I would like people to see my version of the movie, and I intend to make it available for free on my YouTube channel. I will always be indebted to David for that.

CHAPTER 18

LARRY CHARLES' DANGEROUS WORLD OF COMEDY

As I was getting older, as I watched the country go down a dangerous path with the emergence of Trump and all he represented, as the world was plunged into deeper chaos and as I realized I had limited power to change it, I knew that whatever I did next had to count. Not commercially, though I was in need once again of money. But in the formula that had gotten me this far, wherever that was. Impact? The willingness to go too far? I had to do something from my limited power position in the firmament to have impact. To say something that needed to be said and that only I could say. I realized at that moment how far I would have to go.

Larry Charles' Dangerous World of Comedy began to crystallize.

In my travels, I rarely had a chance to look up from my monitor or take stock of where I was except in relation to getting the scene. But when I did, I began to realize how insulated and American my life was. And how much of the world I didn't have a clue about.

And I realized that if I, who traveled to these places and immersed myself in their environments, didn't have a clue, how could an American who hadn't had the privilege of experiencing these places know about them?

I was repeatedly struck by the vibrant comedy scene in places like Morocco, Argentina and Uruguay, the Czech Republic and Thailand. There was comedy everywhere. And comedians plying their trade everywhere. On TV and in movies, but also even stand-up.

I don't think anyone I knew in the American comedy world had any idea that this existed. I certainly hadn't. We had enough comedy right here without some weird comedy from some other strange country, and possibly in some other language.

Here, I had been in these places, places like Morocco with its Islamic/monarchic rule. Or the Czech Republic, with its post-war vigilant, sometimes violent, struggle for democracy. Or Argentina or Uruguay, countries besieged by corrupt regimes and dictators with long histories of bloody coups, or Thailand, where military dictatorships and civil and political instability had become commonplace. And yet comedy thrived in these places too.

One thing I had after years of doing the kind of work I did particularly abroad was a certain credibility and authenticity and integrity. Those were important traits, and I cultivated them because they transcended show business, which had increasingly put a premium on corporate marketing to replace artistry and from which I felt increasingly alienated.

This idea, of comedy in foreign countries, particularly countries under siege, became an obsession of mine.

I love researching, and I began to research the subject extensively. I might start by googling a notoriously dangerous country and comedy. Syria, Libya, Liberia, Somalia. And without exception, the most dangerous countries in the world also had some sort of comedy scene. I would read articles and watch videos and, if they were available, comedy movies and television shows from all these places. Often, they weren't translated, but I had developed and honed my instinct for comedy, especially when directing foreign-speaking actors, so that I could tell innately if they were funny, and how funny they were. And it was exhilarating.

I quickly amassed a large file of dangerous countries and their comedy.

At the same time, back in the USA, it was undeniable that a dark cloud, maybe the darkest ever, was passing over us. In fact, it was hovering, massive and hanging there and blocking out the sunlight. And its name was Trump.

Most people, it seemed in New York anyway, had Trump's number. An unscrupulous con man. He didn't even hide it but instead wore it as a badge of honor. But as I discovered, an equal number of people in New York admired him for exactly the same reason. "Hey, he got away with it." Indeed he still is.

Nationally he was a professional buffoon. But his name recognition was pervasive, and sadly, these days that might count for more than substance, ethics, or intelligence.

And it seemed his star was on the rise. Was it possible that he might become president? When others said, "No way!" I remembered asking the same question of Ronald Reagan in 1980, and the rest, as they say, is history.

But what could I do about it? These two ideas, comedy in dangerous places and my utter disgust and disdain for Trump and the xenophobia and racism and excess and mindlessness that he represented, started to synthesize in my mind.

I couldn't stop Trump. But in my tenuous position, I could expose America to places and people they would never meet and, in doing so, show them that we humans have more in common than the color of our skin or our borders or the random luck of where and under what circumstances we were born.

And the idea of *Larry Charles' Dangerous World of Comedy* coalesced.

My agent at the time, Lindsay Dunn, who had exhibited taste and intelligence and support in many of my other projects, and thus was someone I trusted, was immediately intrigued by the idea and had an inspiring idea of her own. The Russo brothers, Joe and Anthony, who had gone from directing high-quality sitcoms and indie movies to big-budget Marvel extravaganzas such as *The Avengers* and *Captain America*, had used their massive success and newfound leverage to set up a production company. They were actively seeking projects to support, and luckily happened to be fans of my work.

I met with the brothers at the infamous Bob's Big Boy in Burbank, the oldest Bob's still standing. Burbank, of course, had gained notoriety in the 1960s as beautiful downtown Burbank for its extensive studio facilities, particularly NBC, but also its lost-in-time 1950s quality as a town as exemplified by the Bob's Big Boy.

You could understand how it was David Lynch's favorite restaurant. It was quaint and old-fashioned and sort of frozen in time, but also surreal, because of those same qualities.

And Joe and Anthony fit right in. Despite their success, they were two brothers from Cleveland. Enthusiastic fans, not only of my work, but of a host of things that we discussed passionately during our time together having breakfast and drinking a lot of coffee.

Artistically I had always been attracted to Cleveland. It was weird in a way I embraced and loved. Many of my favorite outsider artists hailed from there. Particularly R. Crumb and Harvey Pekar, who had collaborated on the original *American Splendor* comics. As well as the idiosyncratic punk band Pere Ubu.

When we got around to discussing my idea, going to the most dangerous countries in the world to find comedy, they were immediately enthusiastic and wanted to help me get it produced.

Very quickly we went from that breakfast to taking my little idea to Netflix and, with the substantial support of the Russos, sold it with relative ease.

It may have been my most difficult show, yet it was my easiest pitch. And I will forever be indebted to the Russos and their main man, Mike Larocca, for their participation.

But now I had to make it.

We set up a small office in Culver City. I would be working with people who were mostly quite a bit younger and whom I had never worked with or even met before. Many of them had done some extensive traveling in dicey places for past gigs and so had a little experience in that aspect of the journey, but almost none in specifically what we were about to embark on.

So for all of us, it was an adventure.

Research would be the foundation of the first set of decisions that had to be made. I handed over my research to an eager group of researchers, including my son, Francesco, who began to delve deeper into the reality of the many countries and their respective comedy scenes.

As they did, we slowly built an itinerary that would group together as many of these dangerous countries as possible and be achievable in terms of time, budget constraints, and security. Iraq could be grouped with Palestine and Jordan. All difficult to enter but not impossible. Saudi Arabia was a no until the last minute and then their status changed for American visitors and we were able to get visas. This would be our Middle East sweep. Then we could do a West African leg, which included Nigeria and Liberia and then the circuitous path to East Africa and Somalia.

Yes, there were many countries I wished to visit that the State Department had deemed off limits at that time. Syria was a no go at that time. But that is a list that is always in flux, depending on the political realities in those places. I had hoped to visit Ukraine. It was just as Zelenskyy, the former comedian, had been elected, and I thought no one personifies dangerous comedy more than him.

Some countries such as France, where an antisemitic comedian had been jailed, were very accessible. Many times, too accessible. I wanted to do a show that didn't just give lip service to the concept of dangerous comedy but actually lived up to its hyperbolic adjective. So some countries were struck simply because they were too safe.

Some were too far afield. In order to do the Middle East and Africa, we would have to forgo South America and Asia. In my mind, the countries we couldn't make, and these entire continents could be explored in a potential Season 2. It was a beautiful perennial idea in that respect. Dangerous countries would always exist, and so would comedy.

I needed to make sure these were countries that defined "dangerous," so that when you heard we were going there, you might say, "Wow, that sounds dangerous." And it was.

One of the countries I became obsessed with early on was Somalia. The other was Liberia.

So Somalia and Liberia became two must stops on my Dangerous Comedy Tour.

•••

Somalia seemed like the most dangerous country on earth. I kind of
figured in the back of my mind that the State Department would nix
this idea and I'd be able to say *Well, at least we tried*. But shockingly,
without any resistance, they said "yes."

Flying into Somalia was my first indication that this would be
surreal at best. We were coming from Nigeria and Liberia on the
west coast of Africa, and there are no direct flights to Somalia. You
must stop in both Abidjan, Côte d'Ivoire, and Nairobi, Kenya, two
African hubs. Somewhere in those two places, or perhaps somewhere else, I got quite confused honestly, but I remember boarding a
puddle jumper on an airfield for the flight to Mogadishu. The plane
was tiny and cramped and old, and it quickly filled with two types
of people: Somali nationals and mercenaries. It wasn't hard to distinguish between the two. The Somalis were black and dressed in
local mufti. The mercenaries were white and grizzled with crew cuts
and shaved heads and serious expressions and dressed in vaguely
militaristic clothing.

Of all the flights we were on, and some were quite nice, ironically this was the only flight I fell asleep on. But I remember being
jolted awake as the plane made a radical dipping turn. I looked out
the window and saw only churning water. No land. No airport.
Just water. The pilot had missed the narrow landing strip in Mogadishu and almost crashed into the Indian Ocean. What a time to
wake up.

Somalia seemed like a place at war, but with no sides. Just random extreme violence to no discernible end. And a mysterious
American military and business presence there that only made
things worse. Yet it was obvious America saw something in the natural resources of Somalia that was worth exploiting even at the risk
of completely destroying the country, which was where it was at that
time. And honestly, little has changed.

The blame in the media was placed squarely at the feet of the so-called terrorist group al-Shabaab, but I had learned long ago to question and be skeptical of such simplistic explanations.

And there was no place on earth where comedians, like so many innocent people, weren't at risk.

Our first day in Mogadishu at a simple modest, clean hotel surrounded by this fort, our security man, Jason, gave us some guidance in case we found ourselves under attack. It was essentially, follow his lead. I remembered the emergency medical procedures class the crew and I attended back in Culver City. If shot, do this, if wounded, do that, if bleeding out, do this. Though obviously valuable information, it didn't seem very practical. Every situation where that kind of extreme violence might occur seems completely spontaneous and unpredictable. It all struck me as somewhat absurd. At some point during his lecture, I felt obligated to chime in as I often do.

I said, "If we were outside and shooting or bombing or any kind of violence broke out—run. Run in any direction and hide if possible, seek shelter and safety. Jason has as good a chance of getting his head blown off as anybody, and if God forbid that happened, then what?" There could be no reasonable plan in the face of unreasonable unexpected random violence. That was our reality for the next few days. Mogadishu was a testament to that.

And there I met the famous and beloved Somali comedian Ajakis, who had been jailed countless times and lived with a price on his head and whose best friend and equally popular comedian, Adji Jeylani Marshale, had been assassinated just after they had parted one evening. He retold the story with tears in his eyes. Sadly, Ajakis himself passed away last year.

In Mogadishu, we met a number of other comedians—Old Boy, Abrahaa, BBC, and Aw-Daango—still attempting to ply their comedy trade, and although they had barely escaped death numerous times, they never gave up. They talked matter-of-factly about performing despite repeated assassination attempts, by the government and others, as if they were talking about an irritating heckler. It was simply a hazard of their profession.

I also met a former member of al-Shabaab. I was interested in talking to terrorists or former terrorists about humor. Did these groups ever laugh? If so, what did they laugh at? When I asked him what they found funny, he told me that when they killed somebody and dragged his body on the back of a truck, they would laugh heartily.

This man, who did not want his identity to be revealed, was very frank with us about how he was recruited by al-Shabaab. The group seems to be made up of farmers and young, aimless, out-of-work men who get drawn into this web of violence. This mirrored what I was told by a former ISIS member, now imprisoned in an Iraqi army prison.

I had never felt the danger in most places we visited, and we were cautious but as brazen as our security would allow me. But Mogadishu was different. There was no ignoring the destruction, the utter rubble all around us. There was no infrastructure, no currency. No nothing, to be honest. Except soldiers.

Soldiers in different-colored camo patrolled the streets with machine guns. Large armadas of tanks barreled down the potholed unpaved streets through barriers erected every fifty yards or so, and you never knew whose side anyone was on. And what was still standing today might very well not be there tomorrow.

We got caught in a traffic jam as these unidentified multicolored uniformed soldiers with automatic weapons converged on our vehicle and I thought, *Okay, maybe this is it.* I wasn't frightened. More resigned.

We sat quietly in the darkness of the vehicle as men in these different-colored camos, and even men dressed as civilians, argued and gesticulated wildly with their weapons.

The streets quickly emptied, like the Main Street in a Western where a gunfight is about to take place.

We seemed only a moment away from the first barrage, and once that started, it seemed clear that everything around us, and us, would be riddled, decimated, in a hail of bullets.

Then, it grew quiet, and suddenly we were moving again. The situation had been defused. We were alive. Next!

I had promised the crew that I would not be showing up at their houses back in LA to tell their wives and girlfriends and kids that Daddy didn't make it. That was not an option.

And fortunately we all made it home. Changed by the experience. Perhaps more grateful. But safe.

•••

I first became fascinated with Liberia when I stumbled upon a Vice documentary with Shane Smith from the early 2000s. He waded into the hyper-violent civil war that was being waged there. It was far more surreal and graphic and savage than any *Apocalypse Now* fiction could ever approach.

It also introduced the character of the charismatic cannibalistic "General Butt Naked."

I don't know why, but at that moment I knew I'd like to go there someday.

When I did my research, it was even more fascinating than I had originally surmised. Liberia was a country founded by freed American slaves, who in turn wound up enslaving the native people. There had been fighting and rebellions and civil wars ever since. Exacerbated like all wars by outside, specifically American and Western colonial forces, who looked to exploit the situation for their own gain.

The violence and chaos had escalated unabated until the present. And Shane Smith, who would go on to become a media mogul, had the balls as a white man to walk into the middle of it and document it.

Out of all this madness emerged a very pure, fledgling, struggling, but game comedy culture.

Though ravaged by war, with signs of it everywhere, including a preponderance of amputees and other permanently war-wounded lining the streets of Monrovia, it struck me as a fairly mellow place. Perhaps the country was finally able to take a breath after the relentless pounding of the war followed and even overlapped by the Ebola epidemic.

But we were plunged in immediately. Our producers had actually secured an interview with Joshua Milton Blahyi, General Butt Naked.

But it could only be conducted on the very first night we landed in Monrovia. I was tired, but I wasn't about to let this hard-won opportunity be squandered. My exhilaration and anxiety fueled my adrenaline, and we headed out into the darkened Monrovia streets to interview the former general.

We found a lone streetlight to film under, and soon a small crowd gathered in the shadows across the street. Were they simply curious, or were they victims or families of victims who would attack General Butt Naked on sight? And would we be in the way or collateral damage?

As he approached, unassuming now in bucket hat, polo shirt, and shorts and an expanded girth, the answer was still not clear. I felt tension, but was that inside my own mind?

It didn't help that I had made up my mind that I was going to ask him about eating human flesh. But I mean, why was I there otherwise? And that was a question that occurred to me too.

But we had a reasonable conversation in which discussing his childhood and eating human flesh had about the same tone. His childhood was harrowing. Literally given to the tribal elders by his father to grow up and learn to fend for himself in the deep dense forest, he grew into a leader, learning magic and trances that were all put to good use during the war. And I guess it worked. He survived.

He described pre-battle rituals of removing the still-beating heart of a live child for all the other child soldiers and himself to eat as a talisman. He talked quite extensively about sacrificing children until God told him it was enough. He still killed that child, but stopped after that.

When I asked him about humor, he told stories that made him smile and laugh about tricking and trapping and ambushing rival soldiers.

I asked him about how he got his nom de guerre. Literally by fighting naked, believing he was invisible and the bullets would never touch him. He even told me about the origins of the names of other soldiers such as General Rambo, General Osama Bin Laden, General Mosquito, and General Mosquito Spray.

They had an appreciation of the absurdist humor of their struggle, even as they were in the midst of it. From *Buck Privates* to *Catch-22* to Liberia, comedy and war weren't such strange bedfellows after all.

I asked him about the television shows he loved as a kid. He cited the black-and-white half-hour drama *Combat!*, starring Vic Morrow, who was eventually beheaded in the infamous *Twilight Zone* movie incident. And he spoke fondly, without irony, of loving the show *Kids Say the Darndest Things* with, yes, Bill Cosby.

Wow. The interview was going great.

And I asked him about eating flesh. He told me matter-of-factly that it tasted like "Pork rib...barbeque pork..."

He seemed to enjoy our conversation, and so did I. When it was done, we thanked him, and he disappeared back into the darkness from where he'd emerged.

We took a cab ride through the streets of Monrovia with comedian Duke Murphy, who was raised in a refugee camp, where he started doing comedy. In the midst of our ride, he was reduced to tears when we inadvertently passed the spot where his sister had been stabbed to death.

We met Paul Flomo, who also had been raised and started his career in a refugee camp and who'd been led to believe his father had been killed in the war, then he found out many years later he was still alive.

He works often with another survivor of war who lost many family members, Angel Michael, who got his comedy career started by playing an angel with an attitude.

At the once-beautiful Ducor Hotel, now ravaged and abandoned by war, we spoke to female comedians Rosaline Blamo, Mamie, and Super Mama, who shared their humor and exuberance for life side by side with their harrowing tales of witnessing murders on the street right next to them, bodies floating in the river as they crossed, and their own personal rape ordeals at the hands of soldiers.

We met Kekura Kamara, the star of a once wildly popular television comedy show in Liberia, *Malawala Balawala*, which combined local humor with universal physical comedy but was cut short by the war. He told me, however, that his life was saved when he was stopped by soldiers who were ready to kill him or take him prisoner, and instead let him go because they had been fans of the show.

I remember the power going out in the middle of the interview. I kept this moment in the show. This reality was a common occurrence, not just in Liberia but in virtually every country we visited.

We met ex–child soldiers, now street performers, who performed and lived in a cemetery for the benefit and entertainment of other souls broken by the war.

And outside the gates of the cemetery, a one-eyed young man who called himself Special Forces would perform a one-man pantomime, a violent ballet of sorts, as elegant and graceful as it was brutal, of a battle. And he would do it all day long.

How did they live? It wasn't clear. Not to me. Not to them.

I truly loved Liberia. I found the people to be sweet and welcoming. Having it be an English-speaking country made that easier for me, the Ugly American.

We actually stayed at a nice though modest hotel on the main strip of Monrovia. Like most of the places we visited, we rarely got a taste of the local cuisine. The hotel, the Royal Grand, was owned by a Lebanese family, who served first-rate Lebanese food in their restaurant.

There was an election going on when we were there, and that truly defined the environment during our stay. The famed soccer star George Weah was the leading candidate and would go on to win. But his running mate was Jewel Taylor, the ex-wife of the savage former president and war criminal, Charles Taylor.

People took to the streets for their candidates with great zeal, and we often found ourselves caught in fascinating passionate traffic jams of opposing supporters.

Weah and Taylor would be replacing Ellen Sirleaf, the Nobel Peace Prize–winning former president and first female head of state on the continent of Africa, something we here in America still haven't accomplished. She was stepping down, but had brought humanity and hope to this country in the wake of the civilian war and the Ebola epidemic. And the people wanted to build on that and protect it. These may have been the freest elections I had ever witnessed. Everyone cared. Can we say the same about America? Sometimes it seems like even the politicians don't care.

I had wanted to add South Africa to the itinerary, but there was no time or budget to fly that far. A choice would have to be made. In my mind, I imagined doing many iterations of this show, and felt like I'd have a chance to visit South Africa. For now, our third country in Africa was Nigeria. Specifically Lagos. Nigeria was quite different than Liberia and Somalia.

•••

Nigeria is the most populous country in Africa. And one of the most ethnically and linguistically diverse in the entire world.

We tend to generalize about Africa, but there are fifty-four quite different countries with different issues and conflicts and different cultures. It would be like grouping together New York and Tennessee. Once you're there, you realize how absurd any generalizations are.

Nigeria, the country itself, has thirty-six states. That begins to rival ours. And they are quite distinct from each other as ours are too. Lagos is a massive city. One of the biggest in Africa, and even the world. It's on the western coast. In the middle of the country lies the capital, Abuja. Unfortunately, we didn't have the time and resources to explore that area.

Of course, it had been colonized and, like so much of Africa, had undergone a violent history to throw off the shackles of colonization, but remnants still remained.

One interesting sidelight of the history of colonization: Countries colonized by the British had shit coffee. It was a challenge to get a decent cup of coffee in Nigeria. And in countries like Ghana, whose coffee is proudly packaged by Starbucks on their shelves, you realize the best of the crops are sent to the United States, leaving them with the dregs. But ironically, Somalia, though virtually lacking literally everything else, had great coffee. Why? They had been a colony of Italy, and the Italians *really* cared about their coffee.

Nigeria has not escaped violence, civil war, and military coups. But although violence still raged in the north and elsewhere, it was possible not to feel it in Lagos. Sort of similar to Ireland during their war, where Northern Ireland was the center of the violence but Southern Ireland remained relatively unscathed.

Nigeria suffers from many of the same problems as America. Political corruption, organized crime, poverty, the exploitation of their natural resources. And like most countries I visited, you could feel the military presence up close. And often, it was the American military. And what were they doing? The same thing colonial powers had been doing in these regions for centuries, protecting their "interests."

Indeed, the Lagos waterfront looked like Long Beach, with its American oil tankers crowding the dirty waters.

Nigeria was a heavily religious country, and like many religious countries, the religious differences were often at the source of violence. Lagos and the western sections of Nigeria had a predominately Christian presence, as illustrated by its proliferation of churches dotting the landscape the way fast-food franchises do here.

But my primary reason for choosing Lagos, Nigeria, was that it had one of the most developed and commercial and successful cultures in all of Africa. "Nollywood" had pioneered African cinema, and I had been a fascinated fan for many years. And it had gone from movies recorded on home video cameras and played in people's houses to a bonafide industry. Losing some of its funkiness along the way, but retaining its unique flavor and becoming a career choice for many young artistically minded Nigerians. The same with television. It had developed into a legitimate industry with facilities and programming that, like their movies, supplied the rest of the continent.

And most interestingly of all, it had one of the most successful stand-up comedy industries not only in Africa, but anywhere in the world.

This group of comedians were called humorpreneurs. They had managed to parlay their stand-up acts into lucrative gigs and commercial sponsorships that would be the envy of any Western comedy star. They were among the biggest stars in Nigeria. As big as star athletes and movie stars, and were courted by politicians seeking their public support.

Another truism about African comedy was that although there had been a local comedy culture in virtually every country I visited and researched, Western comedy was still the dominant force, both in influence and impact. Every comedian, in fact every person, was a fan of Eddie Murphy and Dave Chappelle and others.

One day while filming a female comedian named Helen Paul under a colorfully muraled trestle under a freeway, there was a car accident on the road right behind where we were filming. When I turned, I heard someone shout, "Larry Charles!" A young Nigerian man had abandoned his vehicle in the traffic and was running toward me smiling and excited. His name was Abba T. Makama, a bold young filmmaker who blended Western humor and Nigerian sensibility into very original work, and he was surprisingly a fan of my work. Now I'm a fan of his as well. We have remained friends as I have tried to do with many of the people I have encountered. But it illustrates the influence of Western comedy.

Another illustration of the influence and impact of Western comedy is *The Daily Show.* Particularly since South African comedian Trevor Noah took over from Jon Stewart.

Every African country I visited or researched had at least one show, and often a few, modeled after *The Daily Show.* Why? Even the most mainstream models of the show like *The Other News* here in Lagos starring Okey Bakassi, which had a desk set and a studio audience and multiple cameras and location pieces and a writing staff and on which I was a guest, could be done quite economically. But in countries where there might not be that many options on mainstream or government-run television, I met many comedians who did similar *Daily Show*–type shows right out of their house using a table and green screen and an iPhone. These shows allowed them to comment and be funny and scathing about political and social events and post the episodes directly on social media, where in many cases they reached millions of people.

This direct form of satire has had a massive impact and influence on me. As I've drifted away from mainstream media in my tastes and desires, I have begun shooting my own videos, sometimes at home but often wherever, using an iPhone with a teleprompter app and simply posting them on Instagram or Twitter or my YouTube channel and being able to directly communicate with an audience without commercials or network notes or any censorship of any kind. It has been liberating, and I have these comedians to thank for that.

This was also true in the Middle East, where the Iraqi comedian Ahmad Albasheer has pioneered his own unique version of this format.

It was fascinating to be the minority in a place for once. The only white man in a predominately "black country" (not including, in all fairness, my camera and sound guy and producer—it just sounds better, but you get the idea). Your perspective changes quickly when you are obviously the minority. There was no hiding my whiteness, and we were stared at in some places like freaks, and like I imagine black people are often stared at in predominately white areas of the United States.

I interviewed many of the major comedians of Nigeria. For each one, I tried to choose an iconic location that illustrated the unique environment of Lagos. The comedian known as Ali Baba, and whose real name was so long, it was almost a joke in itself, whom many credit with being the pioneer of humorpreneurship, lived in a luxurious house, but like much of the affluent sections of Lagos, it was surrounded by rubble and unfinished infrastructure and behind a massive wall with cameras and guards for security.

He had an extensive library of comedy books, including many biographies of famous American comedians, and he loved showing them off to me.

I interviewed the comedian known as Basketmouth. To talk to him, I choose Fela Kuti's New Africa Shrine, a beautiful open-air venue for music at night with amazing art displayed on the walls and ceiling, dedicated to the memory of Fela Kuti, the legendary politically radical Nigerian singer who died of AIDS, but a strange smoky hangout during the day with people in various states of high-ness and inebriation and an ominous air. Fights broke out while we were there, and strangers would walk up to Basketmouth and inter-rupt the interview. But it was called the *Dangerous Comedy Show*, not the *Safe One*.

I met many sexually ambiguous personalities in Nigeria who were much beloved but also much reviled in this still homophobic country. Like Denerele Edun, with his flamboyant dress and person-ality, who had laughed in the face of the abuse he had to endure. I felt his brand would've translated well to the States, where he would be much more accepted. At least by more people.

It was ironic because the flip side of the homophobic culture, which ran rampant through not just comedy but the entire soci-ety and was used as a source of humor, was the casual sexism and misogyny that made it difficult for women in all walks of life, not just stand-up, to be taken seriously, and also spilled into rape jokes, for which Basketmouth had been roundly criticized.

But he thanked his critics, saying that the controversy helped increase his ticket sales.

We met Charly Boy, yet another flamboyant personality who had flirted with his sexual ambiguity for literally decades, but man-aged to combine it with a fierce political determination that saw him leading protests and become a hero of the Nigerian downtrodden.

I interviewed him on a busy bustling street corner in Lagos in the relentless sun and heat.

As we spoke, a crowd gathered. First, just a few, but by the end of the interview, it was a mass. They all knew and loved and admired and respected Charly Boy, who had been uncompromising in fighting inequity his entire life.

Ever the entertainer, the power of the surrounding crowd was not lost on Charly Boy.

Spontaneously he began leading them in a freedom chant. This led quite naturally to a march as more and more people joined. They marched, we filmed. Until Charly Boy had made his point, and on camera, with a simple gesture, dispersed the crowd. It was a stirring moment.

My search for dangerous comedy didn't just include comedians, or even terrorists, but people living in these dire circumstances. Could they even retain a sense of humor? (The answer was always "*yes*.") What made them still laugh? And how did laughter help them cope?

The last wildly popular comedian we interviewed was known as Bovi. Aaron and David, the producers, and our local Nigerian fixer, Terfa Tilley Gyado, and in fact all our fixers in every country, would try to give me options for locations to conduct interviews. I always chose the most challenging and tense to give a flavor of the reality of our environment. I think it really added to the authenticity of the show rather than conducting interviews in hotel rooms. Sometimes I wanted to go places that our security would not allow me. But Bovi's may have been the most challenging and risky of all.

The interview took place in one of the massive open-air markets in Lagos. An almost absurdly dense bazaar of goods, produce, electronics, clothes, people, and anything else you can imagine, crushed together in all directions, including up. It is hard to describe this human mass, but it was like crowd surfing. You didn't really walk—instead you were carried along, and warned to check your pockets. It was quite impossible to move voluntarily, but at the same time incredibly exciting and exhilarating.

This onslaught of humanity and sheer "stuff" inspired groups of desperate roving young men to exploit and take advantage and capitalize in any way they could. Thievery and robbery were apparently commonplace and you could understand why.

Even parking our van was a challenge, as we had to wade into a dangerously overcrowded area where some of these young men, referred to as "rent boys" by the locals, waited and preyed. In our case, they had to be bribed to let the van stay. It was sort of an unofficial parking fee. Not that much different than any parking lot in LA except there were no spots, no signs, no way in or out, and you were forced to negotiate a price and hope the van would still be there when you returned.

We decided to conduct the interview on a balcony that overlooked the marketplace. The din was overwhelming but contributed to the reality, since it was reality. Bovi and I both loved it. The security and crew, less so.

When it was time to leave, Bovi's driver could no longer get close to where we were, and Bovi asked if he could ride with us to meet up with him. Of course we said "yes" and proceeded to our van, but if possible, the marketplace had become even more crowded, and the addition of a celebrity complicated our short journey, rendering it almost impossible to reach our vehicle.

The crew was feeling a little panicky and our security was on high alert, but as I've described before, there are so many frivolous situations in which I get anxious, but in these more urgent situations, I become strangely serenely calm, almost happy. Weird. I interpreted this phenomenon as being the result of surviving so many childhood confrontations, but now I wonder if it isn't also coupled with a low-grade sociopathy.

When the van was finally in sight, the crew, Bovi, and I were quickly shoved in by security, and now some local police who had joined them. The doors were slammed shut, and both Bovi and I smiled at the surreal scene unfolding around us. But the chaos was quickly escalating as we became surrounded by the throngs, but mainly some very rapacious and predatory "rent boys" who wanted their pound of flesh. And despite everything, we would not be moving unless we coughed it up.

For some reason, our driver was offended by the rent boys and defiantly refused to give them anything, though it was crystal clear that this would lead to potential violence. Soon the van was being rocked, and it wasn't hard to imagine the windows being smashed and the doors forced open and us being dragged out of the van. Bovi remained shockingly calm. My cameraman, Matt, was almost frozen by the scene developing around us, and I had to snap him out of it to start shooting. That was always my concern in these situations. If it's going to happen, and it was, making fucking sure we shot it. He picked up his camera. Both Bovi and I suggested we pay the fee, whatever it was. And believe me, although I didn't know, it simply couldn't have been very much.

But by this time it was teetering on the verge of being too late. It sort of felt like the van had driven into a muddy river and was now sinking. We finally coerced the driver to take some cash and crack open the window before it was cracked for us and hand it off to the most vulturous of the "rent boys." You can see him on camera, by the way, as he pressed his predatory visage against the window. And with that, a narrow path opened up.

●●●

I had what I call a "Death Wish List" for countries I wanted to visit for *Larry Charles' Dangerous World of Comedy*. In the Middle East, Iraq was number one. And it was indeed the first stop on our tour.

As Americans, we tend to simplify so much about other countries, even our own. We rarely bother to learn the intricacies and complexities of a foreign nation. And I'm as guilty of this as anybody. But this show taught me how valuable it is to put in the time and learn and expand our knowledge of these places, and that was part of the goal in doing it.

Iraq was a great example. What *was* Iraq? Well, long before it was Iraq, it was many things. For instance, back in the 3000s and 4000s BC, it was the home of the very first acknowledged civilization, the Sumerians. They were the first known practitioners of disciplines such as mathematics, astronomy, writing, law, medicine, and even organized religion. There is very little global respect for, or even remnants of, that legacy.

Iraq was the actual Mesopotamia at some point, and contained the fabled city of Babylon.

Iraq, as we know it, wasn't referred to as Iraq until after World War I. It was named and was ruled by the British for a long time before and afterward.

Of course, this led to a series of coups d'état and civil wars and interventions ever since that still rage to this very day, inspired by this oppressive colonial rule, which in a sad and weird way led us right up to the present.

Yet when we landed in Erbil, the capital and most populous city in the Kurdistan region of Iraq, you might not know or feel any of this at all.

The chaos and violence that have been sown by our military involvement there have perpetuated a series of long-standing civil disputes that have spilled out into wars themselves. Wars within war. Like the attempt of the Kurdistani Iraqis to gain independence from Iraq itself.

Living in a constant state of war takes its toll on a people. Not just in casualties. But in trauma for the living. This trauma produces numbness and bitterness and anger, but also compassion and humanity and a very dark gallows humor in the face of it. Iraq possessed all of these traits.

And Erbil was in some ways an attempt to ignore all of it and show the world what a modern free Iraq could be.

Erbil was a surprisingly modern city. Modern skyscrapers and hotels and malls dotted the landscape. And new construction with large cranes and equipment was present everywhere. Of course, the war raged only a few miles down the road in places like Baghdad, Kirkuk, and Mosul.

Before the producers, Aaron and David, even had a chance to commune with our fixers, we were invited to a live comedy show, outside, which would be attended by thousands. And if we didn't go tonight, we wouldn't have a chance again while we were there.

Comedy show. Live. Thousands of people. Does anybody realize there's a war going on?

Yes. Everyone does, and that's the point.

None of us quite knew what to expect. Our security was on guard. Matt; Ken, our sound man; Aaron; and David were quite nervous. But I was digging it. It was a scene. In the open field adjacent to an amusement park. Not a bombed-out amusement park, but one that was operating rides and selling ice cream. This was life during wartime. Life in the face of war. Life saying *Fuck you* to war.

The name of the comedy troupe was Bezmi Bezm. They did live sketches lampooning politics and social and cultural mores. And though I couldn't understand a word they said, I knew comedy well enough that when I heard the gales of laughter ripple through the crowd, I knew they were funny too.

I talked through a translator to many of the performers and many people in the crowd. And they were in sync. This was as important a part of their survival as any weapon, and perhaps more powerful.

The people onstage and in the audience, including many families, weren't reckless or foolish. But they were beyond fear. Determined to live their lives in the circumstances presented to them. And laughter, like breathing, like eating, like loving, was what would sustain them.

It proved to me that very first night how important, how crucial, how essential comedy was. People need a respite from the relentless reality that overwhelms them. They need to laugh at what scares them. And our first night in Iraq, I quickly learned that lesson and confirmed my thesis and reason for doing the show.

And that lesson became the theme of my time in Iraq.

Next we met Ali al-Khalidi, whose dark humor surpassed virtually anything I'd seen, though you'd never know it from his appearance. Sparkling blue eyes, a tailored suit, and not a well-coiffed hair out of place. He had the demeanor of a precocious child, yet he had hosted a harrowing prank show called *Put Him in Bucca*, which was a reference to a notorious American military prison in Iraq.

Apparently a big issue in Iraq was fake checkpoints in which ISIS would pretend to be Iraqi military. They would stop people, and rather than question them, they'd often take them prisoner or murder them. The premise of the show was: He would set Iraqi celebrities up to meet the Iraqi military and, somewhere along the way, plant fake bombs in the trunks of their cars. Then have actors pretending to be Iraqi police or military pull them over and accuse them of being terrorists and threaten to imprison them or execute them, as hidden cameras watched.

Our translator kept calling me Ray Charles, but other than that, we had a fascinating interview.

After this, I met Mivan Mandalawi. He was a stand-up comedian in a place with no comedy clubs. His English was excellent, and as he riffed on the street, trying out his material on me, across from the only comedy club, the LOL Club, that had existed, now sadly defunct, I realized he'd make a great translator. After the interview he was hired.

Next, we drove into Kirkuk, a city about an hour away from Erbil. It had been the site of fierce fighting, leaving the city, and every building still standing, riddled with bullet holes. It was surreal entering this wasteland. Yet amid the destruction, people still needed to go about their business, shopping for what they could, trying to keep their small shops open. Children being dragged by their mothers as you might see in any American city. Such a strange juxtaposition.

Yet another reminder that we and "they," whoever "they" are, are not that dissimilar. What would we be doing if our cities had been bombed to rubble? Trying to survive. Trying to rebuild. And occasionally laughing.

We were on our way to a prison operated by the Iraqi police that housed ISIS prisoners. This had been one of my goals. To talk to a member of ISIS and ask him what he found funny.

It was a difficult negotiation gaining access, but we had. First we were led into the general's office. He regaled me, with Mivan frantically translating, with his exploits and adventures as a soldier and policeman, often sharing humorous anecdotes about the war, and much like the other soldiers' humorous recollections, they were mostly about the enemy suffering.

Then he led us into a room where an ISIS prisoner was brought, shackled at the hands and feet. The general would not allow us to ask his name, and so he remained nameless.

He was not what I had imagined. A very nonprepossessing slight man in civilian clothes. He had a low-key demeanor, as opposed to the bombastic colorful general. He was, he told us, merely a farmer who had been drawn into the conflict when ISIS destroyed his village. He had a family whom he missed very much. And he shared what he could under the circumstances of what he found humorous, in his life as a farmer, and as a prisoner.

It was not at all what I had imagined or expected. But it was a stark reminder of the reality of war. Not everyone was a fanatic. Or even particularly angry. Some had no choice. And paid the price anyway.

As it turned out, this was the day that Mosul had fallen and the battle raged as we headed back. It wasn't that far from Kirkuk to Mosul, and as we drove along, we could see the smoke from the bombs cloud the air in the distance. You could see it, too, in that episode.

Iraq was like any place that you might spend some time in rather than reading about. Much more diverse and less predictable than any media accounts. You could no more generalize about Iraqis than about Americans. If we could learn this, think how far it would go to create friendship and tolerance rather than suspicion and hate. We as Americans need to learn the expression "That could be us."

For instance, we met an Iraqi "shock jock." His name was Noor Matti. As a child, his father, a communist, and his entire family had been forced to flee Iraq through the mountains on foot to escape execution. After an arduous journey, they wound up in, can you guess? Detroit.

Detroit and American culture had a profound effect on Noor, from dress and food to humor. He'd had a successful assimilation, eventually completely integrating himself into this new environment called America. But something called him back. He sensed a need to return to his home country, but bring back his newly earned

American sensibility, and he wound up starting a radio show modeled on the ones he'd listened to back in the States, like Howard Stern, with pranks, and contests, and call-ins and music.

He had taken the hard way. More fulfilling, but far more difficult. But something that Americans often never need to do.

We met Iraqis who considered themselves Iraqis but also Iraqis who considered themselves Kurds, such as Ako Sangawi, a fierce soldier with a goofy sense of humor who was still an active soldier, even as he was an active comedian making comedy videos in between the fighting.

I wasn't just interested in meeting comedians in dangerous places. As I've said, I interviewed ex-al-Shabaab "terrorists" and ISIS prisoners. In Iraq, as families are displaced due to the war, I thought it would be interesting to talk to a refugee family.

The refugee camp was vast, and normal life was clearly trying to be approximated. But entire families slept in metal huts where it was almost impossible to stand and where power was shut off for many hours a day and water was scarce. This was in stark contrast to their previous lives, when they lived in houses, with family members employed or attending school.

Yet these people dreamed. Not so much of returning to their homes, which for the most part had been destroyed, but to getting out of the camp and facing the future. This sense of hope, this sense of a future, was often accompanied by a sense of humor. I wanted to know what an average refugee family found funny. Was there any humor in their predicament?

Other than the external reality, as I sat on the floor of the hut with them, the universal truth I had stumbled upon had occurred to me again. We are all more the same than different. They were a family, with a teenage son making mixtapes and hoping to make music his life and a young daughter dreaming of a career but for now focusing on her studies. The mom was stoic, trying to make the best without the usual conveniences and appliances available to her. And the dad, beaten down by so many realities, house and job destroyed, forced to run to protect his family, but noble in the strength he projected to hold his family together.

And they laughed. Heartily and warmly. At the stuff families do. The absurdity of the situation. Each other. They were warm and welcoming to me, and I hoped I'd be able to maintain my dignity and hold my family together under the same circumstances.

In another world, it could be the basis of a sitcom. But instead it was reality.

By far the most compelling and inspiring person I met in Iraq was actually living in Jordan. His life defined the world of dangerous comedy. His name was Ahmad Albasheer.

Albasheer, as he is known by his millions of fans, is the host of his version of *The Daily Show*, called *The Albasheer Show*. Using all forms of comedy, he skewers all sides in the Iraqi conflict. This has made him a target of all sides in the Iraqi conflict. The government, and the militias, and anyone in between. That's why when we met him, he was doing the show in Jordan. And before we'd be done, he'd be on the move again to a new country.

Yet his commitment to illuminate the truth and absurdity of this conflict was unwavering. I often wondered if American satirists would be willing to pay that price.

Of course, American satirists would not have risen from such inauspicious circumstances in the first place. He was beaten and banished from his house as a teen by his physically abusive, religiously extreme, and rigid father for listening to Britney Spears. This occurred literally on the first night of the Iraq War. And Albasheer, defenseless, was forced into the streets, scrambling to seek shelter, as the violence escalated all around him.

Soon he would watch his brother and cousin both be killed by rockets in front of him when his house was randomly bombed.

But these traumas and tragedies made him more determined to do something about it.

Somehow, he turned this experience into a desire to be a journalist, which he accomplished. But as a journalist he was kidnapped, imprisoned, and tortured, but he managed to sidestep death by using his sense of humor. A sense of humor he didn't even know he had until thrust into this life-and-death situation. The soldiers laughed and spared him.

Lucky, ballsy, humble, he lands a gig as an on-air reporter for an Iraqi news show. He soon finds it impossible to simply report on the absurdity around him without some editorial comment. Often these are humorous.

This leads to the opportunity to host his own show. And it is almost immediately apparent that he has tapped into a deep need in Iraq for truth and humor beyond simply reporting events, and the show becomes a massive phenomenon. And catches the eyes of the authorities, both in the government and in the extremist communities, and almost as soon as the show is a hit, there is a hit put out on him. He becomes a target. But he's been through so much that, though he has no interest in dying, he is truly willing to in order to do what is clearly important work. This is comedy that counts. That makes a difference. Comedy that people can laugh at, but also need desperately on a much deeper level.

Someday, he could become president of Iraq. But for now, he continues doing his show, although what country he is in, I do not know.

●●●

Another insanely perennially dangerous place was Palestine, where innocent people live under constant siege while the media portrays them as terrorists. Palestine was a must-stop on my Dangerous Comedy Tour.

I'd been to Israel with Bill Maher when we did *Religulous*. And again with Sacha as Brüno sought to broker world peace.

With Bill, we had the opportunity to visit Palestine, specifically Hebron, but Bill timidly demurred. With Sacha, we did enter the West Bank, crossing through the ubiquitous vast prison-like wall to keep Palestinians controlled and out of Israel, except when the Israeli military allowed them, to manipulate an innocent shopkeeper into a terrorist for our Western comedy.

But my mind had lingered long after about Israel and Palestine and the disparity and distorted, inaccurate perceptions. I wanted to find out more. And when I googled "Palestine and comedy," it revealed a treasure trove of comedy activity on the other side of the imposing wall the Israelis had erected, and a peace-loving, freedom-loving people, who despite their dire circumstances, could still laugh.

Perhaps no one personified this spirit better than the comedian Adi Khalefa. One of the most energized, intense, yet sweet and compassionate men I've ever met. Adi played to large adoring crowds, who laughed heartily at his fairly nonpolitical observations of the silliness and absurdities of life in Palestine. He spoke to his audience, and he spoke for them. And used every trick in his comedy arsenal. He was verbal and physical and also emotionally honest, and that truly resonated with the crowds.

He had been to America a couple of times under the mentorship of Mo Amer, the popular Palestinian-American comedian, and had met Dave Chappelle on one of his visits, who offered encouraging words, which he carried with him as daily inspiration. Like a prayer that he would repeat to himself. It kept Adi grounded and focused.

But if he was just a comedian trying to make it, it would not have been as interesting a story. He brought me to meet his brother and mother at the home they all shared. His mom and brother, like him, were sweet and generous and full of humor and laughter. They had no interest in violence. Only peace.

But Adi went beyond that and showed me he wasn't just a comedian trying to make it, though he desperately wanted to. He wanted to perfect his English so he could perform in America. He was driven. But not just driven by career ambition. He had other, loftier, yet humble aspirations.

He took me to his comedy workshop for children. Children who had been traumatized and even injured in the ongoing violence that they all had to live under.

This was an incredibly moving experience. Watching these young people get up on a makeshift stage in an abandoned warehouse across from a theater where a famed director had been assassinated and tell their personal stories, mining their experiences for universal humor, was an unforgettable experience.

When we left Palestine, I got a small taste of what Palestinians must live with every day. A Palestinian cannot just commute back and forth to Israel. There are numerous checkpoints inhabited by Israeli soldiers with automatic weapons. And there are random time deadlines to cross these checkpoints, and once they close, Palestinians who need to get home or to Israel are out of luck. And our time was running out, so we were hurrying a bit. But we were stopped at one of these checkpoints and told to get out of our van. Somehow, we seemed suspicious to the soldiers despite our fixer, Elio's, futile attempts to explain our reason for being there.

●●●

I had been drinking a Coke Zero and left it in the van when we were told to disembark. The soldiers checked the van and came out with the can of soda. They held it carefully and asked whose it was, and I told them, mine. Thinking it seems suspicious in some way, perhaps a bomb, perhaps poison or acid, they had me drink it all down on the spot in front of them. I did. This seemed to convince them that our itinerary was as we said and let us pass.

We got to the border crossing and once again were delayed inexplicably. This time Elio had an idea. He spoke to one of the border officials and told them I was a writer on *Seinfeld*. It worked. Within minutes, the border official was shaking my hand and telling me what a fan of the show he was and ushering us across the border like VIPs.

I discovered on this show that *Seinfeld* was the universal language. I saw bootleg DVDs sold on a blanket in Jordan, where no Jews live. I saw them in video shops in Monrovia. I've seen it everywhere. *Seinfeld*, quite inadvertently, transcends language and religion and ethnicity. And it has to do with the specificity of those things on the actual show. In an almost paradox, that specificity somehow creates a universal which everyone everywhere relates to. And it uses comedy and laughter to achieve it.

•••

I had wanted to go to Mecca for a long time. Going back to *Brüno*. Nothing seemed more offensive than Brüno in Mecca. But as I discovered then, you must be a Muslim to enter Mecca. Of course, like all organized religion, there was some corrupt mechanism that allowed you to quickly convert to enter, but if anything was against Sacha's religion, it was this. And I wasn't thrilled about it either, although to get a one-of-a-kind scene, I'm apt to do anything.

But there would be no time for Mecca on this trip. It had to be short, and it would be too far to travel to Riyadh or Medina so we chose Jeddah, which was a "Mecca" of sorts for the expanding media and comedy industries of Saudi Arabia.

It was the off-season for the Hajj so I was able to interview a couple of vendors who worked the Hajj selling food and other goods. They quickly made it clear that, above all, Mecca, and especially the Hajj, was like Vatican City and Jerusalem and other seemingly holy locations—essentially a tourist trap. And of course, if you think about it, it makes sense. Overpriced hotels and restaurants, tour guides and trinkets. It takes a lot to get past these worldly material distractions and actually have a spiritual journey.

In Jeddah, I was taken on a tour of UTURN Entertainment's studios. They were producing shows of all sorts for the burgeoning and Westernizing Saudi Arabian market, as well as the entire Middle East and beyond.

Like the African comedians who did shows in small studio spaces or even in their houses, UTURN, although it had a facility, was able to produce many shows out of just one or two small studios. Turn this way, there was one show, turn this way, the set for another, etc.

It reminded me of the economy of a sitcom stage and has been instrumental, like the African video content makers, in how I approach doing my own video content in my home.

Many things struck me about UTURN. Despite women still being treated as second-class citizens in many parts of Saudi Arabian culture and society, here you could feel the exciting and incipient change coming. Women, still wearing the traditional Saudi abaya, worked side by side and equally with their male counterparts. They were living a different reality than the official one. It was heartening, even inspiring, to see.

There I met Hatoon Kadi, a wife and mother in traditional dress, but also a Western-educated PhD and comedian. She had an infectious and lovable personality, but make no mistake, her comedy was about the absurd double standards of Saudi Arabian society. And further, make no mistake, she was, and is, wildly popular.

Most of the women I met wore the traditional abaya, but fewer wore the niqab, or veil that covered their face.

Amazingly, one of the most popular comedians on social media in Saudi Arabia, Amy Roko, did.

Both she and Hatoon surprised me with their fierce feminism. They defended the use of the formless abaya and even the niqab as actually liberating. They couldn't be judged on their looks, and it forced a sexist society to look past that to who they were and what they said.

At first, it was a shock to Western ears, but when I thought about the oversexualization of women and the obsession with and harsh judgments of the female body at the expense of virtually everything else in Western society, I wondered what did freedom mean and who was really more liberated?

Going back to *Seinfeld* for a minute, the show was a sensation in Saudi Arabia, and I had the opportunity to meet a comedian who is known as the *Seinfeld* of Saudi Arabia, Fahad Albutairi.

Although far from a controversial comedian himself, he's even played in the States at places like the Laugh Factory, he was married to perhaps the most prominent women's rights activist in Saudi Arabia, Loujain al-Hathloul.

As an outspoken leader of the movement, she was imprisoned many times, and in 2018, in the wake of the murder of Jamal Khashoggi, they were both arrested. Apparently they were forced to divorce and are both free now, but with tremendous restrictions on their movements and words.

It is a stark reminder that even in a country with intimations of expanding freedoms on the surface, living under the yoke of a fundamentalist religious regime is still quite dangerous. And further, a portent of what can happen anywhere to anybody when we allow our freedoms to erode, even here, the land of the free, but also the home of the religious right.

I understood that dangerous places were not confined to simply other countries. There were dangerous places right here at home. For some people, for some comedians, very dangerous places. And among the most profound interviews I conducted were right here in America with Indigenous American comedians, particularly three women who performed as part of a tour called the "Ladies of Native Comedy," Adrianne Chalepah, Deanna M.A.D., and Tonia Jo Hall.

They were comedians, but also college-educated students of media, and they spoke insightfully about the perceptions and distortions white America had perpetuated about the Native experience. It remains one of the most illuminating interviews I did.

I had tried to expand the definition of dangerous comedy. I had written letters requesting interviews with the Unabomber, Ted Kaczynski; the controversial leader of the Philippines, Rodrigo Duterte; and perhaps the most dangerous filmmaker, Werner Herzog. Duterte and Kaczynski didn't respond. Herzog said no, but in a sardonically funny letter. Which of course, I've kept.

I also conducted three-hour interviews both with the philosopher Slavoj Žižek and another OG of dangerous comedy, John Waters. I spoke to Žižek in my old neighborhood of Brighton Beach in a windswept boardwalk restaurant, Tatiana's. And John was gracious enough to invite us to his house, which is also his museum, a home densely packed with mementos and art from his many years of filmmaking.

Both interviews were amazing, impressive and illuminating, but sadly Netflix had no interest in them. I still hold out hope that I can broadcast them somewhere soon.

The sad part of this journey is that there are endless dangerous places in the world. Some are perennially dangerous, like Somalia.

Has it ever been safe there? Others shift, from insanely violently dangerous to somewhat peaceful and often back again based on many circumstances.

Yes, the world is an increasingly dangerous place, and I discovered that humor, like food, like air, like love, is an essential key to survival. I saw Laughter nourishing when there was no food. I saw Laughter heal when there was no medicine. I finally saw Laughter in a new light. Laughter is a miracle.

CHAPTER 19

THE STORY OF THE LARRY DAVID STORY

*I*n 2017, inspired by my encounters with global comedians, I started my own YouTube channel, Larry Charles Projects. It would be a place to put new stuff I'd make and old stuff too.

I immediately thought, to introduce the channel, I should interview Larry David. I actually knew him better and differently than most people. I would venture to say I knew more and remembered more about Larry David's life than almost anybody did. Sometimes even him. I thought it would be an intimate, fresh, uncensored, illuminating and funny, and maybe sometimes quite serious conversation.

Without hesitation and quite graciously, he agreed. I never considered until writing this chapter how, at the time, this was a big ask. I don't know why. Thoughtless, mindless, obliviousness. I mean, Larry is an icon in constant demand. I was sincerely grateful and appreciative but unaware that a "yes" might be a big deal. Perhaps neither was he. This was all operating on an unconscious level. Nevertheless, on a certain closer-to-the-surface level, I knew it was a good idea and I pursued it.

Now, the last time I'd seen Larry, about a year before, in 2019, it had been an awkward encounter. He had asked to have lunch with me, while I was still finishing *Dangerous Comedy*. I didn't realize he had something he wanted to discuss with me, though I felt there was more to it than just a meal and catching up.

The meal began inauspiciously when the waitress naturally recognized Larry, but then mistook me for Sid Haig, the murderous clown from Rob Zombie's *House of the 1000 Corpses*. (I suppose when Sid himself would be recognized in these situations, it was probably a thrill.) If you're going to be mistaken for someone, a psychotic clown might not be your first choice.

But that was merely the prelude to my humiliation. Once the obviously myopic waitress left with our order, Larry proceeded to tell me why he had asked me to lunch.

He told me that HBO was unhappy with our white male directors lineup. He emphasized that HBO, and of course *Curb*, felt I was the exception. But in order for Larry to tell his old friends and regular *Curb* directors, Robert Weide, Bryan Gordon, and David Steinberg, that they weren't being asked back, he asked me to take one for the team, be a martyr to the cause, and also not return for the upcoming season.

Wow. I was not expecting that. I was special. I was flattered. But also fired.

I had to scramble there in the moment for a response. Talk about an improv show. I was in a *Curb* episode.

Cue the *Curb* music.

I wish I had filmed that lunch.

I quickly responded that I understood. As much as I loved *Curb* and especially working in it, I hadn't done that many episodes the past couple of seasons, as they conflicted with the projects I was working on at the time. And *Curb* paid scale, so it wasn't a big financial hit. And I was supportive of bringing in new blood. Women, people of color, other directors with other points of view.

This was what he told me, that it was HBO's idea and he was the unfortunate messenger, once again the victim. And though knowing him as I did, I was skeptical, knowing him as I did, I was also accepting. Again, my loyalty to Larry made me want to believe him.

But as it turned out, when the new season premiered, instead of fresh faces and genders and people of color, there was Jeff Schaffer, who no one could accuse of being anything but a white man, directing all but two of the episodes.

Or was it me? I had lost my temper directing what would be my last show. We were shooting a dinner party scene with seven people. Getting all the coverage and keeping things fresh and spontaneous was a challenge under the best conditions. As I shot, I kept seeing movement through the kitchen door. It was somebody's reflection as they hid behind the appliances. I asked politely numerous times and was told no one was moving. But I saw it with my own eyes. At some point it crossed into that territory where it sounded like I was crazy. Adam, my wonderful AD, insisted there was no movement despite my observing it firsthand. And it was ruining takes. Finally I snapped and kicked everyone out of the kitchen. It was jarring for the actors, and I immediately regretted it, even as I was losing it and despite apologizing. Was that it? If it was, they would have justification. Perhaps the actors had requested I not be asked back. Perhaps it was the HBO executives who hovered on the set. Perhaps it was Larry himself. And regardless who, Larry might not want to tell me.

But it didn't really matter what the reason was. My contribution to the show was extremely limited, and it was fully their prerogative.

Yet for some reason, perhaps shock, perhaps my already very diminished role on the show, perhaps simply life itself, I must confess I wasn't bothered by this news at the lunch or after.

So, a year later, when I thought about asking Larry to do this interview for my YouTube channel, I think we both felt we were on good terms and he readily agreed. Unless he was feeling guilty. And as I said, I didn't think about the massive favor he was doing for me and my modest venture.

I would pay for this myself and felt it was a good investment, not financially, but in attracting viewers to my new channel.

It seemed so simple and smart as so many things do initially. But it wound up being pretty complicated and stupid. And very expensive.

I told Larry this would be as low maintenance an operation as I could muster. And afford. I would come to his house with one other person, who would man the camera and set up the sound.

It would be one angle shot continuously. No other people. No B-roll. No cuts. Just an intimate conversation with LC and LD.

A fellow was recommended to me who did both jobs. I interviewed him, and without bragging or arrogance, he spoke with great confidence of his abilities in both realms. Although his experience was much less than I'd expected, he seemed like this was something he could do with ease.

We arrived at Larry's house and set up on a couple of couches in a den-like room off the kitchen. The DP/sound man checked the shot and the mikes, and he seemed to think it was good. I had relied not only on my memory, but also on research, and I had come prepared with pages of questions.

We spoke for two hours. Maybe more. There was so much to talk about, we only got to *Fridays* and 1980. At the end of the interview, Larry was effusive in his praise. He said without hesitation that this had been the best interview he'd ever done. I reminded him we'd only got to 1980 and he volunteered to do a part two. I was into that too, and promised to arrange it as soon as possible.

Then I reviewed the footage.

I had wanted to shoot the interview with one camera handheld as I had all the interviews in *LCDWOC*. It wasn't easy but it lent a vigor and aliveness and spontaneity to the conversation. The cameraman told me, assured me it would be no problem.

Now normally I might've had a monitor to watch the action, but because the shot was so simple and I wanted to focus on Larry, not the shot, there didn't seem to be a need for one. I often didn't use the monitor on *LCDWOC*. It was understood what we were shooting, and I was right there.

And I did notice some discomfort and asked on numerous occasion early on if he was okay, and other than some heavy sweating, he said "yes."

But as I watched this interview at home, this singular piece of gold, praised by Larry himself, my heart dropped, then my stomach, then my soul.

In cinéma vérité documentary shooting, there are many sins that can be forgiven and overlooked. It can be shaky sometimes. It can be out of focus for a moment.

This was shaky and out of focus for large long swaths of the interview. I'd wait for it to get better, and it wouldn't.

Consolation. The sound was good.

I deemed the footage virtually unusable and brooded for a couple of days. When I emerged from the darkness, I went to see Cosmo Orlando, who was an associate producer on *LCDWOC* but who had gone on to be a busy and successful music video producer. I thought he might know how or who might help me. And he did.

I met an editor, and we talked about various techniques and technologies to improve the picture.

I hadn't planned on cutting away to anything. But as I watched and rewatched the footage, I wondered if we could cover up a lot of the bad camerawork with photos, footage, and clips.

We began to insert photos, clips from old movies, references that Larry made, found footage of him and his pre-*Seinfeld* work on *Fridays* and elsewhere. And this was only a proposed part one.

If I got to a part two, I was immediately enticed by the prospect of drawing on copious clips from *Seinfeld* and *Curb*, which served as a sort of television series autobiography of Larry.

Suddenly this documentary took on a life. It wasn't just Larry and me talking, but vivid, sometimes hilarious cutaways, which reflected and commented on the conversation.

I was very proud of it. It was unexpected in so many ways. The intimacy and honesty with which Larry talked about himself, raw and stripped away of any artifice, were in sharp contrast to his carefully calculated TV image and persona. It was funny and very, very human. I thought people would love it. I hoped he would.

I kept Larry abreast of the entire saga from the footage debacle to this point we had reached. He had even volunteered to redo the interview. But I didn't feel that was necessary. Now that I had landed on a style and language for the movie, I was especially excited at the prospect of filming part two.

I wondered if there was something more that could or should be done with it.

I sent the most recent cut to Larry. He was blown away, speechless. He thought the movie was amazing. His only caveat was that he didn't like how he looked. Or sounded. This was a problem that transcended the movie. This was how Larry David sounded and looked. These were things I could not change. You cannot change someone's perception of themself.

But despite the one reservation, he was very surprised and impressed by the film.

I tried to assure him he looked and sounded great. He looked and sounded like him. But knowing Larry, I knew that issue could raise its "ugly" head again. Still, I didn't dwell on it and hoped it would remain dormant.

My intention was still to put it on YouTube along with an eventual part two and use it to launch my channel. It would be free and I'd never make any money from it, but it might make it easier to do other projects for YouTube.

I thought that the clips, being so specifically pertinent to everything Larry said, would be protected under the fair use rules and I wouldn't have to pay for them if the video was broadcast only on YouTube.

So with all this in mind, proud of the work, a fully produced and finished project out of my own pocket, possibly a calling card to other work, I sent it to my agents, Greg Cavic and Carolyn Sivitz at UTA. I often show things to Greg and Carolyn. And they will be honest about a project's viability from their point of view, often recommending that it might be better suited to YouTube than to the more commercial platforms. Often, that's how far it goes. But rarely do I have a fully produced movie made completely under the radar. And I felt, this was a new piece of work, a piece of work that could beget other work. Besides, other than social media, harangues, weird videos that I was making, it was the only thing I'd fully produced and brought to life since *Dangerous Comedy*.

I thought they would give it some kind encouraging words and then wish me luck on YouTube. What they didn't tell me was that they snuck a peek to the people at HBO, the home of *Curb* itself. And they loved it and wanted to acquire it. For a sum vastly greater than what I had spent. I was thrilled and excited, but mostly shocked.

But first, I had to call Larry. I wanted to get him up to speed on these developments and make sure I had his blessing. If he was uncomfortable for whatever reason, YouTube would be the home for this film and I would be okay with it.

I called and explained the situation to Larry. Initially, he was surprised, but actually surprised in a good way. He seemed quite pleased. I tried to assuage any doubts, assuring him that after it was color corrected, we'd be able to fix any imperfections he felt about himself. He seemed happy to hear that, though I knew once he'd been introduced to that idea, it would not fade away, but would fester like a sore that never heals.

With Larry David, somewhat like Chekhov, if a complaint is voiced in the first act, you can be sure it will be used against you in the third act.

I continued trying to make sure he was cool with this plan. I told him that they were going to pay me a lot and I would be more than happy to give him a share or split any amount of that money. He absolutely refused, as I suspected he would, almost as if I even insulted him with the thought. But I also knew that didn't necessarily mean it was the end of it.

For me, it had the air of déjà vu, redolent of the time back on *Seinfeld*, when Elaine Pope and I had offered to give him co-writing credit on "The Fix-Up," and he refused. Elaine and I won an Emmy for that episode, and Larry was angry. Essentially ending his relationship with Elaine, who had submitted it. I had submitted "The Subway" episode, which I wrote alone, and which didn't receive a nomination. But the incident certainly damaged my relationship with Larry for a while as well, though my conscience had been clear and I think he eventually understood that.

But here again, he was refusing something that he should've accepted.

Yet he seemed to accept on the surface that this would be the movie's fate. He even volunteered that his two daughters had watched it and loved it. This had made him happy.

So with Larry David's full knowledge and full blessing, and with the unexpressed acknowledgment to myself that these issues may yet arise again, we sold the movie to HBO.

We probably had the most interaction we'd had in years. A series of texts and phone calls in which he was extremely positive and constructive. And continuing to give me notes on every pass. This had been a very open arrangement. I understood his discomfort and thought his continued involvement and a sense of control offered the best way to assuage it.

The HBO executives assured me on multiple occasions that the project was all in the family and they would help secure the clips and releases.

And then suddenly, there were mysterious complications and obstacles.

At first, I was led to believe that the overwhelming majority of the clips would fall under the fair use rule and thus would not be subject to the usual fees. Then suddenly, we were getting mixed messages from HBO, which owns *Curb*, and Warner, which owns *Seinfeld*, and which are both owned by the same parent company. Not to mention the dozens of other companies and entities that were the source of the plethora of additional clips.

The laws were muddy and confusing. If HBO gave us the *Curb* clips for free, which they were willing to do, that would mean we'd have to negotiate and pay for everything else. And then Warner refused us permission for the *Seinfeld* clips. Why?

Suddenly, this rights issue became an almost unclimbable mountain of documentation, legal wrangling, and circular Zoom calls. Nothing was getting accomplished. Old issues weren't resolved, and new issues continued to mount. And I couldn't fathom why. There seemed to be no reason or logic behind the logjam. I began to feel there were malevolent entities working behind the scenes to sabotage the project.

There were other clip complications as well. For instance, a big theme in the documentary is how Ayn Rand's *The Fountainhead* had served as a seminal inspiration for Larry.

To that end, as Larry described his relationship to the book and its main character, the uncompromising architect Howard Roark, and how Larry had applied Roark's rigid determinism into his own life, I had used extensive clips from the heated melodramatic King Vidor film version starring Gary Cooper.

Warner owned that movie, too, and simply said we couldn't use the clips, providing only the murkiest explanations. The estate of Ayn Rand was somehow involved. It began to get very labyrinthine.

Was I looking for Rosebud?

In order for me to secure all these clips, I would have to spend the bulk of the money HBO had given me. Was this the plan? In the hopes that it would squeeze the life out of the project but make it seem like it had died of natural causes?

Was I paranoid, or was this business as usual?

Meanwhile, I shared every cut with Larry. And despite him promising no new notes with each new cut, indeed there were invariably new notes. All designed in my opinion to make him seem lighter and funnier and less serious and heavy. I was surprised at how much he had become invested in the public facade.

We talked about things like death and spirituality, subjects you don't hear Larry David wax seriously on. While talking about his children, he wept. It was all revelatory. He asked for it all to be cut.

Nevertheless, I addressed every single one of his notes, hoping to alleviate his anxieties and second thoughts. Each cut was another opportunity for Larry to say he was uncomfortable and wanted to stop it.

But instead, despite the notes, he was always encouraging and marveling at the work itself. Which I very much appreciated.

Slowly, we inched toward our deadline. HBO was already

scheduling marketing meetings and an airdate. And it was fast approaching.

And it seemed like Larry had resigned himself to this inevitability. He seemed okay with it. Almost looking forward to it.

I would never not be aware of the ever-present risk of Larry hiding his true feeling or changing his mind, but all I could go on was his surface behavior, even knowing as well as I do that was only one part of the Larry David equation.

But somewhere, just a couple of weeks from the deadline and everything that would follow, I received a call at my home around eight o'clock in the morning.

When I picked it up, the cacophonous decibel-defying roar from the other side forced me to yank the receiver away from my ear. It was Larry's agent and my former agent, Ari Emanuel, and his equally evil henchman, Lloyd Braun, screaming at me at the same time but not in unison. Yes, let me repeat. Ari Emanuel and Lloyd Braun screaming at me on the phone at 8 a.m. I couldn't understand a word they were saying. And I couldn't get them to stop. Was I in a *Seinfeld*, a *Curb*, an *Entourage*? A hybrid of all three? Yes!

And what were they screaming about? Somewhere amid their earsplitting caterwauling, I was being accused of ripping off Larry.

"You stole from him! You stole from him!" It was like being screamed at by an irate shopkeeper in Brighton Beach.

Larry knew all this was patently false so where were they getting this information? Were they just making it up as a ploy? Was it like the police yelling, "Your children are in danger!"? Without telling me the danger was me.

This was preposterous. Comical if it had been a scene from a movie. But I couldn't get them to stop. During their inhalations of much-needed air, I told them the entire saga that I've told you here. They were undeterred. They wanted money.

I was surprised this was all about money. Especially as I had offered Larry a copious sum at the very beginning of this process and made it clear on numerous occasions after that the offer was still available. He would dismiss the notion before I finished with a firm, "No."

But here I was being attacked falsely by his representatives. I considered saying, "Let us stop talking falsely now. The hour is getting late." But I don't think they would've gotten the reference.

When it was clear that Larry had indeed been offered money, they changed tacks and insisted that Larry receive every cut. "He has a right to a cut!" Again, this information was transmitted by two men screaming at the top of their lungs. And once again I explained, as calmly as I could, that Larry had received every cut and of course he knew that, and if they ever needed to see any documentation of any of this, it exists.

Once their baseless accusations had been repudiated, they still barked and sputtered but eventually hung up. However, I now knew that all my suspicions of behind-the-scenes shenanigans had been grounded in reality. And they weren't over.

But before I could process what had happened or explain to Keely, who stood nearby stunned and appalled by this verbal assault, the horrifying cry of these banshees in suits, the phone rang again.

It was Larry. Mortified. Horrified. Disgusted. His words. About what had just occurred. He swore that he knew nothing about it. That he was clueless that Ari would pull this sort of a classless stunt. He would never have allowed this to occur if he knew. He begged me to believe him.

And because it would be so much easier, I really wanted to believe Larry. In my mind, I could envision a scenario, a very *Curb*-like scenario at that, where Larry was playing golf with Ari and Lloyd. They asked what he was up to. He told them about the documentary. They probably asked him what he got for it and he said nothing, and they took it from there to that 8 a.m. call.

I got off the phone believing Larry. But once I had a chance to process, I knew that just as likely a scenario was Larry saying to Ari, on the golf course, on the phone, at dinner, whatever function they might both be attending, that I had made this documentary about him and he wasn't happy with it and didn't know what to do. And with Larry's full knowledge and support, in fact at Larry's instigation, he allowed Ari to do his thing, which was to bluster and intimidate on Larry's behalf. To be the bad guy while Larry gets to remain the good guy. And then cast himself as the innocent victim on the phone. Perfect. A recurrent theme in his life and work.

But still, I marched on. And despite the many obstacles, we finished. Now the airdate loomed. Ads and trailers began appearing. I was actually excited. It seemed, and I know I had been here before, but it seemed like Larry was going to be okay with the doc after all. Perhaps Ari's overreaction had had some impact on Larry, and he realized, as I had tried to tell him many times, that this was a good thing, that the fans would love it, that it was unexpected but only added to his persona.

I was on the set of my new movie, *Fucking Identical Twins* (eventually changed against my strenuous protests to *Dicks: The Musical*), getting ready to set up the first shot of the morning, many people waiting, when my phone rang. It was Larry.

What he proposed on that phone call and what he was really saying were two different things. And I knew that the issues had not only not died or faded away, but had become more urgent as the airdate approached.

Larry offered to do a live interview with me, where he could be Larry David and be funny in front of a crowd. I was stunned. I asked if he meant for this to be in addition to the documentary, or in lieu of.

He said that HBO would "postpone" the doc till some "later date." I knew that "later date" well. It was "never."

I asked him if I said "no" to the live interview, would the documentary air as planned? He hemmed and hawed a bit, but it was clear. Live interview or not, the doc would be postponed. Indefinitely and beyond, if possible.

I told him it was a lot to process, and I would have to think about it and was keeping everyone waiting on the set. After I hung up, I staggered to the set. Reeling from what had just transpired.

Later I wrote him a text saying I wasn't interested.

That was the last day of February 2022. I never heard back. It was the last time I spoke to Larry David.

●●●

I'm not mad at Larry. I simply wish he could've trusted me more all along the process. I would never have done anything to hurt him. Quite the opposite, I've always tried to protect Larry, as a friend and as a collaborator. And while this wasn't a puff piece, it was not a hatchet job either. Far from it. It was a conversation with a cultural icon by someone who may know him better than anybody.

Our relationship had always been close, but our physical realities had been diverging for a long time. He was among the super wealthy. And though he was Larry David, puncturing wealth and class for laughs on TV, in real life, he enjoyed all the trappings of privilege but made his public happy by complaining about it.

But as with so much with Larry, my strangely individualistic predominant thought, my ultimate conclusion was that the experience had been a positive one. It's hard to explain that to others. Yes, there was a price to pay, but the benefits far outweighed the cost.

On a very pragmatic level, in pursuing various personal and passionate projects, having not given much thought to money over the past few years, we were on the precipice of struggling and making some hard economic decisions that I simply did not want to make. Usually I figure this out. But this time, besides the looming illness and death and hate all around us that the pandemic and the malevolent forces that emerged behind and around it who chose to exploit people's suffering instead of alleviating it, there was also the possibility that I might never work again. My wife jokes that I always say that, and I do. But someday it will be true. So getting this gig got us through the pandemic and took the economic pressure off, despite the fact that there would be no work available for a while.

So why did this happen? I actually think Larry didn't want to hurt my feelings. He would rather perpetuate a lie than tell the truth if it meant avoiding an awkward or uncomfortable situation or even hurting someone. Not because of them. Because of him. He couldn't take it. It's silly in a way. On *Seinfeld*, Jerry always did the firing because Larry couldn't handle it. But as Larry and I had discussed many times and written about many times, we also both knew at the same time that, however you interpreted it, this was an act of emotional cowardice. But knowing it was looming, I also didn't confront him, fearing that what would happen would happen and it happened anyway.

But I haven't exactly been courageous in my emotional encounters in life either. I think I've made that abundantly clear. I guess we're all avoiding something. But every time we turn away, we face something else. An unfinished never-ending emotional encounter. With ourselves.

We've never seen each other or spoken again. We are no longer able to say things to each other that we never dared utter to others. That was part of the fun of our longtime dynamic. Confiding the forbidden. But I wouldn't say I miss it, or him. We had drifted in fundamental ways long before this. And relationships, friendships fall by the wayside. Even after forty years. Maybe especially after forty years. We were so much the same for so long in so many ways and yet increasingly vastly different in perhaps the most important ways. We had lost that connection a long time ago. Perhaps the documentary was a last chance to reignite it. Another illusion. And it failed. Loss is part of the process of growing old. Like the signs for going-out-of-business sales proclaim: EVERYTHING MUST GO! Our friends. Our loved ones. Everything we ever cared about. And us...

EPILOGUE

THE CODE

I never thought I'd be so relieved to see the automatic doors of an emergency room slide open to let me be wheeled in. I was actually grateful. Grateful to be alive. Grateful to have such proficient and cool EMTs surrounding me and assuring me on the harrowing journey to get here. Grateful for all the people, especially Keely, who loved me. Was this the promised land? And would I enter or be denied?

Or was life but a joke? A cosmic joke. Meaningless, trivial, and over.

Perhaps my most significant inadvertent oracle, Larry David, once said, "No Hugging, No Learning." When you're young, that philosophy is easy to follow. And for a long time, that worked for me. No fake emotion or pretending everything was going to be all right. Hugging and learning were anathema to comedy. Coldness, callousness, uncaring, uncompassionate, disdain, skepticism, scoffing at seriousness, these were the building blocks of comedy. And there was no room for genuine emotion.

But from the moment Julia walked into Larry and Jerry's office crying, we knew we could no longer write women as cardboard straight men like Hillary Brooke in *Abbott and Costello*, whose only function was to set up "the boys." A character with no history or backstory who essentially doesn't exist without that interaction.

And I could no longer live that way. Not really feeling. Not really caring. Real emotion began to enter my life. Families, children, loved ones, and hand in hand with that, connection, compassion, caring, tragedy, and loss. You begin to learn there is no separation between the laughter and tears, the joy and sadness.

I only wish I could've learned it earlier.

We all think that the time that we live in is the only time, the most important time, the last time, instead of, oh well, another time. One of an infinite number that exist in multiple realms. It seems like it will go on forever, but the only constant is, it won't. Not in the way we imagine it.

I don't think I realized until I wrote the book, until I read the book, how much I was the agent of my own misfortune. I had lost my temper, been impatient and uncool, betrayed those closest to me, wasn't honest especially with myself. Acted impulsively, selfishly, thoughtlessly, with everyone and everything in my life as well. Why was I rushing past everything? What was I rushing for? What was I rushing to? Death? What was the rush? Did my fear hasten my journey? And what did I miss along the way?

One thing for sure: I wouldn't have those moments back. They are gone, seared into my memory, but laced with regret. Unlike Frank Sinatra, who said in "My Way," *"Regrets, I have a few, but then again, too few to mention,"* I have many. Many, many regrets. And I've mentioned quite a few. But there are no do-overs. We have to live with the results.

When I was wheeled through the emergency entrance at St. John's Health Center in Santa Monica, the first question I was asked was, "On a scale of one to ten, ten being worst, how would you rate your pain?" But I felt no physical pain. The only pain I felt was my psychic pain. And that was a ten.

I certainly missed a certain level of joy that was available to me. And I could've been more generous with the joy and love I doled out. Rare was the time I was with my children, girlfriends, wives, friends, work, and allowed myself to feel the love and luck of my life. The joy of the moment. Instead I only felt pressure. And now in the back of the ambulance careening down the Pacific Coast Highway, that pressure had manifested physically, no longer a metaphor. A reality. My reality. Crushing me. When would it collapse? When would it end?

And I was right in a way. The constant companions of caring and loving are pain and sadness. Bob famously said, *"When you ain't got nothing, you got nothing to lose."* But the unspoken response is, once you have something, you have everything to lose. And you will lose it.

I miss my parents.

I miss everyone who ever loved me who is now gone and so I will never be able to adequately reciprocate.

I miss the chance to say thank you to all those in my past who needed and deserved it.

Although my relationship with my children today is strong, and has taken a lot of work on all our parts to build that, I miss their childhood when I was often checked out, consumed with work, acutely lonely, and acting out by cheating and lying and, perhaps above all, absence.

Although my relationship with my wife, Keely, today is very strong, I miss the years I wasted, foolishly convincing myself that my love toward her was always as true and pure as could be. When in truth, my equivocations, hedging my bets, procrastinating, thinking I was being sensitive to her or my kids were the delusions I fed myself to make me feel better about the damage and hurt I'd caused, and I only wound up causing more before I could start the healing process. I'd chipped away at that purity until it was in danger of breaking and collapsing. You see, even when I'm good, even when I think I'm doing the honorable thing, I'm somehow not and, further, not getting it.

I miss enjoying my early success and instead always worrying about an abstract future.

I miss the many opportunities to be honest and spare people the misery and suffering I caused.

I miss the many opportunities to be loving and generous and sacrificing.

I miss the many years I sleepwalked through my life when I could've been awake to all that was around me.

Shit, I miss everything.

I can't ask for forgiveness unless I can forgive myself, and I'm not sure that's going to happen.

It makes me wary to say I've learned anything. It's an act of hubris, an assumption that I can't be sure of. Sure, I'd like to believe that. But have I, really? Does self-consciousness prevent us from being truly self-aware?

It pains me to think that, as Bob said in "All Along the Watchtower," *"Life is but a joke."* At one time, I could nonchalantly toss off that line with a laugh. Of course it's a joke. Look around us. Look at the absurdities. But what makes us cry also makes us laugh. That is the great paradox.

In the context of the song, the people who abuse and exploit the planet, the innocents, the resources, even each other, they think it's all meaningless. It doesn't matter. It's all temporary. Take what you can any way you can get it, and then say goodbye and dump the detritus on the future generations if they're even here.

But that's a heartbreaking joke. With a decidedly unfunny punchline.

As a comedy writer, perhaps first and foremost, I want to rewrite that joke. Give it meaning. Give it resonance. Make it more than a joke. The joke as something serious, significant, meaningful. The joke as the journey.

Sometimes the destination is less important than the journey. And sometimes the punchline is too.

But seriously, folks, is life but a joke? A question without an answer? A punchline without a setup? A trivial pursuit? A lark? A laugh? Some could certainly argue it is. We're here. We're gone. We remember. We forget. We are remembered. We are forgotten. Are we just the punchline to a cosmic shaggy dog story? Does the universe laugh at us? Our futility? Our delusions? Our dreams? Are we simply randomly thrown into this brief, brutal earthly existence, long enough to suffer but too short to understand? Funny, right?

And ironically, I am the joker who desperately wants to believe life is not a joke. And I am the thief who already knows it's not.

I tried to be loyal to my masters. I tried to do my job and move on. With honor. With grace (sometimes). With respect. I think about death and impermanence every day. I ponder death. Imagine death. Experience death. Everything ends. Not just me. My fear drives me. My hunger and desire drive me. But instead of suffering, it drives me to peace, tranquility, satiation, surrender. I live by a code. Or try to. Nobody's perfect.

ACKNOWLEDGMENTS

With thanks to my intrepid, tireless, and dapper agent, Byrd Leavell, and my relentless soccer-team-hoodie-wearing editor, Amar Deol. And my late, dearly missed parents, Arlene and Irving, who would have been shocked and thrilled I wrote a book. And to my children. Who were afraid I would.

ABOUT THE AUTHOR

LARRY CHARLES rose from the mean streets of Brooklyn and the working-class housing projects of Donald Trump's nefarious father, Fred, to become the director of *Borat*, *Brüno*, *The Dictator*, and *Religulous*, among others. He directed Bob Dylan and an all-star cast (including Jeff Bridges, John Goodman, Jessica Lange, and Penélope Cruz) in the film *Masked and Anonymous*, which he and Bob wrote together. He has also directed numerous episodes of *Curb Your Enthusiasm* and was one of the original writers and producers of *Seinfeld*. He has been nominated for twelve Emmys, winning two; eight Golden Globes, winning one; a Peabody award; and some other stuff too. He has collaborated with a diverse group of cultural icons from Mel Brooks to Michael Moore to Nicolas Cage. In 2018, he created, directed, wrote, and starred in the four-part limited series for Netflix, *Larry Charles' Dangerous World of Comedy*. His new film for A24, *Dicks: The Musical* (formerly and more preferably *Fucking Identical Twins*), premiered at the Toronto Film Festival in the fall of 2023 and won the People's Choice Midnight Madness Award. And yet despite all this, or because of it, he remains kind, humble, and grateful.